SUPER-COLOSSAL
BOOK OF
puzzles
tricks&
GAMES

Sheila Anne Barry

Illustrated by Doug Anderson

STERLING PUBLISHING CO., INC.   **NEW YORK**

Oak Tree Press Co., Ltd.   London & Sydney

OTHER BOOKS OF INTEREST

Biggest Riddle Book in the World
Calculator Puzzles, Tricks and Games
Eye Teasers
Games to Learn By

Junior Magic
Matchstick Puzzles, Tricks & Games
Metric Puzzles, Tricks and Games
Mind Teasers: Logic Puzzles & Games of Deduction

With love to Mark and Lael

ACKNOWLEDGMENTS

My thanks to Mark Weissman and Lael Weissman, who contributed some of the best contests and games, to Esther Nelson for the materials she shared, to Lincoln A. Boehm for his many suggestions and ideas, and to David A. Boehm, for making this book possible. Also thank you to Sterling Publishing Company for permission to reprint and adapt some of the excellent puzzles, tricks, and games from the following books, all of them © Sterling Publishing Co., Inc., unless otherwise indicated: by Paul Castle, *101 Funny Things to Do and Make* © 1956; C. B. Colby, *Strangely Enough* © 1959, 1972 C. B. Colby and *Weirdest People in the World* © 1965, 1973 C. B. Colby; Rudolf Dittrich, *Tricks and Games for Children* © 1964; Lillian and Godfrey Frankel, *Creating from Scrap* © 1962; *Muscle-Building Games* © 1964; *101 Action Games for Boys* © 1952, 1968; *101 Best Games for Girls* © 1952, 1968; *101 Best Games for Teenagers* © 1958; *101 Best Party Games for Adults* © 1953; Walter B. Gibson, *Junior Magic* © 1963 Doubleday, 1977 Walter B. Gibson; Vernon Howard, *Pantomimes, Charades and Skits* © 1959, 1974; *Puppet and Pantomime Plays* © 1962, 1967; Muriel Mandell, *Games to Learn By* © 1958, 1972; Peggy and Robert Masters, *101 Best Games for Two* © 1957; *101 Best Stunts and Novelty Games* © 1954; Esther L. Nelson, *Movement Games for Children of All Ages* © 1975 Esther L. Nelson; *Musical Games for Children of All Ages* © 1976 Esther L. Nelson; Norvin Pallas, *Calculator Puzzles, Tricks and Games* © 1976; *Code Games* © 1971; Charles H. Paraquin, *Eye Teasers* © 1976; Ib Permin, *Hokus Pokus* © 1969; Don Reinfeld and David Rice, *101 Mathematical Puzzles* © 1960 Printed Arts Co., Inc.; Alfred Sheinwold, *101 Best Card Games for Children* © 1956; Walter Sperling, *How to Make Things Out of Paper* © 1961; George J. Summers, *Mind Teasers* © 1977 George J. Summers; Wolfgang Zielke, *Conditioning Your Memory* © 1970.
Many of the puzzles, tricks and games in this book were based on them.

CONTENTS

3. Test Yourself

CONTENTS/(Cont.)

4. House of Cards

5. Quizzes

Card Tricks **183**
The Two Rows—The Two Rows Encore—Mint Date—Mutus Dedit Nomen Cocis—Do As I Do—Do As I Do Again—Coins and Cards—Four-Heap Deal—Card Under Glass—The Rising Card—The Flying Card—Hatful of Cards—X-Ray Eyes—Finding the Lost Card—The Multiplying Cards—Fooled!—The Double Deal

Solitaire Games **210**
Accordian—The Clock—The Cave Man Game—The Wish—Hit Cards—Four-Leaf Clover—Gaps—Perpetual Motion—Pyramid—Stairway to Heaven—Klondike—Canfield—Pounce!—Russian Solitaire—Russian Bank

Card Games for Two or More **230**
Concentration—Pig—Donkey—Donkey Buttons—My Ship Sails—My Bee Buzzes—My Star Twinkles—Through the Window—Through the Wide Window—Go Fish—"Fish" for Minnows—Authors—Bango—The Duck Went Moo—Slap Jack—The Persian Card Game—War—Revenge—Pishe Pasha—Enflay—Snip-Snap-Snorum—I Doubt It—I Doubt It Threesies—Crazy Eights, Wild Jacks, and Go Boom—Whist—Hearts—Calamity Jane

Quizzes for Yourself, Parties, or Your Own Quiz Show **255**
Literature Quizzes—"Bad Guys" Quizzes—Mythology Quizzes—Bible Quizzes—Legends, Tales and Fables Quizzes—Nursery Rhymes Quizzes—Origins of Words Quiz—Interesting Places Quizzes—Where Are These Rivers?—Famous Explorers Quiz—Where Are These Famous Structures?—Where Are These Volcanoes?—Famous People Quizzes—Science Quizzes—Pot Luck Quizzes

6. Quiet Games

Pencil and Paper Games **297**
Fractured Riddles—Ham and Eggs—Funny-Grams—Group Art—Group Lit—Dots—Eternal Triangles—Snakes—Kettle of Fish—Doodlebug—Battleships—Hangman Grows Up—Double Hanging—Tic-Tac-Toe Squared—Tic-Tac-Toe-Toe—Go-Bang—Guggenheim—Eppizootics—Word Bridges—Sprouts—Gibberish—Every Other—Cat-astrophe—Word Hunt—Longest Word—Transmigration of Words—The Big List Game

Games for Travelling **330**
Geography and Other End-Games—Ghost and Double Ghost—Super-Ghost—Botticelli—Hinky-Pinky—

7

7. Quick Contests

8. Party Games for Ages 6-8

CONTENTS/(Cont.)

9

11. Psycho- logical Games

PUZZLES AND PUZZLERS

1

Brainteasers

NEW YEAR'S RESOLUTION

Suppose you made a New Year's resolution to save twice as much each day as you did the day before, starting with a penny a day. On January 1st, you would save one penny; on January 2nd, you would save 2 pennies; on January 3rd, you would save 4 pennies; on January 4th you would save 8 pennies. At the end of January, how many pennies would you have saved?

First try to guess the answer without figuring it out mathematically.

If you don't have a calculator, look up the answer on page 608.

THE TRAVELLERS' DINNER

This puzzle has been stumping the unwary ever since Biblical times! The legend is that many years ago, two Arabs were travelling to Baghdad and stopped at a small town for a meal. One of the Arabs had 5 loaves of bread in his camel-sack, and the other Arab had 3 loaves.

Before they began eating, they were joined by a hungry stranger who asked for food and offered to pay for what he ate. The two Arabs agreed to divide their bread with him, so he sat down and ate. They divided the bread equally, and when the meal was over, the stranger laid down 8 coins of equal value in payment for the food. He said goodbye and went on his way.

The Arab who had had 5 loaves took 5 of the coins as his share, and the other Arab was left with 3. The second Arab was not pleased with this division and argued that he should receive half of the coins. The two Arabs couldn't agree on this, and they argued so vehemently that finally they had to take their case to a judge.

The judge listened to the story of what had happened, and then he said, "The man who had 5 loaves should receive 7 of the coins, and the man who had 3 loaves should receive only one."

Which is the correct division of the coins? Remember, the coins are of *equal* value.

(SOLUTION ON PAGE 608)

THE GARBLES

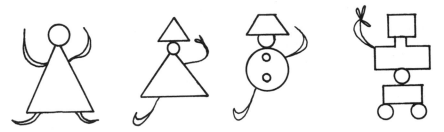

These are Garbles. All Garbles have something in common.

These are not Garbles.

Melissa   Celestine   Stephanie   Duke

Which ones are Garbles?

(SOLUTION ON PAGE 608)

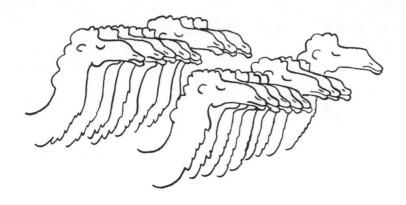

DIVIDE THE CAMELS

Many years ago an Egyptian died and left his estate, which consisted of 17 camels, to his three sons. The eldest son was left half of the camels, the second son was left a third of the camels, and the youngest son was to receive one-ninth of the camels, according to the will.

The sons and their legal advisers could figure no way to make the distribution without cutting up a camel. So they went to the Pharaoh for advice. The Pharaoh, after listening to the problem, thought for a moment and then announced a solution which had not occurred to anyone. What was it?

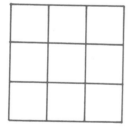

MAGIC FIFTEEN

Fill the squares with numbers from one to 9, no number being used twice. The numbers must add up to 15 in all directions—horizontally in all three rows, vertically in all three rows, as well as the two diagonals.
(For more about magic squares, see page 90.)

(SOLUTION ON PAGE 608)

SEND MORE MONEY

```
  S E N D
+ M O R E
---------
M O N E Y
```

Besides being a message you'd like to send, this is a famous numerical cryptogram. Each letter stands for a number, and no number has been used for more than one letter. Can you decipher it?

(SOLUTION ON PAGE 608)

CROSS-COUNTRY TOUR

You are about to start on a 12,000-mile (19,200 km) auto trip across the country. You are told by your mechanic that your four tires definitely will last 8,000 miles (12,800 km) each, but not a mile more. You can't take any chances, so you have to buy some spares and carry them with you. How many spare tires do you need to buy?

(SOLUTION ON PAGE 609)

WHO IS THE AVON LADY?

Jill, Tracy and Liz each work at two jobs. Each one of them is two of the following: actress, model, private detective, sculptor, race car driver and Avon lady.

From these facts, can you tell which girl is the Avon lady? And which is involved in each of the other occupations?

1. The sculptor and the race car driver used to go to school with Jill.
2. The model bought some make-up from the Avon lady.
3. Liz beat both Tracy and the model at tennis.
4. The actress and the sculptor are roommates.
5. The actress dated the model's brother.
6. Tracy owes the race car driver $10.

(SOLUTION ON PAGE 609)

WHAT IS THE NAME OF THE LARGEST RABBIT IN THE WORLD?

Jim, Mark and Sally each have unusual pets. Jim calls his Jarvis, Mark calls his Marvin, and Sally calls hers Spot. One of the pets is a baboon, another is a penguin, and the third is the largest rabbit in the world.

1. The rabbit played soccer with his owner yesterday.
2. Jim's leg has been in a cast for 2 months.
3. The baboon's owner goes horseback riding every Saturday with one of the other pet lovers.
4. The baboon bit Marvin.

What is the name of the largest rabbit in the world?

(SOLUTION ON PAGE 609)

THE FARFELS

These are Farfels. All Farfels have something in common.

These are not Farfels.

Belinda   **Flo**   **Dmitri**   **Beauford**

Which ones are Farfels?

(SOLUTION ON PAGE 609)

RUSSIAN TUNNEL

During World War II, three Russian V.I.P.'s, Molotov, Vishinsky and Malenkov, were travelling on a train in Russia. Suddenly the train entered a tunnel without the conductor's turning on the lights. The tunnel was long and sooty. At the moment the train emerged, Stalin wandered into the car and noticed that the men had become spotted with soot.

He said to them: "Before I show you a mirror, I have an idea. Your answers will show me which of you is the quickest thinker."

The three men immediately sat up and paid strict attention, for each was anxious to show Stalin how smart he was.

"Now," said Stalin, "each of you gentlemen will please look at the other two, and if you see *one* whose forehead is smudged with soot, raise your hand."

All three quickly raised their hands.

Stalin continued, "As soon as any one of you knows with certainty whether he himself has been smudged or not, drop your hand."

Looking at each other for a few moments, the three men kept their hands raised. Then Malenkov dropped his hand and said, "I know. I am smudged." Could he really have known? Or was he guessing?

(SOLUTION ON PAGE 609)

FAMOUS 45

Divide the number 45 into four parts so that if 2 is added to the first and subtracted from the second, if the third is multiplied by 2 and the fourth divided by 2, the result of each process will be the same.

(SOLUTION ON PAGE 609)

THE MAILBOX MYSTERY

The vice-president of a large corporation had an extremely efficient housekeeper. When he left for his vacation, he instructed her to forward the mail to him at his camp. During July he received no mail, so he phoned his home and asked the housekeeper what had happened. She explained that he had forgotten to leave her the mailbox key.

The vice-president apologized and promised to mail her the key right away. During August, he still received no mail, though the housekeeper had told him there was a batch of mail in the box. When he returned home, he immediately fired the housekeeper. Was he right in doing this? Or was he unfair? Why?

(SOLUTION ON PAGE 609)

AFRICAN THINKING GAME

An explorer goes to Africa to find his friend Diamala, but he doesn't know what tribe Diamala belongs to. There are three tribes in the area, the Elephant Tribe, the Leopard Tribe and the Crocodile Tribe.

A person belonging to the Elephant Tribe always tells the truth.

A person belonging to the Leopard Tribe always lies.

A person belonging to the Crocodile Tribe sometimes tells the truth but sometimes lies.

In order to find his friend Diamala, the explorer must find out what tribe Diamala belongs to. He asks three Africans—each from a different tribe—two questions: "What tribe do you belong to? What tribe does Diamala belong to?"

Agassu answers: "I am not an Elephant. Diamala is a Leopard."

Bantu says, "I am not a Leopard. Diamala is a Crocodile."

Coffi says, "I am not a Crocodile. Diamala is an Elephant."

What tribe does Agassu belong to? What tribe does Bantu belong to? What tribe does Coffi belong to? And finally, what tribe does Diamala belong to?

(SOLUTION ON PAGE 609)

THE TWO BROTHERS

A Saxon king, displeased with the greed shown by his two sons, left a will with an unusual provision: The sons were to mount their horses in a tiny town on the border of the kingdom and ride, without dismounting more than once, to the gate of the king's castle. The son whose horse arrived *second* at the castle gate was to be awarded the entire fortune.

When the king passed away, the sons began their "race," moving along slowly together for days on end. Each tried to go slower than the other and after a while, they got so sleepy they had to dismount and get some sleep at an inn. While they slept, they each had their footmen alerted to notify them when the other left the inn. Actually, they left the inn together. As they were about to mount their horses, one brother whispered a few words to the other, they both laughed, jumped into the saddles and raced the horses as fast as they could to the castle gate.

It doesn't matter to us which brother won the fortune, but can you figure out what the brother whispered?

(SOLUTION ON PAGE 609)

THE WISE KING

During the Middle Ages, a Nordic king had the opposite problem. His sons were good friends, and the king wanted to make sure that they would have no cause for jealousy after his death over the division of his property. He didn't want to provide in his will merely that the possessions were to be divided equally, lest his sons start quarrelling over what each was to get.

Finally the king thought of a foolproof yet simple way of providing for absolutely equal distribution of his possessions. What did he write in his will?

(SOLUTION ON PAGE 609)

DEATH MEETS THE SQUIRE

In a small English town long ago, this story was told:

It was a hot summer Sunday. The squire and his wife were in church when the squire fell asleep. He dreamed he was a French nobleman at the time of the Revolution. He had been condemned to death, and he was waiting on the scaffold for the guillotine to fall. Just then his wife, noticing that he was asleep, tapped him sharply on the back of his neck with her fan. The shock was so great—in view of what he was dreaming—that the squire immediately slumped over, dead.

Could this story be true? Why?

(SOLUTION ON PAGE 610)

GETTING A RAISE

Two young men wanted to marry Susie Johnson. Susie's father wanted to know which one was smarter, so he offered each of them a job in his office.

They started to work for Mr. Johnson on the same day, and they each received a salary of $10,000 a year. At the end of their first day of work, Mr. Johnson called them in and said:

"Bob and Tom, I'm going to give each of you a choice. I will give you each a raise of either $1,000 every year, or $250 every six months. Think this over until tomorrow morning and let me know then which you prefer."

The next morning, Bob told Mr. Johnson he would rather receive a raise of $250 every six months, while Tom said he preferred the $1,000 a year raise. Mr. Johnson immediately fired Tom.

Later on, Tom met Bob and said, "I don't understand it. I guess I asked for too much money."

Bob looked at him in surprise.

Was that the reason Tom had been fired? Which young man asked for the greater raise?

(SOLUTION ON PAGE 610)

THE NIFTIES

These are Nifties. All Nifties have something in common.

These are not Nifties.

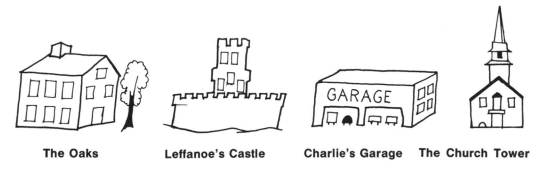

The Oaks   **Leffanoe's Castle**   **Charlie's Garage**   **The Church Tower**

Which ones are Nifties?

(SOLUTION ON PAGE 610)

REVOLUTION IN PLATONIA

After the revolution in Platonia, the dethroned king, his prime minister, and his treasurer were arrested and tried by the revolutionary court. Before sentence was passed, the judge spoke to each of the prisoners.

To the king he said, "If *and only if* both your ministers receive the same sentence will you be executed."

To the prime minister, he said "If *and only if* the king and the treasurer receive the same sentence will you be imprisoned."

To the treasurer, the judge said, "If *and only if* the other two receive different sentences will you be set free."

The judge then pronounced his sentence. "Tomorrow morning one of you will be set free, another will be imprisoned for life, and the third will be executed." He then ordered the guards to lead the prisoners away.

"Wait!" they shouted, "what's to become of us?"

The judge merely replied, "I've already told you," and he walked calmly away. What were the respective sentences?

(SOLUTION ON PAGE 610)

WHO WANTS TO WORK FOR
KING SADIM?

Every month each of the six provinces of the Kingdom of Kardonia paid, as tribute to King Sadim, a quantity of gold proportional to its population. The payments were made in sacks of 16-ounce (448 g) nuggets.

One month the minister of finance reported to Sadim that one province was paying with nuggets that weighed only 15 ounces (420 g).

In a fury, Sadim told his minister: "Tomorrow morning, you shall place no more than 16 of the nuggets from the various sacks on the royal scale. If you cannot identify the guilty province when you learn the weight of these nuggets, you will be executed on the spot!"

How can the minister save his life?

(SOLUTION ON PAGE 610)

CANNIBALS AND MISSIONARIES

This classical puzzle has stumped people for many years. Possibly it is based on a real event.

In deepest Africa there once were three missionaries who had converted three cannibals and were bringing them back to civilization. When they reached the Congo River, they realized they would have a problem ferrying the cannibals across, because their boat could carry only two at a time. It was not safe to let the cannibals outnumber the missionaries at any time—not on either side of the river nor in the boat. To complicate matters further, only one of the cannibals, the king, could row, although all three missionaries could handle the boat.

Using pencil and paper—or coins—or toothpicks—can you figure out how many trips it took them to get across safely?

(SOLUTION ON PAGE 610)

THE CASKET AND THE BASKET

Perhaps not as ancient as the Cannibals and Missionaries, but old enough, is this story of the royal family imprisoned in London Tower. The king (who weighed 200 pounds [100 kg]), the queen (who weighed 110 pounds [55 kg]) and the crown prince (who weighed 95 pounds [47.5 kg]) were all imprisoned in the tower, along with a casket (weighing 80 pounds [40 kg] filled) which contained the royal jewels. Some of their friends managed to rig up a pulley with two baskets and a rope long enough to reach from the tower window to the ground.

Word reached the prisoners that they were going to be moved to another prison the next day, so the king decided to get his family out by the pulley and baskets that very night. He knew that the pulley arrangement would work just so long as there was no more than 15 pounds (7.5 kg) difference in weight between the two baskets.

The king put the casket in one basket, lowered it to the ground, and ordered the crown prince to get into the other basket. Did the royal family manage to escape with their lives and their jewels? If so, how did they do it? Even a mechanical engineer may have trouble with this one!

Note: Actually 1 kilo = about 2.2 pounds, but in the metric version of this puzzle, the royal family and its jewels are a little heavier.

(SOLUTION ON PAGES 610–611)

THE TENNIS NUT

Whenever Rodney can sneak away from work for a morning or afternoon of tennis, he does. He plays tennis every weekend: one match each morning and another in the afternoon.

Since the beginning of July he went to work 26 days, but never for the whole day. On these days he played tennis either in the morning or in the afternoon.

Up to last night, he played 25 matches in the morning and 21 in the afternoon.

Rodney is going to be fired on August 6th. How much time does he have?

(SOLUTION ON PAGE 611)

THE KRIPPIES

These are Krippies. All Krippies have something in common.

These are not Krippies.

June   **Watch**   **Pansy**   **Dragonfly**

Which ones are Krippies?

(SOLUTION ON PAGE 611)

COFFEE, TEA FOR THREE

Abigail, Bridget and Claudia often eat dinner out. Each one orders either coffee or tea after dinner.

If Abigail orders coffee, then Bridget orders the drink that Claudia orders.

If Bridget orders coffee, then Abigail orders the drink that Claudia doesn't order.

If Claudia orders tea, then Abigail orders the drink that Bridget orders.

Who always orders the same drink after dinner?

(SOLUTION ON PAGE 611)

THE DRESSING ROOM MURDER

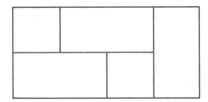

Vera, one of the performers in a play, was murdered in her dressing room. The illustration above shows how the dressing rooms are laid out. Each of the five performers in the play—Vera, Adam, Babe, Clay and Dawn—had his or her own dressing room.

(1) The killer's dressing room and Vera's dressing room border on the same number of rooms.

(2) Vera's dressing room borders on Adam's dressing room and on Babe's dressing room.

(3) Clay's dressing room and Dawn's dressing room are the same size.

(4) Babe's dressing room does not border on Clay's dressing room.
Who killed Vera?

(SOLUTION ON PAGE 611)

THE MUTILATED DICTIONARY

Mark's dictionary had 632 pages. Each page had 25 entries and every seventh entry was illustrated. One day, when he went to use his dictionary, Mark found that his little sister had cut out all the illustrations which were among the first 5 and the last 6 entries on each page.

Can you tell how many illustrations remained in Mark's mutilated dictionary?

(SOLUTION ON PAGE 612)

MADNESS AT THE BIKE SHOP

The owner of the Atlantis Bicycle Shop was quite mad. When he took inventory, instead of counting the number of bicycles and tricycles in his store, he counted the number of pedals and the number of wheels. Once he counted 153 wheels and 136 pedals.

How many bicycles and tricycles did he have?

(SOLUTION ON PAGE 612)

THE PARAGLOPS

These are Paraglops. All Paraglops have something in common.

These are not Paraglops.

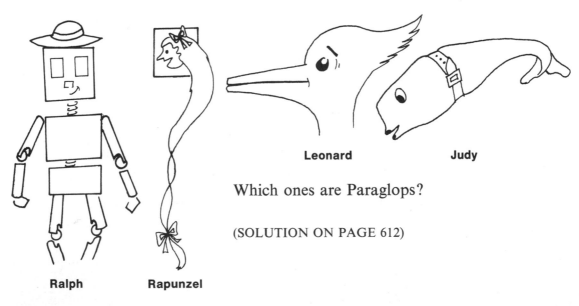

Ralph   Rapunzel   Leonard   Judy

Which ones are Paraglops?

(SOLUTION ON PAGE 612)

NOT COMIN' THROUGH THE RYE

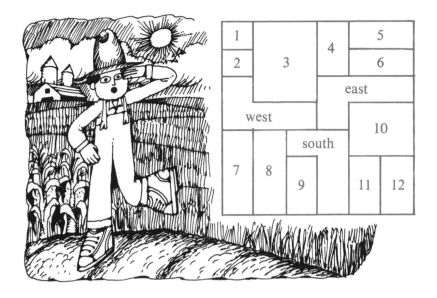

The plan above shows an arrangement of corn, wheat and rye fields. Jack is in the middle of one of the fields and has to meet his father in the middle of another field. On his journey from the field he is in to the field his father is in:

(1) His route takes him continuously through each of the five other fields exactly once.

(2) He is allergic to rye, so he avoids going through any part of a rye field.

(3) No two fields of the same kind border on each other.

Which L-shaped field—east, west or south—is a rye field?

(SOLUTION ON PAGE 612)

THE TERRIBLE TIC-TAC-TOE PLAYERS

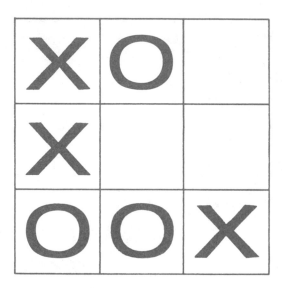

The game of Tic-tac-toe (Noughts and Crosses) is played in a large square divided into nine small squares.

(1) Each of two players in turn places his or her mark—an X or an O—in a small square.

(2) The player who first gets three marks in a horizontal, vertical, or diagonal line wins.

(3) A player will always place his or her mark in a line that already contains (a) two of his or her own marks or (b) two of his or her opponent's marks, giving (a) priority over (b).

Only the last mark to be placed in the game is not given. The next player—X or O—will win, but which player will it be?

(SOLUTION ON PAGE 612)

THE RIBBLES

These are Ribbles. All Ribbles have something in common.

These are not Ribbles.

Lynn   **Ivan**   **The Baron**   **Mrs. Hyde**

Which ones are Ribbles?

(SOLUTION ON PAGE 612)

Optical Illusions

THE CAT DISAPPEARS

Close your left eye. Keep your right eye focused on the dog and move the book back and forth in front of you. At one point, the cat disappears completely! Turn to page 613 to find out why.

COUNT

THE CUBES

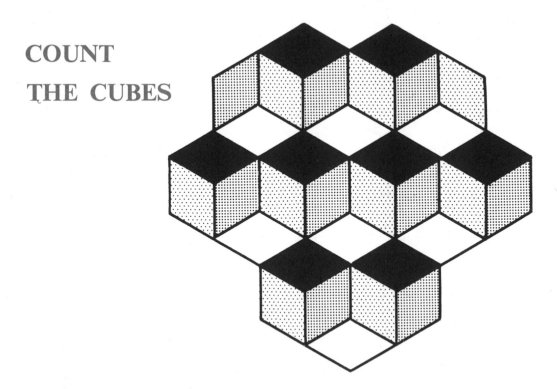

Are there 7 cubes here? Or 8?

(SOLUTION ON PAGE 613)

CHANGING IMAGES

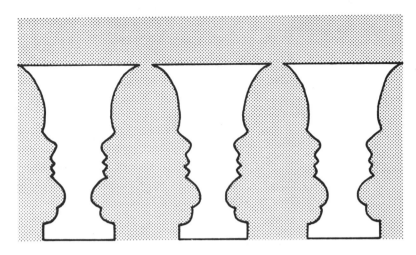

Faces—or vases?

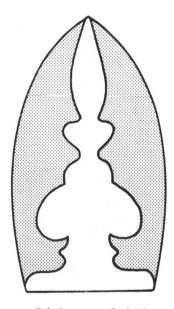

Light—or fight?

(SOLUTION ON PAGE 613)

THE THREE MOVIE BUFFS

Which of these movie-goers is the tallest?

(SOLUTION ON PAGE 613)

GOOFY GEOMETRY

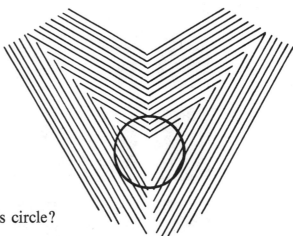

a. What is the matter with this circle?

b. Are the sides of this square bulging out?

(SOLUTION ON PAGE 613)

WHAT'S ON WHITE?

What shows up on the intersecting white lines, even though they are all white?

(SOLUTION ON PAGE 613)

THE FENCE

Concentrate very hard on a point in the white field of intersecting lines for about 30 seconds. Then shift your attention quickly to one of the black squares. What do you see inside the black squares?

(SOLUTION ON PAGE 613)

THE WARPED BARS

Are the white bars straight or do they bulge and bend?

(SOLUTION ON PAGE 613)

NIGHTMARE FOREST

Are the vertical lines straight? Do the cross-bars go straight through them or is their pattern uneven?

(SOLUTION ON PAGE 613)

THE MAD HAT

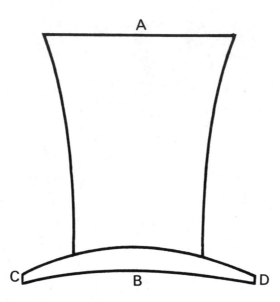

How does the height of this top hat (A–B) compare with the width of its brim (C–D)?

(SOLUTION ON PAGE 613)

CUT-OUTS

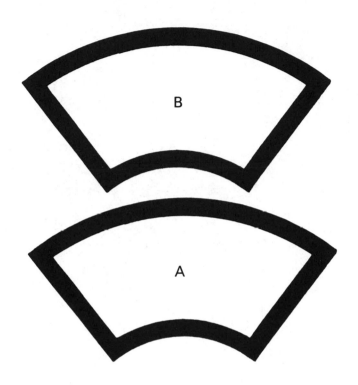

Are A and B the same size?

(SOLUTION ON PAGE 613)

YOUR HIDDEN HOSTS

The owners of this house are shy.
Can you find them?

(SOLUTION ON PAGE 613)

THE UNSURE LINES

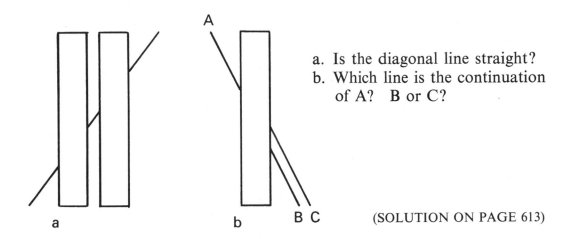

a. Is the diagonal line straight?
b. Which line is the continuation of A?   B or C?

a

b

B C

(SOLUTION ON PAGE 613)

FIND THE HIDDEN SHAPES

Each shape is hidden *once* (same size) in its corresponding diagram. For example, shape #1 is hidden in drawing #1. Can you find the shapes with your naked eye?

1.

1.

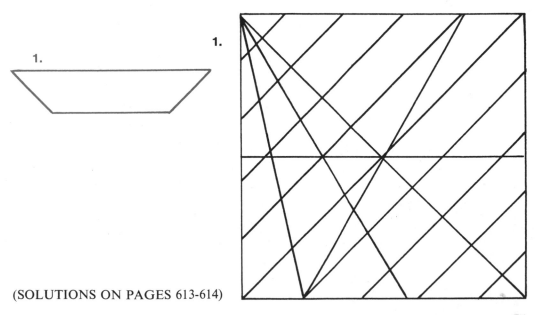

(SOLUTIONS ON PAGES 613-614)

See the instructions for Find the Hidden Shapes on page 51.

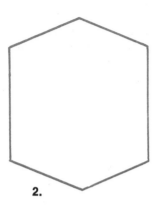

2.

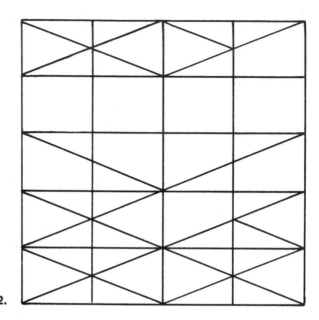

2.

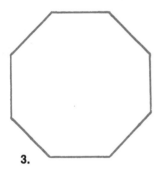

3.

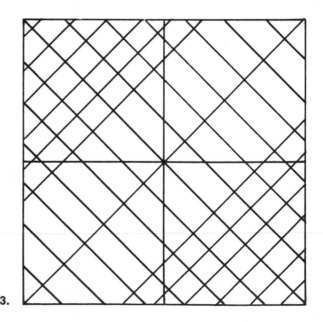

3.

See the instructions for Find the Hidden Shapes on page 51.

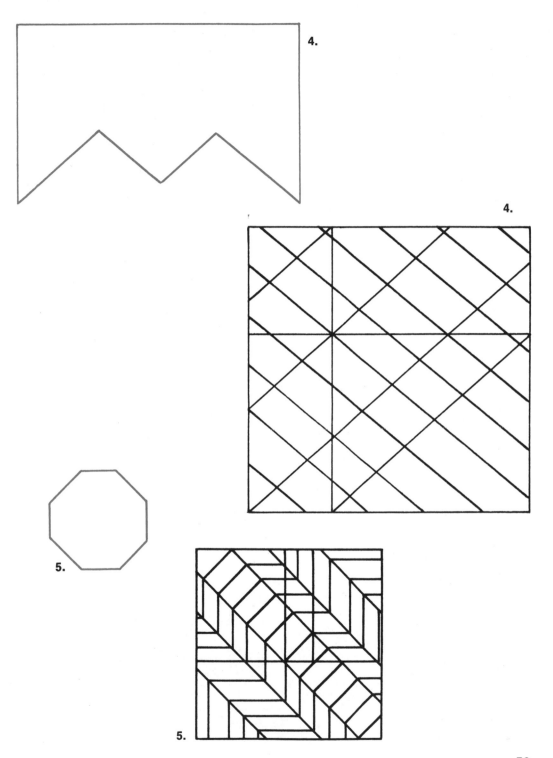

4.

4.

5.

5.

See the instructions for Find the Hidden Shapes on page 51.

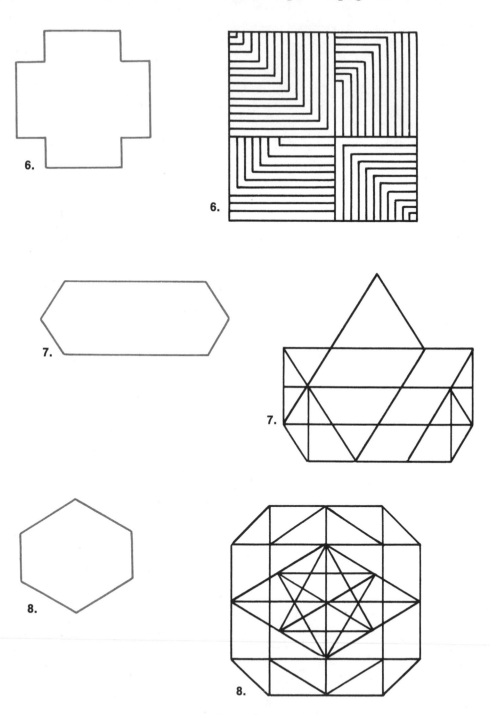

6.

6.

7.

7.

8.

8.

See the instructions for Find the Hidden Shapes on page 51.

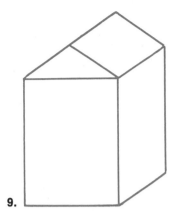

9.

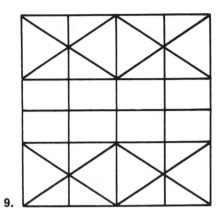

9.

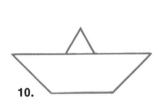

10.

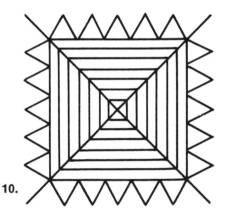

10.

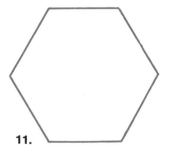

11.

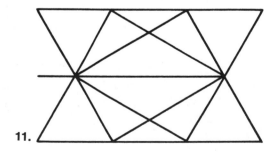

11.

Calculator Puzzles and Games

UPSIDE-DOWN DISPLAYS

Seven of the digits on a calculator, when turned upside down, make reasonable approximations of letters of the alphabet. Solve the following problems by entering the figures and performing the calculations in the order they are given, then read the display upside down to answer the clue. You may want to guess the answer before trying the calculation.

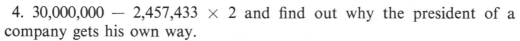

1. The square root of 196 and get a greeting.

2. 44 × 70 and get a musical instrument.

3. 52,043 ÷ 71 and get a snake-like fish.

4. 30,000,000 − 2,457,433 × 2 and find out why the president of a company gets his own way.

5. $7,964^2$ + 7,652,049 and get the name of a large oil corporation.

6. 711 × 10,000 − 9,447 and get a competing oil corporation.

7. 53.5149 − 51.4414 ÷ 29 and find a farmer's storage place. (NOTE: If your calculator prints a 0 before a decimal point, divide by 2.9 instead of 29.)

8. 15^2 − 124 × 5 and get a distress signal.

9. 2 − 1.4351 ÷ 7 and get a name for a wolf. (See note on #7.)

10. 159 × 357 − 19,025 and get a beautiful young lady.

11. 471 × 265 + 410,699 and learn what a snake does.

12. 99^2 − 2,087 and get a rise.

13. 1 − .930394 ÷ .9 and get a telephone greeting. (See note on #7.)

14. 217 × 121 − 8,550 and get a kind of pop.

15. .161616 ÷ 4 and find out what Santa Claus said when you asked him for a yacht. (See note on #7.)

(ANSWERS ON PAGE 614)

THE CALCULATOR MURDERS

Here is a list of the people who worked at the Acme Calculator Company:

Lise Bell
Hi Bishel
Max Carty
Lil Ellis (second victim)
Bill Hess

Bobo Hill
Elsie Lee (first victim)
Eli Shill
Bob Sobel
Ollie Sol

Two of the workers have been murdered. Police believe it is an inside job, and that the killer will strike again. Of course they could wait till everyone except one was murdered, and the person remaining would probably be the criminal, but this would involve considerable criticism of the police force. Besides, there is no firm evidence, and they would like to catch the dastardly villain in the act.

Can you help the police figure out the name of the fiend, his probable motive, and his next scheduled victim? Remember that murders, like wars, may be committed for very trivial reasons.

(ANSWER ON PAGE 614)

MORE UPSIDE-DOWN DISPLAYS

See page 56 for instructions.

1. $31 \times 11 \times 11$ and get a small island.
2. $3^9 + 35,495$ and get a description of married life.
3. $5,016 \times 11 + 2,542$ and get unwelcome arrivals on the first of the month.
4. $1,000 + 852.8667 \times 2$ and get the bottom line on your shoes.
5. $851^2 - 143,667$ and find what a man does when he loses a winning ticket worth $100,000.
6. $0 - 1,234,567 + 6,589,945$ and find what a preacher does.

7. 2,101 × 18 and get the name of a very good book.

8. 60² — 96 and get a gardening tool.

9. 1,234 — 463 and find out what you'll be after eating four gallons of ice cream.

10. 23⁵ — 1,118,998 and find out why you shouldn't trust a girl when she's in bed.

11. 305,644 ÷ 43 and get into hot water.

12. 9,999 — 8,038 × 3 and find what the tide does after it flows.

13. 73² + 9 and get a honey of an answer.

14. 127³ + 4,618,283 — 1,347,862 and find how people occupy their spare time.

(ANSWERS ON PAGE 614)

MAGICALCULATIONS

One of the most useful tricks in the magician's repertoire is the ability to "force" a card. The magician asks a volunteer to select a card at random, but through sleight of hand, the card picked is the one the magician wanted picked.

To perform magic on your calculator, you don't have to master difficult manipulations with your hands. The only digits you manipulate are the ones in your calculator. This is the easiest kind of magic, since the tricks work themselves once you know the mathematical secret.

Tell your friend to choose any number—of any number of digits, scramble it up, subtract and then add it across—and you will be able to predict the result. This is how it works:

1. "Choose a number." (567134, for example)	567134
2. "Scramble it up, any way at all."	−341765
3. "Subtract the smaller number from the larger number."	225369
4. "Cross-add the digits until only one is left." (2 + 2 + 5 + 3 + 6 + 9 = 27 = 9)	9

Your prediction, of course, is "Nine."

You could stop the trick here. But you can make things more interesting. If you know your friend's age or street address, you can keep giving instructions to add or subtract until you reach it. Let's say your friend's address is 182 River Road. Go through the whole trick the way you did before, but then, after your friend cross-adds all the numbers and has only the "9" left: 9

5. "Add your grade in school." (You know your
   friend is in 8th grade.)   8
                                                               ———
                                                                17
6. "What would you rather have—$1000 or $1?
   Add the figure you'd like to have."   1000
                                                               ————
                                                                1017
7. "Subtract the last four digits of your telephone
   number." (You know that they are 0822.)   0822
                                                               ————
                                                                195
8. "Subtract your age." (You know your friend is
   13.)   13
                                                               ———
9. "The result is your address."   182

Probably the most impressive way to perform this trick is to write down the "182" prediction on a slip of paper before the trick begins and hand it to a spectator. Then have your friend do all the calculations and ask to have the prediction read out loud.

You can make this trick even more astounding. The number your friend starts with can be the result of any number of instructions that you give your friend. For example, your friend could start with today's date, multiply by the number of people in his or her family, subtract his or her grade in school, add street address, multiply by number of close friends, subtract number of enemies, and then do the trick with the resulting number.

ANSWER IS ALWAYS NINE

Here is another way to "force" a 9 on your unsuspecting friends:

1. **Put into your calculator any number from 10 to 99. (Your friend chooses 28.)**   **28**
2. **Reverse the digits.**   **82**
3. **Subtract the smaller number from the larger one. (82 — 28 = 54)**   **54**
4. **Divide by the difference in your original two digits. (In this case, the difference is 6: 8 — 2, so 54 ÷ 6)**   **9**

You won't want to do the trick the same way every time. And of course you need to keep things moving fast enough so your audience won't realize that a 9 is coming up all the time.

Here are some other methods:

1. **Pick any number of up to 7 digits.**	4751
2. **Multiply by 10.**	47510
3. **Subtract your original number.**	42759
4. **Divide by your original number.**	9

Or you can do it this way:

1. **Pick any number up to 6 digits.**	4751
2. **Multiply by 100.**	475100
3. **Subtract your original number.**	470349
4. **Divide by 11.**	42759
5. **Divide by your original number.**	9

YOUR CALCULATOR IS CALLING

This simple trick is especially good for displaying your friend's phone number—the last four digits—or his or her address.

Suppose the last four digits of the telephone number are 3823. Before the trick, secretly subtract 1089 from this number:

$$\begin{array}{r} 3823 \\ -1089 \\ \hline 2734 \end{array}$$

Now ask your friend to do the following:

1. **Choose a number between 100 and 1000.**	235
2. **Reverse the numbers.**	532
3. **Subtract the smaller from the larger (532 − 235).**	297
4. **Do you now have a number between 100 and 999? (In this case, the answer is yes, so proceed as follows:)**	
5. **Reverse the digits and add.**	792
	1089
6. **Add 2734.**	2734
	3823
7. **Does this number have any special significance to you?**	

Your friend will have to admit it is his or her own telephone number.

There are two things to keep in mind while you do this trick. Look at Step 4. If your friend says no, the number in the machine is *not* between 100 and 999, substitute the following Step 5, instead.

> **Alternate Step 5: Reverse the digits, put a zero on the end, and add. For example, if the number your friend had was 99 (it cannot be lower than that), reversing the digits and putting a zero on the end would bring it to 990. 99 plus 990 equals 1089.**

The one other possibility is that Step 4 will lead your friend to a zero. This would happen if your friend picked a number such as 101 or 202. Make sure that you're not starting with this type of number. One way to make sure is to tell your friend to select a number in which all the digits are different.

See page 81 for another way to use this trick.

MAGIC MULTIPLIERS

Once you can force a number on your victim, you can perform all kinds of calculations and make up all sorts of tricks. Try this system:

If you multiply 1001 by 111 and then by 9, you get 999999.
a. The number 1001 can be made up from 3 other numbers, multiplied by each other—7 × 11 × 13.
b. The number 111 can be made up from 2 other numbers multiplied by each other—3 × 37.
c. The number 9 is made up of 3 × 3.

To perform the trick:

1. Select any number between 2 and 6.	**5**
2. Multiply it by 1001.	**5005**
3. Multiply it by 111.	**555555**
4. Multiply that by 9.	**4999995**
5. Divide by 7.	**714285**

The number that you have at this point is a peculiar one. (You can read more about ways to use it on page 89.) It is a variation on the number 142857, which keeps coming out to this sequence of numbers every time, but in different order. If you do this trick with the number 2, you'll get 285714. If you do it with 3, you'll get 428571. If you do it with 4, you'll get 571428. If you do it with 6, you'll get 857142.

Now you can get your friend to select a number of your own choice by telling him or her to take

the lowest digit	—1
the lowest even digit	—2
the sum of the 2 lowest digits	—3
the lowest even digit doubled	—4
the middle-sized odd digit	—5
the sum of the 2 lowest digits × 2	—6
the highest odd digit	—7
the highest digit	—8
the sum of the 2 lowest digits × 3	—9

Since you already know what digit your friend will pick, when you give one of these instructions, you carry him or her through some involved calculations—and you'll already know the answer. If your calculator has a memory, you can do these involved calculations first, put them aside in memory, and then retrieve them later for more hokus-pokus.

*   *   *   *   *

Now try this. Tell your friend to pick a secret number:

1. Pick any number from 100 to 999.	**138**
2. Multiply it by 1001.	**138138**

The number will always duplicate itself, side by side.

You can work this stunt in reverse:

1. Pick any number from 100 to 999.	**537**
2. Duplicate it side by side.	**537537**

At this point you know that the secret number (whatever it is) × 7 × 11 × 13, will equal the number now in your friend's calculator. If you want your friend to come out with "13":

3. Divide by 7.	**76791**
4. Divide by 11.	**6981**
5. Divide by your secret number.	**13**

Or if you want your friend to come out with 77, use the following steps instead:

3. Divide by 13.	**41349**
4. Divide by the secret number.	**77**

Or if you want the secret number left:

3. Divide by 7.	**76791**
4. Divide by 11.	**6981**
5. Divide by 13.	**537**

If you want a 1 left, divided by all 4 numbers:

    6. Divide by the secret number.   **1**

*   *   *   *   *

To do the same stunt with a 2-digit number, ask your friend to select any number from 10 to 99 and put it into the calculator three times, next to each other. This is the same as multiplying by 10101. This time you'd be working with 3, 7, 13 and 37. Try it:

    1. Select any number from 10 to 99.   **68**
    2. Put it into your calculator 3 times.   **686868**
    3. Divide by 3.   **228956**
    4. Divide by 7.   **32708**
    5. Divide by 13.   **2516**
    6. Divide by 37.   **68**

*   *   *   *   *

And you can do it with a one-digit number, too. This would be the same as multiplying by 111, and you'd use 3 and 37.

    1. Select any number from 1 to 9.   **8**
    2. Put it into your calculator 3 times.   **888**
    3. Divide by 3.   **296**
    4. Divide by 37.   **8**

TREASURE HUNT BY CALCULATOR

PLAYERS: 6–12
EQUIPMENT: A pocket calculator for each set of partners.
                Pad and pencil for each set of partners.
PREPARATION: See below.

    Each player or pair of players is given a number to put into a calculator. When turned upside down this number will tell them the place to go to find the next clue. Well . . . almost. Remember that only a few letters of the alphabet can be represented by turning numbers upside down. Some of the letters in the clue will be missing, and the players will have to figure out what the complete word is. For instance, if the number 304373 came up in the display, the players would have to figure out that clue is TELEPHONE.

When they solve the first clue and go to the place indicated, they will find a new number which they must add or subtract to the number already in the machine, to get their next clue. Players had better write down each number as they come to it, which will make sure they discover all the clues in order, and help them get back on the track if something should go wrong.

1. 773800
2. −770293
3. +704944
4. −708337
5. +700386
6. +71001
7. −399701
8. +35578
9. −403571
10. +374523
11. −324773
12. +291894
13. −310443
14. +10097
15. +5525902

(ANSWERS ON PAGE 614)

THE NUMBER IS 43,046,721

This stunt works well for a friend whose age you don't know. First memorize the number 43,046,721, or write it on a slip of paper and put it in your pocket.

Then ask your friend to do the following:

1. **Put in the year of your birth.**
2. **Subtract 3.**
3. **Add your age.**
4. **If you have not had your birthday this year, add 1.**
   If your birthday is past, skip this step.
5. **Subtract the current year.**
6. **Add 6.**
7. **Square the amount in your calculator.**
8. **Square the amount** *now* **in your calculator.**
9. **Square whatever amount you have in your calculator** *now.*
10. **Square whatever amount you have in your calculator** *now.*

Then tell your friend the answer—or bring the paper out of your pocket and show it to him or her.

The secret? When your friend put in the birth year plus age this year and subtracted the current year, nothing remained. All that your machine contained was $-3 + 6 = 3$. Knowing there will be a 3 in the machine, you can carry out any calculation you please, like this one for 43,046,721.

If you want to do more with your calculator, turn to page 572 which shows how to make your own biorhythm charts with a calculator.

TRICKS

2

Challenge Your Friends

THE LAST STRAW

PLAYERS: 2
EQUIPMENT: 4 straws, 16 matches or 16 toothpicks
PREPARATION: None

You can play this puzzler with straws, matches or toothpicks. If you play it with straws, use four and cut them in four parts each, so that you have 16 pieces. Take the 16 straws, place them in one straight line on the table. Now challenge any of your friends to play against you. The rules are simple: The two of you alternate in taking 1, 2 or 3 straws at a time from the line. Announce that you will *never* be left with the last straw.

If you go first, you can always win. Here's the secret:

Take 3 straws, leaving 13. At your next turn, leave 9 straws, then 4, then 1. Those are the numbers to remember—13—9—4—and 1. If you have to let your opponent start, you may still be able to bring the combination to 13, 9, 4, and 1, but you can't do it if your opponent knows the secret.

STUCK WITH A TOOTHPICK

PLAYERS: 2
EQUIPMENT: 12 toothpicks or 3 straws (cut them in 4 parts, if you use them,
             as in the previous trick) or use 12 matches
PREPARATION: None

In this contest, the principle is the same: the loser is left with the last toothpick or match or straw. Start by placing 12 toothpicks on the table in 3 rows: top row of 5 toothpicks, middle row of 4 toothpicks, and bottom row of 3. Now each player is allowed to take as many toothpicks as he or she wants from any *one* row at a time. Challenge your friends to beat you at this. You'll always win.

Turn the page for the secret . . .

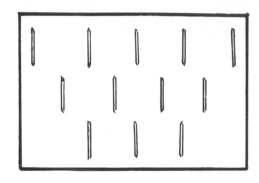

**The starting set-up:
12 toothpicks
in 3 rows**

THE SECRET: When your opponents go first, it doesn't matter much what they do. Try to leave any of these combinations after your turn:

2 rows of equal number
rows of 1, 2, and 3 toothpicks
rows of 5, 4, and 1 or
rows of 1, 1, and 1

If your opponent takes 2 toothpicks on the first turn from the bottom row, leaving you with rows of 5, 4, and 1, your opponent can win, but most players don't know that.

If you have to go first, your best chance is to take 2 from the bottom row, and you will surely win. If you don't want to give away the secret by taking 2 from the bottom row, take 1 from that row, or take 2 from the middle row, or 3 from the top row: these are the most confusing moves, and will probably allow you to bring the combination back to what you want on your next turn.

Let's examine why you win with the above combinations. If you leave 2 equal rows (of 3 each, let's say) and your opponent takes 1, you take 1 from the other row, leaving 2 equal rows again. Now if your opponent takes 2, you take 1, leaving the last. If your opponent takes 1, you take 2, leaving the last again.

Let's say you leave 1, 2 and 3 toothpicks. If your opponent takes 3, you take 2, leaving the last. If your opponent takes the row of 2, you take the row of 3, leaving the last. If your opponent takes the row of 1, you take 1 from the row of 3, leaving 2 equal rows of 2, and you win—as described above. If your opponent takes 2 from the row of 3, you take 1 from the row of 2, leaving 1, 1, and 1, and this, of course, will win for you.

If you leave 5, 4 and 1, you can always convert the next step into 2 equal rows of 1, 1, and 1—or 1, 2, and 3—and win.

YOU CAN'T
WRITE "TENNESSEE"

PLAYERS: 1 or more
EQUIPMENT: Chair
            Table
            Paper and Pencil
PREPARATION: None

Tell your friends that you'll give them a pencil and paper, nothing will be done to hamper their hands, they can sit at a table to write, but they still will not be able to write a simple word like "Tennessee."

Before you let the victims start, let them practice a little foot movement. They must not stop this movement for a second while they are writing. The movement is nothing but a simple circling of one foot under the table. Sit down on a chair and demonstrate the motion. Move your foot clockwise in a circle about as big as a plate. Then let your friends try it.

As soon as they are sliding their feet around satisfactorily, give them pencils and let them try to write a designated word. No matter how hard they try, they will not be able to write anything but strange-looking hieroglyphics.

The secret is that it is difficult to keep two very different motions going at the same time. Your hand wants to start making the same movement that your foot is making. However, if you practice you will be able to surprise your friends by writing any word they call out without stopping the motion of your foot for an instant.

A TOUCHY PROBLEM

Just as with the two movements involved in the last trick you will find that you are clumsy if you try to pat your head gently with one hand in an up-and-down motion at the same time you rub your stomach in a circular motion with the other hand.

Naturally, when you demonstrate the trick to your friends, you will have practiced enough to have mastered the necessary coordination. Some people will get the knack of the trick sooner than others, of course, and then the real fun begins.

Let a whistle be the signal for reversing the motions: pat your head and rub your stomach, whistle, rub your head and pat your stomach, whistle, and so on. Most people get the two movements hopelessly confused.

MORE COORDINATIONS

1. Make a circle with your left foot while you make a figure 6 in the air with your left arm.

Switch the direction of your foot circle.

Now do it with your right arm and foot.

Now use your left arm and your right foot.

2. Make a circle with your left foot while you make a figure 8 in the air with your left arm.

Switch the direction of your foot circle.

Now do it with your right arm and foot.

Now use your left arm and your right foot.

LUCKY PENNY

Stand with your back to the wall with your head and heels touching it. Try to pick up a penny without moving your heels. If you can get it, you're very lucky!

TRICKY DRINKING

PLAYERS: 1 or more
EQUIPMENT: Glass of water
PREPARATION: None

Can you drink without putting your nose into the glass? Yes, you can! With a little agility, you can demonstrate how to drink as shown in the illustration below.

There is no doubt that your nose is well outside the rim of the glass. Your friends will laugh and try to imitate you, but this is a trick which will spill water over them several times before they master it.

KNOT THAT WAY

PLAYERS: 1 or more
EQUIPMENT: String about 20 inches (50 cm) long
PREPARATION: None

Place a string about 20 inches (50 cm) long on a table. Ask your friends to hold one end of the string in each hand and tie a knot—without letting go of the string. Now you can sit back and watch the amusing contortions they go through. No matter how hard they try, they simply will not be able to tie a knot without releasing at least one hand.

Then demonstrate how to do it. Cross your arms as shown in the drawing. Bend over the string and grab the ends in your hands. As you straighten up, by uncrossing your arms, you will have tied a perfect overhand knot.

THE IRRESISTIBLE FORCE

Bend your fingers and put your hands together, so that your fingers meet at the second joint, as in the illustration.

Now move out your third fingers (the tall ones) on each hand, so that they are pointing up and leaning against each other. Get your fingers tightly joined again at the second joint.

Now try to separate your third fingers without separating your other fingers.

STUCK TO THE WALL

Stand with your head, shoulder, one side and its heel tight against the wall. Now try to move the outside leg without moving any other part of your body away from the wall.

QUICK-CHANGE ARTIST

PLAYERS: **2 or more**
EQUIPMENT: **Long-sleeved sweater**
               Jacket
               Door
PREPARATION: None

You can confound your friends with the following exhibition of skill. Make the claim that you can take off the long-sleeved sweater you are wearing under your jacket and put it back on *over* the jacket all the while someone holds one of your hands.

Your friends may say that it's impossible for you to exchange the sweater and jacket in this way because the two pieces of clothing have to be taken off both arms. Tell them that you will do the trick behind the door, and that you will leave the door open just far enough to put your hand through for someone to hold your hand (see illustration). When you push open the door with your free hand, your clothing will be changed. Your sweater will no longer be under your jacket. It will be over it!

THE SECRET: As soon as you are hidden behind the door, slip off your jacket. This is not hard to do with one hand. The jacket will now be dangling from the arm which is being held from the other side of the door. Now use your free hand to slip off the sweater as well, first pulling it over your head and then sliding your free arm out of the sleeve.

At this stage of the trick, both the jacket and sweater are hanging from the arm which is being held. The trick now is to pull the whole sweater through the sleeve of your jacket! As soon as you have pushed and pulled the sweater through the jacket sleeve, it will hang on your wrist below the jacket. To finish the trick, slip your jacket back on and then pull the sweater on again—this time *over* the jacket. Open the door quickly, and watch the surprised looks on your friends' faces.

THE TRICK NO ONE CAN DO

This trick is supposed to have originated in a seaport where sailors and dock hands were once showing off how strong they were. One boasted that he could rip a thick telephone book in half, while another bragged about his ability to bend iron bars. A third claimed that he could keep an automobile from starting up by holding it back with his hands.

A bystander suggested that he knew of a feat of strength that no one could do. All of the strong men were immediately ready to show their strength and were surprised when the bystander handed the first a glass full of water.

"Hold this glass on the palm of your hand for seven minutes," he said, "and keep your arm stretched out straight all the time."

The first man shook so much that the glass fell to the ground and broke before the seven minutes were up, the second got a cramp in his arm, and the third gave up in disgust.

This is a trick that no one can do. If you don't believe it, try it yourself.

Amaze Your Friends

THREE-DIGIT MIRACLE

Take any 3-digit number, 197 for example.

Write it backwards:		**791**
Subtract the smaller number:		**−197**
	Total:	**594**
Now write 594 backwards:		**495**—and add it
		1089

What's so miraculous about that? No matter what 3-digit number you use, you'll *always* come up with 1089!

NOTE: If you get the number 99 as the "total" number, look out. Remember, it isn't 99 at all, but 099. So when you write it backwards, write 990.

Example: 211 is the number you pick:

	211
Write it backwards and subtract the smaller number:	112
Total:	099
Write it backwards and add it:	990
	1089

The only numbers that won't work are numbers that are written the same backwards and forwards—such as 141, 252, or 343.

If you want to see how you can use this to perform other tricks, see page 62.

WHO'S GOT THE STRING?

Number all the players in the group and ask them to tie a string on someone's finger while you leave the room or turn your back. Offer to tell them not only who has it, but which hand and which finger it is placed on!

Ask one of the spectators to make the following calculation for you:

1. **Multiply by 2 the number of the person with the string.**
2. **Add 3.**
3. **Multiply the result by 5.**
4. **Add 8 if the string is on the right hand.**
   Add 9 if the string is on the left hand.
5. **Multiply by 10.**
6. **Add the number of the finger (the thumb is 1).**
7. **Add 2.**

When you are told the resulting number, mentally subtract 222. The remainder gives the answer, beginning with the right-hand digit.

For example, suppose the string is on the left hand, third finger of Player #4:

Player's number (4) multiplied by 2	**8**
Add 3	**11**
Multiply by 5	**55**
Add 9 for left hand	**64**
Multiply by 10	**640**
Add finger number	**643**
Add 2	**645**
Subtract	**−222**
	423

The right-hand digit stands for the third finger. The middle digit stands for the left hand (1 would be the right hand), and the 4 tells the number of the person.

When the number of the person is above 9, the *two* left-hand digits indicate the number of the person.

HOW OLD ARE YOU?

Try this on your friends:

1. **Write down the number of the month in which you were born.**
2. **Multiply by 2.**
3. **Add 5.**
4. **Multiply the total by 50.**
5. **Add the magic number. (The magic number varies from year to year. In 1978 it is 1428;**
   in 1979 it is 1429;
   in 1980 it is 1430;
   in 1981 it is 1431, and so on)
6. **Deduct the year you were born.**

The last two digits are your age.

THE SECRET: What you're doing in Steps 1–4 is forcing your friends to come up with a figure that ends in the digits 50. Once you have that, and you add the "magic number," the last digits of that figure are the digits of the current year. Then it is a simple matter of deducting the year of birth and coming up with your age. For instance:

Your birth month:	7
Multiply by 2:	14
Add 5:	19
Multiply by 50:	950
Add magic number:	1428 (if it's 1978)
	23(78 is the current year)
Deduct the year you were born:	1962
	16—your age.

1425 FOR 15

THE SECRET NUMBER

People who are good at math won't have much trouble figuring out why this trick works. Others will be mystified completely. Tell your friends that you are going to read the numbers in their minds, if they do what you tell them.

Now ask them to think of a number, but not to tell it to you.

Then tell them to double that number (mentally), multiply the sum by 5, and tell you the result. You knock off the zero on the end and the remainder is the secret number.

For instance, your friend may take 7. Doubling makes it 14, and multiplying it by 5 makes 70. Knock off the zero and 7 is your answer. It always works—because doubling the number and then multiplying it by five is just the same as multiplying it by 10. When you take off the zero, of course, you have the original number.

If this is too simple for your audience, tell them that you will guess two numbers at a time. Tell them to think of two numbers from 1 to 9, but not to tell you what they are. Tell them now to

take *either* **number**
multiply it by 5
then add 7
and double the sum.
Then add the other original secret number
and subtract 14.

When they tell you the result, it will be a 2-digit number and each digit will be one of the secret numbers.

For example, if someone thought of 2 and 9, and took 9 first, it would go like this:

$$
\begin{array}{r}
9 \times 5 = 45 \\
+\ \ 7 \\
\hline
52 \times 2 = 104 \\
+\quad 2 \\
\hline
106 \\
-\quad 14 \\
\hline
92
\end{array}
$$

Just as in the first example, you are asking your friends to multiply the original number by 5 and then by 2, or by 10 altogether. The 7 is merely to confuse them, for after doubling it, you get them to subtract the doubled 7 by taking off 14. When the second number is added to 10 times the first one, you naturally get the two secret numbers.

MATH MAGIC

With this fascinating trick, you can add large numbers with remarkable speed and accuracy.

Ask your audience to write down 2 rows of figures, each containing 5 digits, such as:

1st row:	3 4 6 5 8
2nd row:	4 6 8 2 9

Now you put down a third row of figures:

3rd row:	5 3 1 7 0

Ask your audience to put down a fourth:

4th row:	6 2 3 5 3

Now you write a fifth row:

5th row:	3 7 6 4 6

Then you look at the figures a moment and write on a small piece of paper, fold the paper and give it to someone in the audience to hold. Then ask the audience to add up the numbers and call out the total. When they figure it out, call for your slip of paper and unfold it. There—for everyone to see—is the correct total!

HOW IT IS DONE: You work your calculations while you are putting down your rows of figures. When you write the third row, make each of your numbers total 9 when added to the number *just above it* in the second row. (Ignore the top row.) In the fifth row, make each number total 9 when added to the number in the fourth row.

Now you can figure out the grand total very quickly from the *first* line: Just subtract 2 from the last number of the first line (8) and place the 2 in front of the first number.

Audience:	3 4 6 5 8
Audience:	4 6 8 2 9
You:	5 3 1 7 0
Audience:	6 2 3 5 3
You:	3 7 6 4 6
	———————
Grand Total:	2 3 4 6 5 6

EXCEPTIONS: If the audience writes a *first* number that ends in either 0 or 1, you need to mentally reverse the first and second row of figures. When you put down the third row, put down numbers that total 9 when added to the numbers in the *first* row. Ignore the second row until the grand total. Follow the same procedure as usual with the fourth and fifth rows. But figure the grand total by using the *second* line—subtracting 2 from the last number and placing 2 in front of the first number.

Audience:	3 4 6 5 0
Audience:	4 6 9 2 9
You:	6 5 3 4 9
Audience:	6 2 3 5 3
You:	3 7 6 4 6
	———————
Grand Total:	2 4 6 9 2 7

NUMBER WIZARD

You are the number wizard. Ask your friends to choose any number from 1 to 10. Then tell them to add 8 to it in their heads (keeping it secret), double it, divide it by 4 and then subtract half of the original number.

"The answer is 4," you say. And you are right! Even though your friends haven't told you a thing about their numbers.

If you had told them to add 6 to the original number, the answer would be 3.

How does it work? The remainder is always half of the number you tell them to add—everything else cancels out.

Or try this one:

"Take a number," you say. "Add 7, double it, add 16, double it again, divide by 4, and subtract 15. Now you each have the number you started with!"

Mystifying? Still it's simple to figure out, because the doubling, dividing, adding and subtracting equal out, and you have really done nothing to change the original number.

MAGIC NUMBER

EQUIPMENT: Paper and pencil for you and your victims

There actually is a magic number which you can multiply with lightning speed in your head. The number is 142,857. Prepare yourself with paper and pencil and show your friends that the paper is blank. You will use it only to write down the result.

Now give your friends pencil and paper and ask them to multiply 142,857 by any number from 1 to 7. Then ask them, one at a time, to tell you any *one* figure in the result. Suppose the third figure from the left is 5. You know immediately that the entire total is 285,714! You also know that the multiplier was 2.

Suppose the fourth figure from the left is 4: then you know the total is 571,428 and the multiplier is 4.

Do you get it? Every possible total of this magic number, when multiplied by 1 to 6, results in the same series of digits, but it begins at a different point. Multiply them out if you want to check, or run them through a calculator. Therefore, if you know the position of any *one* number in the sequence, you are able to write down the total correctly. In the example above, when your friend told you that 4 was the fourth figure, you put down 428 at the end of the total, and 5, 7, and 1 in front, according to the sequence.

How do you know what the number was multiplied by? Look at the last digit you wrote down. Since $4 \times 7 = 28$ (and this is the only combination that ends in an 8) the multiplier gives itself away. That last digit is different for each multiplication.

Oh yes—if you multiply the magic number by 7, you get another magic number:

999,999!

See page 64 for more about 142,857.

"LUCKY" MAGIC SQUARE

You've already seen the regular magic square (page 16), but would you believe that you can construct a "lucky" magic square all your own out of the date you were born? You can, and it's easy! All you have to do is memorize a basic pattern.

Take the date of your birthday and write it above the magic square, like this:

12/30/(19)64

8	1	7
5	6	3
2	9	4

You'll notice that small numbers appear in the right-hand corner of each box. Those numbers show you the order to follow when you write in the answers to the following questions. (Write the first answer in Box 1, the second in Box 2, etc.).

1. Insert the year (last two digits) in Box 1.

2. You have your choice of which is the next number you want to use, the number of the month (12) or of the day (30). You also have your choice of whether you want to add or subtract either number. Just check quickly to make sure that if you subtract the number twice from the total in Box 1 you will still have a "plus number." "Minus numbers" don't work in this magic square.

Let's say that you decide to add. And that you decide to work with the 12 (the month) first. Add 12 to 64 and you get 76. Write 76 in Box 2.

3. Since you have decided to add, you have to continue to add in this third step. Use the 12 again, but this time add it to the sum that you put in Box 2: 12 plus 76 equals 88. Write 88 in Box 3.

Now your magic square looks like this:

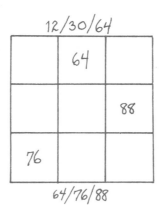

12/30/64

	64	
		88
76		

64/76/88

These numbers are your KEY numbers. Write them underneath the square, as shown above.

4. In the last two steps, you added the month of your birth. Now you are going to work with the day (30). Again you have your choice of whether you want to add it or subtract it. Check to make sure that if you subtract it twice from each KEY number, you'll still have a "plus number." In this case, you can do either one. Let's say you decide to subtract. First subtract from the first KEY number: 64 minus 30 equals 34. Write 34 in Box 4.

5. Now, since you've started subtracting, you must continue subtracting, right through to the end. 34 minus 30 equals 4. Write 4 in Box 5.

You are finished with the first KEY number. Cross it out where you wrote it below the square.

6. Now subtract 30 from the second KEY number. 76 minus 30 equals 46. Write 46 in Box 6.

7. Subtract 30 from that total: 46 minus 30 equals 16. Write 16 in Box 7.

You are finished with the second KEY number. Cross it out where you wrote it below the square.

8. Now go to the third KEY number, 88. Subtract 30 from it, for a total of 58. Write 58 in Box. 8.

9. Subtract 30 from the total you just had (58 minus 30 equals 28). Write 28 in Box 9.

Now you are finished, and your magic square looks like this:

12/30/64

58	64	16
4	46	88
76	28	34

64/76/88

It adds up to 138 in each row horizontally, vertically and diagonally.

If you had subtracted in the first steps, or added in the later steps, you would have gotten a different total perhaps, but you would always get a magic square that added up in all 8 directions. Let's take a look at what would have happened:

12/30/64

70	64	112
124	82	40
52	100	94

64/52/40

12/30/64

16	64	58
88	46	4
34	28	76

64/34/4

Look at the square on the left above. In this combination 12 was subtracted in the first steps and 30 added to the KEY numbers. It adds up to 246 in all directions. You did not have the option of subtracting 30 from the KEY numbers (40 minus 30 minus 30 would have given you a minus number), so this is the only other possible combination you could get using the 12 first.

Look at the square on the right above. In this combination 30 was subtracted in the first steps and 12 added later to the KEY numbers.

And you see that this is actually the same magic square that you came up with originally, with some of the numbers in different spots. You did not have the option of subtracting 12 from the KEY numbers (4 minus 12 minus 12 would have given you a minus number), so this is the only other combination possible.

In every case, though, you created a magic square that added up in all 8 directions.

If you are performing this as a magic trick, ask your friends to tell you which number they want you to begin with and whether they want you to add or subtract. Just remember not to give them that option if subtraction would force you to use minus numbers. Spectators will be particularly impressed by the fact that *they* seem to be making all the decisions! When you finish, you can tell them that the magic number (138 or 246 in these examples) is a lucky number for the birthday person, and give him or her the magic square to carry about for special good luck!

See pages 56-68 for more math magic.

Fantastic Things You Can Do

YOU CAN CRAWL THROUGH A NARROW PAPER HOOP

EQUIPMENT: A strip of paper about 24 inches (60 cm) long
Glue
Scissors

You can crawl through a narrow paper hoop without tearing it.

The exact size you make your hoop depends on your age and size. A strip of paper about 24 inches long should be big enough for most 8–12-year-olds. If you're older, make it just an inch or two longer. The approximate diameter of the 24-inch hoop will be about 7 or 8 inches (20 cm).

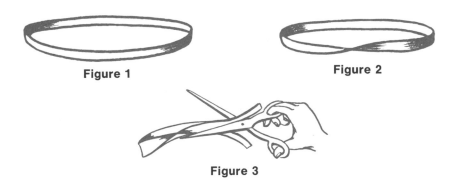

Figure 1
Figure 2
Figure 3

Does it sound impossible? It would be, except that this is a trick. Only you will be able to do it, to the amazement of your friends. This is the secret:

Before you paste the hoop together, give the paper strip a half twist. Your hoop should *not* look like Figure 1, which is simply a pasted hoop. It should look like Figure 2. A mathematician once found out that such a strip does not fall into two parts if you cut it apart lengthwise. Instead, you get a hoop twice the size! Try this amazing thing. Cut the hoop lengthwise with your scissors. Now the hoop is large enough for you to crawl through easily without breaking it. No one will guess what you did in making the hoop—they'll think you're just a sloppy paster!

YOU CAN CRAWL THROUGH A PLAYING CARD

EQUIPMENT: An old playing card
Scissors

This extraordinary trick has been handed down from parents to children for centuries.

Take a playing card that you don't want to use again. Fold it lengthwise, as in Figure 1. Make a series of cuts as shown in Figure 2.

Figure 1

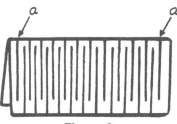

Figure 2

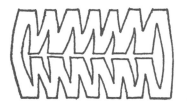

Figure 3

Then cut the *folded* side from *a* to *a*. The result is a structure which, unfolded, spreads apart to form a large ring! It is surely big enough—if the cuts are close together—to let you slip through!

YOU CAN CARRY A COLUMN OF WATER

EQUIPMENT: A glass of water
A drinking straw

Place the straw in a glass of water and suck at the straw. When the water reaches your mouth, place your finger on the top end of the straw as you remove it from your mouth.

Keeping your finger in position, raise the straw from the glass. Trapped inside the straw, and retained by air pressure, is a slender column of water. Walk around with it, if you want to, or run with it!

Now release your finger from the end of the straw, allowing air to come in the top of the column. The water will run out of the straw. Make sure the glass is underneath to catch it.

YOU HAVE A RUBBER THUMB

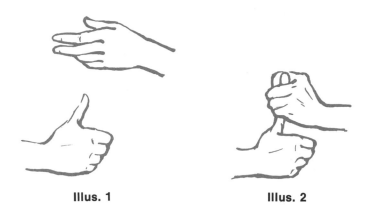

Illus. 1   Illus. 2

Hold one thumb straight up and grasp it tightly with your other hand (see Illustration 1). Illustration 2 shows how this trick appears from the front. The thumb of the top hand is shoved under the index finger of that hand. When the end peeks out, it looks as if it is the end of the thumb on your *lower* hand.

First get into the position in Illus. 1. Now start "pulling" on that lower thumb and make faces as if you are in great pain. Actually, you're not pulling at all. All you are doing is moving your upper hand slowly up the thumb which is being "stretched." Wiggle your lower hand back and forth with great effort, and slowly slip the end of your thumb under your index finger so it peeks out at the top.

"Stretch" your thumb as far as you can without giving yourself away. As soon as the end of your lower thumb starts to appear, slide your upper hand all the way back down to the lower hand with a sudden jerk—as if the stretched thumb were snapping back into place. Then open your hand quickly and begin massaging the "rubber" thumb as though you can still feel the pain.

Younger spectators will be especially pleased by this trick and will watch—fascinated—as you torture your thumb!

Practice the trick in front of a mirror until you get the impression yourself that your thumb is being stretched. If you can't fool yourself, who can you fool?

YOU HAVE A BROKEN FINGER

If you are tricky enough with your fingers, not only can you stretch your thumb, but you can even seem to break off your index finger!

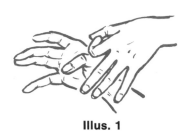

Illus. 1

First, hold your hands as shown in Illus. 1. Then place your bent thumb right up against your index finger, which you have also bent. Now you need to cover up the spot where your thumb and index finger touch. Do this simply by placing the index finger of your upper hand over that place (see Illus. 2). This makes it look like a whole finger, even though it is just the combination of one thumb joint with one index finger joint.

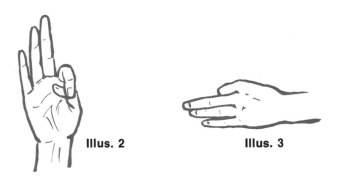

Illus. 2   **Illus. 3**

Now quickly slide the hand with the thumb-part away, without changing the position of any of your fingers (see Illus. 3). Your audience will think that your finger has actually broken off!

Before they can recover from their shock, slide your hands back together. The "broken" finger is together again! Then stretch out your finger normally and rub the "wound." Your puzzled spectators will try to figure out how you did it—so that they can do it themselves.

YOU CAN SEE THROUGH A HOLE IN YOUR HAND

EQUIPMENT: **A newspaper square of about 9 inches (23 cm)**
Scissors
Tape

It is possible to do many things. But would you believe that you can see through a hole in your hand—without having to make one?

Roll the square of newspaper into a tube about one inch ($2\frac{1}{2}$ cm) in diameter. Tape the free end of the paper to the side of the tube.

Take the tube in your right hand and hold it to your right eye so that you can see through it quite clearly.

Now raise your left hand, palm facing you, until it is a few inches in front of your left eye, with your little finger touching the side of the tube. Open both eyes and look straight ahead. Can you see the hole in your hand?

YOU CAN MAKE PEOPLE'S HAIR STAND ON END

EQUIPMENT: A balloon

Blow up the balloon and rub it briskly on some fur or woolen cloth. You can use your sweater to produce a very effective charge of static electricity in the balloon. Then pass the balloon over the hair of your friends. Up it stands! Strangely enough, most people don't feel anything when their hair is attracted toward the balloon, but let someone hold up a mirror for them!

Incidentally, both pet cats and dogs show distinct signs of uneasiness when the balloon is held close to their coats!

You can use this same static electricity to attach balloons to the wall, which is convenient at parties. You can attach playing cards to the wall, too, we've heard, just from the electricity you get by dragging your feet along the carpet, but have yet to see it proved. Maybe it only occurs on a cold, dry day. Want to try it?

YOU CAN DEFY GRAVITY

EQUIPMENT: A pitcher or large drinking glass with straight sides,
or one that is wider at the bottom than at the top
A small ball (like a ball you'd use to play "jacks")

This trick involves carrying a ball in a pitcher (or in a large glass). Put a small ball on the table and cover it with a pitcher. Challenge your friends to carry the ball from that table to another table without touching it and without turning the pitcher right side up.

Impossible? Actually, it's very simple to do. Just start making a circular motion with the pitcher so that you hit the ball and gradually get it to make the same circles as the pitcher itself. By doing this, you create a force (known as centrifugal force) which will press the ball against the inside of the pitcher. Now—without stopping the circular motion—you should be able to lift both the pitcher and the ball. In this way, as long as you keep the ball rotating inside the pitcher, it will not fall out, even though the pitcher is upside down.

Whether you use a glass, a vase, or a pitcher for this trick, the container must have straight sides or, preferably, be wider at the bottom. Centrifugal force causes a ball to find the largest possible circle in which to rotate. As a result, in a pitcher or vase which is larger towards its base, the ball will be drawn up safely inside.

Then you can take a few careful steps and put the circling pitcher down on the other table. You have moved the ball without touching it!

YOU CAN TURN A GLASS OF WATER
UPSIDE DOWN WITHOUT SPILLING IT

EQUIPMENT: Drinking glass
       Postcard or thin piece of cardboard with a glossy surface

Fill a smooth-rimmed drinking glass to the very top with water and lay the postcard or thin piece of cardboard with a glossy surface on top of the glass. Press the card gently to the rim of the glass with your left hand, while you pick up the glass in your right hand and turn it upside down.

Now remove your left hand from the card carefully, and—behold —the water stays in the glass! In spite of gravity, which could be expected to pull both the water and the card to the floor, the card sticks to the rim of the glass and holds the water in.

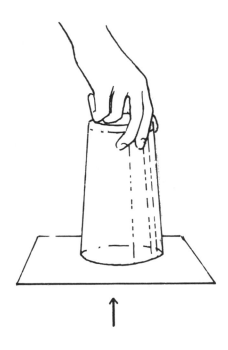

What you have just achieved is the result of air pressure. Since there is almost no air at all inside the glass, the air can press only upwards on the underside of the card and it supports the water.

If you do this trick indoors, do it over a pail or a sink. One clumsy movement can result in a very wet floor.

YOU CAN MAKE PAPER AND CORK DANCE WITHOUT TOUCHING THEM

EQUIPMENT: **A small pane of glass**
2 books
A silk handkerchief or scarf
Tissue paper
Cork
Glycerin

Rest the ends of a glass between the pages of two open books, raising the glass so that it is about ¾ of an inch (2 cm) from the top of the table. Tear some tissue paper into tiny scraps and spread these below the glass. Rub vigorously on top of the glass with the piece of silk. Within a few seconds, the scraps of tissue paper will seem to dance! (They have been attracted by the static charge of electricity that you are producing in the pane of glass.)

Instead of tissue paper you can use tiny pieces of cork, ordinary bottle cork chopped up. These can be made to perform, too, and it is possible to create such a strong charge that the cork will hang from the underside of the glass like miniature stalactites!

If you really want to surprise your friends, however, tell them that the pieces of cork are so obedient to your will that you can make them form an initial of your name. To do this trick, you need to prepare the pane of glass first. Smear an outline of glycerin in the shape of your initial on the underside of the glass.

Now when you rub the top of the glass with the silk handkerchief, the pieces of cork will be attracted to the underside. Where they come into contact with the glycerin, they will actually stick to the glass.

Stop rubbing the glass and the pieces of cork outside the glycerin outline will fall back to the table, leaving your initial clearly "written" in cork chips!

YOU CAN BE A HUMAN PRETZEL

The following feat requires great flexibility of your arms. If you have long arms, you should be able to do it easily. The idea is to make a loop with your arms and stick your head through it.

Follow these steps:

1. Hook your fingers together as shown in Illus. 1.

Illus. 1

2. Keeping your fingers clasped, slip one elbow into the bend of the other so that your arms hold each other. (You should not have to release your fingers.)

3. Your arms now form a noose through which it is possible to stick your head (see Illus. 2).

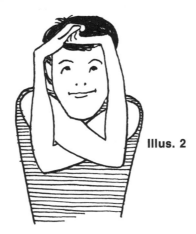

Illus. 2

Try it! While you are doing this, do not release your fingers. They should still be together when they are behind your neck.

4. Now slip your raised arms down slowly over your ears until your head peeks out of the loop made by your arms.

With a little practice, you will be able to demonstrate this at high speed.

YOU CAN LIFT
AN ICE CUBE
ON A STRING

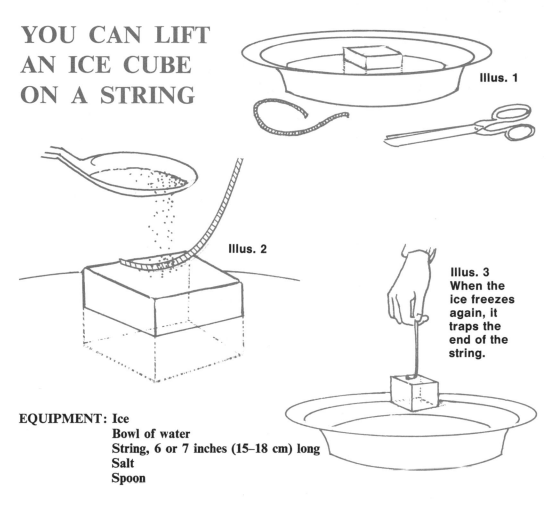

Illus. 1

Illus. 2

Illus. 3
When the ice freezes again, it traps the end of the string.

EQUIPMENT: Ice
Bowl of water
String, 6 or 7 inches (15–18 cm) long
Salt
Spoon

Challenge your friends to take an ice cube out of a bowl of water with a short piece of string as a derrick, without touching the ice directly.

Some will try to loop the string under the slippery cube; others will be completely baffled.

HOW IT IS DONE:

1. Dip the string in the water until it is thoroughly wet.
2. Then lay it across the top of the ice cube.
3. Now sprinkle a spoonful of salt along the line of the string, allowing the salt to fall on both ice and string. (See Illus. 2.) Where the salt strikes the ice, it will melt it a little (you know how salt can melt ice from the sidewalk in winter?) and form a coating with the water in the string. As this re-freezes, it joins in a strong bond with the string. Then you simply pull on the string and you will be able to lift the block of ice clear of the water.

YOU HAVE STRANGE POWER OVER EGGS

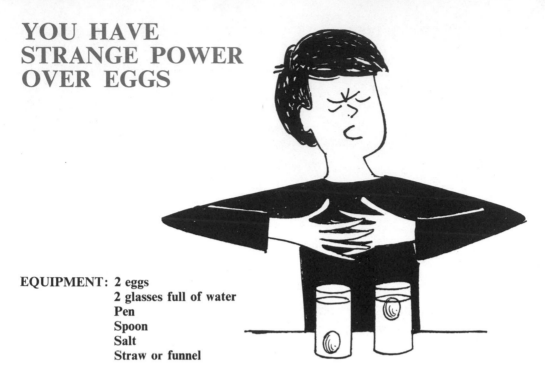

EQUIPMENT: 2 eggs
2 glasses full of water
Pen
Spoon
Salt
Straw or funnel

Announce that you are going to reveal the strange power you have over eggs. You then produce two eggs (fresh or hardboiled—it makes no difference—but hardboiled may be safer) and two glasses of water.

Ask someone in the audience to write the word "sink" on one egg, and another person to write the word "float" on the other.

Now tell your friends that these eggs will do just what they are told.

Saying this, place the "sink" egg in one glass and the "float" egg in the other. Do it gently, with a spoon. The "sink" egg will sink to the bottom of the glass and stay there. When you place the "float" egg in, wave your hand mysteriously over the glass and say a few masterful things to the egg. The "float" egg will sink to the bottom, and then slowly rise to float on or near the top!

If your friends think there is something special about the eggs, produce two more and perform the stunt again, letting any skeptic write the words this time. If they think there is something peculiar about the water, take a sip from the top of each glass, or let them do it.

HOW IT IS DONE: The glass on the left is plain water, and the egg sinks in that. But the glass on the right contains salt water (in a strong solution) at the bottom and a layer of fresh water on top. The fresh will not mix with the salt water if you pour it on top through a straw or funnel and let it slide down the side of the glass. Just an inch or less of fresh water on top is enough. You make the salt solution by dissolving the salt long ahead of time in a glass, and letting it stand. Then pour the solution into a fresh drinking glass so that no salt grains are visible in the bottom. Test with the egg to be sure the salt mixture is strong enough before adding the fresh water. And make sure, before performing the trick, that the glasses look alike.

YOU HAVE
STRANGE POWER
OVER CANDLES

EQUIPMENT: A candle
Matches

Before you begin, let your audience examine, light, and extinguish the candle you use, to prove that it is an ordinary candle. Then light the candle, and let the match continue to burn. As your audience watches, blow out the candle gently. The candle will continue to smoke a little. Wait a split second for the smoke to start up again in a straight line. Then hold the lighted match an inch or more above the candle and say, "Candle light, jump!"

Mysteriously, the candle will light up again!

HOW IT IS DONE: After a little practice, you will discover exactly the farthest distance above the candle that you can hold the match. The reason this works is that the stream of air above the candle is still hot and it acts as a wick, carrying the flame from the match *down* to the candle.

LEVITATION

PLAYERS: 5 or more
EQUIPMENT: An ordinary chair
PREPARATION: None

Four of you can lift even the heaviest person off a chair and into the air with only one or two fingers each. There is no gimmick to this feat. You can really do it, and it's as easy as it looks!

Let one of the group sit in the chair. Then the four of you who will do the lifting stand at the four corners of the chair. At a signal, you each take a deep breath and hold it. Then two of you put one or two fingers under the knees of the person in the chair, and the other two players put their fingers under the person's arms. Still holding your breath, you lift the person out of the chair and up into the air as if he or she weighed almost nothing at all! It is holding your breath that is the key to this feat. Don't let your breath go until the person is back in the chair.

Mind-Reading Tricks

THE MYSTERIOUS TEMPLE

EQUIPMENT: None

THE EFFECT: You leave the room while the group thinks of a number from 1 to 5. When you return, you go around the group, pressing your hands to the temples of each of the players. Feeling their heads, you get "thought waves" from them and—by the time one round is completed—you announce the number the group had in mind!

HOW IT IS DONE: You will *always* guess the right number, because you're not guessing. You have a spy or partner working for you. The spy clenches and unclenches teeth while you press his or her temples. If the number is 3, the spy clenches teeth three times. That way you get the correct "thought wave."

Feel your own temples as you clench your teeth and you will see that this movement causes a ripple which you can feel easily.

Anyone who doesn't know the trick will think you are performing miracles!

THE MAGIC CIRCLE
AND THE MAGIC CROSS

EQUIPMENT: None

THE EFFECT: You announce that there is a telepathic bond between you and your partner. You get it going when you draw the magic circle and the magic cross. Your partner leaves the room while you point out one of the people in the room and say you will "send" the person's name to your partner. When your partner returns, he or she immediately points to the person and says, "You are the one."

HOW IT IS DONE: You draw the magic circle by tracing a large circle on the table or on the floor with your finger. As you do it, you say, "This is the magic circle," and then you wait for a moment, until someone speaks. You and your partner have decided ahead of time that the first one to speak will be the person whose name you "send." Then you trace the magic cross (within the circle), saying, "And this is the magic cross."

PERFORMANCE TIPS: If too many people talk all at once after you draw the magic circle, you can say to your partner, "You're not in the magic circle—you're not getting my message, are you?" Your partner says "No," and you can start again.

Don't worry about what will happen if no one speaks. Someone always does!

ESP TAKES A TRIP

EQUIPMENT: None

This is a good follow-up to the Magic Circle and the Magic Cross, proving that you and your partner can work your ESP in several ways.

THE EFFECT: Your partner leaves the room while a spectator—let's say Pat—decides on one article of clothing which she will take on a trip. When your partner returns, you ask about several articles of clothing. Your partner eliminates everything but the one piece of clothing that Pat has selected.

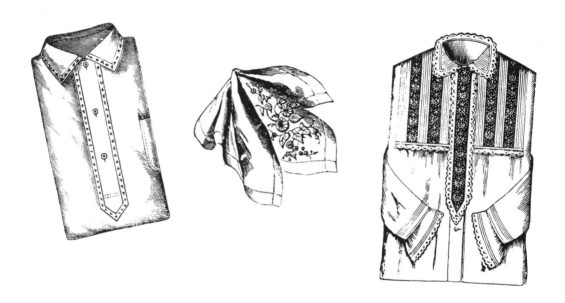

HOW IT IS DONE: Before the act, you and your partner decide on a color. You agree that the object you ask about immediately *after* you ask about something of that color is the one that is "going on the trip."

Let's say that the code color is white. And the object Pat picked is her jeans. You say to your partner:

"Beth is going on a trip. Can she take her shoes?"

"No," says your partner.

"Can John take his eye glasses?"

"No."

"Can Susan take her blouse?" (Susan's blouse is white.)
"No."
"Can Pat take her jeans?"
"Yes."

PERFORMANCE TIPS: You can vary this act by changing the color that you work with. Let it be white the first time, for example, red for an encore, and blue if you do it again.

Or skip the colors altogether. When you open the door to let your partner back in for the guessing part, be careful about the number of fingers you hold against the door. Whatever number you put there will be the number of the correct question. For example, if you put four fingers on the door, the fourth question will be the one to answer "yes" to. This limits you to 10 questions—but that's more than enough.

CUP, DISH
AND SAUCER

EQUIPMENT: A cup
A dish
A saucer
24 lumps of sugar

You can do this mental mystery with ordinary objects from the dinner table, which makes it a specially useful trick. You can do it when everyone is having coffee, and you wish you could get away from the table but you can't.

THE EFFECT: You ask three people to assist you with this telepathic demonstration. For convenience, we will call the first person Andy, the second person Ben, the third Charles.

You begin by dumping the 24 lumps of sugar onto a plate or simply onto the table. Then you give Andy a lump of sugar. You give Ben two lumps, and Charles three.

Now you say: "While I am in the next room, I want one of you to take the cup, another to take the dish, the third to take the saucer—an absolutely free choice among the three of you. Understand?"

After they nod agreement, you add:

"Whoever takes the cup must take the same number of lumps that I have already given him and hide those lumps under the cup. Whoever takes the dish must take twice as many lumps as he already has and hide them in the same fashion. Whoever takes the saucer is to take four times as many lumps and hide them."

Also, you warn: "Don't touch any of the remaining lumps or you may give me a false mental impression. When you are ready, call me back."

When you get back, pass your hand back and forth over the cup, dish and saucer, telling each person to keep concentrating on the item which he chose.

Then, in dramatic style, you point from the cup to one person, say Ben, as you announce: "You took the cup!" Next you point from the dish to another person—Charles—and declare: "You took the dish!" Turning to the last person, Andy, you conclude, "That means you took the saucer!"

You are right on every count!

HOW IT IS DONE: Actually it is a matter of counting, not X-ray vision, that enables you to look through solid tableware. What you count are the left-over lumps of sugar, those that you told people not to touch.

Before you do this trick, you must memorize a list of words, or better still, write them out in the form of a column, with certain letters underlined or capitalized. The words are: CADETS, DICKENS, CUSTARD, DRASTIC, SCORED, SARDONIC.

When you list them:

1. C a D e t S
2. D i C k e n S
3. C u S t a r D
5. D r a S t i C
6. S C o r e D
7. S a r D o n i C

Note that there is no #4 on the list. Also note that the large letters, C, D, S, appear in each word but in different order. Those letters stand for Cup, Dish and Saucer, respectively.

Here is how you use the list to work the trick:

Suppose Andy, the first person, should take the saucer. You have already given him 1 lump of sugar. Whoever chooses the saucer is to take 4 times the number of lumps you gave him.

So Andy takes 4 lumps and hides them.

Suppose Ben, the second person, takes the cup. You have given him 2 lumps of sugar. Whoever takes the cup is to take the same number of lumps that you originally gave him.

So Ben takes 2 lumps and hides them.

Suppose Charles, the third person, takes the dish. You gave him three lumps. Whoever takes the dish is to take twice as many lumps as you gave him.

So Charles takes 6 lumps and hides them.

You gave out 6 lumps to start with. The three persons have taken 12 more. That makes a total of 18. So there will be 6 lumps left, lying over to one side as though they didn't matter. But they matter a great deal!

No. 6 on your list is the word SCORED. Its "key" letters appear in the order S, C, D. That means the *first person*, Andy, took the saucer; the *second person*, Ben, took the cup; the *third person*, Charles, took the dish. You tell them that, making it sound very mysterious, and you are right!

If they had picked the objects in some other order, your key word would be different, but just as accurate, according to the left-over lumps. Two lumps, for example, would spell DICKENS, meaning that Andy had chosen the dish, Ben the cup, and Charles the saucer.

You can use more than 24 lumps of sugar, but make sure you know how many more, so you can ignore them. That is, if you use 28 lumps, mentally subtract 4 from the left-overs before counting through your list.

PERFORMANCE TIPS: You can use other objects, say a coin, a dollar, and a spoon, instead of a cup, a dish, and a saucer, since they also conform to the initials C, D, S. And you can use matches instead of lumps of sugar.

SNEAKY THUMBELINA

EQUIPMENT: Any three objects

THE EFFECT: Leave the room while the other players place three objects on the floor. They decide which object they are going to think about.

When you return you study the objects very carefully. Then you announce which one the group is thinking of.

HOW IT IS DONE: You are secretly in cahoots with another player. While you pretend to study the objects carefully, you are just covering up a sneaky look at your partner's thumbs.

If the object is the one on the right, your partner's thumbs are crossed so the right one is over the left.

If the object is the one on the left, your partner's left thumb is crossed over the right one. If it is the middle object, both your partner's thumbs are held together, side by side.

Be sure to practice this ahead of time with your partner so that you get the "left" and "right" of it straight.

SEEING THROUGH A SEALED ENVELOPE

EQUIPMENT: 4 cards, each about 3 x 4 inches (7.5 x 10 cm) in size
An envelope which is just large enough to hold a card comfortably
PREPARATION: Draw a different symbol on each card: a circle, a square, a triangle, an X.

THE EFFECT: Show the cards to the spectators. Call their attention to the symbols on the cards.

While you turn away, someone puts one of the cards into the envelope, seals it, and hides the other cards. You take the envelope, hold it to your head, concentrate, and name the symbol on the card. When the envelope is opened, this proves to be correct.

You can repeat this mental test with the same success. You can also vary it by having four different people take an envelope from a packet and place a card in it. You can name all four cards as easily as one. You may even let the spectators inspect the envelopes before and after the trick, proving that it is impossible to see through them.

HOW IT IS DONE: Although the cards seem to be identical in size, they vary slightly in their dimensions. That is the subtle secret of the trick. One card, which bears the circle, is just the size of the envelope, slipping in easily but snugly.

The card with the square on it is cut 1/16th of an inch (1–2 mm) short. This is too slight a difference to be noticed, even when you handle the cards as a group.

The card with the triangle is cut slightly narrow. The spectators won't notice that either. The difference is about 1/16th of an inch.

The card with the X is cut both short and narrow. This too is normally undetectable.

After a card is sealed in the envelope, however, you can check the difference swiftly and secretly by holding the opposite edges of the envelope between the thumb and finger and pressing slightly.

If there is no "give" in either direction, the "circle" card is in the envelope. If there is "give" from top to bottom but not sideways, it is the "square" card. If the envelope yields to sideways pressure only, it contains the "triangle" card. If pressure shows slack in both directions, the X card is inside.

PERFORMANCE TIPS: Practice the handling of the envelopes. You need to do it in a smooth, casual way. When you show the cards, stress the fact that they differ only in their symbols. Put one, then another, in an envelope and hold it to the light to prove that it is impossible to see through it.

Then when the card is sealed in the envelope and handed to you, take it by the edges, say at the top and bottom, pressing it as you do. Transfer the envelope to your other hand, which naturally takes it by the opposite sides, pressing them the same way. Then lift the envelope to your forehead, so that you can concentrate upon its contents and pick up a "mental impression."

By then, little concentration is necessary, because you know what card is in the envelope.

"READING" WITH YOUR FOREHEAD

EQUIPMENT: A small square of paper for each player (except you)
A pencil for each player (except you)

THE EFFECT: Everyone but you is given a small square of paper and a pencil. Each player writes a word or a short sentence on the paper. Then they fold their papers neatly in quarters.

You select one of the players to be your assistant, and that player collects the folded papers and gives them to you.

You take one of the papers and press it (still folded) to your forehead. Then you announce the message and, incredibly, it is the exact message that one of the players wrote.

You open up the paper to make sure the player is telling you the truth. Can you do it again? (Sure, you can.)

You take the next paper and hold it to your forehead, as if the message is going right through into your mind. Then you announce the message. It is, word for word, the sentence of one of the other players.

This goes on while you total up a perfect score.

HOW IT IS DONE: The assistant that you pick is working in cahoots with you. Before the trick, you two decide what that player's "message" will be. And your assistant makes sure that his or her paper is at the *bottom* of the pile that is given to you.

Then, when you take the top paper from the pile to "read" it mentally, you announce the message that you two decided upon in advance. Your assistant says, "That's mine! I wrote that!"

When you look at the paper to "check," what you're seeing is one of the other messages, one that belongs to someone else in the group. You remember it, put the paper aside and press the next message to your psychic forehead. When you announce the message, you report what you've just seen written on the previous piece of paper!

Each time you open a paper to "check" and make sure you got it right, you are reading the next message.

PERFORMANCE TIPS: Don't perform this trick more than once. The other players might get suspicious about the fact that your assistant's message is always read first. But it's a mighty impressive trick the first time, and no one will be able to figure out how you did it unless they know the secret.

THE NINE SLIPS

EQUIPMENT: **A sheet of paper with smooth edges**
            Pencil
            A hat—or deep bowl

THE EFFECT: Tear a sheet of paper into nine slips, all the same size. A spectator—Linda— writes any name on a slip, folds it, and drops it into a hat or deep bowl.

Now she writes other names on the remaining slips, folds them the same way and mixes them in the hat.

While Linda concentrates on the original name, you read through the slips one by one and finally announce the name that Linda has in mind!

HOW IT IS DONE: Use a sheet of paper with smooth edges. If necessary, cut any rough edges with a pair of scissors beforehand. Fold the paper into thirds—both ways—so it can be torn into nine equal pieces (see Illus. 1).

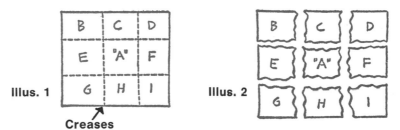

Illus. 1

Creases

Illus. 2

Do this neatly, so the slips look alike, but one of them—the original center of the sheet—will be slightly different. It will have four rough edges, whereas every other slip will have at least one smooth edge (see Illus. 2).

Illus. 3
Drop the
slips in
the hat.

Illus. 4
Find the slip
with all
rough edges.

Hand the slip with the four rough edges to Linda first, or put it on top of the others so that she uses it to write the name she has in mind.

More names are written on the remaining slips, but you can always pick out the right one by its four rough edges.

PERFORMANCE TIPS: Stress the fact that you are trying to catch one thought out of nine and that the slips are merely incidental. Go through them one by one, name by name; then start over and stop on the chosen one. That makes it look like real mind reading.

I'VE GOT YOUR NUMBER

EQUIPMENT: 7 square cards
PREPARATION: Write a number on each card, as described below.

THE EFFECT: You show the seven square cards to the group. One person, George, let's say, notes a number, and you lay the cards face-down in a circle. You tap the cards in a jumbled way while George spells his number mentally, letter by letter.

For example, suppose George spells "T-W-E-L-V-E," and on the final letter, says "Stop!" You turn the cardboard square up and, by an amazing coincidence, it is George's number—12!

HOW IT IS DONE: Each number is spelled with a different number of letters, so the count works automatically. The numbers on the cards are:

> 2—T-W-O
> 5—F-I-V-E
> 7—S-E-V-E-N
> 11—E-L-E-V-E-N
> 16—S-I-X-T-E-E-N
> 13—T-H-I-R-T-E-E-N
> 17—S-E-V-E-N-T-E-E-N

When you place the cards in a circle, you arrange them as follows:

> 2
> 7 13
> 16 11
> 17 5

Make the first two taps on any cards, but on the third tap, hit the 2, so that if George is spelling "T-W-O," he will say "Stop!" as he completes his spelling and you will turn up his card.

For the next tap, jump two cards clockwise, hitting the 5. The next jump is two more, to the 7; then to the 11, and so on around the circle, automatically turning up the right number on the word "Stop!"

PERFORMANCE TIPS: When you show the cards, don't say anything about spelling. Just say:

"Here are some cards with numbers from 1 to 20."

And you run through them, numbers up—

"And I want you to take one, look at it, remember it, and mix it with the rest, numbers down."

You hand George the cards, numbers down so that he can do this, while you turn away. Then you reach for the cards, saying:

"Let me have the cards so I can go through them while you keep thinking of your number—just that number and no other. I'll try to catch your thought . . . Now I have it!"

You don't have it, of course, but you have set your circle in the correct order.

You continue: "As I tap the cards, I want you to spell your number mentally, like 'O-N-E' for 1— or 'T-E-N' for 10—
and on the last letter say 'Stop!' "

Go about your tapping slowly, as if you are concentrating deeply. This allows time for the spelling.

Instead of jumping two cards, you can move diagonally across the circle, as though you are drawing a seven-pointed star. This amounts to the same as jumping, but makes it look more like a jumbled, meaningless sequence.

Super-Memory

Have you ever wondered how memory artists can remember long lists of words—maybe 100 of them—that have no relation to each other?

How many words do you think *you* can remember, if someone calls them out to you? If you want to test yourself, take a look at the words on page 141. These are easy lists to memorize, because all the words in them are related, but see how you do.

Now suppose the words weren't related. Suppose they had nothing to do with each other. How many do you think you could hold in your mind? Most people can only remember and repeat about seven words—without making a mistake or getting confused!

How do the memory artists do it? They use tricks called *mnemonic devices*. Memory schools charge enormous prices for courses that teach these tricks—but one of them is here in the next section. It is 2,500 years old; the ancient Greeks used it, but it's every bit as good today as it was then. If you study it for half an hour, you'll be able to repeat 25 words —just the way the memory artists do—and you'll be able to say them backwards, too, and if anyone wants to know, you'll be able to tell them what number the word is in order! And you'll be able to do it instantaneously, without hesitation!

Do you want a Super-Memory? Here it is.

THE MEMORY TRICK

The first thing you have to do is memorize a sequence of words, picture words, which lead you automatically to connect ideas. These picture words have been chosen carefully. They have to be distinctive enough so that you won't get confused later about their meaning and their order. They are called *stereotypes*, but you don't have to know that. All you have to do is memorize them thoroughly, so that you can recite them while you are sleepwalking. You have to repeat them forwards, backwards, and any other way you can think of. Here they are:

1. Lighthouse

Visualize a solitary, lonely lighthouse, one that stands way off by itself. It even looks like a "1".

2. Eyeglasses

Think of it as "two," two eyes, two glasses for reading.

3. Stool

A stool usually has three legs. That's why it's a symbol for three.

4. Window

Four, because it is a rectangle with four corners.

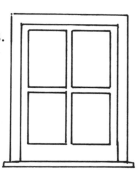

5. Hand

Because it has five fingers.

6. Cube

Because it has six sides. You can imagine a six on the dice.

7. Rain

You can remember this in a number of ways, whichever is easiest for you. If it rains on St. Swithin's Day, it will rain for the next seven weeks—if you know that saying, fine. If not, "seven" rhymes with "heaven"—the general direction that rain comes from. Or you might think of "Come, Seven!" and connect that with "Come rain and come shine." Or that seven is lucky and with your luck it will rain next weekend. Take your pick or make up your own.

8. Gate

Sounds like eight.

9. Cat (think of a black cat)

Because a cat has nine lives.

10. Toes

Because you have ten—probably.

11. Suspension bridge
The towers at each end form an 11.

12. Lunch table
Lunchtime—noontime—12 o'clock.

13. Fire
Right or wrong, 13 has always been taken for an unlucky number. One unlucky accident could be a fire.

14. Fort
Sounds like fourteen.

15. A tennis match
In scoring tennis, the first point counts 15.

16. Girl dancing
In honor of Sweet Sixteen parties.

17. A magazine.
Because of the magazine *Seventeen*.

18. Soldiers

At age 18 you are old enough to join the army.

19. A man with a lasso

The man is alone (one) and the loop of the lasso forms a 9.

20. Cigarettes

Cigarettes are usually packed in 20's.

21. Card playing

In Blackjack the best hand adds up to 21.

22. A swan or pair of swans

The number 2 looks like a swan. Imagine a pair of swans moving along together.

23. A swan and a frog

The frog is leaping like a coiled spring, the shape of 3.

24. A Christmas tree

For Christmas Eve, December 24th.

25. Stars

Imagine five 5-pointed stars in the sky.

This sequence of picture-words is only an example. It would be better for you to choose the word-pictures by yourself, to choose words that have real meaning for you. You could eventually go ahead and expand your list to 50 or 100 or more, but right now, start with 25 words, these or your own. It should take you about 20 minutes or half an hour to memorize 25 picture-words like these.

Once you've learned the words, this is how the memory trick works:

Let's start with 10 words that you have to remember: 1-lion 2-boot 3-honey 4-Uncle Fred 5-car 6-paper 7-luck 8-boat 9-hair tonic 10-iron.

1. In order to remember the lion, imagine in your fantasy that a *lion* is prowling around the lighthouse (symbol for 1). Later, when you want to remember word #1, think of your lighthouse, and you will see a lion skulking around it. It will be easy to remember that lion is the first word.

2. Your glasses are about to be crushed by a *boot*. Actually *see* the glasses with the boot coming down on top of them.

3. A jar of *honey*, which was standing on a stool, fell over. The golden sticky mess is spreading all over the stool. How are you going to get it off?

4. Uncle Fred looks out the window. See his face in the window clearly.

5. A hand is waving from a *car*. Imagine the hand as being over-sized—gigantic, in fact. The stranger the picture in your fantasy, the more it will impress itself on your mind.

6. Your cube is half wrapped in *paper*.

7. When the rain started you found a hiding place. So you say to yourself "What *luck*!" In your fantasy, you must hear this so loudly that it almost hurts your ears!

8. A *boat* is at the dock but you can't get to it because the gate is locked.

9. Your cat rubs itself with *hair tonic*. Its coat becomes very shiny. Can you smell it?

10. An *iron* falls from the table. Where to? Onto your feet, naturally.

If you have really painted each single picture with your fantasy, you will be able now to repeat all of the 10 words easily in any order, or when you hear the number.

Try it. Close the book so you can't see the pictures.

Did it work? If it didn't, maybe you didn't memorize the beginning picture-words well enough. Or maybe you said to yourself, "This is childish nonsense." That attitude has a negative effect and it will prevent your using the memory trick. If you use it, childish or not, you will find yourself in great company. Cicero, the great Roman statesman used it (he was famous for his speeches, and this trick may have helped with them). Charles de Gaulle, General and President of France, used it, too.

If you failed in your first experiment, go through the picture-words again and make sure that you have them very clearly in your mind. If someone says 3—do you automatically see the stool (or whatever image you selected), without reaching around in your mind for it? Once you have really memorized those picture-words, you shouldn't have any trouble with the rest.

Can you see the lion—hear him—padding quietly around the lighthouse? Does it almost hurt to imagine the glasses about to be smashed by the boot? Can you feel the sticky honey? Make the pictures in your mind so vivid that you can hear, feel, and smell them. Make the mental pictures strange. Make them weird. It is easier to remember them that way, because the extraordinary remains in your memory more easily than ordinary things. If something is not *extraordinary*, you pay little attention and forget it fast. It doesn't matter if the extraordinary something is extraordinarily funny, shocking, dreadful or silly. It works. Try it again. The second round should be easy.

That is the whole technique, the entire secret. The most costly books and the most expensive courses won't teach you any more, no matter what they promise; they will just give you variations on the same method. These are the only tools you need.

And don't worry that you'll start thinking about a lion when you try to remember a new list of words or things or ideas. The newest impressions always take the place of the old ones.

Mark Twain once told the story of a memory specialist who astonished his audience for hours with an endless sequence of remembered words and numbers. But he left the theatre without his umbrella or hat as he walked out into the rain. Maybe now you'll understand how that can happen . . .

Ventriloquism

YES, YOU!

WHO, ME?

CAN YOU DO IT?

If you think that being a ventriloquist requires special vocal chords, you are wrong. *Anyone* can be a ventriloquist—that is, anyone with just a little skill who will practice a lot!

Ventriloquism is simply creating the illusion that your voice (or a voice a little bit different from yours) is coming from a different place than your own mouth. Ventriloquists don't "throw" their voices. They only give that illusion. The reason that ventriloquists usually have dummies is to *misdirect* the attention of the audience.

When a performer bends his or her head slightly, as if watching the dummy's face, it looks like ordinary conversation. Actually this angle not only helps to cover up the ventriloquist's lip movements, but it also focuses the attention of the audience on the dummy. Many professional ventriloquists really do move their lips all the time, and can't perform without moving them!

It is easier to practice ventriloquism if you get yourself some kind of temporary dummy—even a hand monkey will do. The important thing is that it has a mouth that you can move with your fingers. Hold the dummy on your lap, or at least lower than your own eye level, so you can look down at it. Practice until you can make the dummy's head and mouth move without having to concentrate on it. This is important:

when you choose a puppet or doll for your dummy, be sure to pick one that is easy to manipulate. Your hand movements are almost as important as your voice in ventriloquism!

WHAT IS YOUR "OTHER" VOICE LIKE?

Before you learn voice techniques, you need to find out what "other" voice comes naturally to you and is easiest for you to use. Is it the voice of a little boy? A little girl? An old man? A duck? Here's how to find out:

Take a long wooden pencil and clench it between your teeth.

Stand in front of a mirror and watch to see that your lips don't move but stay slightly parted as you speak. Say the vowels—A - E - I - O - U.

What does your voice sound like? Without shaping your lips, it may sound slightly cracked and higher than usual. Do it again. You will soon begin to *feel* your vocal chords working.

To help you repeat these sounds over and over, touch your tongue to the roof of your mouth, near the back of your upper front teeth. Take a deep breath. Let it out slowly, making a groaning sound as you let out the air, putting a steady pressure on your vocal chords. The groan will be like a prolonged "ah." Repeat this until you produce a clear, humming sound, like the buzzing of a bee.

Now vary the pressure on your vocal chords as you drone on, and you will notice a change in the tone of the humming. When you have mastered the hum, go back to saying the vowels in the same way. You are beginning to develop a dummy voice. Every person has a natural "other" voice, and you can develop it with practice. After all, it took years to train you to speak. It won't take nearly as long to train yourself to become a ventriloquist.

TALKING WITH YOUR DUMMY VOICE

Now you are ready to practice what is called "near" ventriloquism.

Notice that when you have the pencil in your mouth, you can move your tongue without moving your jaw or your lips. Practice saying the major consonants T - D - G - L - N - K - R and S. The "S" sound is the most difficult and gives your tongue the most work.

The other consonants B - P - F - V and M are impossible to pronounce without moving your lips. Remember this when you choose a performance script and avoid those sounds as much as possible.

Practice the vowels and consonants that you *can* pronounce and don't waste time and effort on the others. When you hit a difficult sound, you will either have to slur over the sound or move your lips. But if your face is turned away from your audience at that moment it won't spoil your performance.

MAKING YOUR DUMMY DIFFERENT

In your "other" voice, try to read from a book (any book) and *mimic* and sing in the voice of your character so that it sounds peculiar. Talk in a stilted fashion as you read, or a baby-like fashion, or in any manner that is different from the way you normally talk. You want to make your dummy not only different in age but different in manner.

Developing an interesting dummy character is half of the battle. All the great ventriloquists have been very different from their dummies. If the dummies are loud and raucous, the ventriloquists are gentle and subdued. The greater the contrast, the better.

If your own speech is rapid, let your dummy speak slowly and painfully. If you are naturally serious, your dummy could be silly or nutty. If you're cheery and bubbly yourself, your dummy could be a moaner and groaner. Try reading rapidly with the pencil between your teeth. After some practice you will be able to read faster and faster, stressing those words which come through easiest and clearest. This gives a slight artificiality to your dummy's speech. With experience you will find which words sound funny to your audience and you can build your script around them.

TALKING TO YOUR DUMMY

After you can read and sing easily in your dummy voice, try reading alternate paragraphs in your natural voice (without the pencil). Choose some book that has lots of dialogue—a play would be good.

Keep using the pencil for your dummy voice so you will remember to change character. After about two weeks of daily practice, you won't need the pencil anymore.

Keep your lips slightly parted (otherwise the sounds can't come out) and read without the pencil, still looking in the mirror now and then. Repeat the words you're not sure of. Some performers keep their lips pursed but parted when talking in the dummy voice. You may prefer to do that, too.

Move your lips and head when you speak in your natural voice and let the dummy sit quietly, with its head tilted to watch you. When you use the dummy voice, keep your own head (as well as your lips) still. Movement draws attention, and you want the audience to shift its attention to the speaker, whether it's you or the dummy.

CHOOSING A PERMANENT DUMMY

After you can switch back and forth easily, you are almost ready to put on a performance. First you need to choose a permanent dummy. The hand monkey may do if you want your dummy voice to be animal-like. If your dummy character is a little girl, you can use a doll that sits on your lap or slips over your hand.

The dummy should *look like* (not contrast with) the character your dummy voice is mimicking. You can make your own funny-looking hand puppet if you don't find the one you want elsewhere.

If you don't want to use a hand dummy, you can use a screen or curtain with a pair of shoes showing under it to represent the dummy. Then you can talk to the "person" behind the screen and answer in your dummy voice. The illusion is not as complete as with a dummy, but you can do an act like this on the spur of the moment when you may not have a dummy with you.

HINTS AND TIPS

When you work out your script, try to keep the sentences fairly short. Let the dummy interrupt you in the middle of a speech, or you interrupt. That makes the act more interesting and life-like. If you can interrupt rapidly in the dummy voice, your audience will get the illusion of two people talking *at the same time*!

Another trick most ventriloquists use is switching from a whisper to a loud voice. Whispering holds an audience's attention more than

If you are learning ventriloquism with a friend, you can put on a combined performance—both of you and your two dummies. A staged argument can create a sensation, with the dummies bickering and the ventriloquists trying to keep them apart.

anything else, because people have to be quiet to hear you. The dummy's whisper-switch-interruption needs practice, but it is very effective.

YOUR FIRST PERFORMANCE

Get a few friends together and try out your act on them. Try it out on your family, too. Use a play or a joke book or riddle book to get ideas for your script, but change the jokes to suit your character. Maybe add a song. After you memorize an act about 5 minutes long, put on the show in your living room. Have as much light as possible shine on the dummy, and sit so that your face is more or less in shadow. You are trying to create an illusion and the more help you can get from the setting, the better.

Remember that your friends and family will be your *toughest* critics. Ask them to give you *constructive* criticism after you finish. Run through the act a second time to find the spots that need improvement. There are bound to be some slips in any performance, and you can work out the difficulties later in practice sessions before the mirror.

THE ILLUSION OF DISTANCE

The illusion of distance ("throwing your voice") is not necessary unless you want to put on a stage performance of "distant" ventriloquism, but you should know some of the principles.

It is very difficult to judge distance and direction. If you want to see *how* difficult, get someone to blindfold you and make sounds in different parts of the room. See if you can tell where the sounds are coming from. It's a tricky assignment.

You can create the illusion of distance when you hold your dummy at arm's length and let it speak softly. Then draw it closer and raise the volume of the dummy voice at the same time.

You might put your dummy in a trunk and walk away. Then you can use the muffled voice to cry, "Let me out!" and carry on a conversation, perhaps with your back or your side to the audience, varying the volume of your voice.

With practice, you can seem to be throwing your voice to distant parts of the room simply by lowering or increasing the strength and tone of your dummy voice. If you want the voice to come from a cupboard across the stage, try this:

Take a deep breath and then lift your tongue up and curl it slightly, back in the middle of your mouth. Then speak farther back in your throat. That will make your voice sound muffled.

The acting you do is just as important as your voice. If your dummy is in a cupboard, *look* at the cupboard. "Relate" to it. Even if you turn away, keep thinking about the dummy in the cupboard and the audience will, too.

TEST YOURSELF

3

TEST YOUR VISUAL MEMORY 1

There are 8 simple words in each of the following 4 columns. Work with one column at a time: read it aloud and then try to repeat the words in the correct order silently to yourself. Read the column aloud again. Then immediately close the book and write as many of the words as you can remember—in their original order, if possible.

After you have finished all 4 columns, compare your list with the originals.

street	boy	hat	salt
light	desk	coat	pepper
lamp	school	shirt	stove
pole	chalk	shoes	pan
bank	blackboard	tie	water
clock	words	rack	sink
night	book	closet	faucet
policeman	teacher	door	drip

(SEE PAGE 614 FOR YOUR SCORE.)

TEST YOUR VISUAL MEMORY 2

Study the 10 figures here for 2 minutes, trying to remember them so you'll recognize them when you see them again. Then turn to page 614 for further instructions.

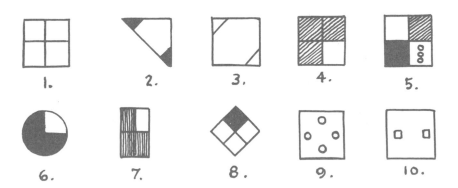

TEST YOUR VISUAL MEMORY 3

Take both tests on this page before you look at the scoring section, to get a good idea of your artistic and visual memory.

Study the design for Test #3 for only ten seconds. Then close the book and immediately draw the design on a separate sheet of paper, as accurately and carefully as you can, freehand. Allow one minute. Then go on to the next test.

TEST YOUR VISUAL MEMORY 4

Follow the same directions as for the previous test, except that you may study this design for 20 seconds.

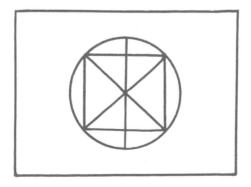

(SEE PAGE 615 FOR YOUR SCORE.)

TEST YOUR OBSERVATION 1

To test your ability to perceive and remember details, study the picture on this page for two minutes. Make only mental (no written) notes. Then turn to page 615 and answer the questions there without looking at this page again.

TEST YOUR OBSERVATION 2

Study the picture on this page for five minutes, but don't make any written notes. Then close the book and, on a separate sheet of paper, write down as many items as you remember from the scene. (Don't break any single item into its component parts, such as the table top, table legs. It's simply one item, a table.) Then turn to page 615 for a list of the items that appear in the drawing.

144   Test Yourself

TEST YOUR KNOWLEDGE OF WORD MEANINGS 1

The idea of this test is to select, from a group of words, a word that means either *the same as* or *the opposite of* the key word. For example:

Deep: ocean   shallow   thoughtful   useful

The key word is deep and the answer is shallow–in this case the opposite of deep.

Write down on a separate sheet of paper the word you think is correct in each case. Allow no more than 10 seconds for each part.

1. **Gradual: brisk, elevated, inward, sudden**
2. **Vapid: insipid, obedient, hopeful, stubborn**
3. **Querulous: uncomplaining, silent, fragile, poetic**
4. **Devout: worshipped, strong, impious, penitant**
5. **Contemptible: unable, corrupt, despicable, somber**
6. **Energetic: sensitive, virtuous, apathetic, heroic**
7. **Gaunt: haggard, unhappy, prosaic, insipid**
8. **Eternal: vigilant, sky, changeless, temporary**

(SEE PAGES 615–616 FOR YOUR SCORE.)

TEST YOUR KNOWLEDGE OF WORD MEANINGS 2

Follow instructions for the previous test.

1. **Envious: covetous, snide, possessive, unhappy**
2. **Reserved: studious, dumb, reticent, ticket**
3. **Identical: heterogeneous, alien, close, distant**
4. **Moderate: modern, slow, temper, extreme**
5. **Romantic: youth, male, silent, prosaic**
6. **Liberal: sublime, generous, lavish, party**
7. **Round: soft, large, circular, ellipse**
8. **Cruel: vicious, hasty, angry, modest**

(SEE PAGE 616 FOR YOUR SCORE.)

TEST YOUR REASONING 1

Time yourself on this test. Allow three minutes to write your answers on a sheet of paper. Don't spend too much time on any question. If you don't get it promptly, go on to the next.

1. A motor boat was rented by a man and his wife, his two daughters and their husbands, and three children in each daughter's family. How many were in the boat?

2. What is the well-known proverb which expresses the idea that a person who is prompt usually derives an advantage over people who come late?

3. In the following series, two pairs are wrong. Rewrite the series correctly.

2   5   3 6   5 9   1 4   6 8

4. The moon bears a relationship to the earth as the earth bears a relationship to what body of our solar system?

5. Count each S in the following series that is followed by an R, provided the R is not followed by an A. How many such S's are there?

A R S R T O S R A S R S G S R Y D S R A

6. Freezing water bursts pipes because:
    (a) the cold weakens the pipes
    (b) the ice stops circulation of the water
    (c) water expands when it freezes

7. If an argument or difference of views is settled by mutual concession, it is called:
    (a) restraint
    (b) injunction
    (c) compromise
    (d) deadlock

8. Supply the words that will make this a clear sentence:
    It is usually very_____to become_____with people who are_____timid.

9. Give the two numbers that should come at the end of each of these series of numbers:

$$\begin{array}{cccccccc}
8 & 1 & 6 & 1 & 4 & 1 & — & — \\
81 & 27 & 27 & 9 & 9 & 3 & 3 & 1 & — & —
\end{array}$$

(SEE PAGE 616 FOR YOUR SCORE.)

TEST YOUR REASONING 2

Follow the same instructions as for the previous test.

1. One number is wrong in the following series. Write the series correctly.

4   8   16   32   65   128

2. One number is wrong in the following series. Write the series correctly.
2   4   15   256   65,536

3. If the earth were nearer the sun:
    (a) the stars would become invisible
    (b) our months would be longer
    (c) the earth would become warmer

4. It is colder nearer the poles than at the equator because:
    (a) there is more ice at the poles
    (b) the poles are further from the sun
    (c) the sun shines more obliquely at the poles

5. What well-known saying expresses the idea that students stop working when the teacher leaves the room?

6. What his neighbors and friends say about a man constitutes:
    (a) his character
    (b) his personality
    (c) his outlook
    (d) his reputation
    (e) his psyche

7. The ohm is used in measuring:
   (a) electricity
   (b) water power
   (c) rainfall
   (d) wind velocity

8. Supply the words that will make this a clear sentence:
   A reasonable_____of sleep is usually_____ if a person is to_____ a high _____of efficiency.

9. A contest of any sort always has:
   (a) an umpire
   (b) an audience
   (c) ticket takers
   (d) opponents
   (e) victory

(SEE PAGE 616 FOR YOUR SCORE.)

ARE YOU THOROUGH?   1

Thoroughness consists of attention to detail and accuracy in following directions. Study the figure on page 149 briefly. The lower part of this page contains questions which you are to answer, referring to the figure when necessary. Work rapidly, since there is a 2-minute time limit, but remember you are aiming for thoroughness. Write your answers on a separate sheet of paper.

What numbers are:
1. In the triangle but not in the square, circle or rectangle?
2. In the circle but not in the square, triangle, or rectangle?
3. In the square but not in the circle, triangle, or rectangle?
4. In the rectangle but not in the circle, triangle, or square?
5. In both triangle and circle but not in the square or rectangle?
6. In both circle and square but not in the rectangle or triangle?
7. In both square and triangle but not in the rectangle or circle?

(SEE PAGE 616 FOR YOUR SCORE.)

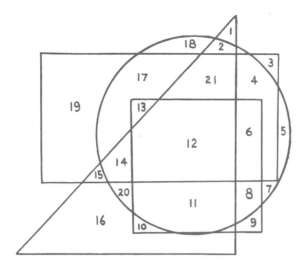

ARE YOU THOROUGH? 2

Referring to the diagram in the preceding test, and following the same instructions, answer the following questions in 2 minutes:

What numbers are:
1. In both triangle and rectangle but not in the square or circle?
2. In both circle and rectangle but not in the square or triangle?
3. In rectangle and triangle and circle but not in the square?
4. In rectangle and circle and square but not in the triangle?
5. In triangle and square and circle but not in the rectangle?
6. In rectangle and square and triangle but not in the circle?
7. In rectangle and square and triangle and circle?

(SEE PAGE 616 FOR YOUR SCORE.)

TEST YOUR ARTISTIC PERCEPTION

In each of the following pictures, one vital detail is missing. On a separate sheet of paper, list the missing items by number. Allow 3 minutes.

(SEE PAGES 616–617 FOR YOUR SCORE.)

11.

12.

13.

14.

15.

16.

17.

18.

19.

20.

TEST YOUR SENSE OF WORD RELATIONSHIPS 1

In each of the following groups of four words, pick the word which doesn't belong. Allow one minute to list your answers on a separate sheet of paper.

1. breakfast, grapefruit, dinner, supper
2. cow, horse, dog, tiger
3. book, magazine, newspaper, letter
4. recline, rest, sleep, slumber
5. forest, woods, grove, tree
6. hen, goose, duck, swan
7. France, New York, Scotland, Australia
8. shout, cry, whimper, yell
9. slippers, stockings, boots, shoes
10. view, landscape, scenery, picture
11. Venus, Earth, Mars, Sun
12. gloaming, twilight, evening, dawn

(SEE PAGE 617 FOR YOUR SCORE.)

TEST YOUR SENSE OF WORD RELATIONSHIPS 2

In each of the following groups of four words, pick the word which doesn't belong. Allow two minutes to list your answers on a sheet of paper.

1. marsh, morass, quagmire, atoll
2. zephyr, typhoon, current, breeze
3. docile, tractable, cordial, grudging
4. paragon, perfection, ideal, superfluous
5. remedy, curare, antidote, physic
6. hydrogen, oxygen, carbon, water
7. Sirius, Arcturus, Tauri, Castor
8. Guernsey, Hereford, Shorthorns, Civet
9. ulna, biceps, triceps, deltoid
10. tibia, femur, fibula, pelvis
11. Mohammed, Moses, Darwin, Buddha
12. parishioner, minister, prelate, pontiff

(SEE PAGE 617 FOR YOUR SCORE.)

TEST YOUR SENSE OF WORD RELATIONSHIPS 3

In each of the following examples there are two key words, related in a way which you will have to determine. Next a problem word is given, followed by four optional words. From those four words pick the one which has the same relationship to the problem word as in the key words. For example:

Key Words	Word	Words to Choose From
Cattle: hay	man: ?	eat, drink, bread, dessert

The answer, of course, is "bread." Now try the following problems. Allow 10 seconds for each.

	Key Words	Word	Words to Choose From
1.	Clock: watch	trunk: ?	suitcase, train, redcap, taxi
2.	Phone: hear	telescope: ?	distance, enemy, seek, see
3.	Author: book	sculptor: ?	artist, clay, stone, statue
4.	Horse: carriage	locomotive: ?	track, steam, coal, cars
5.	Illness: crisis	drama: ?	stage, ticket, climax, act
6.	Best: quality	most: ?	goods, income, quantity, produce
7.	Crowd: people	herd: ?	dog, cows, silo, barn
8.	Past: future	history: ?	prophet, dictator, army, prediction

TEST YOUR SENSE OF WORD RELATIONSHIPS 4

	Key Words	Word	Words to Choose From
1.	Fang: lion	thorn: ?	stick, hurt, rose, injure
2.	Battle: duel	chorus: ?	duet, song, choir, orchestra
3.	Disease: cleanliness	accident: ?	hospital, doctor, caution, insurance
4.	Portrait: painter	symphony: ?	opera, conductor, cello, orchestra
5.	Water: thirst	air: ?	hydrogen, oxygen, suffocation, life
6.	Yard: distance	hour: ?	time, clock, year, calendar
7.	Imitate: create	copy: ?	picture, originate, learn, depend
8.	Arm: elbow	leg: ?	skin, foot, bursa, knee

(SEE PAGE 617 FOR YOUR SCORE.)

TEST YOUR COMPREHENSION

There are seven numbered proverbs on the left side of this page, and fourteen lettered statements on the right. Each proverb has close application to two of the statements from the right-hand column. For example, "Every cloud has a silver lining" has a close relationship to statement (b), "It is a long lane that has no turning," as well as to one other statement.

On a separate sheet of paper list numbers 1 through 7, then match up two letters, (a) through (n), for each number.

1. They counsel best who live best.

2. Anyone can hold the helm when the sea is calm.

3. Every cloud has a silver lining.

4. More is obtained from one book carefully read than from libraries skimmed with a wandering eye.

5. They are truly wise who gain wisdom from the mishaps of others.

6. Cowards die many times before their death.

7. As for me, all I know is that I know nothing.

(a) Wisdom is often nearer when we stoop than when we fly.
(b) It is a long lane that has no turning.
(c) Learn and profit by observing other people's experiences.
(d) They who fear too much suffer more than those who die.
(e) Jack of all trades, master of none.
(f) Untempted virtue is easiest to keep.
(g) Concentrate your energies for best results.
(h) It's an ill wind that blows no good.
(i) Learn to see in another's calamity the ills you should avoid.
(j) A good example is the best sermon.
(k) An unassaulted castle is easily defended.
(l) Practice what you preach.
(m) The valiant never taste of death but once.
(n) The doorstep to the temple of wisdom is a knowledge of our own ignorance.

(SEE PAGE 617 FOR YOUR SCORE.)

TEST YOUR MATHEMATICAL JUDGMENT

Don't try for exact answers on this test. The time element won't allow it, and the test is not for accuracy but judgment. Your reasoning power will determine how well you do at approximating the right answer to these problems. There are four possible answers for each problem. Working quickly, write down on a separate sheet of paper the answers that seem most likely to be right. Allow $2\frac{1}{2}$ minutes.

1. A man left $\frac{1}{3}$ of his net estate to charity and $\frac{1}{2}$ of the remainder went to each of his children. If each child got $10,000, what was the total of his net estate?

$20,000 $140,000 $30,000 $70,000

2. A factory employs 200 women, 150 single men and 650 married men. If each group is expanded proportionately until there are 1150 total employees, how many additional women will be hired?

13   1100   30   563

3. If you buy 5 pens at $.25 each and 12 ornamental weights at $2.00 a dozen, what will the total cost be?

$1.10 $4.96 $3.25 $15.00

4. A dealer marked some goods at $.60 a yard (meter) but sold them at a 20% discount and still made a profit of 20% of the cost. What was the cost of the goods per yard (meter) to the dealer?

$.12 $1.30 $.40 $.08

5. Based on her average time, a typist can copy a page in $3\frac{1}{2}$ minutes. How many pages can she copy in 98 minutes?

6   19   160   28

(SEE PAGE 617 FOR YOUR SCORE.)

TEST YOUR SENSE OF NUMBER RELATIONSHIPS 1

The numbers in each of the left-hand series below follow a definite "rule" or pattern. You are to determine this numerical relationship or rule. Then from among the numbers to the right choose the one number which correctly continues the series. For example:

10 11 13 14 16 17   17 18 19 20 22   Answer: 19

Studying the left-hand numbers we discover that the "rule" here is to add 1, then add 2, add 1, add 2, etc. Therefore we now must add 2 to 17 and the answer is 19. Another illustration:

4 6 9 13 18 24   26 27 29 31 33   Answer: 31

The rule here is add 2, add 3, add 4, etc.

Study these illustrations till you understand the numerical principles involved. Then, on a separate sheet of paper, write down your answers to the following problems. Allow 2 minutes.

A. 31 33 31 34 31 35	30 31 34 35 40
B. 5 5 5 3 3 3	0 1 2 3 4
C. 7 9 11 13 11 9	7 9 11 13 15
D. 12 36 18 18 54 27	18 27 36 54 81
E. 21 22 20 23 19 24	16 18 25 29 30
F. 3 6 12 21 24 30	32 36 39 60 99

(SEE PAGES 617-618 FOR YOUR SCORE.)

TEST YOUR SENSE OF NUMBER RELATIONSHIPS 2

See the explanation and instructions in the preceding test. Allow 2 minutes.

A.	1	2	3	1	2	3		0	1	2	3	4
B.	90	45	50	25	30	15		0	5	15	20	10
C.	22	25	28	31	34	37		38	39	40	41	42
D.	72	36	40	20	24	12	16	4	8	12	16	20
E.	5	10	7	14	11	22	19	16	20	24	32	38
F.	95	92	46	42	21	16	8	2	4	6	8	10

TEST YOUR SENSE OF NUMBER RELATIONSHIPS 3

See the explanation and instructions for previous tests. Allow 2 minutes.

A.	24	27	9	18	21	7	14	11	17	22	28	33
B.	44	40	42	14	10	12	4	0	2	6	7	10
C.	3	6	5	5	8	7	7	6	7	10	13	14
D.	1	2	5	11	12	15	21	22	24	25	27	30
E.	14	16	13	17	12	18	11	15	16	17	18	19
F.	9	10	8	24	6	7	5	3	6	15	16	20

TEST YOUR SENSE OF NUMBER RELATIONSHIPS 4

See the explanation and instructions for previous tests. Allow 2 minutes.

A.	76	38	36	18	16	8	6	1	2	3	4	5
B.	81	27	54	18	36	12	24	4	8	21	24	48
C.	90	82	74	66	58	50	42	32	34	36	38	40
D.	21	20	22	20	23	20	24	16	20	24	28	29
E.	6	9	7	10	8	11	9	7	10	12	13	14
F.	8	10	12	10	12	14	12	10	12	14	16	18

(SEE PAGE 618 FOR YOUR SCORE)

ARE YOU A GOOD ORGANIZER? 1

In each of the areas below are geometrical pieces that you can fit into a perfect square. On a separate sheet of paper, draw these shapes so that you form a square from each set of pieces. If you can visualize them readily and then form the parts into a whole, you're a good organizer. Allow 5 minutes.

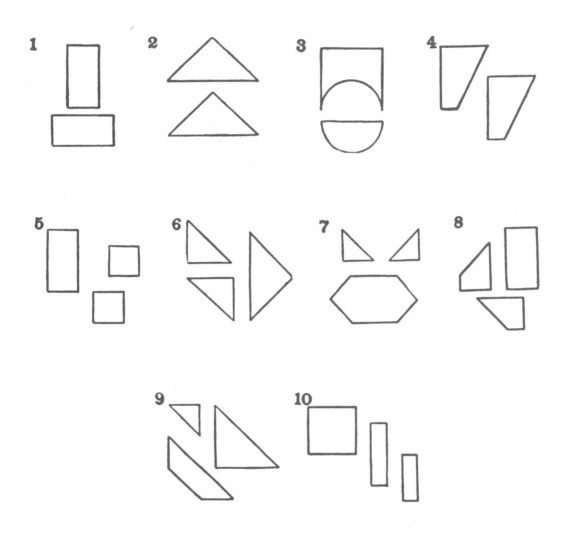

(SEE PAGE 618 FOR YOUR SCORE.)

ARE YOU A GOOD ORGANIZER? 2

Follow the instructions for the previous test, but allow 4 minutes.

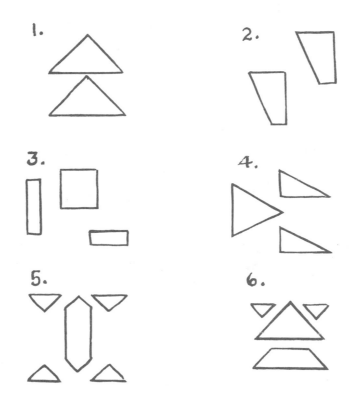

1.

2.

3.

4.

5.

6.

(SEE PAGES 618–619 FOR YOUR SCORE.)

VISUAL ANALYSIS TEST   1

To analyze the problems below, you need to ask yourself, "A is to B as C is to what?" For instance, in the first example below, B is the same as A, only larger, so you would choose figure 2 (from among the 5 optional figures) for your answer. In Example 2, the answer is 1, the same shape but smaller and hollow. When you think you understand the examples, go on to the test below. Allow 2 minutes to jot the answers down on a separate sheet of paper.

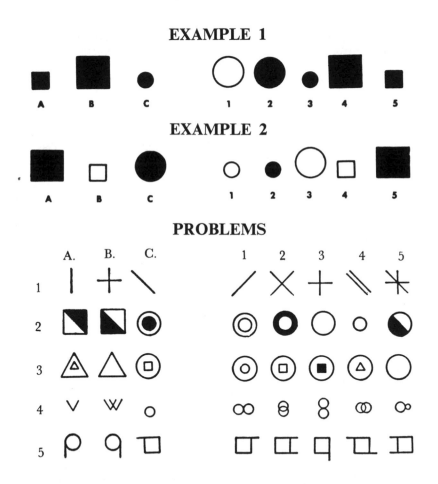

(SEE PAGE 619 FOR YOUR SCORE.)

VISUAL ANALYSIS TEST   2

Follow the instructions for the preceding test.

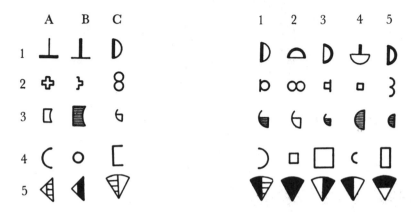

(SEE PAGE 619 FOR YOUR SCORE.)

VISUAL ANALYSIS TEST   3

Follow the instructions for the preceding test.

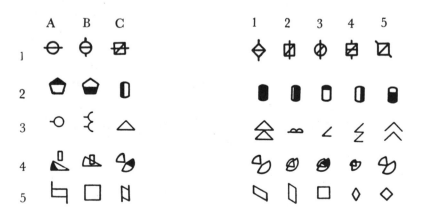

(SEE PAGE 619 FOR YOUR SCORE.)

VISUAL ANALYSIS TEST 4

See the instructions for Visual Analysis Test #1. Then proceed with the following 10 figure examples. Allow 5 minutes.

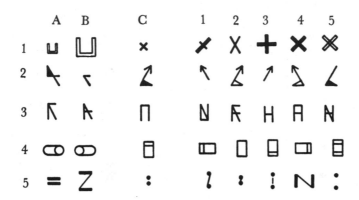

(SEE PAGE 619 FOR YOUR SCORE.)

VISUAL ANALYSIS TEST 5

See the instructions for Visual Analysis Test #1.

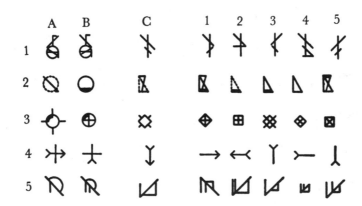

(SEE PAGE 619 FOR YOUR SCORE.)

HOW WIDE-RANGING IS YOUR KNOWLEDGE? 1

These words or names are connected with some particular field of knowledge or activity. Name the fields or activities. Allow 3 minutes.

1. Darwin
2. outriggers
3. Pavlova
4. Chippendale
5. a cappella
6. Titian
7. Ionic, Doric
8. Adam Smith
9. sisal
10. transformer
11. iconoscope
12. seismograph
13. cracking process
14. Bessemer process
15. conservation of energy
16. binomial theorem
17. Aesop

(SEE PAGE 619 FOR YOUR SCORE.)

HOW WIDE-RANGING IS YOUR KNOWLEDGE? 2

These words or names are connected with some particular field of knowledge or activity. Name the fields or activities. Allow 3 minutes.

1. marimba
2. gerund
3. philatelist
4. John Milton
5. Poseidon
6. Dead Sea scrolls
7. Genghis Khan
8. Plato
9. sourdough
10. Roald Amundsen
11. cantilever
12. bronchoscope
13. caries
14. catamaran
15. Beethoven
16. ichthyology
17. marathon

(SEE PAGE 619 FOR YOUR SCORE.)

TEST YOUR CONCENTRATION   1

Concentration is the ability to disregard other matters and focus your attention on a particular task. It is essential to constructive thinking. When you take the following tests, have the radio going, the television set on, or provide some other distraction.

In each line of numbers, you will find one or more pairs of adjacent numbers whose sum is 10.

Example: 2 6 4 7 1 5 0 3 7 8 2
         (6 4)   (3 7) (8 2)   3 pairs

List by line the pairs you can find in the lines below within 3 minutes.

(a) 4 1 8 4 9 1 3 0 4 8 5 9 6 8 4 7 6 9 4 0 1 3 2 8 3 7 5 4 4 8

(b) 9 8 6 4 3 8 5 8 1 3 8 5 6 7 0 9 4 8 2 3 1 5 8 7 4 0 9 8 6 1

(c) 3 1 8 6 0 3 9 4 1 2 3 7 0 4 8 6 9 0 5 1 2 8 5 0 9 9 4 8 6 7

(d) 7 5 5 0 1 2 8 4 8 9 8 1 5 8 4 8 7 3 9 1 5 8 4 7 6 9 4 1 3 2

(e) 6 2 4 8 3 4 0 9 2 8 4 3 8 5 1 3 8 4 8 6 7 4 1 8 3 7 9 8 0 4

(f) 6 9 3 8 1 3 5 6 7 8 3 4 5 7 8 3 7 5 7 2 9 4 3 1 2 9 4 3 8 6

(g) 8 5 9 4 8 3 7 4 9 8 1 3 8 7 4 1 8 2 0 7 4 6 5 1 4 7 5 5 6 3

(h) 5 3 4 7 6 3 5 9 8 2 3 7 6 6 3 0 1 4 6 2 2 5 7 9 3 4 2 3 8 5

(i) 4 9 3 9 6 3 0 3 6 8 5 5 8 9 1 4 0 8 6 7 6 3 4 7 2 9 5 8 3 5

(j) 1 1 9 2 7 5 1 6 8 7 4 5 6 1 3 9 2 4 3 6 7 4 8 4 3 9 5 6 9 9

(SEE PAGES 619–620 FOR YOUR SCORE.)

TEST YOUR CONCENTRATION   2

The idea here is to subtract (mentally) a series of 7's from 100 until no further subtraction can be made. As you make the mental subtractions, call them off orally to a person who is following the scoring on page 620.

Allow only 45 seconds. If you make a mistake, the person helping you is to correct you immediately. Continue your subtractions *from that point* correctly.

For best results, complete the series within 45 seconds without making more than one mistake.

TEST YOUR CONCENTRATION 3

The idea of this test is to subtract mentally first 1's, then 2's alternately from the number 50. As you make the mental subtractions, call them off orally to a person who is following the scoring on page 620.

Allow only 45 seconds. If you make a mistake, the person helping you is to correct you *immediately*. Continue subtractions *from that point* correctly.

For best results, complete the subtractions within 45 seconds without making more than one mistake.

TEST YOUR CONCENTRATION 4

In each of the ten lines of letters below you will find one or more combinations of consecutive letters which spell common words. On a separate sheet of paper list the words that you find, line by line. When you put together the words from each group of letters, they should form a meaningful sentence.

Allow 3 minutes.

1. P T A O C I F N I J R Q T S E J L I U V T E W H X O L P Y O U

2. F R L D O J V U L H Q R C W E L L V X A G L T E F T H E X R C

3. C M I U V N T X E Z B J M I N O R V H I G T A S K S M J E J X

4. W H I C H A Q E V F R T I Y T H L D Y O U C N I J R N E Z E F

5. D L E Q G H T S V X A R E Z U I O C A L L E D E T J Q V N I R

6. X N I Q J E V K F F I H R D L J I Q H U I Y I H T L R U P O N

7. T O Q L R T S D E V H P E R F O R M I D X V Y O U M T Q W Z Z

8. B R W I L L L J A Q H A V E W J H G B U T R J I A L I T T L E

9. E O C J D I F F I C U L T Y R D W I T H C J R Q A K S H L D U

10. V J B I Q T H E I U B J L I H V B I G G E R B L O N E S R Z X

(SEE PAGE 620 FOR YOUR SCORE.)

TEST YOUR IMAGINATION 1

The pictures below relate to famous nursery rhymes and tales. See if you can figure out appropriate *titles* for each picture. Allow two minutes.

(SEE PAGE 620 FOR YOUR SCORE.)

TEST YOUR IMAGINATION   2

The pictures on this page are incomplete in that some of the detail has been omitted. Nevertheless, each should suggest some scene or figure to you. Allow yourself three minutes to see if you can come up with the artist's identification of these figures, or ones you think are just as appropriate.

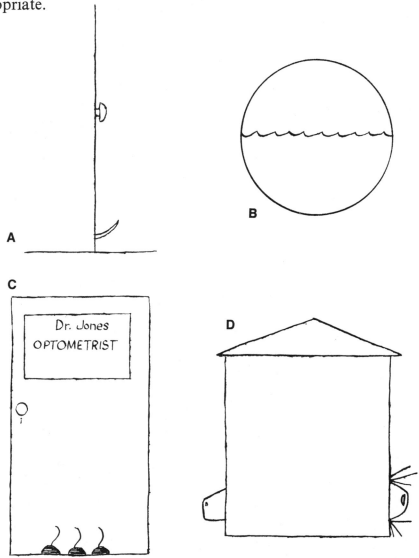

(SEE PAGE 620 FOR YOUR SCORE.)

TEST YOUR MECHANICAL
COMPREHENSION 1

Examine each picture intently for not more than 10 seconds. Then answer the question for it, without looking at the picture again. Proceed through all five pictures before consulting the answers.

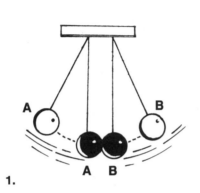

1.

2.

1. Assume that A and B are wooden balls suspended in such a way that they just touch each other when at rest. If A is drawn aside and let fall against B, B will be thrust to the right. Will A bounce back an equal distance, or will it be brought to rest by the impact?

2. Under which jacket will the snow melt faster?

3.

4.

3. Which parachute will reach the earth first?

4. Assuming that C is the power shaft, will shaft A or shaft B turn faster?

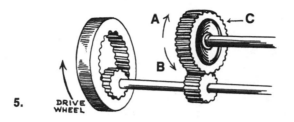

5. DRIVE WHEEL

5. Notice the direction in which the drive wheel moves. Does gear C move in the direction of the arrow marked "A" or the arrow marked "B"?

(SEE PAGE 620 FOR YOUR SCORE.)

TEST YOUR MECHANICAL
COMPREHENSION 2

Examine each picture intently for not more than 10 seconds. Then answer the question for it. Proceed through all five pictures before consulting the answers.

1. Which bottle is colder?

2. If each man pushes with equal force, in what direction will the ball move?

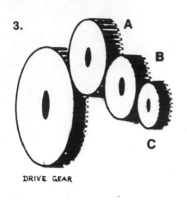

3. What gear wheel will make the greatest number of turns in a minute?

4. Is the job easier for A or B?

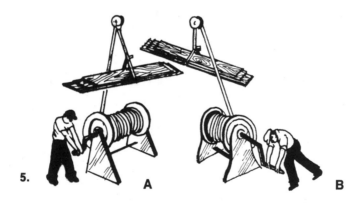

5. With which windlass can a person lift the greatest weight?

(SEE PAGE 620 FOR YOUR SCORE.)

ARE YOU ACCURATE? 1

The paired columns of numbers below consist of some exact duplicates and some which differ slightly. Working quickly but as accurately as possible, jot down on a separate sheet of paper the key numbers of those pairs which are *the same*.

Allow 1½ minutes only, and if you cannot finish in the allotted time, note the number at which you stop.

1. 650	650	14. 36015992	360155992
2. 041	044	15. 3910066482	391006482
3. 2579	2579	16. 8510273301	8510273301
4. 3281	3281	17. 263136996	263136996
5. 55190	55102	18. 451152903	451152903
6. 39190	39190	19. 3259016275	3295016725
7. 658049	650849	20. 582039144	582039144
8. 3295017	3290517	21. 61558529	61588529
9. 63015991	63019991	22. 211915883	219915883
10. 39007106	39007106	23. 670413822	670143822
11. 69931087	69931087	24. 17198591	17198591
12. 251004818	251004418	25. 36482991	36482991
13. 299056013	299056013		

(SEE PAGE 620 FOR YOUR SCORE.)

ARE YOU ACCURATE? 2

Follow the same directions given for the previous test.

1. 10243586	10243586	14. 3484657120	3484657210
2. 659012534	659021354	15. 8588172556	8581722556
3. 388172902	381872902	16. 3120166671	3120166671
4. 631027594	631027594	17. 7611348879	76111345879
5. 2499901354	2499901534	18. 26557239164	26557239164
6. 2261059310	2261659310	19. 8819002341	8819002341
7. 2911038227	2911038227	20. 6571018034	6571018034
8. 313377752	313377752	21. 38779762514	38779765214
9. 1012938567	1012938567	22. 39008126557	39008126657
10. 7166220988	7162220988	23. 75658100398	75658100398
11. 3177628449	3177682449	24. 41181900726	41181900726
12. 468672663	468672663	25. 6543920817	6543920871
13. 9104529003	9194529003		

(SEE PAGE 620 FOR YOUR SCORE.)

ARE YOU PRECISE? 1

The idea in these tests is to replace familiar digits with unfamiliar symbols. Each number from 1 to 9 is represented by a symbol, thus:

1	2	3	4	5	6	7	8	9
‐	И	⊐	L	U	O	∧	✕	＝

Study the above symbols for a few minutes. Now, on a separate sheet of paper copy the two lines of numbers below. Allow yourself $2\frac{1}{2}$ minutes to write the correct symbol below each digit. You may, of course, keep the book open in front of you.

    1 5 4 2 7 6 3 5 7 2 8 5 4 6 3 7 2 8 1 9 5 8 4 7 3
    6 2 5 1 9 2 8 3 7 4 6 5 9 4 8 3 7 2 6 1 5 4 6 3 7

(SEE PAGES 620–621 FOR YOUR SCORE.)

ARE YOU PRECISE? 2

See the instructions for the preceding test. However, do all three rows on this page as quickly as you can, instead of observing a specific time limit. Time yourself carefully to determine how many seconds it takes you to complete the three rows. Remember to try for accuracy as well as speed.

1	2	3	4	5	6	7	8	9
‐	И	⊐	L	U	O	∧	✕	＝

    3 1 2 1 3 2 1 4 2 3 5 2 9 1 4
    6 3 1 5 4 2 7 6 3 8 7 2 9 5 4
    6 3 7 2 8 1 9 5 8 4 7 3 6 9 5

(SEE PAGE 621 FOR YOUR SCORE.)

ARE YOU PRECISE? 3

Follow the instructions for Precision Test—No. 2.

```
1   2   3   4   5   6   7   8   9
—   и   ⊐   ∟   ∪   ∩   ∨   ✕   =
```

```
1 9 2 8 3 7 4 6 5 9 4 8 5 7 6
9 3 8 6 4 1 5 7 2 6 2 4 8 1 3
4 9 5 1 7 5 2 6 9 3 7 8 4 1 8
```

(SEE PAGE 621 FOR YOUR SCORE.)

TEST YOUR SPACE PERCEPTION

There is no time limit on this test, but don't use a pencil or any other device to figure out the answers. Just use your imagination and mental perception to judge or guess at the answers and write them on a sheet of paper.

1. If you held the figure 124 up before a mirror what would it look like?

2. A clock reads 11:45. If you changed the small hand for the large hand and the large hand for the small hand, what time would it show?

3. Imagine that you fold a square sheet of paper in half, then fold it in half again. Now imagine that you take an office paper punch and punch it once through the folded paper. Now "unfold" the paper. How many punched holes will there be in it?

4. Assume that you fold a square sheet of paper once on the diagonal, then fold it again so it forms a triangle, then punch a hole through the folded sheet. Now "unfold" it. How many holes?

5. A clock reads 5 minutes after 3. Exchange the hands. Now what time does it show?

6. What would the abbreviation "&" look like if held up to a mirror?

(SEE PAGE 621 FOR YOUR SCORE.)

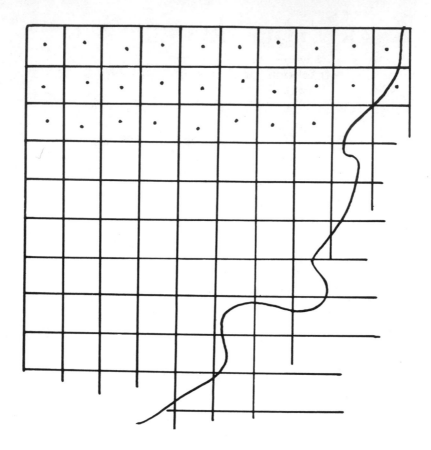

HOW IS YOUR MANUAL DEXTERITY?

Rule a sheet of paper into 150 half-inch (15-mm) squares (10 squares by 15).

With a sharp pencil held lightly in writing position, tap a dot within each square. Go from left to right in the top column, then from right to left in the second column, from left to right in the third, etc. Don't stop to correct errors. Try to work as rapidly as possible and still retain accuracy.

Allow only 30 seconds.

(SEE PAGE 621 FOR YOUR SCORE.)

TEST YOUR SENSE OF SPATIAL RELATIONSHIPS

The first row of cubes shows you how many cubes are contained in each pile. Study them to understand how the sum is arrived at, then figure out the number of cubes contained in each of the piles below. You may use any method of calculation, and you may make notes on paper. Allow 3 minutes.

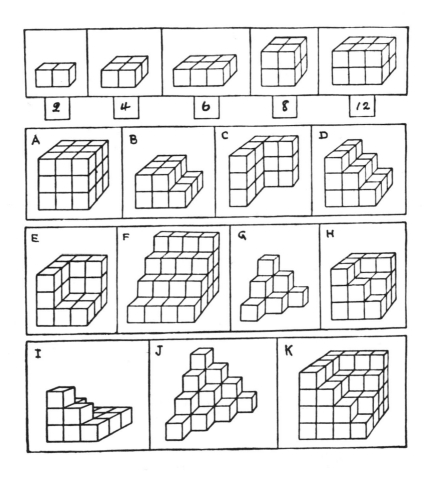

(SEE PAGE 621 FOR YOUR SCORE.)

OFFICE MACHINE APTITUDE TEST 1

Study the following Key which gives a letter as symbol for each digit from 0 to 9:

0	1	2	3	4	5	6	7	8	9
E	H	G	V	N	Y	T	F	W	Z

Below are listed 15 lines of 4 letters each which you are to transpose into numbers according to the above Key. For example: WFYV would be 8753. Work as rapidly but as accurately as possible writing down the appropriate numbers on a separate sheet of paper.

Allow ½ minute.

1. T	E	V	G		9. N	E	H	Y
2. G	W	Z	H		10. E	V	T	H
3. H	T	F	N		11. H	F	H	T
4. V	N	H	E		12. H	G	V	H
5. G	F	E	Z		13. Y	G	V	Y
6. H	N	E	V		14. T	Z	V	Y
7. F	H	V	G		15. N	H	N	Z
8. Y	W	E	Z					

(SEE PAGE 622 FOR YOUR SCORE.)

OFFICE MACHINE APTITUDE TEST 2

Follow the directions for the previous test.

1. H	N	W	G		9. V	T	Z	H
2. H	E	V	N		10. F	N	Y	T
3. H	V	Y	V		11. N	G	T	F
4. G	V	Z	Y		12. T	V	E	N
5. H	Y	W	Y		13. W	G	V	F
6. Y	E	Z	G		14. Y	Z	V	E
7. N	Z	E	N		15. F	G	N	V
8. Y	W	E	H					

(SEE PAGE 622 FOR YOUR SCORE.)

COPYREADING APTITUDE TEST   1

The lists below consist of 15 pairs of names. On some lines the names are exactly alike. On some lines slight differences or errors appear. On a separate sheet of paper list by number the lines containing one or more errors.

Allow 40 seconds for the test.

1. Sheppard Novelty Co.	Shepard Novelty Co.
2. Roberts and Lennon, Inc.	Roberts and Lennen, Inc.
3. Joseph Pape and Sons	Joseph Pape and Sons
4. Thompson Co.	Thompson, Inc.
5. Simplex Shoe Corp.	Simplex Shoe Corp.
6. Leibster & Bros.	Liebster & Bros.
7. Silver Standards Co.	Silver Standard Co.
8. Oppenheimer and Powers	Oppenheimer and Powers
9. Powers and Oppenheimers	Power and Oppenheimers
10. Northern Texas Petroleum	No. Texas Petroleum
11. Royaltone Corporation	Royalton Corporation
12. G. H. Furnath Co. Inc.	G. H. Furnath Co. Inc.
13. Harold Jacobsohn Co.	Herald Jacobsohn Co.
14. Terrell Express Co.	Terrill Express Co.
15. Hart Wallder and Sons	Hart Wallder and Sons

(SEE PAGE 622 FOR YOUR SCORE.)

COPYREADING APTITUDE TEST   2

Follow the same instructions for the preceding test.

1. Knappe and Johns	Knapp and Johns
2. Greenland Masonite Products	Greenland Masonit Products
3. Magic Seal Supplies	Magic Seal Supply
4. Seton Hall College	Setan Hall College
5. Imperial Coats, Inc.	Imperial Coats, Inc.
6. Shagmoor Furs Co.	Shagmore Furs Co.
7. Personnel Institute of America	Personell Institute of America
8. Pritchard and Kayella	Pritchard and Kayella
9. D. C. Victor Elec.	A. C. Victor Elec.
10. Elfrein and Mattick	Elfrein and Mattrick
11. Hector's Bar-B-Q	Hector's Bar B-Q
12. Raymodna and Sharpe	Raymond and Sharpe
13. The Marquisea Company	The Marquisea Company
14. Thorp Noland and Son	Thorp Noland and Son
15. Parke Davis and Co.	Park Davis and Co.

(SEE PAGE 622 FOR YOUR SCORE.)

PATTERN VISUALIZATION TESTS

The following tests (8 in all) are based on patterns that can be folded into solid forms. Without actually cutting out and folding the patterns, study the figure on the left in each test and decide which figures among those on the right of the line could be made from the pattern figure. Sometimes more than one correct figure is possible. Then, on a separate sheet of paper, list the answers for all 8 tests before consulting the scoring page. Allow time as marked.

TEST #1—allow 2 minutes.

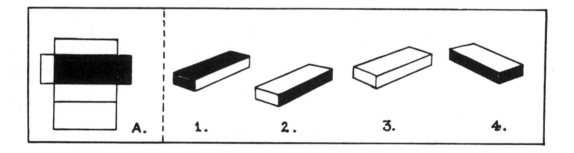

TEST #2—allow 2 minutes.

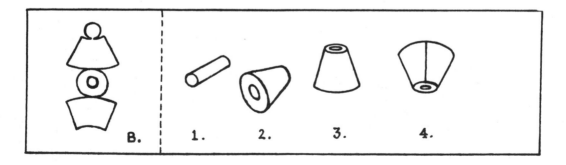

(SEE PAGE 622 FOR YOUR SCORE.)

TEST #3—allow 3 minutes.

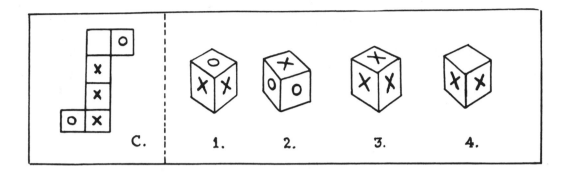

TEST #4—allow 3 minutes.

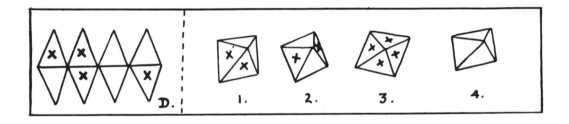

TEST #5—allow 3 minutes.

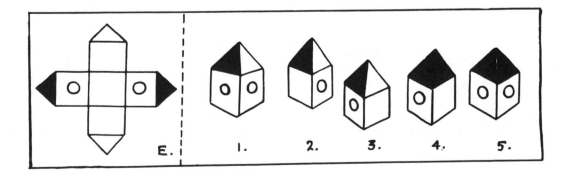

(SEE PAGE 622 FOR YOUR SCORE.)

TEST #6—allow 3 minutes.

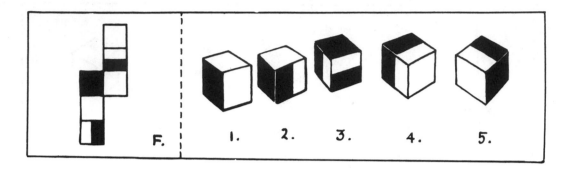

TEST #7—allow 3 minutes.

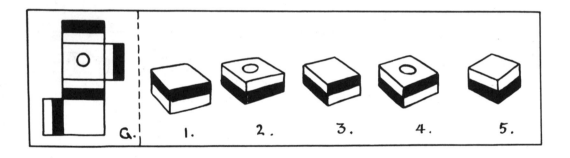

TEST #8—allow 2 minutes.

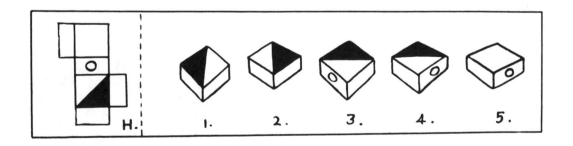

(SEE PAGE 622 FOR YOUR SCORE.)

HOUSE OF CARDS

4

Card Tricks

The card tricks in this section are very simple to do. Most of them depend upon subtle principles rather than sleight of hand. All you need is a pack of cards, and you can start doing them immediately, either as part of a magic act or as an act all their own.

No intricate shuffles, no deft deals, no trick decks are needed. But here is an important tip, and one that applies to other types of magic as well: The more smoothly, the more neatly you handle the cards, the more effective your tricks will be.

If you handle a pack of cards clumsily, people take for granted that your tricks must be easy; otherwise, they think, you couldn't do them. But when you shuffle the cards briskly and deal them rapidly, you give them the idea that skill is needed in even the simplest of tricks.

THE TWO ROWS

THE EFFECT: You tell a spectator—say, Geoff—to deal two rows of cards, each row containing the same number of cards, so that he'll have the number firmly fixed in his mind.

He can use any number of cards in each row from 3 or 4 to 20; it is entirely up to him. You are going to give him instructions on how to re-arrange the rows in various ways. While he is re-arranging them, you either turn your back or go into another room (as long as he can hear you from there).

When Geoff is ready, tell him to take away cards from either row, but to state *how many* cards he takes, and from which row, *top or bottom*.

When he does that, tell him he can do what he wants—take more cards from either row—or add cards, or transfer them from one row to the other—as long as he tells you how many cards were moved and says which row—or rows—are involved.

At one point, you suggest a number for Geoff to take away, but he never tells you how many cards either row contains.

Then suddenly you say, "Stop!" And you name the exact number of cards that remain.

HOW IT IS DONE: The number of cards in each row *does not matter,* as long as they are equal at the start. For example, assume that Geoff puts 7 cards in each row:

```
   TOP:  *  *  *  *  *  *  *
BOTTOM:  *  *  *  *  *  *  *
```

You don't see these cards, but you take a high number of your own—say 20—and imagine or visualize the rows as containing 20 cards each. Then you ask Geoff to take away cards, add them, or move them as he chooses, but to tell you what he does. Like this:

He moves 3 cards from the bottom row to the top, and says so. That leaves the rows like this:

```
   TOP:  *  *  *  *  *  *  *  *  *  *
BOTTOM:  *  *  *  *
```

Working from your "key" number 20, you mentally move 3 from bottom to top, saying to yourself: "Twenty-three in the top row—17 in the bottom row."

Now, suppose Geoff takes away 2 from the bottom row, stating that fact. He has:

```
   TOP:  *  *  *  *  *  *  *  *  *
BOTTOM:  *  *
```

You say to yourself: "Two from 17 leaves 15 in the bottom row—with 23 still in the top row."

Geoff decides to add one card to each row. He announces that fact and performs the action, so that the rows stand:

```
   TOP:  *  *  *  *  *  *  *  *  *  *
BOTTOM:  *  *  *
```

Mentally, you add one to each of *your* rows, giving you 24 in the top row and 16 in the bottom row.

Now comes the important part: You tell Geoff to count the number of cards in the bottom row and take that many away from the top row. He takes 3 (the number in his bottom row) from the 11 cards in his top row, which gives him:

```
   TOP:  *  *  *  *  *  *  *  *
BOTTOM:  *  *  *
```

Meanwhile, you are the doing the same with your imaginary rows, subtracting 16 (bottom) from 24 (top) so you have 8 cards in your top row.

Then you tell Geoff to take away his bottom row entirely. That leaves him with a single row:

```
*  *  *  *  *  *  *  *
```

You too eliminate your imaginary bottom row (16 cards) and that leaves you with a single row of just 8 cards, identical with the row now on the table!

From then on, you can let Geoff add or subtract cards as he wants, providing he states the exact number in each case. You go right along with him, for you are both working with the same number.

Assume that he simply takes away 4 cards. He then has:

* * * *

You do the same and announce your final total: "Four!"

PERFORMANCE TIPS: Your aim should be to keep the trick intriguing and at the same time reasonably simple, in order to avoid any false steps. That is why it has been described in such exact detail. When you do it, keep these points in mind:

First you tell Geoff to deal a row of cards, and then another with the same number, so he has the number fixed in his mind. As he does it, you add: "It can be a small number or a large one, anything from 2 up to 20, but be sure you deal the same number twice—and don't change it—at least not yet!"

Here you give him the impression that you are already beginning to "get" the number. Then you say:

"Now take away or add cards to either row, but tell me how many cards you move and what you do with them. You can simply move them from one row to the other, if you want."

With that done, you continue: "Now move a few more and tell me again. From these partial thoughts, I am trying to get a full impression."

After a few such moves (as already described), you say, "Stop! I think I have it. Just to make sure our minds are tuned, I want you to count the cards in the smaller row, without telling me. Take that row entirely away. You've done it? Good. Now, take the same number from the other row, so as to fix it firmly in mind. Add a few more, or take some away if you prefer, but this time, tell me how many. That's enough. I have it!"

You can do this trick with coins or with matches or toothpicks, as well as with cards.

THE TWO ROWS ENCORE

This makes a good follow-up to The Two Rows. The tricks are similar, but there is enough difference between them to throw observers off the trail.

THE EFFECT: Tell one of the spectators—Suzie, let's say—to take an odd number of cards and put them down in equal rows. The extra card can go in either row. Turn your back while Suzie lays out the cards.

The rows might be:

```
*  *  *  *  *  *  *
*  *  *  *  *  *
```

Now ask Suzie to name a small number, less than the number of cards in either row. Suppose she says, "Five." You tell her to take 5 cards from the long row and put them aside.

The rows will then stand:

```
      *  *
*  *  *  *  *  *
```

Next, tell Suzie to count the cards in what is now the short row and to take that many away from the other row, without stating the number (which happens to be 2, in this case).

This leaves:

```
      *  *
*  *  *  *
```

Then tell Suzie to take away the first row entirely, and to concentrate upon the number of cards in the remaining row:

```
*  *  *  *
```

After much concentration and exchange of "brain waves," you name the number: "Four."

HOW IT IS DONE: This trick works itself. Your "key number" for the climax is *one less* than the number that Suzie named at the beginning!

In this case, Suzie picked up 5, and that meant there would be 4 at the finish. If she had picked 3, there would have been 2 left, and so on.

PERFORMANCE TIPS: You need a few rehearsals in order to make this trick work smoothly and effectively. Play up the mind-reading angle at every stage. When Suzie adds the "odd" card to one row, act as if you are "picking up" the number of cards even then.

After Suzie chooses her number, continue to "concentrate." When you tell her to remove the first row, you can say, "Your mind seems to be going from one row to another. Take away the first row entirely. You've done that? I thought so . . . Now count the cards in the one remaining row. Count them mentally, one by one. Fix on the final number and keep it firmly in mind. I am counting to myself now. One, two, three, four! That is the number!"

> **Note:** If Suzie picks the number *one* at the start and removes only one card, the rows will be the same and the trick won't work. If she says, "One," simply say, "That's too small. Let's make it larger." Or you can tell her to double it, and take 2 cards from the long row. Or at the start, you can say, "Name any number above one—but less than the number of cards in either row."

MINT DATE

EQUIPMENT: A coin
        A hat
        A deck of cards
        A scarf or an ordinary large handkerchief
        A decorated empty box

THE EFFECT: You begin by borrowing a coin from a member of the audience. You place it in a colored silk scarf (or an ordinary handkerchief) and place the entire bundle in an empty box. Ask the person who lent you the coin to hold the box.

Ask another person from the audience to shuffle a deck of cards and then divide it into four equal piles. The backs of the cards should face upwards. You take the top card from each stack and put them into a hat without any comments.

Now ask the volunteer who is holding the box to open it, unwrap the scarf, and read the date on the coin. You immediately produce four cards from the hat and their face values are the same as the date on the coin. If, for example, the coin was minted in 1976, you produce an ace, a nine, a seven and a six.

HOW IT IS DONE: Before the performance, pick up any coin and note its date. Now pick out four cards, the numbers of which make up the date. Place these cards in the hat.

Place the coin and the scarf together on your table. When you're ready to do the trick, palm the coin in your hand when you pick up the scarf.

Show the audience that the scarf is empty and, under cover of the scarf, switch the borrowed coin (you must ask for a coin of the same denomination) with the palmed coin.

Hold the scarf with your left hand so that it hangs loosely. Place your right hand, holding both the palmed coin and the "real" coin, under the scarf and slip the palmed coin between the fingers of your left hand. Let the spectators see the outline of the coin under the scarf so they know it is where it should be.

Placing the scarf and coin in the box afterwards is only for effect. It has no significance at all so far as the trick is concerned.

It also does not matter which cards are picked, since none of them will be used. You put the cards you need in your pocket beforehand.

PERFORMANCE TIPS: To keep from mixing up the two stacks of cards in the hat, you might put one stack on its side and the other on its end.

Or, if you use a felt hat, put the "real" cards on one side of the crease and the "cheating" cards on the other side. Then you will not have trouble figuring out which pile is which. You can also deposit the palmed coin in the hat.

MUTUS DEDIT NOMEN COCIS

THE EFFECT: Give the spectator—Sally Ann—a packet of 20 cards to lay out on the table *face down* in sets of two. Then turn your back and ask her to select one of these sets of two, look at the cards in it, and remember them.

Other spectators can look at a set, too. If there are ten people watching, each one can look at a set of two and remember it.

Turning around now, you gather up the sets, keeping them together, and lay the cards out on the table *face up* in four rows of 5 cards each.

"Which one or two rows are your cards in?" you ask Sally Ann.

As soon as she points to the rows which house her two cards, you announce what they are. And you do the same thing for any other spectators who point out the rows their two cards are in.

HOW IT IS DONE: This trick is based on code words, which you need to memorize. The words are "Mutus" (pronounced MEW-tus), "Dedit" (DEAD-it), "Nomen" (NO-mun), "Cocis" (COCK-us).

M U T U S						1	2	3	2	4
D E D I T						5	6	5	7	3
N O M E N						8	9	1	6	8
C O C I S						10	9	10	7	4

The layout—numbered by sets

When you lay out the cards, instead of just putting them down in any old order, you follow the letter pattern in the words. For example, you put the first set (two cards) down in the spots occupied by the M's—the M in Mutus and the only other M spot, the M in Nomen. Then you put the second set of two cards into the spots reserved for the U's—both of them in Mutus. And so on for set #3: start with the T in Mutus and then go to the T in Dedit, and on until you have laid out all the sets.

So when you ask Sally Ann to point out the rows (horizontally) in which her cards are located, it is a simple question of finding the two identical letters.

If Sally Ann says both cards are in the first row, you know automatically that it is the set of U's in Mutus. If they are in rows 1 and 2, you know she had the T's in Mutus and Dedit. If they are in rows 1 and 3, she had the M's in Mutus and Nomen. If they are in rows 1 and 4, she had the S positions in Mutus and Cocis.

If the cards are only in the second row, she had the D's in Dedit. If they are in the second and third rows, she had the E's in Dedit and Nomen. If they are in the second and last rows, they are the I's in Dedit and Cocis.

If Sally Ann says her cards are only in the third row, she had the N's in Nomen. In the third and fourth rows, she had the O's in Nomen and Cocis. And if they are just in the last row, she had the C's in Cocis.

PERFORMANCE TIPS: This trick works well only if you memorize the words thoroughly. Practice until you can lay out the cards in the four-word pattern with speed and assurance. Once you can do that, it is simple to remember the code when it comes time to find the sets. As you start placing the pairs, you can say, "I'll place these here and there, so they will be all mixed up," but all the while, you are setting them down according to your formula.

For a repeat, it is a good idea to lay out the pairs differently. You can change the order of the words, and use other formulas, too, instead of Mutus Dedit Nomen Cocis. (Some of those are Latin words, but as far as we can tell, they don't have any secret meaning.)

Here are three other arrangements:

```
T  A  R  O  T
E  N  D  E  R
I  O  N  I  C
S  C  A  D  S

M  O  T  O  R
S  H  E  E  R
N  I  N  T  H
M  I  L  L  S

S  A  L  A  D
Z  I  P  P  S
T  I  T  L  E
O  O  Z  E  D
```

It doesn't matter whether you work this as a mind-reading trick or a memory stunt. It is puzzling and entertaining, in either case.

DO AS I DO

This classic trick will really bewilder your audience, but it is easy to do once you learn to handle the cards in a convincing way.

THE EFFECT: You take two packs of cards and let a spectator—Joyce—choose either pack. You shuffle one pack, and she shuffles the other.

To show that all is fair, you then exchange packs, so that each of you shuffles the other's. Finally, you hand your pack to Joyce and say, "From now on, do as I do, and let's see what happens."

You deal your pack in three heaps on the table. Joyce does the same thing with her pack.

You lift the top card of the middle heap and peek at it. Joyce does the same, and you remind her, "I am remembering my card, so I want you to remember yours."

Now you gather the heaps and give your pack two or three cuts. Joyce does the same with her pack. Remarking that the peeked-at cards are now "well buried," you exchange packs again. Then you say:

"I am going to look through your pack and take out the card that I found in mine. You look through my pack and find yours. Then we'll put them face down on the table."

Once you each pick out your cards, set the packs aside. Dramatically, you turn up the two cards. They are identical! By an amazing coincidence, you have each taken the same card from a different pack!

HOW IT IS DONE: After a few shuffles and exchanges, take a peek at the bottom card of the pack that you hand to Joyce. Here is one way to do it:

Let's say the bottom card is the 9 of Clubs. You take her pack and say:

"Now do as I do."

Lift off about 2/3 of the pack, set it to the right. Then lift off the top third and put it further to the right.

with the 9 of clubs at the bottom → rest of pack | Joyce peeks at the top card. → second third | top third

Joyce does the same with the pack you gave her.

Peek at the top card of the middle heap, but don't bother to remember it. Still keep thinking of that bottom card of the other pack. Pick up the left-hand heap of your pack, put it on the middle heap and place both heaps on the top heap.

Joyce does the same with her pack. In the process, she plants the bottom card—the 9 of Clubs that you secretly noted—squarely on the card at which she peeked!

You cut the pack twice or three times, and chances are the two cards will remain together. So after you exchange packs again, simply look through Joyce's pack for the 9 of Clubs, and remove the card just below it, say the Jack of Diamonds.

That will be the card she looked at. Meanwhile, she is looking through your pack, finding the Jack of Diamonds and taking it out as you instructed. So the two cards turn out to be identical.

PERFORMANCE TIPS: Do this trick with confidence. If you miss a chance to note the bottom card, or if it gets lost in a chance shuffle, simply exchange the packs again and proceed from there.

Sometimes you may "spot" the bottom card of the pack that Joyce is shuffling. In that case, you don't have to note yours. Instead of exchanging packs, you would say, "Just put your pack on the table and cut it as I do mine."

Don't worry about which pack is which after the trick has passed the preliminary stage. Just refer to a pack as "your pack" or "my pack," according to convenience or the way it develops.

If Joyce starts to shuffle her pack after looking at her card, don't give up the trick. Just say, "That's good. Now let me shuffle your pack while you shuffle mine." At the same time, hand her your pack.

It generally takes a good shuffle to separate the chosen card and the "key" card above it, so chances are the trick will work anyway. If it misses, try again, preferably with Do As I Do Again, which follows.

DO AS I DO AGAIN

THE EFFECT: The effect of this trick is almost identical to the last one. You and Joyce shuffle the two packs and exchange them. Each of you notes a card and these, when drawn from the other's pack, are the same.

HOW IT IS DONE: During a shuffle, note the *top card* of your pack before handing it to Joyce. Then tell her, "Now do as I do."

In this case, lift off 2/3 of the pack and carry it well to the right. Then lift off the top third of that heap and bring it back a short way, setting it between the other two, so that it becomes the middle heap.

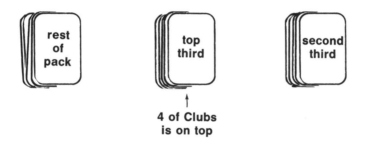

4 of Clubs
is on top

You do this with Joyce's pack. She does the same with yours. Now you say, "Look at the top card of the middle heap and remember it."

Joyce looks at the card you noted, say the 4 of Clubs, while you are peeking at a card in her pack.

Exchange the packs again. Joyce looks for her card in your deck, and you look for your card in hers. You both come up with the 4 of Clubs.

PERFORMANCE TIPS: This version has the advantage that the card is "forced" on Joyce, so the trick cannot possibly miss. Furthermore, you can include a shuffle in the routine after the top card of the middle heap has been noted by Joyce. You simply say, "Now do as I do and shuffle the pack thoroughly." Then you follow with the final exchange.

The best plan is to work the original Do as I Do and save the second version for a repeat. In the original trick, Joyce actually takes a random card from deep in the deck. The second trick depends on an odd handling of the heaps, which works best when you're dealing with a smart spectator who is looking for something else.

COINS AND CARDS

THE EFFECT: Run through the faces of a pack of cards, showing that they are well mixed. Announce that you will predict the card that a spectator—Richard—selects at random. Write something on a slip of paper, fold it and set it beside the pack, which you place *face down* on the table.

Now you tell Richard to take any old coin from his pocket and add the figures on the date. "Whatever the total," you say, "we will count down that many cards in the pack and use the number of spots on that card to find our predicted card."

Richard looks at a coin and names the date, which we'll suppose is 1961. When added, the figures 1, 9, 6 and 1 give a total of 17. Then Richard counts down 17 cards and happens to turn up the 7 of Clubs. So you tell him, "Go right ahead and count down seven more."

Richard turns up the seventh card. It is the 10 of Diamonds. You tell him to open the slip of paper. To his astonishment, he finds the written message, "the 10 of Diamonds," which hits it on the nose!

HOW IT IS DONE: Beforehand you must arrange 13 cards in descending order: King (13), Queen (12), Jack (11), 10, and so on down to Ace (1). These cards can be of any suits, so the setup is quick and easy to arrange. Put this set on top of the pack. Then count any 10 cards from the bottom and put them on top of the set.

When you run through the face-up pack to show it is well mixed, watch for the card just below your setup—in this case the 10 of Diamonds. That is the 24th card from the top, and it is the one you must predict.

The trick is sure to work every time, with the following exceptions:

1. Some coins dated before 1901.
2. Coins dated 1969.   (total of 25)
3. Coins dated 1978.   (total of 25)
4. Coins dated 1979.   (total of 26)
5. Coins dated after 1986.

The lowest possible total will come from 1901 or 1910, bringing the count to the eleventh card. There Richard will find a King, with a value of 13, so you tell him to count 13 more which will bring him to the 24th card.

Other dates work just as well. The higher the sum of figures contained in the coin's date, the lower the value of the card from which the count is continued. So 1-9-6-0 would end on the 16th card—an 8—which would carry the count on to 24.

A date of 1-9-7-7 totals 24 and brings the count squarely to the 24th card, so there is no need to go on further. Just tell the person to read the prediction; and there it is!

PERFORMANCE TIPS: When you run through the pack, thumb the cards rapidly as you reach the set-up group and no one will notice their numerical arrangement. After Richard deals that 24th card, take the rest of the pack from him and shuffle it while he is reading the prediction and turning up the card. That will really mix the set-up group, in case anyone wants to look at the pack.

Don't repeat this trick the same day; once is enough.

FOUR-HEAP DEAL

THE EFFECT: You shuffle the deck thoroughly and spread it *face down* along the table so that a spectator—Jennifer—can remove any four cards, which she lays face down in a row.

Gather up the pack and hand it to Jennifer. Then turn your back and tell her to turn up the first of the four cards and note its value: 1 for Ace, 2 for deuce, and so on. All face cards (Jacks, Queens and Kings) count 10.

On that first card, Jennifer deals enough additional cards (*face down*) to total 12. For example, on a 7 she would deal five cards, on a 10 or a King, two cards.

Now Jennifer turns up the next card in the row and repeats the process, and continues with the third and fourth cards. Here is a sample result:

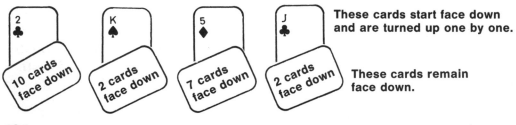

2 ♣ — 10 cards face down
K ♠ — 2 cards face down
5 ♦ — 7 cards face down
J ♣ — 2 cards face down

These cards start face down and are turned up one by one.

These cards remain face down.

Now you tell Jennifer to count down into the pack and turn up the card which is the total of all the face-up cards. She is to look at it and remember it. Then you call out the name of a card, say "Queen of Hearts," and it proves to be the chosen card.

HOW IT IS DONE: You need a pack of exactly 52 cards, so be sure to remove any Jokers beforehand. All you have to do is get a look at the bottom card after the shuffle—in this case, the Queen of Hearts—and the rest is automatic. (See page 192 for a way to sneak a look at the bottom card.)

For example, if four Aces were turned up, Jennifer would have to deal 11 cards on each, making 48 in all. Only 4 cards would be left in the pack. She would gather the 44 face-down cards, drop the 4 cards from the pack on top and count down the total of the Aces, exactly 4 cards.

With four 10's or face cards, she would deal 2 on each, making 8 face-down cards and leaving 40 cards in the pack. She would gather up the 8 cards, drop the rest of the pack on top and count down the value of the 10's (or face cards), which would come to 40.

Tell Jennifer she can gather the face-down heaps in any order she wants and place the rest of the pack face down on the pile. Tell her to add the totals of the face-up cards. In the example in the illustration, the cards would add up as follows: 2 for the 2 of Clubs, 10 for the King of Spades, 5 for the 5 of Diamonds, 10 for the Jack of Clubs, for a total of 27.

PERFORMANCE TIPS: It is a good idea to illustrate beforehand just what you want Jennifer to do. Deal a card face up, then add face-down cards to bring the numerical total to 12, saying that you will have her do that with several heaps. Show her how to gather the face-down cards and drop the pack on them.

Then shuffle the pack, spot the bottom card and go right into the routine. If you are using this method to "force" the card, or as a mind-reading act, it is best to turn away as much as possible. But if you do it as a prediction, by writing the name of the bottom card on a folded slip of paper before Jennifer draws the four cards from the pack, you can watch the process and help in the gathering of the face-down piles.

As long as Jennifer does most of the dealing and is convinced that you could not have manipulated the cards in any way, the trick is 100 per cent effective.

CARD UNDER GLASS

EQUIPMENT: **A plastic glass**
One playing card

THE EFFECT: You show both the front and back of a card to the audience. Then, holding it between your right thumb and index finger (if you are right-handed), you carefully place a glass on top of the card. You concentrate very hard to find the point of balance, but at last you succeed and the glass balances on top of the card.

HOW IT IS DONE: The illustration below reveals the secret.

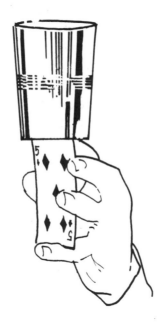

As you can see, your right index finger, hidden by the card, supports the glass. If you use a very small glass, you can put some water in it. This makes the trick all the more dramatic, but be sure the glass is not too heavy.

PERFORMANCE TIPS: This is really a very simple trick and should be done as one of a series of tricks. Unlike the glass, it can't really stand on its own.

Do the trick above the eye level of the audience, so they can't see your index finger at work.

THE RISING CARD

THE EFFECT: You show the audience an ordinary pack of cards, still in the package. Open the package and hold the deck in your outstretched right hand. Say a bit of hocus pocus over the pack and slowly a card slides up out of the box.

HOW IT IS DONE: Cut a slit about ½-inch (15 mm) wide and 1½ inches (35 mm) long on the back of the package (see the illustration). With your right index finger, push the card up.

When you cut a slot in the card box, you can make the cards "crawl" out of the box "by themselves."

PERFORMANCE TIPS: This trick works best when the pack of cards is not quite full. Be sure to follow up this trick rapidly with another one, or switch the package for an identical deck so that no one gets a chance to see the back of the pack.

THE FLYING CARD

EQUIPMENT: 2 empty glasses
2 cones—made of glossy paper in different colors
2 identical pairs of cards from 2 different decks

THE EFFECT: You place two empty glasses on the table in front of you. Put a card into one of them, with its face toward the audience, and place a glossy paper cone over the glass.

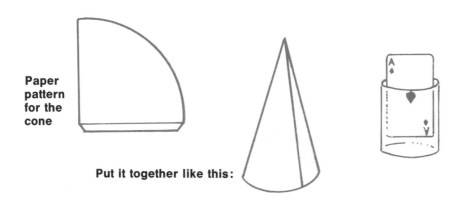

Paper pattern for the cone

Put it together like this:

Show that the other glass is empty. Then place the other cone over it, and tell the audience that you are going to make the card fly through the air from one glass to the other.

Say a little hokus pokus over the cone that has the card under it, and announce that the card has made the journey. "Now," you tell them, "comes the hard part," making the card come back home. Very solemnly, you concentrate and triumphantly remove the cone from the original glass, announcing that the card has come home.

Of course, everyone says that's nonsense, and you can pretend to be hurt because they don't trust you. Tell them you'll do the same thing—but a bit differently.

Now, with the glass containing the card in one hand, and a paper cone in the other, you approach the audience and ask them to concentrate on the card and on the color of the cone. Place the cone over the glass and put them on the table.

Repeat the same routine with the other glass, putting into it a card of a different color and rank.

Now, after some nonsense, chatter and hokus pokus, you remove the cones and everyone can see that the cards have changed places!

HOW IT IS DONE: For this trick you use not two cards but four. If, for example, you have decided to use the 2 of Diamonds and the Ace of Spades (low cards are easiest to tell apart at a distance), you must use the same two cards from another deck.

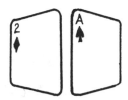

Paste these cards back-to-back.

Paste these back-to-back, too.

Glue together the Ace from one deck to the deuce of the same deck. Glue together the Ace and deuce from another deck, all back-to-back, of course.

After you have shown the first card, the glass, and the paper cone to the audience, turn and put the glass on the table. See to it that the "back" of the card is turned forwards. This happens automatically if you set the glass down without turning your hand.

Do the same with the other glass. Miraculously (it seems), when you lift the cones the cards have changed places.

PERFORMANCE TIPS: Be careful not to turn your back completely to the audience at any time. The cone-and-glass contraption must be visible to the spectators straight through if they are to accept the trick.

It is best to use cylindrical glasses, but if you don't have any that are wide enough to contain the cards, you can manage with jam jars. Or you can use a miniature deck just the size you need.

HATFUL
OF CARDS

EQUIPMENT: A hat
A ball-point pen
10-12 cards from an old or incomplete deck
PREPARATION: See below

THE EFFECT: In this trick you are able to predict which card a member of the audience will draw. You pick a card at random from the deck, write something on it with your pen, and put it in the hat.

Then you fan out the rest of the cards in your hand so that the audience can see they are not alike.

Put the fanned-out cards *face down*. Then ask a member of the audience to draw a card and put it into the hat without looking at it or showing it to anyone. When you hand the hat containing two cards to the spectators, they find to their surprise that written on one card is the suit and number of the other card!

HOW IT IS DONE: You never wrote a single word on the card you put in the hat—you only pretended to! What you did was place the 9 of Diamonds, in this case, in the hat. You did not choose it at random—it just looked that way.

Beforehand you wrote "9 of Diamonds" on all the *other* cards. Since the writing was along the side of the card that is covered automatically by the next card in the fan, the audience wasn't able to see the writing when you fanned out the cards. As for the card on the top of the pile, you hid the writing with your thumb.

PERFORMANCE TIP: If you include mind-reading in your act, this trick will go right along with it.

X-RAY EYES

EQUIPMENT: A deck of cards, still in the package
PREPARATION: See below

THE EFFECT: After you hand a deck of cards over to the audience to be shuffled, you replace the deck in its package. You tell the spectators that you will prove that you have X-ray eyes which can see right through the package.

Holding the pack of cards in your outstretched hand, you announce the suit and number of the cards before you take them out of the package and hand them to the audience for inspection. You seem to have X-ray eyes.

HOW IT IS DONE: Actually, you have a little square "window" cut in the lower right corner of the back of the package. Don't make the window any larger than can be covered by your thumb, so you can show the back of the package to the audience. At the same time, make the window big enough so that you can see the suit and number, which are found in the corners of all decks of cards.

PERFORMANCE TIPS: Remember to insert the cards into the package so that the face side appears through the hole. Another good thing to remember is that an upside-down six looks like a nine, and vice-versa.

FINDING THE LOST CARD

EQUIPMENT: Envelope large enough to hold 4 playing cards,
3 inches (8 cm) of cellophane tape or about 1½ inches (4 cm)
of double-stick tape (which sticks on both sides)
A hat
Letter opener
Assorted cards

PREPARATION: See below

THE EFFECT: You ask a member of the audience—Gerry—to draw four cards at random from the deck and hand them over to you. Without looking at them, you put them in the envelope and seal it. Then you place the envelope in a hat and make a few magical motions over it.

Handing the hat to Gerry, you show her where to stand so that everybody can see. You take the envelope, as everyone watches, and hand it to her. She opens it with a letter opener to see if all the cards are still there.

It turns out that one of the cards is missing. You suggest that Gerry check to see if she has misplaced it at her seat. When she turns around, the rest of the audience sees that the card is stuck to her back!

HOW IT IS DONE: Loop the cellophane tape into a circle, sticky side out (see illustration).

Place this ring in the hat so that the sticky side faces outwards. Even if you were to show the empty hat to your audience, they would not be able to see the transparent tape which, by the way, should not be pressed firmly to the sides or bottom of the hat.

The envelope should also be large enough so that when a card is hidden behind it, the flap can be folded down and sealed without touching the card.

When the cards have been drawn from the deck and are about to be placed in the envelope, hold them so that the backs of the cards face you.

The last card, or the card closest to you, is not placed in the envelope, but is slipped outside it.

Hold the last card against the back of the envelope as you seal it. If you don't show the back of the envelope to your audience, no one will suspect that you have put only 3 cards in it.

The envelope and the loose card are placed in the hat so that the card is near the tape. When you take the envelope, card and sticky loop out of the hat again, it is very easy to press the card against the tape, and it will adhere immediately. The card will be hidden behind the envelope.

When you lead Gerry to the "proper position" (so that "everyone can see"), you put your hand on her back and press the card against it. You won't even have to use much pressure. Then you can give her the envelope to open.

PERFORMANCE TIPS: You can do the same trick in a slightly different way. Ask two members of the audience to pick three cards each. Ask the volunteer whose card you have kept outside the envelope to assist you. The assistant should take the cards out of the envelope and find one of his or her own cards is missing. The rest of the trick goes on as before.

FOOLED!

EQUIPMENT: **A scarf**
2 old or incomplete decks of cards
Glue
Cardboard

THE EFFECT: Holding five cards in your left hand where everybody can see them, you lay a scarf over your left hand. When you remove the scarf there are only two cards left. It is obvious—or at least the spectators will think so—that the other three cards are in the scarf. They can even see the outline of them. Naturally, they will demand to see what is underneath the scarf.

After you refuse to show them for a while, you give in. There is a card under the scarf. Printed on it in large letters is the word "FOOLED"!

The audience now wants to see the other side of the card. Written on the other side are the words, "NO, I'M SORRY."

At this point you drape the empty scarf over the cards and when you remove it after a moment, all five cards have reappeared!

HOW IT IS DONE: Strips of four different cards have been glued to another card, making it appear as if five cards have been fanned out. When the card on the upper right (see the illustration) is placed over the false cards, it is impossible to see the forgery.

The Spread

The "fifth" card

The "5" Fanned-Out Cards

At the top left you see the front of the Spread. The strips of cards have been glued to another card. The card at the top right is used "as is." When you show the 2 parts together (below), it looks as though 5 cards have been fanned out.

For this trick, you have to ruin two decks of cards, so use old or incomplete decks. On the opposite side of the four glued-together cards, glue another card which is identical to one of the cards on the front.

For example, in the illustration the Jack of Hearts (below) has been used twice: once in the "foursome," and once on the back of the foursome as a "twosome" with the 6 of Spades. Also glue a card to the back of the 6 of Spades—another identical 6 of Spades.

**Back of
the Spread**

**Back of
the "fifth" card**

The Jack of Hearts has been pasted to the back of the "Spread." When you turn the Spread over, the Jack of Hearts appears to be the only card there.

**Back of the
"5" Fanned-Out Cards**

Make the card with the captions "FOOLED" and "NO, I'M SORRY" from a piece of cardboard the exact size of a playing card. Keep the cardboard card hidden behind the other two cards.

When you first pick up the cards, the audience will think you are holding five cards. As you put the scarf over your hand, push the "FOOLED" card up into the hand that is holding the scarf. At the same time, turn your other hand so that the twosome is facing the audience.

PERFORMANCE TIPS: There are several variations of this trick. Here is one of them: display the "five" cards and then put them into a hat. Remove two of the cards and ask the volunteer to pick up the other three. But they have vanished!

THE MULTIPLYING CARDS

EQUIPMENT: A flat plate
20 playing cards

THE EFFECT: One by one you place about 10 cards on a flat plate and ask a member of the audience to count them. The volunteer does this and returns the cards to the table, but you shake your head and look doubtful. Then you ask another volunteer to check the number of cards once more. You personally hand the volunteer the cards. To everyone's surprise, there turn out to be twice as many cards as before!

HOW IT IS DONE: The illustration gives the trick away. You have hidden the extra cards under the plate. You hold them in place with your right hand, which is holding the plate. Using your left hand, you push the cards on top of the plate under your right thumb, and with your left hand, you take the plate, uniting the two piles. Throughout this procedure, hold the plate at a slight angle forward so that no one can see the pile of cards under the plate.

PERFORMANCE TIPS: It will be very easy to pick up both the plate and the concealed pile of cards at the same time if you place them both at the very edge of the table, an edge of the cards overhanging the table, in fact.

THE DOUBLE DEAL

This trick is based upon a neat but simple mathematical stunt, and it becomes a real puzzler when you allow the spectators to mystify themselves!

THE EFFECT: Give Dorothy a pack of cards and tell her to deal off any number up to 20 while your back is turned. When she does that, tell her to deal another heap with the same number of cards—to make sure she doesn't forget that number.

Then tell her to deal a third heap of 10 cards, gather all the heaps together and deal them into two separate piles, alternating left and right. Dorothy then is to pick up either pile. From it she deals the original number of cards onto the other heap.

Finally, Dorothy counts the remaining cards in her hand and concentrates on that number. You immediately announce the number of cards she is holding.

And the entire trick is done with your back to the audience.

HOW IT IS DONE: The trick hinges on the third heap of cards you tell Dorothy to deal, the pile of ten. At the finish, she will have just half that number, so by announcing "Five," you are sure to be correct.

For example, suppose Dorothy deals off 8 cards. Told to deal the same number again, she deals off 8 more, making 16. Now you say, "Deal ten more." That brings the total to 26.

Then Dorothy deals the cards into two heaps which will contain just 13 cards each. From one of these, she deals the original number —8— into the other. That leaves exactly 5 cards, the number you proceed to name.

PERFORMANCE TIPS: Since the result is "set" beforehand, stress the fact that Dorothy has her free choice of any number. When you tell her to "Deal 10 more," do it casually, as though those extra cards did not particularly matter.

> **Note:** When you repeat the trick, change that number. If you tell her to "Deal 6 more," the final total will be 3. If you tell her to "Deal 12 more," the total will be 6, and so on.

Solitaire Games

ACCORDION

Deal the cards one at a time face up, in a row of 4 from left to right. Go slowly so that you can keep comparing the cards you deal with their neighbors. Whenever a card matches its immediate neighbor at the left, or the card third to its left, you move the new card over onto the one it matches. The matching may be in suit or rank.

Suppose that the first four cards you turn up are:

The 8 of Spades matches the 8 of Clubs and also the Jack of Spades. You may move it over upon either card. Here it is just a guess which play will turn out better. Later on, you will find that one play is better than another, when you have a choice, because it opens additional plays. Keep watching for new plays you make possible when you consolidate piles.

For example, suppose that you deal:

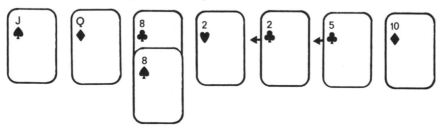

You can move the 2 of Clubs onto the 2 of Hearts. Then you can move the 5 of Clubs onto the 2 of Clubs, since they are next to each other.

Move the entire pile of cards—not just the top card. When you create a gap in a row because you moved a pile away, shove all the piles leftward to close up the gap.

TO WIN THE GAME: You must get the whole deck into one pile. You won't succeed very often. You really can consider it a win if you end up with 5 piles or less.

THE CLOCK

Shuffle the deck, and then deal it into 13 piles of four cards each, all face down.

Arrange 12 of the piles in a circle, to represent the numbers on a clock dial. Put the thirteenth pile in the middle of the circle. Start by picking up the top card of the thirteenth pile. Suppose it is a 5. Shove it face up under the 5-pile and pick up the top card of the 5-pile. Suppose it is a Queen. Put it under the 12-pile and pick up the top of the 12-pile—and so on.

Jacks represent 11, Queens 12, Kings 13; other cards have their spot value.

TO WIN THE GAME: You must get all the cards face up. You lose if you come to the fourth King before all the other cards have been moved face up to their proper hour piles.

Wastepile

THE CAVE MAN GAME

(No More Clubs)

Discard all 2's to 6's, leaving a deck of 32 cards. Shuffle them well and then deal three cards *face up* in a column at your left. If any one of them is a Club, throw it out to start a wastepile. Then deal a new card to take its place. If the new card is a Club, throw it out and deal another —and so on—until you have three non-Clubs in the column.

Then deal four more columns of three cards each, from left to right. From this array of 15 cards, throw all the Clubs into the wastepile.

Gather the cards again (except for the Clubs that you threw out), and shuffle them together. Deal a second time in the same way as the first, and again throw out all the Clubs. Then gather the remaining cards, shuffle again and deal a third time.

TO WIN THE GAME: You must discard all eight Clubs in the three deals.

THE WISH

If you win this game the first time you try it, you will get your wish —so they say.

Use a deck of 32 cards, as in The Cave Man Game. Shuffle them well and then count off four cards at a time *face down*. Then turn them *face up*. Be careful to keep the pile squared up so that you cannot see what any of the cards are below the top.

Deal the whole deck into piles of four cards in the same way.

Then lift off the top cards in pairs of the same kind—two 7's, two Queens, and so on. Keep going as long as you see any pairs.

TO WIN THE GAME: You must clear away all the cards in pairs.

HIT CARDS

Deal the cards one at a time *face up* into a single wastepile. As you deal, count "Ace, two, three . . ." and so on up to the King. Whenever the card you deal is the same as the rank you call, it's a hit! Throw all the "hit" cards out of the deck. After you count "King," start over again with "Ace, two . . ." and so on. When you have dealt the entire deck, pick up the wastepile, turn it face down, and continue dealing. Also continue counting, from where you left off.

TO WIN THE GAME: You must *hit* every card in the deck. But you lose if you go through the deck twice in succession without a single hit.

FOUR-LEAF CLOVER

You will have good luck all day if you win this game—they say.

Discard all four 10's from the deck. You won't be using them at all. Shuffle the remaining 48 cards well. Then deal 16 cards *face up* on the table in four rows of four cards each.

Whenever you can, throw out from these rows any two or more cards of the same suit. These can be (a) two or more cards that total 15 each, such as 9 and 6 or 8, 4, 2, and Ace (Ace counts 1); (b) three cards, the King, Queen and Jack.

After you throw out a batch of cards, deal from the deck to fill the spaces left in the 16-card layout.

TO WIN THE GAME: You must throw out all 48 cards (deal out the whole deck).

TIPS: In making fifteens, try to remove as many cards as possible, so as to bring in as many new cards as possible. For example, when you have a choice remove an Ace and a 2 rather than a 3.

GAPS

Deal out the whole deck *face up* in four rows of 13 cards each. Pick out the four Aces and put them aside, leaving *gaps* in the rows. Examine the card at the left of each gap. The next-higher card of the same suit may be moved into the gap.

For example, if the 8 of Diamonds is at the left of a gap, you may fill the gap with the 9 of Diamonds. Moving in the 9 of Diamonds leaves a gap—which you fill in with the card that is one rank higher than the card to the left of the gap.

Whenever you create a gap at the left end of a row, fill it with any 2 that you please.

TO WIN THE GAME: You must get all four suits in order, one in each row, from 2 to King, going from left to right.

When a King lies to the left of a gap, that gap is dead; you cannot fill it. Usually, all four gaps go dead after a while. Then gather up all the cards except the Aces and the cards which are in proper sequence with a 2 at the left end of a row.

Shuffle the cards well and deal them again so as to re-make the four rows of 13, but leave a gap in each row just to the right of the cards that were not gathered up. That allows you to bring one additional card into its proper place on each row, to start you on a new series of plays.

When you are blocked again, gather and redeal the cards in the same way. You are allowed three deals in all.

Make the most of whatever choice you have when you play. You often can choose the order in which you move the cards and which 2 you use to fill a left-end gap. A good choice will open up many more plays than a poor one.

PERPETUAL MOTION

Deal four cards face up in a row from left to right. If any of them are of the same rank (6's, Aces, Kings, etc.) move them onto the one farthest to the left.

Then deal four more cards from left to right on the four piles (count a space as a pile if you moved any of the first four cards). Play in the same way, if you can, moving two or more cards of the same rank upon the leftmost card of that rank.

All these moves must be one card (the top card) at a time. Do not move a whole pile at a time.

Continue dealing the deck, four cards at a time on the previous piles, making what moves you can each time.

When you have used up the deck, pick up the piles from right to left. That is, put pile #4 (at the right), still face up, on pile #3 (at its left). Put them together on pile #2 and then put the whole bunch on pile #1. Don't get the cards mixed up.

Then turn the whole pile face down, forming a new stock. Go through it again in the same way. You may deal out the stock this way any number of times, until you finally win the game or are blocked.

Whenever the four cards you deal at one time prove to be of the same rank, throw all four cards out, reducing the size of the stock.

TO WIN THE GAME: Throw out the entire deck in batches of four of a rank.

You'll see why the game is called Perpetual Motion the first time you play it. It should really be classed an an action game!

PYRAMID

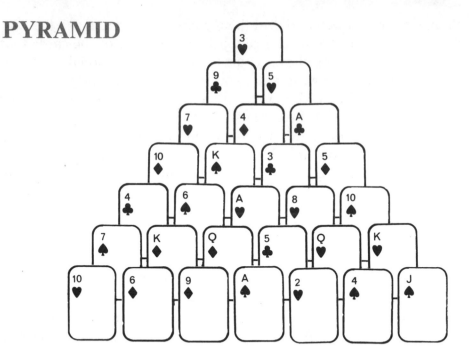

A sad thing about many solitaire games is that you play a round —or five rounds—and then it's over. You have no special feeling of victory (unless you've played out and won) and no standard with which to compare your score.

Here's a game that keeps you counting and scoring all the time. You can play it against yourself, against another player, or against "par."

Lay out the cards in the shape of a pyramid, starting with one card at the top and placing two cards which overlap it, then three overlapping them, and so on until you have a large triangle with seven cards at the base.

Each card has its own numerical value (face value) and Kings count as 13, Queens as 12, and Jacks as 11.

Your job is to remove all the cards that add up to 13 (two at a time), with this catch: you cannot remove a card unless it is "open"—not covered by any other card.

For example, in the pyramid above, you can remove the 9 and the 4, and the Jack (11) and the 2 from the bottom row. This opens up the King and Queen of Hearts in the next row up. You can remove the King alone, because he counts as 13 by himself. You can also remove the Queen (12) and the Ace (1) from the bottom row.

Place all the cards you remove in a "removed" pile, face up. The top card in this pile can be used again to form another 13-match. Right now, the card on top of the "removed" pile is an Ace. You can match it with the Queen of Diamonds, which is still in the pyramid and remove that.

Now you start dealing out the rest of the pack, one-by-one. If you cannot make a match with the card that you turn up, start a separate "discard" pile. Don't mix up this pile with your "removed" pile! In order to win the game, you need to dispose not only of the whole pyramid, but of the cards in your hand as well! You get two re-deals (three times through the deck) to give you opportunity to do it.

Let's say the next usable card that comes along is the 3 of Spades. You could use it to match up with one of the 10's which are open in the pyramid. As Kings come up from the deck, you can put them in the "removed" pile automatically.

The second time you go through the cards in your hands, you have some idea of their order, and that should help you plan and scheme a little to clear away additional cards from the pyramid and from your hand.

HOW TO SCORE: A match is six games. Score each game individually as follows:

50 points—if you get rid of your pyramid in the first deal (once through the cards in the deck). From that score, deduct one point for each card left in the deck. You get two more deals anyway to reduce the number of cards in the deck.

35 points—if you get rid of the pyramid during the second deal, after deducting one point for each card left in the deck (you get another deal to reduce that number).

20 points—if you get rid of your pyramid on the third deal, after deducting one point for each card left in the deck.

0 points—if you never do succeed in getting rid of your pyramid, after deducting one point for each card left in the pyramid, and deducting one point for each card left in the deck. That's right, a *minus* score.

"Par" is 0 for 6 matches. If you do better, you've won!

STAIRWAY TO HEAVEN

This little-known game is more like a braintwister than solitaire. But be warned that you need a gigantic playing area—a large table top or the floor—to set it up.

First remove all the Hearts from the deck and place them in the shape of a stairway, like this:

The Stairway to Heaven

Then remove the King of Spades. He is going to climb the stairway, come back down, and then climb up again. Your object is to have him finish on the top step of the stairway, or the step next to it.

Now shuffle the remaining cards and set them down in seven rows *face up*.

How Kings Get to Heaven

Select two cards from the top row of your layout. Deduct the lower card from the higher one. The difference is the card (on the stairway) on which you place the King.

For example, suppose you selected 5 and 9. The difference would be 4, and you would put the King on the 4 of Hearts. If you had selected Queen (12) and Jack (11), the difference would have been one, and you would have placed your King on the Ace of Hearts.

After your first move, the top row of your layout holds only four cards. Pick another two cards from that row. Deduct one from the other, and you'll find out how many steps the King can take next. Let's say you picked a King (13) and a 6. The difference is seven, so the King can move seven spaces up the stairs. If he started at the 4 of Hearts, he would now be on the Jack of Hearts (11).

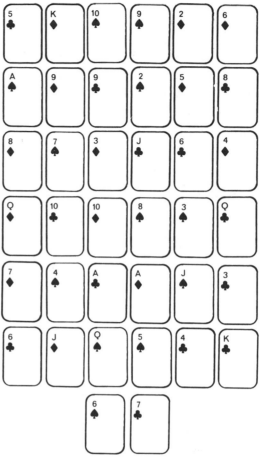

The remaining cards—except for the King of Spades—are set down in 7 rows, like this.

Now there are only two cards left in your top row, a 10 and a 2. The difference is 8, so the King can move 8 steps. When he gets to "heaven," the gates are locked, and he has to go back down again. He heads back towards the bottom, in this case ending up on the 7 of Hearts (up 2 steps and down 6).

Now you start on the next row of cards, repeating the same process of taking two cards, subtracting one from the other, and moving the King that number of steps. He must head all the way down to the first rung and start up again, until he gets to the top step.

The catch? You have to use up *all* the cards in the layout to get him to the top step! It's up to you what cards you subtract from each other, but you'll have to do some fancy figuring to get the King where you want him!

Note: For an easier game, use any cards in the layout to work out the numbers with which you move the King—not just the ones in the same row.

KLONDIKE

Lay out seven cards in a row, face down, except for the first card. Then put card #8 face up squarely on top of the second card in the row, and lay down another layer of face-down cards, one for every pile you've started. Then put a face-up card on the third pile, and finish off the row with a layer of face-down cards. Continue in this way until you have a face-up card on every pile.

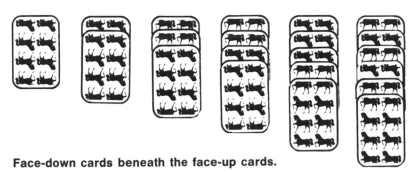

Face-down cards beneath the face-up cards.

Your layout will look like this:

Put the Aces above the spread—here.

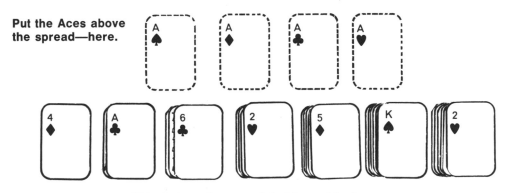

This is how the completed layout looks.

Now you are ready to play.

First, look over the spread carefully. You can move a card if

1. It is an Ace. Put it up above the spread. This is a "point."

2. It is a Deuce of the same suit as an Ace that you put up (another point).

3. Since you are going to be building up complete sets of each suit up at the top, starting with the Aces and going all the way to Kings

(if you can), make sure there are no threes and fours or any other cards you can put up. Every one of them will be a point. Just make sure that you build each Ace-to-King with cards of the same suit.

You can also move a card if

4. It is one rank lower than another card in the layout and of a different color. For instance, if you have a 9 of Hearts and an 8 of Clubs face up in the spread, you can move the 8 of Clubs onto the 9 of Hearts. Leave the top of the 9 showing, though. If a 10 of Spades (or Clubs) opens up, you can move the 9 onto it.

Every time you move a card from the spread onto another card, you "open up" a new card. It could be an Ace, which you can put at the top, or another scoring card, or it might be a card that will help you open up another card somewhere else. The more cards you open up, the closer you are to winning the game. If there is no face-down card under the card that you move, you have a vacant column, and you can move a King—but only a King—into it.

When you're sure there are no further moves you can make from the layout, you start turning over cards, one by one, from the rest of the deck. Study the spread carefully before deciding you can't use the card, because you won't get another chance at it. You can only go through the deck once.

Keep a sharp eye on the sets that you are building at the top, so that you don't miss any cards that fit into them.

When you have finished going through the cards, the game is over. The cards you have managed to place up at the top are your points. Five rounds of Klondike make a game and give you your total score.

Some people don't go through the cards one-by-one, but instead count them off in three's. If you choose the counting-off-by-three's method, you can go through the deck as many times as you want.

CANFIELD

A shorter, faster game than Klondike, Canfield is played much the same way, but it starts from a different basic layout.

For Canfield, count out 13 cards into one packet and put them in front of you *face up* and a little to the left. These 13 cards become a sort of "bank" from which you draw new cards to play with.

Then lay out a row of four cards, face up.

Check the four-card spread carefully to see whether you can make any moves within it. You can't put any cards on the 13-pile. Your object is to *unload* them. If you have a 5 of Hearts as one of your four cards, for example, and a 4 of Clubs is the top card on your 13-pile, you can move the 4 off the 13-pile and onto the 5. But if you have a 6 of Clubs on top of your 13-pile, you can't put the 5 on it. The 13-pile is *only* for unloading.

Now start turning up cards from the deck, three-by-three, placing them on one of the four cards, if possible, in the same pattern you used for Klondike with each card a rank lower than the card you put it on.

As Aces appear, put them at the top of the spread—as you did in the two previous games, and build up a set in each suit, going from Ace to King.

When you open up a vacant column among the four cards in your layout, move in a card from the 13-pile to take its place.

In Canfield, as in Klondike and Russian Solitaire, the cards you play up at the top of the spread are your score.

This version is the one used for Pounce! (see page 223), but there is another more traditional way to play this game.

In the other version, before placing the four cards in front of you, put one card (the 14th) up above, where the Aces usually go. Instead of building from Aces, in this version, you start building the suits from that "up" card and continue until you have built right through King and Ace and all the way back to the card that comes before it in sequence. You can't use this version so easily in Pounce!, but it's fine for regular solitaire or in a two-way competition.

POUNCE!

NUMBER OF PLAYERS: 2–6
EQUIPMENT: A pack of cards for each player

There is more action in this card game than in any other that has ever been invented! Actually, it isn't a game all its own, but one that has been put together.

Two or more people play their own games of solitaire—but when they put their Aces up at the top of the spread, *anyone* can build on them. It's an exciting game for three, a wild one for four, and if you have enough room (and long arms) you can even go on to six players! And then look out!

Each player needs a deck of cards, and the backs of each pack must bear a different design or emblem or color from the others, because eventually, at the end, the players sort out their own cards in order to see who won.

You can play it with any solitaire game that builds up Aces in suits, but it is most often played with Canfield or Klondike. When playing Klondike in a game of Pounce!, you may run through the deck as many times as you want. Canfield makes for the fastest game.

Whichever solitaire game you choose, all the players lay out their spreads, but no one starts playing until a signal is given. Then anything goes. Play as rapidly as you can. Aces that you play to the top of the spread now go in the middle of the table. Try to get as many cards up there as rapidly as you can. These are your points. In case of a dispute, the player whose card got there first is the one who gets to leave it (that means the card that is lowest in the pile). But it is against the rules to use more than one hand to put cards in the middle. And you can play only one card up there at a time.

The first one to get rid of all the cards onto the bases (into the middle) wins the game.

If play comes to a standstill before any of the players get rid of their cards, sort out the cards that have made it into the middle. The player with the most cards in the middle wins.

When the game is Canfield, you can play a shorter game: the one who gets rid of the 13-pile first wins. It doesn't matter where the cards go—into the middle or onto building piles—as long as they move *somewhere*.

RUSSIAN SOLITAIRE

Some people say this is the most difficult solitaire game in the world to win. But it is one of the most intriguing.

Lay out the cards exactly as in Klondike. But instead of stopping after you finish the seven piles, lay out the rest of the deck, too, starting at the second pile—like this:

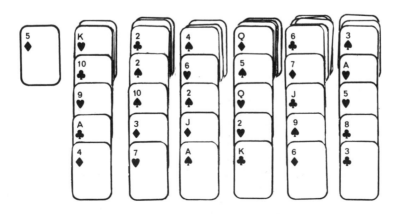

Let's follow this layout to see how the game works.

First of all, an Ace is lying exposed at the bottom of a pile. That goes up to the top, just as in Klondike, where you will be building up Ace-to-King suits.

In the rest of the layout, you will be building *down* by suit, starting with whatever cards are available, and moving onto them the next lower card in the same suit. For example, the 6 of Diamonds is lying open. You can put the 5 of Diamonds on it—and *only* the 5 of Diamonds. That is the card in the first pile. Take it and put it on the 6. Your piles are uneven, but that is part of the game.

When you moved the 5 of Diamonds, you created a vacant spot in the first column. That vacant spot (just as in Klondike) can be filled only by a King. You have your choice of which King. Suppose you decide to move in the King of Hearts. You have to move the entire column of cards on top of him to the #1 spot. There is only one card underneath the King. Turn it over: it's the King of Diamonds, and it is now the leading card of the second column.

Your next move might be to put the 4 of Diamonds on the 5 of Diamonds. That opens up the Ace of Clubs, which you can put up at the top to count as another point.

You might then move the 6 of Hearts down onto the 7. Remember that when you move the 6, all the cards on top of it must move, too!

Now your layout looks like this:

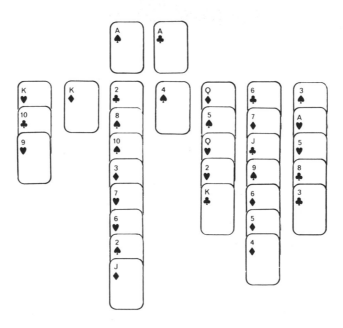

There are quite a few moves left in this game. Eventually, your layout may look like this:

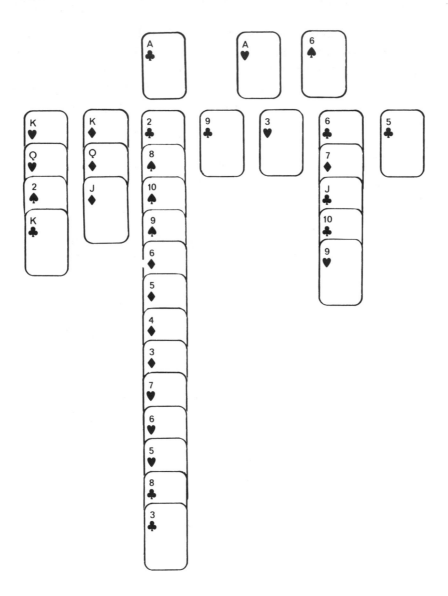

And there are more moves after that. But for all the action, you finish with a total of eight points. Frustrating? Yes, that is Russian Solitaire! But there's something intriguing about shifting around those long columns of cards. Try it.

Play five rounds of this game, totalling up the number of points in each for your total score.

RUSSIAN BANK

NUMBER OF PLAYERS: 2
EQUIPMENT: A deck of cards for each player. They must have different backs.

This is an unusual solitaire game for two. It is not played simultaneously like Pounce! Here the players take turns. And the game is played by very exact rules. These rules govern the order in which you can move the cards. If you move one card when you should move another, according to the rules, your opponent can call "STOP" and your turn ends. In very strict play, your opponent can stop you if you even *touch* a card when you should move another first. (A fairer rule is that you can't call a stop until a player actually picks up a wrong card.) More about the rules later.

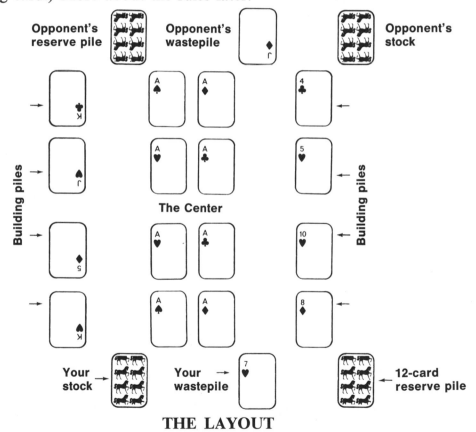

THE LAYOUT

You each deal from your own deck a pile of 12 cards, *face down*, which you place to your right. This is your *reserve pile*.

Above the reserve pile, you deal out a line of four cards, *face up*, extending toward your opponent. These eight cards (four from each of you) start the *building piles* and they are common property.

Put the balance of the deck *face down* at your left. This is your *stock*.

BASE CARDS: All Aces are base cards. Whenever an Ace becomes available, you move it into the space between the building piles. Place the Aces in two columns, parallel to the building piles. They are called "The Center." You may build cards on the Aces—in the same suit and in upward sequence—2, 3, 4, 5, 6, 7, 8, 9, 10, Jack, Queen, King.

BUILDING PILES: On these piles, build downward and in alternate colors, as in Klondike and Canfield. You may move the 4 of Clubs, for example, onto the 5 of Hearts or the 5 of Diamonds. You can put the Jack of Hearts on any black Queen. You cannot build a King onto another card in the building piles, but you can put it on a Queen of the same suit in the Center.

Move cards one at a time from and to the building piles. This is different from Klondike and Canfield, where you move the pile as a unit.

You can move "available" cards. An available card is one that is free to be moved because it is (a) the top card of your reserve pile, (b) a card you turn up from your stock, but have not yet put on your wastepile (cards in the wastepile are *never* available), (c) an uncovered card in a building pile. (A card covered by another in a building pile is not available.)

THE FIRST MOVE: Look at the building piles. If there are any Aces— or other base cards that belong in the Center—move them there. Then turn up the top card of your reserve pile.

The Rules

1. You must turn up the top face-down card of the reserve pile *before making any other move* (except in the First Move).

2. Whenever an available card can be moved into the Center, *you must move it there before you can make any other move.*

3. If the reserve card can be moved to the Center, this move must be made ahead of a move from a building pile.

4. You may play available cards from the building piles to the Center in any order.

5. After you have made all possible moves to the Center, you are free to move cards in the building piles to make additional cards available, create spaces, and so on.

As you move the cards in the building piles, you are allowed to move any available card from a building pile into a space. A space is created whenever all of one building pile is removed.

For example, suppose one building pile consists of a 9 of Clubs, and an 8 of Diamonds. There is a 10 of Hearts on another pile, and there is a space. If you move the 8 of Diamonds into the space, you can uncover the 9 of Clubs and move it onto the 10 of Hearts. Then, when you put the 8 of Diamonds back on the 9 of Clubs, you have *two* spaces instead of one. Look for such opportunities to create spaces. They help you get rid of your own cards.

6. You must move the top card of your reserve pile into a space before you can fill the space with a card from your stock.

7. You must fill all spaces in the building piles before turning up a card from your stock.

8. Once you've done all this, you can turn up the top card of your stock. You must play it to the Center, if possible. If not, you may put it on a building pile, if possible. (See also *Loading,* below.) If you can't find a place for it anywhere, you must put it face up on your wastepile, and this ends your turn. Your turn continues as long as you can find a place for the cards you turn up from your stock.

9. The wastepile is a single pile placed between your reserve pile and your stock. If you put a card on your wastepile, your turn ends, even if there was actually a place to play the card!

10. *Loading:* You may build available cards not only on the base cards in the Center, and to the building piles, but also upon your opponent's reserve card and wastepile: this is called *loading.* You can load in suit and sequence—but the sequence may go down or up or both ways, as you please.

For example, if your opponent's reserve card is a Jack of Diamonds, you may move the 10 of Diamonds onto it. Then if you turn up a Jack of Diamonds from your stock, you can put it on the 10 of Diamonds.

11. Stopping: If you violate any of the rules above, your opponent can call "STOP!" And if your error is proved, your turn ends.

12. End of the game: When your stock is exhausted, you immediately turn your wastepile over to form a new stock. When your reserve pile is exhausted, you continue without it, playing from your stock.

The first player to get rid of the reserve pile and stock pile wins the game. Winner scores 30 points plus 2 points for each card left in the other's reserve pile and 1 point for each card in the other's stock and wastepile.

Card Games for Two or More

CONCENTRATION

PLAYERS: 2 or more

Concentration is a card game which can bridge a span of generations—a four-year-old can play with adults or teen-agers. It can also bridge the language barrier, because it is played in silence.

Lay out a deck of cards *face down* any-which-way on the table. Don't let them overlap each other, and don't put them down in rows or patterns. Players take turns, and the object of the game is to turn up cards that match in number.

The first player—Burt—turns any two cards face up in their places. If they form a pair (two deuces, two 7's, two Kings), he removes them, puts them in his private stock and gets another turn. If the cards do not form a pair, Burt turns them face down again exactly as they were before. *All the players try to remember what these cards are and where they are!*

The second player—Maxine—turns up two cards, but now does it one at a time. If the first card is the mate to one which was previously turned up and put back, she tries to remember that card's location in order to turn up a matching card to form a pair.

Each time a player forms a pair, he or she takes the pair into stock, gets another turn, and continues to play until two unmatched cards turn up. The game ends when all the cards have been paired off and removed. The winner is the player with most cards in stock.

TIP: Sometimes your opponent's second card is the mate to a card which was turned up earlier. If you think you remember the location of both cards, but you're not sure of the earlier one, turn over the one you're *not* sure of first. Then, if you're wrong, you have another chance to form a matching pair.

Children who haven't learned to read numbers yet are often surprisingly good at Concentration. Simply call out the card number as you turn it over and call out the number on the cards that the child turns over. The picture cards may be confusing at first (you can eliminate them from the deck, if you want), but after a few games, watch out for that four-year-old!

PIG

PLAYERS: 3–13 (5 or 6 are best)
EQUIPMENT: 4 playing cards of a kind for each player in the game.
              For example, 5 players would use 20 cards: 4 Aces, 4 Kings,
              4 Queens, 4 Jacks, and 4 10's. For 6 players you would
              add the 4 9's.

This is a hilarious game for children or for adults to play with children. Anybody can learn it in two or three minutes and one extra minute makes you an expert!

Any player shuffles and deals four cards to each player. The object is to get four cards of a kind in your own hand, or to be quick to notice it when somebody else gets four of a kind.

First you look at your own hand to see if there are four of a kind in it. If nobody has four of a kind, you put some unwanted card *face down* on the table and pass it to the player at your left. At the same time, you receive a card from the player at your right.

Look at your cards again, with the newly-received card. If still nobody has four of a kind, you again pass a card to the left and get a new card from the right.

When you finally get four of a kind, you stop passing or receiving cards, and put a finger to your nose.

The other players must be quick to notice this, must stop passing, and put fingers to their noses. The last player to put up a finger is a PIG.

DONKEY

This is the same game as Pig, except that when you get four of a kind, you put your cards *face down* on the table, instead of putting your finger to your nose. In the process, you still get a card from your right and pass it along to the left, but you place your four of a kind untouched on the table.

As the players see what has happened, they each put their cards down quietly on the table, whether they have four of a kind or not. The idea is to keep up the passing and the conversation while some player plays on without realizing that the hand has ended.

The last player to put down his or her cards loses the hand. This makes the player a "D." The next time that player loses, he or she becomes a "D-O." This keeps on until finally some player becomes a "D-O-N-K-E-Y."

The D-O-N-K-E-Y loses the game. The winner is the player who has the smallest number of letters.

DONKEY BUTTONS

PLAYERS: 3–13 (5 or 6 are best)
EQUIPMENT: Buttons – or pennies, candies, or matchsticks (one fewer than the number of players)

This is the same game as Donkey, except that when you get four of a kind, you shout "Donkey!" and quickly grab a button from the middle of the table. Since there is one fewer button than there are players, the last player to grab doesn't get a button. That player becomes a "D." The game continues until someone is a D-O-N-K-E-Y. At the end of the game, the D-O-N-K-E-Y has to bray "heehaw" three times.

MY SHIP SAILS

PLAYERS: 4–7 (4 or 5 players are best)

The object of the game is to get seven cards of the same suit. Deal seven cards to each player, one at a time. Look at your hand and pass one card to your left. At the same time the player to your right passes a card to you. The play goes on, as in Pig or Donkey, but the difference is that you are trying to get all your cards in the same suit instead of the same value.

There are many different ways to end a hand. When you get seven cards of the same suit, you may put your cards down immediately and say, "My ship sails!" Or you can say nothing, but put your finger to your nose, as in Pig.

If it takes too long to finish a hand, try one of the shorter games— My Bee Buzzes or My Star Twinkles.

MY BEE BUZZES

This is the same as My Ship Sails, except that you need only six cards of the same suit to win the hand. Each player gets seven cards, but six cards in the same suit (and one extra card) win. It takes less time to finish a hand in this game than in My Ship Sails.

MY STAR TWINKLES

This is the same as My Ship Sails except that you need only five cards of the same suit (and two odd cards) to win a hand. It takes only two or three minutes to play a hand.

THROUGH THE WINDOW

PLAYERS: 3–13 (the more the merrier)

The object of this game is to win the most cards. You deal four cards to each player. You (the dealer) begin by saying, "I looked through the window and saw—." Just at this moment, and not before, you turn up one of your four cards, so that all the players can see it.

Each player (including you) must try to say an animal or thing beginning with the same letter of the alphabet as the card that has been turned up. For example, if the card is an Ace, you might call out, "Ant!" "Alligator!" "Apple!" or anything else that begins with the letter A. If the card is a 9, you might call out "Noodle!" or "Nut!"

The first player to call out a correct word takes the card and starts a separate pile of captured cards. Then the person to your left says, "I looked through the window and saw—," turning up a card.

The game continues in the same way (in turn to the left) until all the original cards in each hand have been turned up and captured. Each person keeps his or her own separate pile of captured cards. The one who captures the most cards wins. The captured cards have nothing to do with your original cards, since you each had four chances to turn up a card.

When a word has been used once to win a card, no player can use it again. For example, if you used the word "Stone" to capture a 7, neither you nor any other player can say "Stone" to capture another card beginning with "S."

THROUGH THE WIDE WINDOW

This is played exactly like Through the Window, except that when you turn up a card, you must call out two words: an animal or object and a word describing that animal or object.

For example, if someone turns up a King, you might call out, "Kissable Koala," or "Kinky Kangaroo." You can use a single word more than once in the game, but you can't repeat a pair of words. If you call out "Quivering Quail" on seeing a Queen, for example, anybody may use the word "Quivering" and anybody may use the word "Quail" for another Queen, but nobody is allowed to use the two words together.

When grownups play with children, the best rule is to have the grownups say two words (the descriptive word as well as the object or animal) while children need to say only one word.

GO FISH

PLAYERS: 2–5

If only two play, deal seven cards to each. If four or five play, deal five cards to each. Put the rest of the pack *face down* on the table, forming the stock.

The object of the game is to form more "books" than any other player. A book is four cards of a kind, such as four Kings, four Queens, four 7's.

The player at the dealer's left—Rod—begins by saying to another player: "Jane, give me your 9's." Rod must mention the name of the player he is calling and he must say the exact rank of the card (Ace, King, Queen, etc.), and he must have in his hand at least one card of the rank that he calls for.

Jane must hand over all the cards she has of that rank, but if she has none, she says, "Go fish!"

When told to "go fish," Rod must draw the top card from the stock of cards. If he picks up a card of the rank he asked for, he shows the card immediately before he puts it into his hand, and his turn continues. Otherwise, the turn passes to the player on his left.

If Rod gets some cards from Jane, he keeps his turn and may ask anyone for more cards. He may ask Jane again, or some different player, and he may ask for a card of any rank in his new question.

When he gets the fourth card of a book, he shows all four, places them on the table and continues his turn.

If he runs out of cards, he may draw one card from the stock at the next turn and then ask for a card of that rank. After the stock is used up, if he has no cards, he is out of the game.

The game ends when all 13 books have been laid down. The player with the most books wins.

FISH FOR MINNOWS

This is a simpler version of Go Fish, and it is particularly good for very young players. Deal out all the cards. It doesn't matter if they don't come out even.

At your turn, you ask for some rank of card, and the player you ask hands over one card only (if possible). The object is to form *pairs* instead of books of four. As soon as you get a pair, you put the cards face down on the table. The one who puts down the most pairs, wins.

AUTHORS

Since a set of 4 cards of the same rank is called a book, it's not surprising that this variation of Go Fish is called Authors. You can play it more seriously, though, and with greater skill.

All 52 cards are dealt out, even though they may not come out even. When it is your turn, you ask for a single card by naming both its rank and suit. For example, you might say, "Bill, give me the Jack of Spades." Your turn continues if Bill comes up with the Jack of Spades. Otherwise, the turn passes to the person on your left. As soon as you get a book, you show it and put it down on the table. The game ends when all 13 books have been laid down.

TIPS FOR SKILLFUL PLAY: When a player asks for cards and gets them, but doesn't put down a completed book, you can tell that he or she has two or three cards of that rank. For example, suppose John asks for Queens and gets one from the player he asks. John doesn't put down a book of Queens, but asks some new question and is told to "Go fish." You know that John had to have at least one Queen to give him the right to ask for Queens. He received a Queen, so he has a total of either two or three Queens, and not four because he has not put down a book.

In the same way, you learn something even when a player gets nothing. Suppose Bill asked somebody for a 9 of Hearts and is told to "Go fish." You know that Bill has at least one 9 in his hand.

Little by little, you build up information about the cards the other players hold. If you know that another player has Queens, but you have no Queens yourself, it doesn't help you very much at that moment. But if you pick up a Queen when you're told to "Go fish," you know how to proceed!

BANGO

PLAYERS: 2–10
EQUIPMENT: 2 decks of playing cards

Did you ever want to play Bingo but didn't have a set? With two decks of cards, you can play Bango, which is very much like it.

Each player gets five cards from one of the decks. The players put the cards face up in front of them.

Then the dealer takes the *other* deck and turns up the first card, announcing its rank and suit: "The 3 of Clubs."

If any player has the 3 of Clubs, that player turns the card face down.

The dealer then announces the next card, and so on, until one player has turned all five cards face down and is the winner. That player deals the next game.

THE DUCK WENT MOO

PLAYERS: 3–8

This funny game is played by "animals." Each player chooses which animal he or she wants to be. You can be a Duck, a Cow, a Pig, a Mouse, a Horse, a Dog, a Cat, a Chicken, or any other animal that makes a special sound.

The players need to remember who is who, because remembering is what wins the game.

The object of the game is to get all the cards in the deck.

The cards are dealt out one by one until the entire deck has been given out. Then one by one, each animal turns over one card, putting it down in an "open" discard pile in front of him or her where everyone can see it. No animal (not even the one lifting the card) should see it before anyone else. As soon as a card comes up which matches in number the card that is showing on someone else's open pile, the action starts.

The two animals with the matching cards each try to make the other's sound. For example, suppose a Cow turns up a 4 of Diamonds, and a Duck has a 4 of Hearts sitting open. The Cow has to make the duck sound and the Duck has to make the cow sound. The first one to make the correct sound wins that round and gets all the cards in the opponent's open pile. The cards go under the victor's pile, and the game continues, with the loser turning over the next card.

If an animal makes a wrong sound, or makes it at the wrong time, the penalty is one card to every player.

When the players' closed piles are gone, they turn over their open piles and continue playing until one animal has all the cards.

SLAP JACK

PLAYERS: 3–8

The object of this game, too, is to get *all* the cards in the deck. The only way to get the cards is to be the first one to slap a Jack when it appears in the middle of the table.

The dealer passes out the cards, one by one, until the whole deck has been dealt. The players don't look at their cards, but just make them into neat piles and start playing. Each player in turn rapidly lifts a card so that no one (including himself or herself) sees what it is until it hits the middle of the table. If the card is a Jack, the first one to slap it gets not only the Jack, but all the cards under it. That player puts all the new cards into his or her pile, and continues to play.

If anyone slaps something that turns out *not* to be a Jack, that player has to give one card to each player from the top of his pile or her pile (without looking at it first).

In case of dispute, lowest hand on the Jack wins.

THE PERSIAN CARD GAME

PLAYERS: 2

This simple card game is a good one for two beginners or for a child to play with an adult. You need an ordinary deck of cards, which you divide equally between the players. The cards rank from Ace down to Two, which is low.

To start the game, the players turn the top card of their piles face up on the table, at the same time. If they turn up cards of different suits, nothing happens, and they turn up the next cards. They continue doing this until they simultaneously turn up cards of the *same suit*—such as two Diamonds, two Spades, two Hearts or two Clubs. When that happens, the player with the *higher* card wins all the cards the other player has turned up. These go at the bottom of his or her pack.

The player who captures all the cards in the deck is the winner. Sometimes, you may go completely through the deck once or twice without turning up cards of the same suit. In that case, the game is over, and the one with the larger number of cards is the winner.

WAR

PLAYERS: 2 or 3

Never was a game more aptly named than War. It's a long—sometimes interminable—card game in which the tides of fortune swing back and forth. It requires no skill. All you need to be able to do is turn over the cards and recognize their denominations. Children love it.

It starts out rather like the Persian Card Game and the object is the same, to capture all the cards in the deck. Divide the pack of cards in two (if three are playing, remove one card and deal the 51 cards out equally).

At the word "Go," both players turn their top cards face up on the table. The one who turns over the higher-ranking card wins the "trick" and takes both cards, placing them face down at the bottom of his or her pile. The rank of cards is Ace-King-Queen-Jack-10-9-8-7-6-5-4-3-2.

When both players turn over cards of the same rank, they call, "War!" On top of their war cards, each player puts one card face down and then another card face up. Whoever now has the higher card on top wins all the cards in the war. If the face-up cards also match, it is "Double War!" Each player again plays a face-down card and then another face up. The one with the higher card wins all the cards in the war.

The player who wins all the cards in the game is the winner.

REVENGE

PLAYERS: 2

Like revenge, this game moves slowly, it goes on and on, you think it is never going to end, and you actually do get revenge on the other player many times during the game. This is popular with children, too.

Divide the pack card by card. The object of the game is to get rid of all your cards by putting them onto the other player's pack. You do it by coming up with a card that is one rank higher—or lower—than the card your opponent has just turned up.

Let's say your opponent starts the game by turning over the top card in his or her pile—and it's a 6 of Hearts. If you turn up a 7 of any suit, you can place it on your opponent's 6. Suppose the next card you turn up is an 8. Over it goes, onto your opponent's pack, and you get another turn. Each time you get rid of a card, you get to take another turn.

You can build down, too. If the next card is another 7, you can place that on the 8 that you just put down. If the next card is not in sequence, your turn ends.

Gradually, as you play, you build up long sequences of cards, so that large numbers of cards follow each other in order. Eventually, when you get the chance to put a card on your opponent's pile, you don't put on just *one*—you put on 15 or 20 or more! This is what makes the game such fun. Your opponent can be within two cards of winning when you suddenly zap him or her with almost the whole deck—now that's revenge!

You can give your opponent the cards from the top of your deck or from your discard pile, but be careful. If you are in the middle of a sequence, you don't want to break it by taking a single card from the discard deck. Then again, that one card from the discard pile may lead to an even longer run!

When you have gone through your pile of cards, turn them over and start again. The game goes on until one player is out of cards.

PISHE PASHA

(*pronounced PISH-uh PAY-sha*)

This game is played the same way as Revenge, but with one added element. Whenever an Ace comes up, it is put out in the middle of the table and built on, as in Klondike. And there is no choice about putting cards up in the middle. Even if you are in the middle of a steady run of cards, you *must* interrupt it to play a card to the building suits, when it belongs there. Often, two decks are used for this game.

ENFLAY

PLAYERS: 2

Remove all the twos, threes, fours, fives and sixes from a deck of playing cards. You will be playing with the 32 remaining cards, which rank from the 7, which is low, to the Ace, which is high.

Deal eight cards to each of the two players and place the rest face down in a pile on the table. The first player—Frank—starts by placing a card from his hand face up on the table. The second player—Gale—must turn up a card of the same suit, if she can. She then sets those two cards aside, out of play. The one who played the higher-ranking card now plays the next card—any card at all—as long as it is of a different suit from the previous one.

If Frank cannot match Gale's card, he must take a card from the pile on the table and add it to his hand. Then it is his turn to play.

The first player to get rid of all of his or her cards is the winner. Players score one point for each card remaining in their opponent's hand. The first person to get a score of 50 or 100 points—depending on how long you want to play—wins.

SNIP-SNAP-SNORUM

PLAYERS: 3 or more

Here's a card game with fast action. It depends entirely on the luck of the deal, so there's no need to ponder and the game goes fast. It is an excellent game for three, but more can play.

Deal out the entire deck so each player has the same number of cards. The first player—Andy—places a card *face up* on the table and calls out its number, say, "Three." Now the player to the left—Michele—must either put down a 3 or say "Pass." If Michele has the matching card, she plays it on top of the first card and says "Snip."

If the next player—Steve—has a 3, he puts it down and says "Snap," and the play continues around the circle until the last 3 is played. The one who puts it down says "Snorum."

The four matching cards are then pushed aside and the player who said "Snorum" puts a new card on the table, to be matched up in the same way.

If a card is played for which a player has all three matching cards, he or she calls out, "Snip-Snap-Snorum," and plays all of them at once.

You win when you get rid of all your cards.

If a small child is playing, it's a good idea to remove all the picture cards from the deck so there won't be too many cards to handle.

I DOUBT IT

PLAYERS: 3 or more
EQUIPMENT: A single deck of cards for 3 or 4 players; 2 decks, shuffled together, for 5 or more players

Deal two or three cards at a time to each player so that everyone gets an equal number of cards. When only a few cards are left, deal one at a time as far as the cards go.

The object of the game is to get rid of all your cards.

The player to the dealer's left puts any number of cards—from one to four—*face down* in the middle of the table and says that they are all Aces.

The next player puts down any number of cards, too—from one to four—and says they are all deuces.

The third player does the same—and says that the cards are all 3's.

And the play continues, each player going in turn, putting down any number of cards—from one to four—and saying that they are the next higher-ranking cards, all the way from Ace to King.

As each player puts down his or her cards, any other player may say, "I doubt it."

If this happens, the cards must be turned face up immediately. If the statement was true, the doubter must add the entire central pile to his or her hand. If the statement was false, the liar takes the central pile.

When players use two packs, they are not limited to putting down four cards. They may put down as many as eight at a time.

When someone puts down the last cards in his or her hand, another player must say, "I doubt it," or the game would be over. Then, if the statement is true, the game is won.

If a player has no cards at all of the kind that need to be put down, he or she may not skip the turn. The player must put down one or more cards anyway, and try to get away with it.

If two players say "I doubt it" at the same time, the one nearest to the player's left is the one who must pick up the central pile, if the statement is true.

I DOUBT IT—THREESIES

Deal out the cards equally, as far as they go, and put the remaining cards face down in the middle of the table.

Each player in turn puts down exactly three cards. Instead of starting with Aces automatically, the first player may choose any card at all.

For example, you might say, "Three 9's." The next player must say, "Three 10's," and so on.

When only one or two cards are left, draw enough cards from the ones face down in the middle of the table to make up a total of three.

CRAZY EIGHTS,
WILD JACKS,
AND GO BOOM

PLAYERS: 2–4 (If more want to play, use a second deck and you can double the number of players.)

Each player is dealt seven cards. The rest of the deck goes to the middle of the table with one card turned up (the top one) beside the pack.

The object of the game is to get rid of all the cards in your hand, and there's only one way to do it: each player, in turn, places a card on the turned-up card in the middle, which matches it in rank or suit.

For example, let's say that the turned-up card happens to be the Queen of Hearts. Ginny, who goes first, has a Queen of Diamonds, which matches it in rank. She places it on top of the turned-up card.

Albert, who follows, has a 3 of Diamonds, which matches Ginny's card by suit. He places it on top of the Queen.

Bea, who goes next, doesn't have a 3 or a Diamond in her hand. So she has to pick from the deck until she gets one, adding all those cards into her hand on that one turn! She could play an 8—because in this game of Crazy Eights, an 8 can be any card you want it to be. But because of this, 8's are very valuable, and she may not want to throw it away so early in the game. She has to be careful, though, because if she's caught with the 8 in her hand at the end of the game, the winner will get 50 additional points.

Let's say that Bea does put down an 8. Then she gets a chance to call the next suit that has to be played—Hearts, Spades or Clubs. She naturally wouldn't want to call Diamonds, because she doesn't have any. If she knew that one or more of the players was out of a certain suit, she would call it just to catch them.

The first person to get rid of all the cards in his or her hand wins the round and gets the following points:

> **50 points for each 8 caught in another player's hand**
> **10 points for each face card in another player's hand**
> **1 point for each Ace**
> **and face value for all other cards**

If the game is at a standstill because no one can put down a card and the deck is gone, then the players count up the points in their hands. The one with the lowest score is the winner. The winner is awarded all the points in the hands of the other players—subtracting the points in the winner's own hand.

For example, Ginny has 5 points in her hand and Albert, the winner, has 3. Albert gets 2 points there. Bea has 10 points in her hand, so Albert gets them—less his own score—another 7 points. Albert's score for the round is 9.

The players go on with another round, and 100 points wins.

Note: If you want a change from Crazy Eights, you can play Wild Jacks. Here you follow the same rules, but you use Jacks instead of 8's. Or you can play Go Boom—the same game—with no wild cards at all.

WHIST

PLAYERS: 4 (2 partners)

Deal 13 cards to each player, one card at a time. The last card of the deck belongs to the dealer, who shows it to all the players. Let's say it's the 8 of Diamonds. Diamonds then will be especially valuable in that game. They are the "trump suit."

In every set of four cards, played by the four people in the game, the highest Diamond will be the card to win the round or "trick." The object of the game is for partners to win as many tricks as they can.

The first player—Chris—is the one who sits on the left of the dealer. Chris puts down any card she wants on the table. She plays the King of Clubs. Because she led off with a Club, the next player—Gregg—*must* also put down a Club, if possible. If Gregg doesn't have a Club in his hand, he can put down any other card. Let's say he puts down the only Club in his hand, the Queen of Clubs.

The third player, Diane, also has only one Club in her hand, the Ace of Clubs, and she must play it. Aces are high in this game, and so far Diane is winning the round.

Then you, the dealer, come along with the 2 of Diamonds, since you don't have any Clubs at all. Because Diamonds are the "trump suit" for this game, you take the "trick"—all the cards the players put in the middle of the table. You or your partner set them aside, and you start off the next trick with any card you want.

If you hadn't had a Diamond in your hand to take the trick with, Diane would have won it because she had the highest Club.

You and your partner keep the "tricks" you have won together. You don't keep them in a single pile, but pile them up in batches of four, overlapping like this:

so that you can see at a glance how many tricks you have won.

After all tricks have been played and you have all run out of cards, you score like this:

The partners who won the majority of tricks score 0 for the first 6 tricks and 1 point for every other trick they have won. These scoring tricks are called "odd tricks." If you won 10 out of a possible 13 tricks, you would have 3 odd tricks, and score only 3 points.

Additional points are scored for "honors," the Ace, King, Queen and Jack of the trump suit, in this case the AKQJ of Diamonds. If you and your partner have two of these cards and the other also has two of them, no score is given for honors. If you have 3 honors, you score 2. If you have all four of them, you score 4. The first side to reach 7 points wins the game.

HEARTS

PREPARATION: If you're playing with some number other than 4, remove
enough deuces from the deck to make the deal come out even.

Deal one card at a time to each player. Aces rank high. The object
of the game is to avoid winning any Hearts—or to win all 13 of them.

The player at the left of the dealer makes the opening move and
each of the players in turn puts one card in the middle of the table. These
rounds of four cards are called "tricks," as in Whist. You win a trick when
you play the highest card of the suit that started the round. After you win
a trick, you start the next trick.

Keep score on paper. Every Heart you capture counts one point
against you. The game can stop at any time, and the player with the
lowest total score is the winner. If you have all 13 Hearts, you've won.
Subtract 13 from your score. Some people double that score and subtract
26 points for getting all the Hearts.

CALAMITY JANE

PLAYERS: 3–7 (4 is the best game)

This is the most popular variation of Hearts. When most people say
they want to play Hearts, they mean this game.

It is played exactly like the previous Hearts game, with the following
exceptions:

1. After the players look at their hands, they pass any three cards
they choose *face down* to the player at their left. Then, after they have made
their choice, they take into their hand the three cards that have been
chosen for them by the person to the right.

2. If you capture the Queen of Spades (Calamity Jane) in one of
your tricks, it counts as another point against you. Some people score
Calamity Jane as 13 points against you—a real calamity—so that in one
deal, you could get 25 points against you (12 points for Hearts and 13 for

Calamity Jane). If you capture all 14 cards, 13 Hearts and Calamity Jane as well, you would win! This is called "Shooting the Moon." And if you do it, you can deduct 25 points from your score.

3. The player with the lowest score—when another player scores 50 (or 100 if you want a longer game)—wins.

QUIZZES

5

Quizzes for Yourself, Parties, or Your Own Quiz Show

Here are 44 quizzes which you can use in many different ways. Each one is divided into four sections:

2 point questions which are relatively easy
3 point questions which are more difficult
5 point questions which are pretty hard

With them you can make up your own quiz games, played under your own rules, but here are some other suggestions of how to use them.

ONE PERSON can test his or her knowledge and keep score. For example, the highest possible score on five quizzes is 200 points (40 per quiz). A score of 110 or better is good; a score of 153 or more is excellent.

TWO PEOPLE or TWO PARTNERS can play competitively—one team trying to answer the odd-numbered questions, the other team trying the even-numbered questions. If there is no one to act as Quizmaster and Scorekeeper, write down your answers for the entire quiz on a separate sheet of paper *before* checking with the answer page; then go on with another quiz in the same way.

The two team members must agree on the answer before it is given. If they can't agree quickly, they can toss a coin.

However, it is usually more fun if another person (or team) acts as Quizmaster and Scorekeeper, checking each answer as it is given. This person (or team) can then play the winning contestant on another set of quizzes, with the losers acting as the Quizmaster-Scorekeeper on the new round.

THREE PEOPLE or THREE PARTNERS can play competitively at the same time and on the same quiz games by answering only questions 1, 2 and 3 in each set of questions, ignoring question 4. Again, unless there is a Quizmaster, write the answers down before you check them with the answer page.

FOUR PEOPLE or FOUR PARTNERS can play, of course, by using all four questions in each set. Here again, teams should agree on their answers.

LARGE GROUPS can team up in groups of three or four or by playing different quizzes (four teams taking one quiz, another four a different quiz, etc., and then matching scores). However, there should always be a Quizmaster-Scorekeeper.

Ordinarily each quiz should be played straight down the page, starting with the 2-point questions, going on with the 3-pointers, and then to the difficult 5-pointers. However, if you're going to play at least five quiz categories in one complete game, you might try limiting contestants to one turn per category—but giving them the right to pick the point value of the questions they will try to answer (easy, middling, or difficult).

Another way to score is to *credit* a contestant with the proper number of points for a *correct* answer, but *deduct* for an *incorrect* answer. In no case, however, should you put a contestant's total score below 0 as the game progresses. For instance, if a contestant gains a credit of 3 on the first round, but tries a 5-point question on the second round and misses, he or she goes back only to 0, not to minus 2. If you play the game this way, you should keep score like this:

	Team 1		Team 2		Team 3	
	Game	Running Total	Game	Running Total	Game	Running Total
Game 1	3	3	2	2	5	5
Game 2	−2	1	3	5	−5	0
Game 3	3	4	2	7	5	5
Game 4	3	7	−3	4	3	8
Game 5						
Total						

The Quizmaster decides whether or not a "borderline" answer is close enough to be accepted. No partial credit allowed.

LITERATURE—QUIZ 1

Two-Point Questions

1. Margaret Mitchell wrote the book on which one of the most famous movies of all time was based. The movie starred Clark Gable and Vivian Leigh. Name the book.
2. Name the famous British author who first described Russia as "the bear that walks like a man." One of his best remembered poems is "Gunga Din."
3. In what famous "legend" do we find Ichabod Crane?
4. In 1877, Anna Sewell wrote the autobiography of a horse, a book that profoundly influenced legislation on humane treatment of animals. Name the horse.

Three-Point Questions

1. Which tragic American poet lamented the loss of a love named Lenore?
2. Jonathan Swift wrote a book which he intended as a great political satire. Instead, it has become one of the most famous in the juvenile book field. Name it.
3. Tell whether or not each of the following people was purely fictional or actually lived: Beau Brummel, Lady Godiva, George Babbitt, Cyrano de Bergerac, Minnehaha, and Copernicus.
4. Name the great American poet, born in 1878 in Galesburg, Illinois, who has written epic poems about Abraham Lincoln.

Five-Point Questions

1. In Walter Scott's story, "Ivanhoe," a romantic character named Locksley appears. With which legendary robber character of English folklore is Locksley identified?
2. In "A Study in Scarlet," the letters R-A-C-H-E were written in blood on the wall. Inspector Lestrade thought the murderer had been interrupted while trying to spell out the name Rachel. But what was the correct interpretation made by Sherlock Holmes, who understood German?
3. The poet Dante was banished from the city of Florence and compelled to wander over Europe. He remained true through the years to the great love of his life. In 1292 he wrote a poem about her, entitling it "The New Life." Name the woman he so deeply loved.

4. From the John Milton epic, "Paradise Lost," name the Fallen Angel and his two children.

(ANSWERS ON PAGE 622)

LITERATURE—QUIZ 2

Two-Point Questions

1. In a novel Robert Louis Stevenson wrote in 1896, young David Balfour is sent to sea by a cruel uncle. Was that book "Kidnapped" or "Treasure Island"?
2. Getting nowhere at writing comedies for the stage, this French writer switched to science-fiction 100 years ago and wrote "20,000 Leagues under the Sea" and "From the Earth to the Moon." Who was he?
3. In the 17th century, Cervantes wrote a book in which a poor country squire, crazed by the idea of chivalry, carried his enthusiasm for it to such a point that the excessive chivalry of the times was soon laughed out of favor. Name that great book.
4. A famous London detective of 19th century literature loved no woman but deeply admired a clever swindler named Irene Adler. Name that detective (whose best friend was a doctor).

Three-Point Questions

1. In 1516, Sir Thomas More wrote a book about an imaginary land where people lived in great peace and happiness under pure socialism. From the title, we added a word to our language to characterize any scheme which is too visionary and impractical. Name the book.
2. Name the book written by an English tinker during his twelve years in prison at Bedford for "unlawful" preaching. His name was John Bunyan.
3. Name the King involved in Tennyson's "Idylls of the King."
4. Thanks to re-runs of old movies on TV, everyone knows that William Bendix starred in "The Hairy Ape." But who wrote the play on which the movie was based?

Five-Point Questions

1. In Sheridan's play, "The Rivals," one of the female characters constantly confuses words that are similar in sound but different in meaning (for instance, saying "Allegories are things that live on river banks"). Her name has become a symbol in our language for such mistakes. What is it?

2. An obscure pirate named Alexander Selkirk was marooned for four years on a South Pacific island. A great English author based a fictional book on Selkirk's experiences there. Name the book and the author.

3. Women have made a great contribution to the field of English literature. Name the women who wrote the following books: (a) "Adam Bede," (b) "Sense and Sensibility," (c) "Mrs. Miniver."

4. The longest sentence in literature runs for forty pages! It is spoken by a character named Molly Bloom. Name the novel and the author.

(ANSWERS ON PAGES 622-623)

LITERATURE—QUIZ 3

Two-Point Questions

1. In an attempt to show that good can triumph over evil, Dickens wrote a novel about a little orphan who runs away to London and resists the evil influence of Bill Sikes and Fagin. Name that orphan.

2. A Phrygian slave who lived in the 6th century B.C. told his short stories through animals who speak and behave like human beings. Name the author of those famous fables.

3. Name the Rodgers-and-Hammerstein-like team of England which collaborated on such excellent musicals as "The Pirates of Penzance" and "The Mikado."

4. What did the soothsayer warn Julius Caesar to beware of?

Three-Point Questions

1. Who woke up one night from a deep dream of peace, to find an angel in his tent?

2. Name the sailor in Tennyson's narrative poem who returned home 10 years after his shipwreck, to find that his wife had remarried, presuming him to be dead. He then nobly disappeared.

3. Name the author and famous short story in which two men living on an island off Charleston, S. C., find an old hidden treasure parchment that leads them to the treasure of Captain Kidd.

4. What is the name given that part of the 16th century in which British achievements in poetry and drama reached brilliant heights?

Five-Point Questions

1. A novel by Nathaniel Hawthorne relates a story of the persecution of Clifford Pyncheon by his cousin, Judge Pyncheon—but Clifford and his sister Hepzibah find peaceful years when the Judge dies. Hawthorne named the book after the home in which Clifford and Hepzibah lived. Give its title.

2. One of John Milton's great poems describes the pensive life. A companion poem describes the pleasures of a more joyful meditative life. Name both poems.

3. In "The Merchant of Venice" three suitors for Portia's hand must choose from three caskets of gold, silver, and lead. One of the caskets contains her portrait. Which casket is it, and who chooses it?

4. Name the play by Eugene O'Neill which used the device of having the inner thoughts of the characters in the play break through the regular dialogue in the form of soliloquies.

(ANSWERS ON PAGE 623)

LITERATURE—QUIZ 4

Two-Point Questions

1. What was the pen name of William Sydney Porter, who became famous for his short stories with a "twist" ending?
2. Which famous sailor in the world's great literature was surrounded by water but had not a drop to drink?
3. Sax Rohmer made a fortune out of what menacing Chinese character, usually addressed as "Doctor"?
4. Which Edgar Rice Burroughs series about a jungle hero got Johnny Weissmuller started in the movies?

Three-Point Questions

1. In what book do you find ruthless Wolf Larsen, who ran his ship with no concern for the welfare of his crew?
2. In what book does Sir Brian de Bois Guilbert die of his own passions?
3. What was the name of the fictional Minnesota town that was the home of Dr. Will Kennicott in Sinclair Lewis' novel, "Main Street"?
4. What was the name of the fictional New Hampshire town that was the locale for Thornton Wilder's play, "Our Town"?

Five-Point Questions

1. Name the Mississippi town that Thomas Sutpen came to in 1833, in William Faulkner's novel, "Absalom, Absalom!"
2. Which country was the locale of each of the following novels: (a) "The Brave Bulls" by Tom Lea; (b) "The Wall" by John Hersey?
3. Which country was the locale of each of the following novels: (a) "The Bridge of San Luis Rey" by Thornton Wilder; (b) "A Fable" by William Faulkner?
4. In a great satire by Rabelais, name the following two famous characters: (a) The Last of the Giants, whose immortal achievement is his voyage to Utopia in quest of the "Oracle of the Holy Bottle"; and (b) his father.

(ANSWERS ON PAGE 623)

'BAD GUYS"—QUIZ 1

Two-Point Questions

1. In 1818 Mary Shelley, wife of the poet, wrote the forerunner of all "monster" stories with her tale of a monster created by a young medical student. Name the monster, played by Boris Karloff in the movies.
2. The F.B.I. shot down this Public Enemy No. 1 outside a movie theatre. Name him.
3. Robert Louis Stevenson wrote a novel about a doctor with a split personality. Name the hideous person and personality whom the good doctor became under the influence of a drug.
4. This gangster, enriched by Prohibition days, was nicknamed Scarface. Who was he?

Three-Point Questions

1. Incited by the captain's cruel treatment, the crew of a British ship staged the most famous mutiny of all time in 1789. They set the captain adrift in an open boat with 18 companions; then sailed the ship to Tahiti. Who was that captain?
2. This warrior in the army of Duncan, King of Scotland, aspired to be king himself and murdered Duncan at the urging of his wife. Who was he?
3. In Goethe's great drama, "Faust," by what name was the devil called?
4. This Russian monk had great evil influence on the church and court. Friends of the Czar murdered this monk to end his influence. Name him.

Five-Point Questions

1. Sheriff Pat Garrett shot and killed this famous outlaw whose real-life name was William H. Bonney. By what nickname was he best known in fact and fiction stories of the early West?
2. Name the tyrannical German official whose assassination set off the wave of reprisal terror that produced the massacre of Lidice in World War II.
3. Edward Teach became famous as a ruthless pirate. By what nickname was he known?

4. Teach's sailing master was a cruel and reckless man whom Teach once shot in the knee "just for a lesson." When Robert Louis Stevenson wrote "Treasure Island," he immortalized that man's name by using it as that of a sailing master in the book. Who was he?

(ANSWERS ON PAGE 623)

"BAD GUYS"—QUIZ 2

Two-Point Questions

1. This Roman emperor had his own mother executed, murdered his wife, killed a girl who wouldn't marry him, and then put many Christians to death after accusing them of burning Rome. What was his name?
2. This Sioux Indian chief headed the Indian forces which massacred General Custer's men. Name him.
3. This miserly character hated the Christmas spirit until Christmas ghosts reformed him. Who was he?
4. This King of the Huns was so cruel in warfare that he was called "The Scourge of God." However, when he ravaged Italy in 452 A.D., Pope Leo I persuaded him to spare Rome. Name him.

Three-Point Questions

1. Othello has become the symbol of all overly jealous husbands. But who was the villain whose insinuations drove Othello to murder Desdemona?

2. This pirate had his headquarters on an island off Louisiana. He pillaged shipping in the Gulf of Mexico. However, for helping General Jackson at the Battle of New Orleans, he was pardoned by President Madison but soon went back to piracy! What was his name?

3. In Dickens' "Oliver Twist," what was the name of the unscrupulous old man who taught young boys to become thieves and pickpockets?

4. In the short story by Stephen Vincent Benet, against whom did Daniel Webster contend for the unfortunate Jabez Stone?

Five-Point Questions

1. In "Les Miserables," Jean Valjean was persecuted and hounded by an overzealous detective. Name him.

2. Name the general who, in Richard Connell's famous short story, "The Most Dangerous Game," lived on a Caribbean island (alone except for his huge servant, Ivan) and hunted helpless men whom he lured to the island as "game" for his hunting sport.

3. Name the Italian statesman who wrote "The Prince," a book based on the theory that maintenance of power justifies deceit and treachery in government.

4. As Spanish governor of the Netherlands in the 16th century, this tyrant executed over 18,000 people to maintain order. Later he conquered Portugal with the same brutality. He had the title of Duke. Name him.

(ANSWERS ON PAGE 623)

MYTHOLOGY—QUIZ 1

Two-Point Questions
1. Who holds the world on his shoulders?
2. In Greek mythology, Aurora was the goddess of the morning and Boreas was the god of the north wind. What display of strange lights was named after them?
3. Name the half-horse, half-man creatures that lived in the mountains of Thessaly.
4. Aphrodite was the Greek goddess of what?

Three-Point Questions
1. By what stratagem did Hippomenes defeat Atalanta in a foot race?
2. The king-size cleanup job of all time was accomplished by Hercules when he diverted a river through stables that had never been cleaned. Name the stables he cleaned.
3. Who was the watchdog of Hades?
4. Who changed Odysseus' comrades into swine?

Five-Point Questions
1. The ancient Greeks had a myth about an animal, born from the blood of Medusa, that rode through the sky at will. Identify and name that animal.
2. The staff of Hermes, herald of the gods, has become the symbol of physicians. Name it.
3. Name the boatman who ferried the dead across a river in Hell.
4. Name the father-and-son team who learned to fly on wings of feathers and wax invented by the father.

(ANSWERS ON PAGES 623-624)

MYTHOLOGY—QUIZ 2

Two-Point Questions
1. Who was the Roman god of love?
2. When he made his trip to Colchis, what was Jason in quest of?
3. Who performed twelve great labors?
4. On what mountain did the Greek gods live?

Three-Point Questions
1. Name the man-eating, one-eyed shepherds who, according to Homer, dwelt in Sicily.
2. Who finally cut the Gordian knot with one stroke of his sword?
3. Which handsome youth fell in love with his own reflection in a pool and was changed into a flower that bears his name?
4. Name the Roman god whose two heads faced in opposite directions.

Five-Point Questions
1. Why did Perspehone have to spend four months of each year in Hades with Pluto?
2. Who was the bravest Trojan warrior in the Trojan War, and by whom was he finally slain?
3. Which Greek sea-god had the power to change his shape and form at will? (A word of that meaning in our language was derived from his name.)
4. For what animal did Daedalus build the labyrinth in Crete?

(ANSWERS ON PAGE 624)

MYTHOLOGY—QUIZ 3

Two-Point Questions

1. This hero of Homer's "Iliad" was dipped in the River Styx by his mother, at birth, to make his body invulnerable. Because she held him by his heel, that part of him remained vulnerable. Who was he?
2. Which beautiful Greek woman had "the face that launched a thousand ships"?
3. Who was the Greek god of wine?
4. Name the principal river of Hades.

Three-Point Questions

1. Who killed Achilles and by what means?
2. Give the name of the band of adventurers who sailed with Jason in his quest of the Golden Fleece.
3. In the Nibelungenlied, who won the treasure of the Nibelungs?
4. In Norse mythology, who was the god of thunder?

Five-Point Questions

1. Procrustes was a tyrant who fitted people to his bed by cutting off their limbs if they were too long or by stretching them to death if they were too short. Which Greek hero slew him?
2. The Trojan War, according to legend, was fought because a prince of Troy abducted the beautiful Helen, wife of the King of Sparta. Name (a) Helen's husband at the time and (b) the prince who abducted her.
3. If a man looked at Medusa, one of the three Gorgons, he was immediately turned into stone. Which Greek hero slew her, and by what means did he avoid looking directly at her?
4. Because he offended the gods, this son of Zeus was condemned to stand in water up to his chin. The water receded whenever he wished to drink, and when he was hungry luscious fruits overhead would swing beyond his grasp. Name him.

(ANSWERS ON PAGE 624)

THE BIBLE—QUIZ 1

Two-Point Questions
1. Name the Philistine giant whom David slew.
2. Who was the cousin and forerunner of Jesus who called on the people to prepare for the Messiah?
3. Name the most sacred city of Palestine.
4. Name the prophet who was swallowed by a great fish.

Three-Point Questions
1. Name the large fresh-water lake, in the upper region of Palestine, which is closely associated with the ministry of Jesus.
2. Name the "father" of the Hebrews.
3. What was the name of Paul before his conversion to Christianity?
4. In their conquest of Canaan, the Israelites took a large city by marching around it and blowing their trumpets. Name the city and tell what happened there.

Five-Point Questions
1. Name the three sons of Noah.
2. After serving his Uncle Laban for seven years in order to marry one of his uncle's daughters, Jacob was given a daughter he didn't want and married her. However, by serving another seven years, he won the wife he originally desired. Name each of these wives.
3. What official title did Pontius Pilate have?
4. How many years is Methuselah supposed to have lived?

(ANSWERS ON PAGE 624)

THE BIBLE—QUIZ 2

Two-Point Questions
1. Which strong man of the Bible slew a thousand Philistines?
2. Which Jewish king dazzled the Queen of Sheba with his opulence and wisdom?
3. Who was the "Doubting Apostle"?
4. What twin cities were destroyed because of their wickedness?

Three-Point Questions
1. Who was the first Christian martyr?
2. Name the sister of Moses, who led the people in singing and dancing after the Red Sea was crossed.
3. Who was sold by his brothers to a band of Midianites, who then took him to Egypt where he rose to power and influence?
4. What prophet was taken up to heaven in a chariot of fire?

Five-Point Questions
1. Name the three officials before whom Jesus was tried.
2. Name the three successive kings of Israel before their kingdom became divided.
3. Jonah got himself into a lot of trouble by disobeying God's command to go to a certain designated city, sailing, instead, to a city in the opposite direction. Name those two cities.
4. Name the rich man who buried the body of Jesus in his own sepulcher.

(ANSWERS ON PAGES 624–625)

THE BIBLE—QUIZ 3

Two-Point Questions

1. On what tower being built to reach the heavens, was work stopped because of a confusion of languages?
2. Which King of Israel was once a shepherd boy?
3. Name the Philistine woman who betrayed Samson.
4. What city in Galilee was the home of Jesus in his childhood?

Three-Point Questions

1. Many a teen-age son rebels against the authority of his father, but what was the name of King David's son who raised an army in rebellion against his father?
2. Name the place of the final conflict between the forces of good and the forces of evil, as foretold in Revelations.
3. Name the woman for whom King David had such a passionate love that he arranged the death of her husband in battle in order to be able to marry her.
4. The second Book of the Old Testament gets its name from a Greek word meaning a way out. What is that name?

Five-Point Questions

1. Name the member of the early Church whose deceitfulness to the Church was denounced by Peter. Since then, his name has been applied to habitual liars.
2. For which Babylonian king did Daniel read the handwriting on the wall?
3. Name the Persian king who captured Babylon in 538 B.C. and allowed the Jews to return to Jerusalem.
4. How many plagues did Moses cause to be visited upon the Egyptians before the Pharaoh released the Israelites?

(ANSWERS ON PAGE 625)

LEGENDS, TALES AND
FABLES—QUIZ 1

Two-Point Questions

1. This legendary hero of Switzerland was sentenced to shoot an apple from his son's head. Name him.
2. Name the cruel master who in "Uncle Tom's Cabin" had poor Uncle Tom flogged to death.
3. Which legendary king of Phrygia asked the gods to make everything he touched turn to gold?
4. What will-o'-the-wisp source of water did Ponce de Leon seek in Florida?

Three-Point Questions

1. In Frank Stockton's famous short story, a barbaric princess must show her doomed lover which of two doors to pick, in an arena. Tell what awaits him behind each door.
2. In which book is the Indian Uncas the hero?
3. Name the spectral ship that haunts the southern seas near the Cape of Good Hope.
4. The end result of the appearance of the Angel Moroni to Joseph Smith was the founding of a new religious sect called The Latter-Day Saints. What is another name for this sect?

Five-Point Questions

1. In American folklore, which famous Negro steel driver beat a steam drill down through the rock, then died with his 40-pound hammer in his hand?
2. Which 17th century English statesman and general told his troops to trust in God but keep their powder dry?
3. Name the common-sense squire who attended the overly chivalrous Don Quixote on his adventures.
4. In Chaucer's "Canterbury Tales," in honor of which saint was the party of pilgrims going to Canterbury?

(ANSWERS ON PAGE 625)

LEGENDS, TALES AND FABLES—QUIZ 2

Two-Point Questions
1. Who was the merry chaplain of Robin Hood's band?
2. Name the woman who rode nude through the streets of Coventry.
3. Which famous sailor hitched a ride out of the Valley of Diamonds on a fabulous bird called a roc?
4. Who was Tom Sawyer's best pal?

Three-Point Questions
1. Name the Three Musketeers in the novel of that name.
2. Name the imaginary monster in "Through the Looking-Glass."
3. Name the fabulous Arabian bird that dies, burns itself to ashes, and then rises to new life from its own ashes.
4. Name the boy hero of "Treasure Island."

Five-Point Questions
1. A Norse myth tells of two children who were kidnapped by the moon while drawing water. Under what names did they turn up in nursery rhymes?
2. Name the sculptor of Greek legend who fell in love with his own statue of Aphrodite, whereupon the goddess gave the statue life and he married her!
3. Attila the Hun was called the Scourge of God, but which conqueror was called the Nightmare of Europe?
4. Which nephew of King Arthur seized the kingdom in Arthur's absence? On his return, Arthur killed this nephew but was mortally wounded in the combat.

(ANSWERS ON PAGE 625)

LEGENDS, TALES AND
FABLES—QUIZ 3

Two-Point Questions

1. The Egyptian priests told of a great island or continent in the Atlantic Ocean which sank beneath the sea thousands of years before their time. Can you name that legendary land?
2. Name the triangular stone at an old Irish castle that gives the gift of a glib tongue to all who kiss it.
3. This hero of the Arabian Nights spied on 40 thieves and learned that the words "Open Sesame" gave access to their treasure cave. Who was he?
4. Name the steep, high rock on the bank of the Rhine River where a beautiful siren (for whom the rock was named) lured river boatmen to their death.

Three-Point Questions

1. Name the runaway slave who befriended a lion in a cave by pulling a thorn from its paw. Captured later, he faced that same lion in the Roman arena and was spared.

2. Name the sword that young Arthur pulled from its position in a huge stone from which no one else could move it. Thereby he became the English king.
3. Name the Scottish king who, in his refuge on the Isle of Rathlin where the British drove him, learned the lesson of patience from a spider spinning its web. Seven years later, he was victorious at Bannockburn.
4. In Greek legend, the tyrant Dionysius of Syracuse condemned a man to death, but allowed him to go home and settle his affairs first, provided someone acted as his hostage. The man's best friend volunteered as hostage, and when the condemned man returned for execution, Dionysius was so impressed by their friendship that he granted a pardon. Name the two friends.

Five-Point Questions
1. An English drinking society had a theme song about a Greek poet who loved his wine. Francis Scott Key, who knew the melody, wrote the words of "The Star-Spangled Banner" to that tune. Name the Greek poet for whom the music of the song was originally written.
2. Alexander the Great built a city to commemorate the name of his favorite horse. Name his horse.
3. Name the half-human dragon-monster that Beowulf slew.
4. Peter Pan taught Wendy and her brothers how to fly. Give the full names of Wendy's brothers.

(ANSWERS ON PAGE 625)

NURSERY RHYMES—QUIZ 1

Two-Point Questions
1. When Polly put the kettle on, what was in it?
2. How old was the pease porridge in the pot?
3. What did Little Jack Horner pull out?
4. Where was Little Boy Blue?

Three-Point Questions
1. For what three people did the black sheep have his three bags of wool?
2. What did the Old Woman Who Lived in a Shoe give her children?
3. Monday's child is fair of face. What is Tuesday's child?
4. What did Simple Simon go fishing for?

Five-Point Questions
1. What was the only tune that Tom the Piper's Son could play?
2. When Bobby Shaftoe went to sea, what did he have on his knee?
3. What did Wee Willie Winkie cry as he ran through the town?
4. What did Old Mother Goose ride on when she wanted to wander?

(ANSWERS ON PAGES 625–626)

NURSERY RHYMES—QUIZ 2

Two-Point Questions
1. What frightened Little Miss Muffet away?
2. What did Jack jump over?
3. What did Tom the Piper's son steal?
4. How did Georgie Porgie make the girls cry?

Three-Point Questions
1. Of what occupations were the three men in a tub?
2. What did mother cat tell her kittens they couldn't have, because they'd lost their mittens?
3. What did Wynken, Blynken and Nod sail off in?
4. Why would a person "Ride a cock horse to Banbury Cross"?

Five-Point Questions
1. When the owl and the pussycat went to sea, which objects did they take with them?
2. Name at least six of St. Nicholas' tiny reindeer.
3. In the nursery rhyme that begins "Monday's child is fair of face," etc., what is said of the child born on the Sabbath?
4. In the case of the Ladybird whose house was on fire, what was the name of the only one of her children who was still there?

(ANSWERS ON PAGE 626)

ORIGIN OF WORDS

Two-Point Questions
1. In Greek mythology, the Titans were a race of huge, godlike creatures in the earliest days of Creation. Which word did we get from their name?
2. The Greeks called the word-pictures which the Egyptians carved into stone "hieros" (for sacred) and "glyphe" (for carvings). What word did we get from this?
3. The Latin "scintilla" meant spark. Name our word of similar meaning.

4. The Greek word "bakterion" meant a small staff. When scientists first saw some germ cultures under magnification, some of the germs looked like a staff. What English word was derived from the Greek?

Three-Point Questions
1. In Greek mythology, one of the rivers of Hades was called the Lethe. The dead who drank from it forgot the past. In Greek, lethargos meant forgetting. Which related word do we have in English?
2. The Iliad tells of Stentor, a Greek herald in the Trojan War, who had the voice of 50 men. What corresponding adjective do we have now?
3. The Laconians of ancient Greece said very little, believing in action, not words. What word did their name give us?
4. A French soldier named Nicholas Chauvin carried his admiration for Napoleon to an absurd degree. Which word in our language today means excessive patriotism and prejudice?

Five-Point Questions
1. Almost 900 years ago, a murderous sect in India practiced political executions at their own whim. They ate the drug, hashish, to whip up their courage, and were known as hashashin (hashish eaters). What word of closely related meaning did we get from the Indian word?
2. When the Arabs were a sea-going people, they had a title, "Amir-al-bahr," meaning commander of the sea. It has been changed a bit in getting to us, but which word in our language comes from this title?
3. Since Popes generally had no children of their own, the early Popes sometimes favored their nephews with important positions in the church. The Latin "nepotis" meant nephew. What related word do we still use?
4. When the Athenians wanted to banish a dangerous politician, they voted on it by writing his name on a ballot which they called an "ostrakon." If 5,000 ostrakons were cast against him, he was exiled. Name the word we got from that ancient Greek ballot.

(ANSWERS ON PAGE 626)

INTERESTING PLACES—
QUIZ 1

Two-Point Questions
1. Which continent is called the Dark Continent?
2. Which continent is really a large island?
3. On which continent did Western culture arise?
4. Name the extensive mountain system in Europe which forms a 15,000-foot-high border between France and Switzerland.

Three-Point Questions
1. Do most of the earth's land masses lie north or south of the Equator?
2. The deepest trough in the earth's surface lies near the island of Mindanao in the Philippines (35,400 feet deep). Name the mountain range which constitutes the *highest* upward thrust in the earth's surface.
3. Is the North Pole a land area or an ocean area?
4. Name the sea which Columbus thoroughly explored on his last three visits to America.

Five-Point Questions
1. Name the wide, beautiful street along the waterfront in Shanghai.
2. Give the number of the famous U. S. Route which connects Chicago with Los Angeles.
3. Name the most famous of the old Roman highways, connecting Rome with Brindisi.
4. Name the island in the Pacific Ocean, 2,000 miles off Chile, where hundreds of huge, partly finished, monolithic statues pose one of the great mysteries of archeology.

(ANSWERS ON PAGE 626)

INTERESTING PLACES—QUIZ 2

Two-Point Questions
1. The Labrador Current carries many icebergs into or near the ocean trade-lanes. In which ocean does that current originate?
2. Name the island in the Tyrrhenian Sea, six miles off Italy, where Napoleon was first exiled.
3. Name the historically important body of water which lies between France and England.
4. Name the sea in Palestine which lies almost 1,300 feet below sea level.

Three-Point Questions
1. Name the river which, rising in the Black Forest of Germany and flowing into the Black Sea, is one of the most important water trade routes in Europe.
2. Name the largest city in Africa. It is one of the most important trade centers of the Mediterranean and is the site of many famous mosques.
3. Which two European countries are connected by the Brenner Pass?
4. Name the great mountain system of South America, which ranges from Venezuela to the Tierra del Fuego.

Five-Point Questions
1. Name the Italian city where Michelangelo and Galileo are entombed.
2. In which Chinese city is there an area known as the Forbidden City, because during the reign of the Manchu emperors no people other than the members of the imperial household could enter it without special permission?
3. Name the street in London where an infamous debtors prison stood from the 12th to the 19th centuries.
4. Name the famous rocky hill or cone which rises above the harbor at Rio de Janeiro.

(ANSWERS ON PAGE 626)

INTERESTING PLACES—QUIZ 3

Two-Point Questions
1. What is the Scandinavian word for a narrow inlet of sea, penetrating deeply inland between high cliffs?
2. Name the most sacred river of the Hindus.
3. Name the island west of Norway which was discovered and settled by the Viking Naddodd in 868 A.D.
4. Which is the longest river in Italy?

Three-Point Questions
1. Name the body of water which separates the mainland of South America from the Tierra del Fuego. It bears the name of the great explorer who first sailed through it.
2. What is the name commonly given the vast, treeless plains in the central part of Argentina?
3. One of the South American countries is called the Shoestring Republic because of its long, narrow length. Name it.
4. Name the Italian city where Columbus was born.

Five-Point Questions
1. Name the small, volcanic island in the South Pacific which Fletcher Christian and eight other mutineers from the "Bounty" colonized in 1790.
2. Name the carved-figure memorial to the heroes of the Confederacy, sculptured near Atlanta, Ga.
3. Name the street in England on which the Bank of England is situated.
4. On which African river is the 343-foot-high cataract known as Victoria Falls?

(ANSWERS ON PAGES 626–627)

INTERESTING PLACES—QUIZ 4

Two-Point Questions

1. Which large tract of land, purchased by the U. S. from Russia in 1867, was known as "Seward's Folly" (Secretary of State William Seward arranged the purchase) because it was thought to be just an area of "icebergs and polar bears"?
2. Which river in South America discharges so much rainwater into the Atlantic that the natural salt content of the ocean is reduced for almost 100 miles?
3. Which island off the African coast was Napoleon's final place of exile?
4. Name the world's most extensive desert.

Three-Point Questions

1. Which Oriental city is known, because of its extensive waterways, as the Venice of Siam?
2. A French game of ball known as *paille maille* was once played on a street in London and gave the street its present-day name. What is that name?
3. Name the group of islands north of Scotland famous for a breed of ponies which originated there.
4. In which state is the geographical center of the United States?

Five-Point Questions

1. In which Canadian bay do the highest tides in the world occur?
2. Name all five of the Great Lakes.
3. What name is given the area of the North Atlantic which is famous for its floating seaweed? The Portuguese name for it means the Sea of Little Grapes.
4. Which park in London contains "Rotten Row"—a corruption of the French "route de roi" (way of the king)?

(ANSWERS ON PAGE 627)

WHERE ARE THESE RIVERS?

QUIZ 1

Two-Point Questions
1. Hwang Ho.
2. Yukon.
3. Danube.
4. Rio Grande.

Three-Point Questions
1. Brahmaputra.
2. Don.
3. Fraser.
4. Oder.

Five-Point Questions
1. Mekong.
2. Yenisei.
3. Murray.
4. Parnaiba.

QUIZ 2

Two-Point Questions
1. Nile.
2. Amazon.
3. St. Lawrence.
4. Volga.

Three-Point Questions
1. Irrawaddy.
2. Tigris.
3. Mackenzie.
4. Ural.

Five-Point Questions
1. Ob.
2. Magdalena.
3. Euphrates.
4. Lena.

(ANSWERS ON PAGE 627)

FAMOUS EXPLORERS

What land or body of water did the following men explore?

Two-Point Questions
1. Vasco de Balboa.
2. Ponce de Leon.
3. Hernandes de Soto.
4. Ferdinand Magellan.

Three-Point Questions
1. Hernando Cortez.
2. Francisco Pizzaro.
3. Father Jacques Marquette.
4. John Cabot.

Five-Point Questions
1. Francisco de Coronado.
2. Jacques Cartier.
3. Sir Walter Raleigh.
4. Eric the Red.

(ANSWERS ON PAGE 627)

WHERE ARE THESE FAMOUS STRUCTURES?

Two-Point Questions
1. The Parthenon.
2. The Great Sphinx.
3. The Colosseum.
4. Westminster Abbey.

Three-Point Questions
1. The Taj Mahal.
2. The Pantheon.
3. The Alhambra.
4. St. Mark's Cathedral.

Five-Point Questions
1. The Mosque of St. Sophia.
2. The Duomo.
3. The Escorial.
4. Mosque of Omar.

(ANSWERS ON PAGES 627–628)

WHERE ARE THESE VOLCANOES?

Two-Point Questions
1. Mt. Vesuvius.
2. Fujiyama.
3. Mauna Loa.
4. Popocatepetl.

Five-Point Questions
1. Asosan.
2. Krakatoa.
3. Wrangell.
4. Colima.

Three-Point Questions
1. Lassen Peak.
2. Paricutin.
3. Mt. Etna.
4. Kilimanjaro.

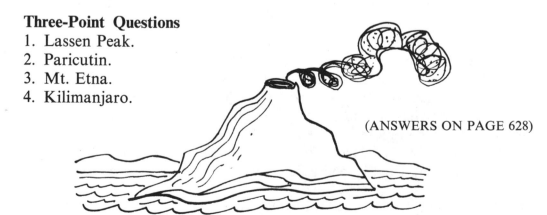

(ANSWERS ON PAGE 628)

FAMOUS PEOPLE—QUIZ 1

Two-Point Questions
1. Who was the "Lady of the Lamp" who founded modern nursing?
2. This famous American poet wrote "Leaves of Grass."
3. Legend says that a falling apple gave this mathematician the idea of the Law of Gravity.
4. In silent movie days, she was known as "America's Sweetheart."

Three-Point Questions
1. Accused of corrupting the youth of Athens, this Greek philosopher was compelled to drink a poisonous cup of hemlock.
2. This hated king of England was forced to sign the Magna Carta.
3. This great Italian sculptor and goldsmith wrote his autobiography.
4. This Portuguese navigator discovered what Columbus failed to find: the sea route from Europe to India (by way of the Cape of Good Hope).

Five-Point Questions
1. Name the German scientist who discovered X-rays.
2. This Italian artist often painted hair in a rich red tone.
3. Name the German socialist who collaborated with Karl Marx in helping complete "Das Kapital."
4. These twin brothers, from Belgium, became famous for their balloon ascents and bathysphere descents. What is their surname?

(ANSWERS ON PAGE 628)

FAMOUS PEOPLE—QUIZ 2

Two-Point Questions

1. This Macedonian king conquered the entire known world by the time he was 32.
2. In 1905 he wrote the Theory of Relativity.
3. This King of England defied the Pope and married Anne Boleyn.
4. Which husband-wife team discovered radium?

Three-Point Questions

1. He was the first Englishman to sail around the world, and in 1588 he defeated the Spanish Armada.
2. This saint of the Catholic Church founded the Franciscan Order in the 13th century.
3. The editorial policies of this famous newspaperman helped bring about the Spanish-American War.
4. A German soldier and storyteller, this "Baron" became famous for his "tall tales."

Five-Point Questions

1. This Chinese physician turned revolutionary and overthrew the Manchu dynasty, then became the first president of the Chinese Republic.
2. Name the Prussian general who became an American major-general in the Revolutionary War, and taught our forces drilling and discipline at Valley Forge.
3. This great French writer detested superstition and fanaticism, and wrote the epic satire "Candide."
4. The central idea of this Greek philosopher (that number is the principal order of the universe) laid the foundations for the pseudo-science of numerology.

(ANSWERS ON PAGE 628)

FAMOUS PEOPLE—QUIZ 3

Two-Point Questions

1. This American frontiersman, with little schooling, was three times elected to Congress, then helped Texas in its fight for independence. He was a hero of the Alamo, where he was killed.
2. From his job as editor of the Nazi newspaper, *Der Angrif*, this spellbinding orator became propaganda minister of the Reich.
3. At the age of 15, she married the French prince who later became Louis XVI. At 38, she died beneath the guillotine.
4. This Italian traveler journeyed all the way to the court of Kublai Khan in China, starting in 1271 and returning to Venice 24 years later!

Three-Point Questions

1. This great Austrian expert in neuropathology developed psychoanalysis in the treatment of neurotic disorders and became the Father of Modern Psychiatry.
2. Name the Greek mathematician who is known as the Father of Geometry. He lived about 300 B.C.
3. His official title was "King of Kings of Ethiopia, the Conquering Lion of Judah and the Elect of God." His capital was at Addis Ababa.
4. As this Egyptian king added weight, he lost popularity and was finally deposed by the army. He fled to exile in Italy.

Five-Point Questions

1. Teddy Roosevelt picked him as the best man to build the Panama Canal—and he finished the job five months ahead of time.
2. This Russian revolutionist became president of the short-lived Russian republic in 1917, but Lenin and the Bolsheviks overthrew him.
3. This Roman naturalist was the most famous Roman killed when Mount Vesuvius destroyed the city of Pompeii.
4. In 18 years as Inquisitor-General, this fanatic put over 2,000 people to death at the stake as "heretics." He was the leading figure of the dreaded Spanish Inquisition.

(ANSWERS ON PAGE 628)

FAMOUS PEOPLE—QUIZ 4

Two-Point Questions

1. He is best remembered for his last words: "I regret that I have but one life to lose for my country."
2. Born a peasant girl at Domremy, France, she became a legendary heroine of her nation as "The Maid of Orleans."
3. This Swedish chemist invented dynamite, made a fortune on it, and then established the famous annual prizes for those who contribute most for mankind's benefit. Who was he?
4. He faced the Indians fearlessly, but he sent John Alden on a personal mission to Priscilla, rather than face her himself.

Three-Point Questions

1. His discovery of gold in the Sacramento Valley of California led to the Gold Rush of 1849; then he died penniless.
2. This Greek philosopher dramatized his belief in upright, simple living, by carrying a lantern with him "in search of an honest man."
3. This reformer changed the course of history when he nailed his "95 Propositions" to the door of a church in Wittenberg, Germany.
4. He made a fortune in tea, and spent a fortune in unsuccessful attempts to win the America's Cup in yachting.

Five-Point Questions

1. She became a heroine of France when she stabbed to death in his bath the infamous Marat of the French Revolution.
2. This young American naval officer performed "the most daring act of the age" when he burned the frigate *Philadelphia* after it had been captured by the Tripolitanian pirates.
3. This Persian religious leader conceived the idea of Good opposing Evil in life, and the "free will" of man to choose between them. He founded a great religion which bore his name.
4. The chief fame of this British chemist rests on his discovery of oxygen in 1774.

(ANSWERS ON PAGE 628)

FAMOUS PEOPLE—QUIZ 5

Two-Point Questions

1. This sixth President of the United States was the son of a man who had already been President of the United States.
2. The most famous woman aviator of all time, she disappeared in 1937 on a trip from New Guinea to Howland Island.
3. He invented the incandescent electric lamp.
4. She married Napoleon Bonaparte and became the first Empress of the French.

Three-Point Questions

1. With African elephants as his "tank corps," he crossed the Alps and brought terror to Rome in 218–217 B.C.
2. He defended Loeb and Leopold, but his most famous case was his defense of a science teacher against prosecution by William Jennings Bryan.
3. This Polish astronomer was the first man to publish the theory that the planets revolve around the sun, not the sun around the earth.
4. She was the founder of Christian Science.

Five-Point Questions

1. Chosen president of the Turkish Republic in 1923, he performed an astounding job of modernizing that nation.
2. Known as the greatest of all orators, he is said (in legend) to have overcome a speech defect by practicing oratory with pebbles in his mouth!
3. This French mathematician propounded a theory (the Theory of Probabilities) which became the basis of rate making in the insurance business.
4. This famous Roman general was first the ally of Julius Caesar but later his political and military enemy. He was defeated at Pharsalus and later assassinated in Egypt.

(ANSWERS ON PAGES 628–629)

SCIENCE—QUIZ 1

Two-Point Questions

1. One of the three states (conditions or forms) in which matter exists is the solid state. Name the other two.
2. Name the precious metal which is the most malleable of all metals.
3. Does sound travel faster in warm or cold air?
4. From which ore is aluminum made?

Three-Point Questions

1. When a physicist divides the weight in air of a body heavier than water by the weight in air of an equal volume of water, which property of the first object is he trying to determine?
2. When two liquids of different concentration are separated by a porous membrane, the liquids tend to pass through the membrane and mix. What is the name of this process?
3. Why is it impossible for a machine with moving parts to have 100% efficiency?
4. It is fundamental that energy, though continually changed or transformed, is never destroyed or diminished (although it can be dissipated into an irrecoverable form). What is this principle called?

Five-Point Questions

1. Newton's Second Law of Motion holds that the acceleration of a body is in the direction of, and in proportion to, the force that produces it. Describe Newton's First Law of Motion.
2. Describe Newton's Third Law of Motion.
3. What is the valence of carbon in most of its compounds?
4. Which element, contained in all acids, determines the characteristic properties of a particular acid?

(ANSWERS ON PAGE 629)

SCIENCE—QUIZ 2

Two-Point Questions
1. In the worship of which two heavenly bodies by the ancient Egyptians and Babylonians did the science of astronomy begin?
2. What is the instrument called by which atmospheric pressure is commonly measured?
3. What is the approximate speed of light per second?
4. Against which dread disease did Edward Jenner develop vaccination?

Three-Point Questions
1. Which ancient civilization was the first to separate religion from science, in trying to determine the nature of the universe?
2. Name the Greek doctor who founded the first scientific system of medicine.
3. Name the famous astronomer of ancient Alexandria whose theory that the earth was the center of the universe prevailed until disproved by Copernicus.
4. Name the young professor at Pisa who, according to legend, used the Leaning Tower of Pisa in experiments which disproved the theory Aristotle had propounded, that a heavy body falls faster through space than a light body.

Five-Point Questions
1. Name the Greek philosopher who tried to devise one all-embracing system of knowledge which would include everything known to man. His former pupil, Alexander the Great, sent him collections of plants from all over the known world to help him in his study of biology.
2. Name the French chemist who demonstrated that it is an element in the air (oxygen) which supports combustion.
3. Name the Austrian priest and botanist who, through his patient experiments crossing and hybridizing many generations of peas, discovered what characteristics are passed on in heredity, and thereby founded the modern science of genetics.
4. Name the Russian chemist who succeeded in arranging the elements into a comprehensive, periodic table of their atomic weights.

(ANSWERS ON PAGE 629)

POT LUCK—QUIZ 1

Two-Point Questions

1. In our own solar system, which planet is nearest the sun?
2. Is "Solon" famous as the name of a planet, a foreign-make automobile or an Athenian lawmaker?
3. In Salisbury Plain, England, there is a group of ancient stone circles believed to have been temples of the Druids over 4,000 years ago. What is that group of historic ruins called?
4. To "rook" is a slang term meaning to steal from, but in which popular game is a rook used?

Three-Point Questions

1. The Phoenician wife of King Ahab of Israel was a cruel and willful woman. She favored the idolatrous worship of Baal and persecuted the Prophets of Jehovah. What was her name?
2. Which President of the United States coined the now-famous expression, "To the victors belong the spoils"?
3. Sitting Bull led the Indian forces which annihilated the cavalry troop of General Custer on June 25, 1876. Of which great Indian tribe was he a member?
4. In many parts of the world, especially Asia, people still use a counting device that goes back before recorded history. It is a board with beads on it. What is this primitive computer called?

Five-Point Questions

1. What is the square root of .09?
2. According to the Bible, one of Noah's descendants was a mighty hunter. His name is frequently used to denote a successful hunter. Can you give us that name?
3. The Japanese call this movie character Miki Kuchi; the French call him Michel Souris; and in Sweden he is known as Musse Pig. What did Walt Disney call him?
4. The ancient Greeks dedicated a temple to Athena at Athens which is regarded as the finest example of Grecian architecture. It has been called "the one perfect thing created by the hand of man." Can you name that great temple?

(ANSWERS ON PAGE 629)

POT LUCK—QUIZ 2

Two-Point Questions

1. Who is the famous king renowned in song as loving tobacco, food and music?
2. When Roman citizens appeared in public, they wore a loose outer garment made of a semi-circular piece of cloth. Name that garment.
3. What was the name of the Governor of New York who bought the Island of Manhattan from the Indians for $24?
4. In Greek mythology, a woman opened a box Zeus had commanded her to leave closed. She thereby loosed trouble in its many forms upon the world. What was her name?

Three-Point Questions

1. Which book of the New Testament was written by a physician?
2. When she was a child, this girl's mother was executed by order of her father, who practically ignored the child thereafter. Nevertheless, the child later came to the throne and survived many plots against her life and reign. She ruled a great nation for 45 years. What was her name?
3. In the song "Comin' Through the Rye," is the reference to rye meant as a river, a field of grain or a bottle?
4. In what country would you find a gila monster?

Five-Point Questions

1. For uncounted centuries, seals have found their way to a group of islands in the Bering Sea to raise their young. Can you name those islands?
2. An expression has crept into the English language which means to be obsequious, to acknowledge the superiority of another, or to flatter another. The expression is kow-tow. In which language did it originate?
3. Natives of the far Pacific, off the coast of Asia, have taught a large bird (which cannot fly) to stand in shallow waters and catch fish. Can you name that bird?
4. Within two pounds, state how much a cubic foot of water weighs.

(ANSWERS ON PAGES 629–630)

POT LUCK—QUIZ 3

Two-Point Questions

1. Name the author and the play (a tragedy) from which came the world-famous expression about something being rotten in Denmark.
2. In Greek mythology, who ruled the underworld?
3. When Cortez reached Mexico, he found an Indian civilization whose culture and learning exceeded anything he had expected to find in the New World. Which Indians were they?
4. Here is an inscription on a famous statue: "Send these, the homeless, tempest-tossed to me. I lift my lamp beside the golden door!" Can you name that statue?

Three-Point Questions

1. Edmund Burke once described the clergy, the nobility, and the mass of the people as "three estates of mankind." Then he pointed to a group of men attending a meeting of the British Parliament and said, "Yonder sits the Fourth Estate, more powerful than the others." Whom did he mean by the Fourth Estate?
2. Is the bat (the flying variety) more closely related, biologically, to a bird, a butterfly or a cow?
3. Name the inventor in the field of communications who gave the Almighty full credit for his invention by sending this question as its first message: "What hath God wrought?"
4. We know what a ringmaster is in a circus, but do you know what a bushmaster is?

Five-Point Questions

1. A furor was created in England on Christmas Day, 1950, when which famous object involving the history of England and Scotland was stolen from Westminster Abbey?
2. Is a "Janizary" a rare bird, a Roman temple dedicated to the god Janus, or a member of the Sultan's guard?
3. Most green plants get their food from a chemical process for which sunlight provides the energy. What is that process called?
4. Europe and North America might have had an Oriental culture today, had it not been for a Greek general who persuaded the Athenians to build a navy as a defense against the Persians under Xerxes. In 480 B.C., this great Athenian defeated the Persian navy at the

Battle of Salamis and thereby changed the course of history. What was his name?

(ANSWERS ON PAGE 630)

POT LUCK—QUIZ 4

Two-Point Questions

1. In April, 1933, a motorist driving along the shore of a lake in Scotland, saw a marine monster that is thought to be a survivor from prehistoric times. Can you give the name of that monster as given it by the press?
2. In the story "Gone With the Wind," which Southern city was burned to the ground?
3. The *Titanic* was sunk by hitting an iceberg. What sank the *Lusitania?*
4. Can you name the great comet which flashed within view of the earth in 1910?

Three-Point Questions

1. What member of the bird family avoids its egg-sitting responsibilities by laying its eggs in the nests of other birds?
2. Which two legendary children, who are later said to have founded Rome, were saved from death and nursed by a female wolf?
3. Only one of the great cities of the world is situated on two different continents. Can you give either its old or its new name?
4. Brazil is the largest republic of South America. Can you name the smallest?

Five-Point Questions

1. What are the common names for these medical terms: (1) caries, (2) myopia, (3) missing patellar reflex?
2. In Shakespeare's plays, which famous king found himself in such need of a horse that he'd have swapped his kingdom for one?
3. In 1929 a British doctor observed a moldly growth from which penicillin was discovered. What was that eminent doctor's name?
4. In which war did the "Black Death" play an important part—the Crimean War, World War II, the Mexican War, or The Hundred Years War?

(ANSWERS ON PAGE 630)

QUIET GAMES

6

Pencil and Paper Games

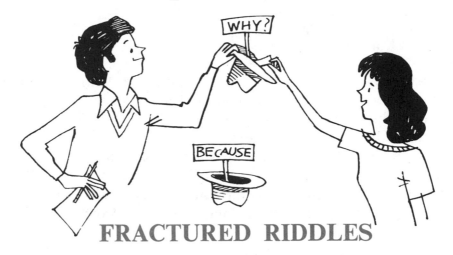

FRACTURED RIDDLES

PLAYERS: 2 or more
EQUIPMENT: Paper and pencil for each player
PREPARATION: None

Give each player 10 or 12 slips of paper or a small pad. Half of them write down on their slips riddle-type questions beginning with "Why?" The others write down as many answers, each starting with "Because." You can use real riddle questions and answers, or make up your own. The less sense and the more nonsense, the better.

When you're all finished, drop the questions into one hat and the answers into another. Shake well and serve: One player draws a question slip and reads it; the next draws an answer slip and reads that. The riddles probably won't make sense, but sometimes they do in a crazy sort of way.

Here are a few samples of what you might get:

Why did your brother set the barn on fire?
Because the mailman was late that day.

Why did Bell invent the telephone?
Because he wanted to get to the other side.

Why don't you grow up?
Because you're in my way.

You'll find some riddles on page 580 which may give you more ideas.

HAM AND EGGS

PLAYERS: 4 or more
EQUIPMENT: Paper and pencil for each player
PREPARATION: Make up a list of "companion" words

There are a great many words in our language that have been used together so often that mentioning one of them immediately makes you think of the other: words such as "Salt" and "Pepper." This game gives you an idea of how many you know.

Pass out a sheet of paper and pencil to each player. Then ask a question, such as "What goes with Cats?" The answer would be "Dogs." The players write their answers as the leader quickly calls out the words to be matched. The person with the longest list of "correct" words is the winner.

Here are some combinations to start off with:

Black and white
Laurel and Hardy
Democrat & Republican
Soap and water

Law and order
Boys and girls
Thunder and lightning
Weak and strong
First and last
Shoes and socks
Bread and butter
Adam and Eve
Abbott and Costello

Brother and sister
Right and wrong
Hide and seek
Big and little
Hands and feet
High and low
Hat and coat
Cops and robbers
Jack and Jill
Mutt and Jeff

Bow and arrow
Knife and fork
Night and day
Dancer and Prancer
Romeo and Juliet
Paper and pencil
Lock and key
Hit and run
Brush and comb
Good and evil
Pen and ink
Donner and Blitzen
Army and Navy
Down and out

FUNNY-GRAMS

PLAYERS: 6–20
EQUIPMENT: A sheet of paper or small pad for every player
                 A pencil for every player
PREPARATION: None

A leader reads a list of 4 or 5 letters of the alphabet. Each person is to write a message using these letters as the first letters of each word, in the order the letters are read.

Suppose the letters given are A, B, D and R. One message might read, "A Bear Does Roar." Others might be, "Annie Bathes Daily, Remember?" or "Anxious Baboons Don't Rest."

After the players have finished making up their Funny-Grams, they take turns reading them out loud, and that's when the fun begins.

Note: After using easy letters to begin with, you can slip in some harder ones—Q, Y, J, etc., and the messages will get even sillier and funnier.

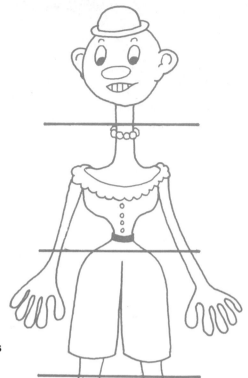

GROUP ART

PLAYERS: 4 or more
EQUIPMENT: A sheet of paper and pencil
         for every group of 4 or 5 players
PREPARATION: None

So you've heard that nothing really good ever came out of a committee? You haven't played Group Art.

Divide the group into smaller groups of 5 players each (or 4 if that works out better). The first player in each group starts at the top of a page and draws the head of a person and the start of a neck. The player then folds over the paper so that only the last bits of the neck lines are showing and passes the page to the next player, who continues the drawing, finishing the neck, putting in shoulders and arms and completing the drawing all the way down past the waist so that 6 lines are sticking out when the paper is folded and passed: 2 lines for each arm, and 2 lines for hips.

The third player continues the arms and draws in hands, completes the bottom of the subject's torso and draws in the upper legs, leaving 4 lines showing when the paper is folded and passed, all for legs.

The fourth player draws in the knees and calves of the creation, down to the ankles, and the fifth finishes off with shoes. If you want to play with a group of 4, the fourth person can finish off the drawing.

Now unfold the sheet and you have a truly original artistic effort —put together by a group. You see? It isn't true what they say. Groups can come up with greatness.

GROUP LIT

PLAYERS: 5 or more
EQUIPMENT: Paper and pencil for each player
PREPARATION: List of installments, as shown below, or your own variations

Like Group Art, this game proves that really fine stories can be written by a team. Your team can be 5 to 10 people. If there are more players, divide up into separate teams. But while the team in Group Art may come up with only one drawing, the team in Group Lit will come up with as many stories as there are players!

Each player is going to write a section of the story, as instructed by the Leader, at the top of a sheet of paper. Then the players will fold back the part of the page they wrote on and pass the paper along to the next player, who does the same thing. As you can see, each player is writing on a different sheet for every installment the Leader calls for.

These are some ideas for installments. The Leader can use these or make up new ones.

1. Write a boy's name and a brief description of him.
2. Write a girl's name and a brief description of her.
3. Write where they met.
4. Where were they supposed to be at the time?
5. How they met.
6. His first words to her.
7. Her first words to him.

At this point, if you're playing in a team of 7 players, the players get back the papers they started. It doesn't matter, just keep them going around. There can be as many installments as you want—as long as the paper holds out.

8. What happened next.
9. What the neighbors said.
10. The consequences.
11. Where they are now.
12. The outlook for the future.

At the end, unfold the papers and each player reads aloud the story he or she has in hand, putting it all together so it reads smoothly. And there you have it—5, 10, 15, or 20 possible plots for the best seller lists—or for unforgettable television viewing!

DOTS

PLAYERS: 2
EQUIPMENT: Pencil and paper
PREPARATION: None

Take a large sheet of paper and make as many rows of dots as you want. Then each player takes a turn and draws a line connecting one dot with the next in any direction—except diagonally—and in any part of the diagram.

Try to connect the dots so that they make little squares. The one to draw the line that finishes a square initials the closed square and then is required to draw an extra line. The player with the most initialed squares wins.

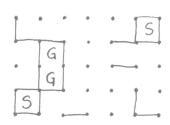

ETERNAL TRIANGLES

PLAYERS: 2
EQUIPMENT: Pencil and paper
PREPARATION: None

This game is similar to Dots. Cover a sheet of paper with dots starting with one in the first row, 2 in the second, 3 in the third, and so on as far as you care to go, as in the diagram here.

Each player in turn draws a line connecting two of the dots either horizontally or diagonally, and the object is to form an enclosed triangle. The player who adds the line which forms the enclosed triangle, initials it and goes again until he or she fails to form a triangle.

The player who makes the most triangles wins.

You can make this game more difficult if you score extra points for larger triangles made at a turn. If you use colored pencils to mark off the larger triangles, you can score them up at the end of the game, or you can score them in the margin as you go along.

SNAKES

PLAYERS: 2–4
EQUIPMENT: Pencil and paper
PREPARATION: None

Here is another relative of Dots.

Set up a bunch of dots on your paper, the same way you did for the previous games. Now, starting anywhere you like, take turns drawing in lines from dot to dot, but don't make boxes. Instead, make a long, stiff snake. No diagonal lines allowed. No skipping spaces.

The winner is the last one to be able to draw a line without connecting the snake to itself.

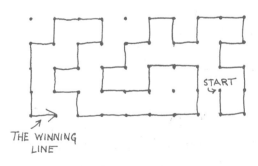

THE WINNING LINE

KETTLE OF FISH

PLAYERS: 2 or more
EQUIPMENT: 36 index cards or small slips of paper
Paper and pencil for each player
PREPARATION: Write out a story, like the one below.

Preparing this game is a game in itself, but playing it is hilarious. Once you have made it up, you can use it over and over again.

First write out the story, in which you substitute a dash (———) for almost all of the nouns. The story should be a meandering tale without much plot, something like this:

> I was walking down the road with ——— in my hand, wondering whether I would ever find ———. Somehow or other I tripped over ——— and while I was getting up, I noticed ——— lying in the ditch. I reached in my pocket and took out ——— and then I got into ——— which was coming down the road. By the time I got to ———, it was noon and I was very hungry so I ate ——— and ———. Then I felt so ill I went to the doctor. He gave me ——— and told me I had ———, etc.

Next take the 3 dozen index cards or slips of paper cut to a size of about 2″ × 3″ (5 cm × 7.5 cm). On the slips or cards the players write a noun or name together with a brief description and the appropriate article. Try for odd combinations and as much variety as possible. Here are a few to give you the idea:

> A pretty kettle of fish
> An old-fashioned nosegay
> Some rotten tomatoes
> Your mother's wedding gown
> The cop on the corner
> A model-T Ford
> George Washington's wig
> Four empty bottles

Place the cards face down in a pile and choose to see who will read the story. Whenever you reach a dash, you turn over one of the cards, taking turns, and read what it says for the missing word.

DOODLEBUG

PLAYERS: 2
EQUIPMENT: Paper and pencil for each player
PREPARATION: None

Each player draws the following diagram:

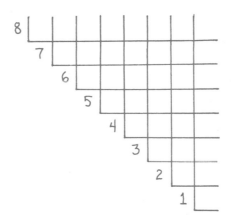

Choose to see who goes first. The first player—Eve—writes a number between 1 and 8, not in one of the boxes, but elsewhere on her paper. She shields her pencil and paper with her other hand, trying to hide what she has written from the other player—Adam. If Adam can guess the number Eve wrote, he gets to write it in the appropriate line of his diagram, and it is his turn to write a hidden number. If Adam guesses wrong, Eve gets to place the number on the appropriate line of her diagram, and she gets another turn.

Note: It's a good idea to cross off the hidden doodle numbers after each turn so that no arguments can arise as to which was the number just written.

The object of the game is to be the player who fills all the boxes of the diagram first. The diagram will then contain eight 8's, seven 7's, six 6's, etc.

Hint: When you doodle a number, either hold your pencil as still as possible so as not to give a clue to the number, or move it wildly to confuse your opponent.

BATTLESHIPS

PLAYERS: 2
**EQUIPMENT: Paper and pencil for each player. (If graph paper is available
that saves time and effort and it's neater.)**
PREPARATION: Each player makes up a 10-square chart (see below).

The object of this popular game is to sink the enemy's ships
before the enemy can sink yours.

Each player has a battleship—made up of 5 squares
a cruiser—made up of 4 squares
a destroyer—made up of 3 squares
a nuclear sub—made up of 2 squares

The first thing each player does is to hide his or her ships. Draw
their outlines into your chart, like this:

Ships can be placed horizontally or vertically, not diagonally.

War is declared.

The first player—Jan—calls out a square by letter and number,
say F5.

The other player—Mike—must tell her whether or not it is a hit.
Look at the sample game below; you see that it was a miss. Jan puts an
O in that box, to show that it was called and it was a miss.

Now it's Mike's turn. He calls B3, which just happens to be
Jan's nuclear sub. Jan admits it is a hit, but she doesn't tell Mike what
kind of ship he hit. Mike puts a big X in that square in his chart. Jan
shades hers.

It's Jan's turn. She calls another square, D6—a hit, Mike tells her. It is his destroyer, but he doesn't tell her that. Jan puts an X in D6. Mike shades D6 in his chart.

Mike's turn. He calls B4. Why? Mike knows that at least one other square is connected to the first hit, since no ship fits in less than 2 squares. It is a hit. But this time, Jan must not only admit to the hit, she must admit that the ship is sunk. Now Mike knows that he sank Jan's submarine, so he darkens in both submarine squares. He knows from that that he doesn't have to try to make more hits right around that area. The next time Mike's turn comes up, he'll call a square on the other side of the chart, or further down.

The charts now look like this:

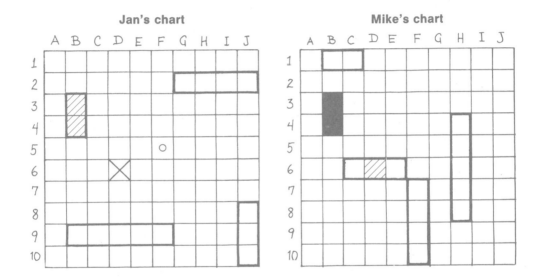

The game goes on in the same way until one player has sunk all the other player's ships.

About the charts: This game is often played with each player keeping up two charts, one to represent his or her own ships and the squares the enemy has called, and the other to show the calls the player has made and the hits scored. The two-chart method may be helpful when an adult is playing with a small child who may make mistakes in recording his or her own hits. Then the adult can help clear up any confusion. Otherwise, one chart seems to do the job very well.

HANGMAN GROWS UP

PLAYERS: 2
EQUIPMENT: Paper and pencil
PREPARATION: None

You need to know how to play Hangman, in order to play Hangman Grows Up. Just in case you don't know how, here is a speedy explanation.

Draw a gallows (an upside down L), think of a word (don't say it aloud) and dash off a string of dashes, one for each letter in the word. Then print the alphabet at the bottom of the page.

Your opponent must guess, one letter at a time, the word you've chosen. If a guess of a letter is correct, write it in at the appropriate place so your opponent can see it and strike it off in the alphabet below. If the letter appears in your word more than once, put it in wherever it belongs.

If your opponent guesses wrong, strike the letter out of the alphabet and draw in a head at the end of the gallows.

For each wrong letter guessed, draw in another body part; two more wrong guesses would give two eyes; another two would supply ears, a sixth would give a mouth; the seventh a torso, and the next four would add arms and legs. If you want to make the game longer, go on to hands and shoes.

> **Note:** Long, complicated words are easier, not harder than short words. Short words containing the less frequently used letters are the most difficult to guess, words such as *why, fox, bay, ski, tax,* and even *yore*. Even if your opponent guessed *o-r-e* quickly, think of all the letters that would probably come up before getting to Y!

Hangman Grows Up

If you have become expert at Hangman, you'll be ready for Hangman Grows Up. Instead of words, substitute other categories for the dashes. You might do it with proverbs or famous sayings (see page 584 for a supply of these), or with famous books or movies or plays. How about famous people in history? Athletes? Song titles? The possibilities are endless. But because you get more clues than in regular Hangman, two parts are hung every time you miss.

G O N E   W I T H
T H E   W I N D

A B C D E F G H I J K L M N O P Q
R S T U V W X Y Z

Double Hanging

If an adult and child are playing together, they might want to try this variation on the game to make it more of a contest.

When it is the younger player's turn, he or she chooses two words and strings them out under the gallows. Then as the adult guesses, the younger one puts in the letters wherever they belong in both words. But when a letter appears in only one of the words a part is hung for the miss on the other word. If the letter appears in neither word, two parts are hung.

Z E U S

_ O R _

A B C D E F G H I J K L M N O P Q R S T U V W X Y Z

TIC-TAC-TOE SQUARED

You probably know how to play tic-tac-toe (Noughts and Crosses, see page 38):

But Tic-tac-toe Squared will be a bit more of a challenge. Make the same tic-tac-toe box that you always make, but then close the edges:

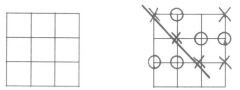

And play the X's and O's on the intersections instead of in the boxes. You need 3 in a row to win.

TIC-TAC-TOE-TOE

If you get tired of Tic-Tac-Toe Squared, try this variation. Draw five lines across and five lines down, for a 4-box playing area (16 boxes in all):

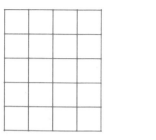
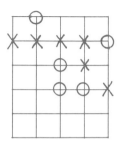

And play the X's and the O's on the intersections again, but this time you need four in a row to win.

GO-BANG

PLAYERS: 2–4
EQUIPMENT: Graph paper. Pencils
PREPARATION: None

There are any number of names for this game. People play it all over the world and call it something different. Even within a country it is called by other names.

You can play it on paper or on a pegboard with pegs or on a checkerboard—on any surface that is marked off in boxes. If you play it on paper, it is much easier to use graph paper.

The object of the game is to take turns writing in X's and O's, as in Tic-Tac-Toe Squared (on the intersections), until you get five X's or five O's in a row. If you are a skillful player, this game can go on and on!

> **Hint:** Beware of a row of three X's or O's. When you see it, quickly stop it with your mark, because once your opponent gets four in a row—with nothing limiting it on either end—the game is over.

Three people or four can play this game, but it is best as a contest for two players. If you play with as many as four, use triangles and squares as well as X's and O's.

```
        O wins                          ∇ wins


            X                              X  X  X  X
            X                              X  X [∇]
    O  O  X  X  X                  O  O  O  X  X [∇]
  [O  O  O  O  O] X                O  □  O  O  ∇ [∇] ∇
    O  O  O  X                     ∇  □  □  □  □ [∇]
    X  X  O  X                               [∇]
            X
```

GUGGENHEIM

PLAYERS: 5 or more
EQUIPMENT: Paper and pencil for each player
PREPARATION: Trace the Guggenheim frame on each sheet and write in the names of categories.

Guggenheim say: Do not be fooled by apparent simplicity of Guggenheim. Guggenheim easy to play, difficult to win.

Give each player a pencil and the sheet of paper with the Guggenheim framework on it. It should look like this:

	Animal	City	Flower	Food
H				
O				
S				
P				
I				
T				
A				
L				

Leave blanks for each item except the categories (Animal, etc.) and the Guggenheim word (in this case, HOSPITAL). If you don't want to select the word ahead of time, ask the players for an 8- to 10-letter word which will be the Guggenheim subject. Then have them fill in the initial letters of HOSPITAL, as it is filled in here, down the side of the page.

The players get about five minutes to fill in the blanks, without collaboration. You can give them more time, if you want. As the model shows, the first category (Animal) must line up with the first letter of the Guggenheim word, and it must begin with that letter. And so on, down the line.

Players who choose obvious answers, such as those in the illustration, are *not* likely to win. The idea is to get unique items and places to fill in the squares—without consulting a dictionary or atlas or any other book!

The score can be figured in different ways: each player can get a point for the number of people who did *not* write the same word. For example, if you have 15 players, and Gordon's word was not repeated by anyone present, Gordon would get a score of 15. If two other people wrote down Gerry's word, she would score 13. If six people wrote Min's word, she would get a score of 9. If everyone wrote down Arthur's word, everyone would get 1 point.

Another way to keep score is to give 5 points to any person who has a unique word; 3 points to players whose word was only repeated once, and 1 point to a 3-person word, with no score at all for the others.

The highest number of points wins.

For a super game, choose words with double letters like GUGGENHEIM and BOOKKEEPER and use more column headings, such as Vegetable, Mineral, Nation, Athlete, Actor, Politician, Dessert, Monster, Dog, Author, Cartoon Character, Nursery Rhyme Character, Fairy Tale Character, Hero, River, Mountain, Television Detective, Comedian, Beverage, Emotion, Characteristic, Part of Body, Game, College, City, Flower, Clothing.

	Animal	*City*	*Flower*	*Food*
H	Hyena	Honolulu	Honeysuckle	Ham
O	Ostrich	Oslo	Orchid	Orange
S	Steer	Sydney	Sweet Pea	Spaghetti
P	Pig	Plymouth	Poppy	Pizza
I	Iguana	Indianapolis	Iris	Ice Cream
T	Tiger	Tokyo	Tulip	Toast
A	Alligator	Adelaide	Apple blossom	Apricot
L	Leopard	London	Lily	Lettuce

EPPIZOOTICS

PLAYERS: 2
EQUIPMENT: Paper and pencil for each player
PREPARATION: None

Each player draws a square made up of 6 lines in each direction—so that you have 5 boxes horizontally and 5 boxes vertically.

The first person calls out a letter—P, for example. Both players insert a P in one of the squares, anywhere they want. The next player calls out another letter, and they each place this in one of the squares. Each player in turn calls out a letter until 25 letters have been announced. They must write down each letter before the next one is called. There is no restriction on the letters you can use, and you can repeat them any number of times.

Each player, as the letters are called, tries to arrange them within the squares in such a way as to make them spell the maximum number of words horizontally and vertically; the best you could hope to get would be 10 5-letter words!

Proper nouns do not count. Neither do foreign words. And no erasing is allowed!

If you are given a letter which you cannot manage to work into the words you are trying to form, you have to put it down anyway, wherever you think it will do the most good—or the least harm!

For instance, if you have s-e-p-a-r and want to make s-p-e-a-r out of them, you cannot. But you can count the 3-letter word "par" as one of your words. If you have s-u-n-a-p, you can count either "sun" or "nap" but not both.

Scoring is 10 points for a 5-letter word, 5 points for a 4-letter word, and 3 points for a 3-letter word.

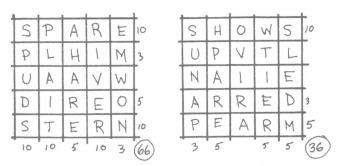

The same letters can give you 66 points—or 36!

Schizophrenic Eppizootics

Each player can use 2 Eppizootics squares at the same time, putting the letters in either one, as they are called.

Here are a few hints: Plan to use flexible words—those which still remain words despite the change of a letter or two, so that you can make the best use of the letters your opponent chooses. Try not to give the more common letters, which you can reasonably expect your opponents to give you. Save the "toughies" like "K" or "X" for late in the game when they will give your opponents the worst jolt.

WORD BRIDGES

PLAYERS: 2 or more
EQUIPMENT: Paper and pencil for each player
PREPARATION: None

Be an architect of words and see who can build the longest Word Bridge with pencil and paper. Each player draws 6 horizontal lines across the paper, and then one gets first choice in selecting a word of 6 letters. Write the word vertically down the page, one letter at the beginning of each line. Then write the word up from the bottom, one letter at the *end* of each line.

```
F  ........................................  R
E  ........................................  E
N  ........................................  D
D  ISINTEGRATIO  N
E  ........................................  E
R  ........................................  F
```

Each game lasts 3 minutes. At the word "Go" you each start to fill in the 6 bridges with words starting and ending with the letters that are already there. The longer the word the better. When the game is over, you score as follows:

The player with the longest word for each bridge gets 5 points. Then add up the total number of letters used for all 6 words. The player with the highest total score subtracts the next highest score and adds the difference to his or her total score. The first player to win 50 points, or 100 points, if you want to play a longer game, is the winner.

SPROUTS

PLAYERS: 2
EQUIPMENT: Paper
           Pencil for each player
PREPARATION: None

In this game you start with just three or four dots on a piece of paper, and join them together. But it's not like the other games you've played because here the line doesn't have to be straight. It can be straight, if you want, but it's more interesting when it "sprouts" in

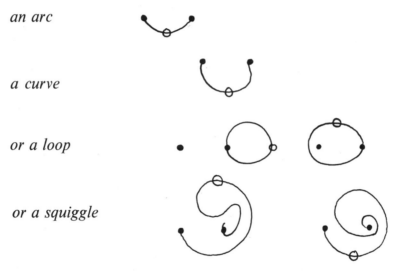

an arc

a curve

or a loop

or a squiggle

For example, start with good solid dots—in fact, let's call them *blops*. Then take turns joining one blop to another and after you finish, put a new blop somewhere on the line.

What's the catch? You may not cross a line

(dotted line is illegal)

and no blop may have more than 3 sprouts coming out of it. As soon as you attach your third sprout to the blop, put a slash through it (it makes it easier to see) so that you know that blop is out of play. When you get expert, maybe you'll decide to leave the slashes out.

The winner is the one who makes the last possible move.

Here is a game you might play:

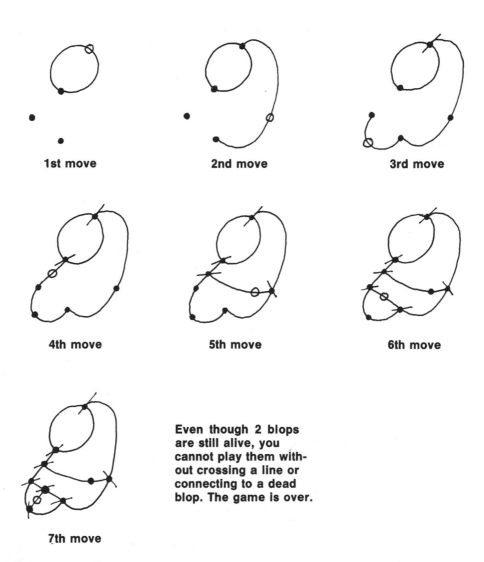

1st move

2nd move

3rd move

4th move

5th move

6th move

7th move

Even though 2 blops are still alive, you cannot play them without crossing a line or connecting to a dead blop. The game is over.

Part of the fun of Sprouts is that while you're sprouting and blopping, you're creating a very weird picture. Try it!

GIBBERISH

PLAYERS: 2 or more
EQUIPMENT: Paper and pencil for each player
PREPARATION: None

Each player writes out a well-known proverb, running the letters all together, like this:

Astitchintimesavesnine.

Now break it up at odd intervals, like this:

Ast it chint imesa vesni ne.

Exchange papers and see who can be first to write out the proverb correctly. If you want to make the game last longer, each can write a number of proverbs, 5 apiece, or even 10—for the others to solve. You might find yourself looking at what seems to be a brand new conglomeration but turns out to be the same proverb you have given your opponent!

For more proverbs, see page 584.

EVERY OTHER

PLAYERS: 2 or more
EQUIPMENT: Paper and pencil for each player
PREPARATION: None

Crossword puzzle fans should do well playing Every Other. It's a game which you first make up for each other, and then solve.

Armed with pencil and paper, each player makes out a list of 10 words (or any number you agree on), but omits every other letter. To put it another way, write down every other letter, starting with the second letter of each word you've chosen. Then, next to each word, write a synonym or brief definition—preferably humorous or tricky.

For example, your list might contain:

- I - F - R - N - E   **meaning REMAINDER (difference)**
- I - T - O - A - Y   **meaning WORDY BOOK (dictionary)**
- A - H - O - A - L - **meaning OF THE LATEST STYLE (fashionable)**

As you can see, it's easier to make them up than to puzzle them out! Set a time limit for each phase of the game, and after you've played it a few times, try playing without any definitions!

CAT-ASTROPHE

PLAYERS: 2 or more
EQUIPMENT: Pencil and paper for each player
PREPARATION: None

For a long-playing pencil and paper game, choose a simple 3-letter word like "cat." Set a time limit of from 15 to 30 minutes, and at a signal, start listing as many words as possible containing the word you've decided on. The word may occur in any part of the longer word, but it must be intact.

For instance, if "cat," is your word, you may use *catastrophe, cater, abdicate, prevaricate, scatter*, etc., but not *castle* or *intact*.

If you choose the word "pen," your list might contain *penny, repent, open,* etc.

The player with the longest list is the winner.

WORD HUNT

PLAYERS: 1 or more
EQUIPMENT: Paper and pencil for each player
PREPARATION: None

This game is simple and fun, and once you start playing it, you don't want to stop.

Take a word of about 8 or 10 letters, and see how many words you can form from the letters in it, changing their order, of course. If a letter appears twice in the original word, you can use it twice to make words with it. If it appears only once, you can use it only once. No proper names, no foreign words allowed.

You can play the game with various rules. The most common way is to use any words of 4 or more letters. No fair adding an "s" to a 3-letter word.

You might want to play by allowing only 5-letter words.

Winner is the one with the longest list.

Hint: It is easier to keep track of your words and not duplicate them if you set up your page by numbering down in the left-hand margin, and then starting each column of words with a different letter (see below):

HAPPINESS

1	happen	apse	pine	sane	nape
2	hasp	aspen	pane	sine	
3	hiss	ashen	pass	spine	
4			pain	shine	
5				snip	
6				snap	
7				spin	
8				shin	
9				ship	
10				shape	
11				snipe	

Here are some words to start with. If you want to test yourself against this book, you'll find lists of 4-and-more letter words on pages 631 and 632. Allow yourself 10 minutes for each hunt, 1 point for each word.

AMELIORATE
Poor	0– 25
Fair	26– 50
Good	51– 80
Very Good	81–100
Excellent	over 100

DEVELOPING
Poor	0–20
Fair	21–30
Good	31–40
Very Good	41–60
Excellent	over 60

IRREGULARLY
Poor	0–15
Fair	16–25
Good	26–35
Very Good	36–45
Excellent	over 45

CONSTRUCTION
Poor	0–20
Fair	21–30
Good	31–45
Very Good	46–60
Excellent	over 60

ESTABLISH
Poor	0–20
Fair	21–30
Good	31–40
Very Good	41–60
Excellent	over 60

PRECIOUS
Poor	0–15
Fair	16–25
Good	26–35
Very Good	36–45
Excellent	over 45

LONGEST WORD

PLAYERS: 2 or more
EQUIPMENT: Paper and pencil for each player
PREPARATION: None

You start this game with a one-letter word (A or I) and add letters one at a time. Each time you add a new letter it must form another word, and at no time can you change the order of the previous letters. But you may add the new letter at the beginning or the end, or insert it anywhere inside the word. The object is to see who can form the longest word.

Here is a sample game:

A
AY
SAY
STAY
STRAY
ASTRAY
ASHTRAY
ASHTRAYS

When you arrive at the final word, tell it to your opponents. They must then play the game in reverse and take the letters away one by one until they arrive back at the original one-letter word.

TRANSMIGRATION OF WORDS

PLAYERS: 1 or more
EQUIPMENT: Paper and pencil for each player
PREPARATION: None

How many steps from lamb to wolf? We made it in nine.

The idea is to progress from one word to the other by changing one letter at a time. With each one-letter change, you must form a new word. For instance, this is one way to get from lamb to wolf:

lamb
lame
lane
sane
sale
sole
sold
gold
golf
wolf

Maybe you can do it in fewer steps.

Start by selecting a pair of 4-letter words at random—or you can choose a pair with amusing or contrasting association. Both players write down the same pair of words, and set a time limit of 5 or 10 minutes. Now see who can transmigrate in the fewest steps. In case of a tie, the one who finishes first is the winner.

THE BIG LIST GAME

Are you a list-maker? If so, this ultimate list game is what you've been waiting for.

On the following pages are the rules for 6 different categories:

Boys' Names
Girls' Names
Animals
Food Plants
Countries, States and Islands
Important Cities of the World

What you need to do is write down every item you can think of that fits into the list you're working on. Let's say you pick *Animals*. First read the rules of the category. Then write down every animal you can think of that begins with A, then with B, and so on through the alphabet. If you can come up with at least one animal for every letter, you get an automatic bonus score of 200 points. Then look at the list on pages 599 through 601 and find the number ratings for all the animal names you wrote down. For example, *Ape* is worth only one point, because it is such a familiar creature. But *Anoa* would be worth 10 points, because it is little known. Then see how you made out, with the Rating Chart on the "rules" page.

Note: Keep your list divided by letter, so that all A's are together, all B's, etc. It is easier to score that way.

You can play this game in a group and see who scores the highest, or alone and compete against yourself. After you've done the same category a few times, you become an expert.

Happy list-making!

BOYS' NAMES

See the instructions for The Big List Game on page 323.

This is an almost endless category, and you'll find more names than you care to know about in the list on pages 590 to 595—and many rare names have been left out for space purposes. If you come up with a name which does not appear in the list in the book, and it is:

(1) in a name book or
(2) in the dictionary or
(3) known to you because you know someone by that name, or
(4) accepted by the group,

give yourself 10 points for it. Do *not* give yourself 10 points if the name is pronounced exactly the same way as another name which is listed—but spelled differently. Give yourself the number of points for the name that sounds the same. Foreign names *are* allowed.

Allow yourself half an hour to make up your list.

BONUS: For a bonus of 200 points, you must come up with a name for every letter of the alphabet.

Rating Chart

Over 200	Excellent
175–200	Very Good
150–175	Good
125–150	Fair
Below 125	Poor

(SEE LIST ON PAGES 590-595.)

GIRLS' NAMES

See the instructions for The Big List Game on page 323.

Here is another category that goes on and on. Again, many rare names have been left out for space purposes. If you come up with a name which does not appear in the list and it is

(1) in a name book or
(2) in the dictionary or
(3) known to you because you know someone by that name, or
(4) accepted by the group

give yourself 10 points for it. Do not give yourself 10 points if the name is pronounced exactly the same way as another name which is listed—but spelled differently. Give yourself the number of points for the name that sounds the same. Foreign names *are* allowed.

Allow yourself half an hour to make up your list.

BONUS: For a bonus of 200 points, you must come up with a name for every letter of the alphabet.

Rating Chart

Over 200	**Excellent**
175–200	**Very Good**
150–175	**Good**
125–150	**Fair**
Below 125	**Poor**

(SEE LIST ON PAGES 595-599.)

LAND ANIMALS—MAMMALS

See the instructions for The Big List Game on page 323.

All the animals listed in this category are mammals. No birds or insects, fishes or marine mammals are included. The list does not include breeds of dogs or cats, either. If you come up with the name of an animal which does not appear in the list on pages 599 to 601, and it is

    (1) in the dictionary
    (2) in some other reference work
    (3) agreed to by the group, if you are playing this game at a party,

give yourself 10 points for it. Any mammal on earth is fair game.

Allow yourself about 20 minutes to make up your list.

BONUS: In this category, give yourself a bonus of 200 points for a complete alphabet, even if you don't have an animal name for U, Q or X.

Rating Chart

Over 100	Excellent
70–100	Very Good
50– 70	Good
30– 50	Fair
Below 30	Poor

(SEE LIST ON PAGES 599-601.)

FOOD PLANTS

See the instructions for The Big List Game on page 323.

If it grows and is eaten—or used to spice other foods—it belongs in this list. Here you'll find fruits and vegetables, grains and nuts and herbs from all over the world. If you come up with an edible plant that does not appear in the list and it is

(1) in the dictionary or
(2) in some other reference work or
(3) accepted by the group

give yourself 10 points for it.

Allow yourself 20 minutes to make up your list.

BONUS: **In this category, give yourself a bonus of 200 points for a complete alphabet even if you don't have a plant name for the letter U.**

Rating Chart
Over 100	**Excellent**
70–100	**Very Good**
50–70	**Good**
30–50	**Fair**
Under 30	**Poor**

(SEE LIST ON PAGES 601-603.)

COUNTRIES AND DEPENDENCIES OF THE WORLD

See the instructions for The Big List Game on page 323.

In this category, you'll find every nation in the world, plus the states of Australia, Brazil, Canada, China, Malaysia, Mexico, the U.S.A., the U.S.S.R., and Yugoslavia. You'll also find the principal islands and island groups. If you come up with a place that does not appear in the list in the book and it is

(1) listed in an atlas as a country, state or island, or
(2) listed in the dictionary in the same way, or
(3) accepted by the group

give yourself 10 points for it.

Allow yourself half an hour to make up your list.

BONUS: In this category, give yourself a bonus of 200 points for a complete alphabet even if you don't have a place for X.

Rating Chart
Over 200	Excellent
150–200	Very Good
125–150	Good
100–125	Fair
Below 100	Poor

(SEE LIST ON PAGES 603-605.)

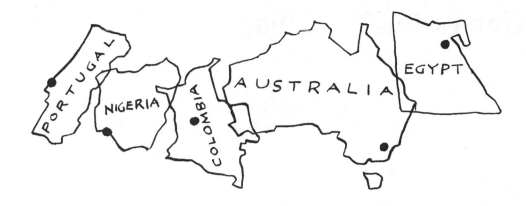

IMPORTANT CITIES OF THE WORLD

See the instructions for The Big List Game on page 323.

In this category you'll find the capitals of most of the countries of the world, plus major populated areas. If you come up with a city which is not in the list and it is

(1) mentioned in an almanac as a major populated area
(2) listed in an atlas as a major city
(3) accepted by the group

give yourself 10 points for it.

Allow yourself half an hour to make up your list.

BONUSES: **If you are able to list both city *and* the country it is in, double the listed rating.**
In this category, give yourself a bonus of 200 points for a complete alphabet even if you don't have a city for X.

Rating Chart
Over 200   **Excellent**
175–200   **Very Good**
125–175   **Good**
100–125   **Fair**
Below 100 **Poor**

(SEE LIST ON PAGES 605-607.)

Games for Travelling

GEOGRAPHY AND OTHER "END-GAMES"

PLAYERS: 2 or more
EQUIPMENT: None
PREPARATION: None

These are ideal games to play on a car trip, especially for the person holding the map!

In basic Geography, the person who starts the game gives the name of a city or state or country or island or body of water or mountain. It is up to the next person to name another place—whose name begins with the same letter that the first place ended with.

Here is a sample game:

> PLAYER #1: Brisbane.
> PLAYER #2: England.
> PLAYER #3: Denmark.
> PLAYER #4: Kentucky.
> PLAYER #5: York.
> PLAYER #6: Kansas.
> PLAYER #1: Suva.
> PLAYER #2: Atlanta.
> PLAYER #3: Australia.

When a player can't think of a place that begins with the right letter, that player is out. The game continues until there is just one person left in it, the winner.

For a name like "Islands" the last letter is "s", "River" is "r"; the first name doesn't count if "Islands" and "River" are announced as part of the name.

No place name may be said more than once. Since, after the game has been going for a while, some players take very long (and boring) amounts of time to come up with a name, it is a good idea to set a time limit for each player. The shorter the time limit, the more interesting the game.

Hint: One of the problems with the game is that once you get started naming places beginning with A, it seems that most of them end with A, too, and the game can get bogged down. Here are some A's that don't end in A, to use when you need them:

Aberdeen	Alsace	Arctic Circle
Abilene	Amalfi	Arctic Ocean
Abingdon	Amarillo	Arezzo
Acapulco	Amazon River	Arkansas
Adelaide	Ames	Armentieres
Adrian	Amherst	Armidale
Aegean Islands	Amsterdam	Arnhem
Afghanistan	Anaheim	Arno River
Aiken	Anchorage	Asheville
Alamo	Anderson	Assisi
Albany	Andes Mountains	Athens
Albion	Andover	Atlantic City
Albuquerque	Annapolis	Atlantic Ocean
Alderney	Ann Arbor	Auburn
Aldershot	Antibes	Austin
Aleutian Islands	Antioch	Avignon
Algiers	Antwerp	Avon River
Alice Springs	Anzio	Ayers Rock
Allentown	Appalachian Mountains	Azores

OTHER END-GAMES

You can play Geography with any other subject your group is interested in. If you're into theatre, you can do it with plays or movies. The only problem is that so many titles end in E that you quickly run out of E's. It makes the game more interesting if you either outlaw any title that ends with E, after a certain point in the game, or agree to use the next-to-last letter when E titles run out.

You can play it with songs if you're into music, with characters in books, with athletes' names, or names of movie stars. Make up your own rules to ease your way over the rough spots (like that E problem), and have a good trip!

GHOST AND DOUBLE GHOST

PLAYERS: 2–4
EQUIPMENT: None
PREPARATION: None

Ghost is a game of word building. The first player says a letter—any letter—which begins a word and the next player adds a letter to it. The object of the game is to force one of the other players to complete a word by the addition of his or her letter, and avoid forming a complete word yourself. Three-letter words don't count.

The player who ends the word gets the "G" of the word *Ghost*. The second miss makes for an H, the third an O. Whoever becomes a G-H-O-S-T first loses.

You must have a word in mind when you add a letter to the word-in-process. If the other player can't think of a word which can be formed from the letters already given, you may be challenged. Then, if you can produce a word, it counts as a miss for the player who challenged you. If you are bluffing, with no real word in mind, you lose and become a fifth more of a ghost than you were before.

That's plain Ghost. In Double Ghost the first player starts by giving two letters. Then the next player can add one letter either at the beginning or at the end.

Here is a sample game:

JOE: RT.

FLO: ORT.

JOE: ORT-H.

FLO: (She doesn't want to make it "north," but "northerly" is a word.) ORTH-E.

JOE: ORTHE-R.

FLO: (Suddenly realizing that "northerly" ends on her, but that "northern" will end on Joe) ORTHER-N.

JOE: (hoping that Flo will not think of the word "northernmost," and will challenge him) ORTHERN-M.

And the game continues until NORTHERNMOST is reached and Joe becomes a G of a ghost.

SUPER-GHOST

Only for people with wonderful vocabularies: try playing Double Ghost adding two letters each time!

BOTTICELLI

PLAYERS: 2–10
EQUIPMENT: None
PREPARATION: None

Botticelli (pronounced Bah-ti-*CHELL*-ee) is one of the great guessing games, and it can be played by anyone from 8 up. The more knowledgeable the group, the more fun the game.

One player thinks of a person, real or fictional, living or dead, and tells the group only the first letter of the person's last name. The others have to guess who it is, but they are only allowed to guess if they already have someone in mind. For instance, let's say the subject is Botticelli, the Italian artist. Here is part of a game:

MARK: I am a famous person whose name begins with B.

HAL: Are you a famous composer? (*He is thinking of Beethoven.*)

MARK: No, I am not Bach.

LIZ: Are you a character from the comics?

MARK: No, I am not Charlie Brown.

LAEL: Are you a comedy writer?

MARK: No, I am not Mel Brooks.

JIM: Are you an actor?

MARK: No, I am not Charles Bronson.

HAL: (*Still trying for Beethoven but he can't ask the same question the same way twice*) Are you a composer who went deaf?

MARK: No, I am not Beethoven.

(*Hal revealed too much. It would have been better if he had known some obscure fact about Beethoven that would disguise his idea so that Mark would not have thought of Beethoven so easily.*)

LIZ: Are you a U.S. President?

MARK: (*stumped*) I challenge you.

LIZ: Buchanan!

(*Liz, having stumped Mark, gets a leading question, which will help the group find out who Mark is. The leading question must be one that can be answered "yes" or "no."*)

LIZ: Are you male?

MARK: (*must answer a leading question truthfully*) Yes.

LAEL: Are you a famous painter? (*She is thinking of Botticelli.*)

MARK: Yes, but I am not Bosch.

(*Mark had to admit that Lael had guessed the right category. But he didn't have to admit that he was Botticelli as long as he could think of another painter beginning with B.*)

JIM: Are you a famous general?

MARK: (*stumped again*) I challenge you.

JIM: Napoleon Bonaparte! I get a leading question. Are you alive?

MARK: No.

HAL: Are you a famous comedian?

MARK: No, I am not Jack Benny.

LIZ: Are you a pioneer?

MARK: No, I am not Daniel Boone.

LAEL: (*Still trying for Botticelli*) Are you a famous Italian painter?

MARK: Yes, but I am not Michelangelo Buonarroti.

(*Now Lael is stumped. She doesn't know any more facts about Botticelli that she can use to ask another question. She cannot repeat her last question without changing it a little. She has to wait for a chance at a leading question before she can pinpoint the person. If she gets to stump Mark again, before anyone else does, she can ask if it is Botticelli, and then she will be the next one to think of a person.*)

BOTTICELLI FOR EXPERTS

For a much more difficult game, the players restrict their questions each time they get information through leading questions.

For example, once the players know that the subject is male, they can ask questions about only male subjects. Once they know, from a leading question, that the person is dead, they can ask questions only about dead people. Don't try this unless you're really a super-Botticelli player!

HINKY-PINKY

PLAYERS: 2 or more
EQUIPMENT: None
PREPARATION: None

You can play Hinky-Pinky anywhere—at home, out walking, in train, car or plane, and even by mail. Anyone can go first by merely announcing, "I have a Hinky-Pinky," a "Hink-Pink" or "Hinkity-Pinkity."

A Hinky-Pinky consists of a phrase of two 2-syllable rhyming words, such as "Silly filly." You describe your Hinky-Pinky and the other player must guess what it is.

For instance, you might say, "I have a Hinky-Pinky meaning an unpleasant part of the face," and the other players must guess the answer. In this case, the answer is "a horrid forehead."

A Hink-Pink consists of two one-syllable words. An example might be "an enormous boat." The answer, of course, is "a large barge."

Hinkity-Pinkities are rare, with 3 syllables apiece. Would you believe a 4-syllable one? How about "Kojak couldn't hold onto a whirly bird"? The answer would be "Telly dropped a helicopter."

As you can see, it's as much fun to make up Hinky-Pinkies as it is to guess them. You can make your definitions easy or hard.

Try these:

1. King Kong.
2. Powerful sleepwear.
3. Revolting couple.
4. Hamlet's mother.
5. A less healthy heart.
6. A wicked insect.
7. Small space vehicle.
8. A fat ape.
9 A hen who doesn't want to be picked up.
10. Order to serve an animal cooked to your taste.
   (hinkety-pinkety)

(SOLUTIONS ON PAGE 632)

336 Quiet Games

SENTENCE UP MY SLEEVE

PLAYERS: 2
EQUIPMENT: Paper and pencil for each player
PREPARATION: None

Did you ever see a magician "force" a card? He asks you to select a card, but actually the card you take is the one he wants you to have. (You'll find a few of these tricks in Chapter 4.)

The object of this game is to force a sentence on your opponent in such a way that he or she doesn't recognize it as a "force."

To begin with, each of you writes a simple sentence on a slip of paper and then pockets the slip. Now you start a conversation together in which you take turns saying a sentence. Your sentences may be statements or questions, but don't forget that you must actually converse, with your remarks following each other in some sort of sense and sequence.

Meanwhile, you are trying to guide conversation in such a manner that you can use your secret sentence. You aim to be able to use it logically, so that your opponent can't spot it as the pre-arranged sentence. Your opponent, meanwhile, is trying to jockey the conversation to the point where he or she can use a different sentence on you! And at the same time, both of you are trying to spot the phony sentence. If you suspect a sentence is being forced, call STOP. If you're right, you get 2 points. If you're wrong, your opponent gets 2 points. If you "get away" with your sentence—use it without your opponent's recognizing it—you get 5 points.

By the way, it's perfectly fair to try to look guilty when you're delivering an innocent sentence—and vice versa!

Some examples of secret sentences:
Elephants wear trunks when they go swimming.
It is dangerous to play football in August.
All dogs enjoy eating peanut butter cookies.

Games for Travelling

COFFEEPOT

PLAYERS: 2–12
EQUIPMENT: None
PREPARATION: None

In this game "coffeepot" becomes a verb—a verb which you (or your group) think up secretly and which your opponent must guess by asking a series of questions. In each question the word "Coffeepot" is used for the hidden verb, and the questions must be answerable by "yes" or "no."

Suppose you are on the guessing end of the game. You might start with, "Do people Coffeepot?"

"Do I Coffeepot?"

"Do you Coffeepot?"

"Do all human beings Coffeepot?"

If the answer to the last question is no, you will need to narrow down the field and find out if only boys Coffeepot or perhaps only old people, or only married women, etc. After you find out, or if you don't seem to be getting any results, try another tack: Do you need any tools to Coffeepot? Do you Coffeepot only in certain places or at certain times of the year or of the day? Do animals Coffeepot? Is Coffeepotting fun? Difficult? Part of a job? A natural function?

Too old to coffeepot?

Too young?

After you have narrowed down the field and think you are pretty sure you know what "Coffeepot" is, you get three guesses. It's a good idea, though, to ask as many specific questions as possible before you guess.

Suppose you've found out that young people Coffeepot but not small children; that you Coffeepot outdoors; that you don't Coffeepot in the dark; that you Coffeepot in warm weather; that you use a long pole to Coffeepot; that neither you nor your opponent Coffeepot yourselves; and that Coffeepotting takes skill, strength and practice. You think the answer may be "to pole vault." Then you might check to make sure by asking, "Do you need a very high hurdle to Coffeepot?" If the answer is yes, you know that you are right.

If you're playing Coffeepot in a group at a party, let one person go out of the room while the others decide what Coffeepot is. Then the guesser comes back in and asks each player one or more questions. When the guesser gets the answer, he or she selects the next one to guess.

If you're in close quarters in a car, and more than two want to play, let one person select the Coffeepot word, while the others ask the questions.

DANCE DARINGLY IN DENMARK

PLAYERS: 2 or more
EQUIPMENT: None
PREPARATION: None

This game is a grown-up version of "A My Name is Alice."

One player starts by saying, "I'm taking a trip to Afghanistan (for example). What will I do there?"

The next player must answer with a verb and another word beginning with the same letter as the name of the place.

"Act arrogant," would be a possible answer.

Then player #2 poses a similar question: "I'm taking a trip to Barcelona," for example.

Player #3 answers that you will "Bake Biscuits in Barcelona," and then throws a C to Player #4, who may "can candy in Canberra," and so on.

When a player fails to answer for the third time, with a reasonable period elapsing after each question, that player is ruled out of the game. Winner is the last player left.

20 QUESTIONS

PLAYERS: 2 or more
EQUIPMENT: None
PREPARATION: None

Twenty Questions is a far better game than most people realize, or it can be if you use a little imagination when you choose your subject. It is one of the simplest guessing games, and people of all ages can play it.

One person thinks of a person, place or thing and announces to the group whether it is animal, vegetable or mineral.

Animal is anything from a human being to a sponge in the "animal kingdom," but it can also be anything made from an animal skin (like a leather wallet) or it can be part of an animal, like the great white shark's jaws or a strip of bacon. It can also be groups of people—like all the people who live in downtown Burbank, or all the people who go out on blind dates. It can be supernatural creatures, like Superman or Frankenstein, or nursery rhyme characters like Mary, Mary, Quite Contrary. It can also be part of a fictional person, like Dracula's tooth.

Vegetable is anything in the plant kingdom. It can be something that grows on trees or in the ground. It can be something made from things that grow—like paper or a book, like perfume, or spaghetti. It can also be penicillin (made from bread mold), a hot water bottle or skis—or some specific thing, like the Pines of Rome, the poison apple the Wicked Queen prepared for Snow White, or all the French fries that McDonald's serves in a year.

Mineral is just about everything else—rocks and stones, but also water, salt, glass, plastic or the Emerald City of Oz.

Back to the game: One player announces the classification of the subject and then the guessers get 20 questions in which to find out what it is. The questions must be ones that can be answered "Yes," "No," "Partly," or "Sometimes." The player who guesses what it is becomes the next player to select the subject.

Think out your questions very carefully so that you eliminate many possibilities each time. Questions that are too specific too soon can be a complete waste. If you think you know the answer and are not too near 20, continue to pin it down with general questions before you ask a direct one.

Here is a sample game:

The subject is The Three Bears. Animal.
1. Is it human? No.
2. Is it 4-legged? Yes.
3. Is this a carnivorous animal? No.
4. Is it bigger than a bread box? Yes.
5. Is it bigger than I am? Partly. (The idea being that Pappa and Momma Bear are bigger, but Baby Bear isn't.)
6. Is more than one animal involved? Yes.
7. Are they land animals? Yes.
8. Are they dangerous? Yes.
9. Are they found in North America? Yes.
10. Are they hairy? Yes.
11. Are they bears? Yes.
12. Are they bears who attacked people? No.
13. Are these bears fictional? Yes.
14. Are there more than 3 of them? No.
15. Are they the Three Bears? Yes.

Other ways to play: If the group is large, set up teams. One selects the category while the other does the guessing. You can set up more than two teams, if you have a lot of people, and play the game as a tournament. Or if you have a large group (20 or more), break into smaller groups of approximately 5–10 people each. Each group sends a representative out of the room. These players meet and decide on a subject, and then return— each going to an opposing group—to stump them and win for their teams.

BUZZ, FIZZ-BUZZ, RAGS AND BONES,
AND SUPER-BUZZ

PLAYERS: 2 or more
EQUIPMENT: None
PREPARATION: None

BUZZ

In this game the players do nothing but count, starting with "One." But instead of saying any number that has 7 in it, or that is a multiple of 7 (14, 21, 28, 35, 42, etc.), they must say "BUZZ."

A game goes like this: the first person says, "One," the second "Two," the next "Three," and on until it is someone's turn to say "Seven," but that player must say "BUZZ" instead.

The game should proceed at a good clip, and anyone who doesn't say BUZZ when it should be said, or who says BUZZ when it *shouldn't* be said, is OUT.

FIZZ-BUZZ

FIZZ-BUZZ is more difficult and demands an enormous amount of concentration, but it can be hilarious. Just as 7 (and its multiples) are BUZZ, 5 and its multiples are FIZZ. So a game goes like this:

> 1, 2, 3, 4, FIZZ, 6, BUZZ, 8, 9, FIZZ, 11, 12, 13, BUZZ, FIZZ,
> 16, BUZZ, 18, 19, FIZZ, BUZZ, 22, 23, 24, FIZZ, 26, BUZZ,
> BUZZ, 29, FIZZ, 31, 32, 33, 34, FIZZ-BUZZ, 36, BUZZ,
> 38, 39, FIZZ, 41, BUZZ, 43, 44, FIZZ, 46, BUZZ, 48, BUZZ,
> FIZZ (50), FIZZ (51), FIZZ (52), FIZZ (53), FIZZ (54),
> FIZZ-FIZZ (55), FIZZ-BUZZ (56), FIZZ-BUZZ (57), FIZZ (58),
> FIZZ (59), FIZZ (60) . . .

You get the idea. Same rules apply.

You can play this game with many variations. One of them is based on 3's and 4's—BUZZ is 3 and FIZZ is 4. But when it comes to multiples, it gets more complicated, as you must call out the factors. Here is a sample game:

> 1, 2, BUZZ, FIZZ, 5, BUZZ times 2, 7, FIZZ times 2, 9, 10, 11,
> BUZZ times FIZZ, 13, FIZZ, BUZZ times 5, FIZZ times
> FIZZ, 17, BUZZ times 6, 19, FIZZ times 5 . . .

And so on. As you go along, you might encounter such fancy items as

"BUZZ times BUZZ times FIZZ" (36) or "FIZZ times FIZZ times 2" (32), and others where there is more than one way of saying the number. It's up to you what form you give it, as long as you FIZZ-BUZZ it right.

RAGS AND BONES

In another variation, 3 is BUZZ, 5 is RAGS and 7 is BONES. In this game, the count in the 50's goes like this:

RAGS (50), RAGS-BUZZ (51), RAGS (52), RAGS (53), RAGS-BUZZ (54), RAGS-RAGS (55), RAGS-BONES (56), RAGS-BONES-BUZZ (57), etc.

SUPER-BUZZ

Super-Buzz is a party game. The object is for the crowd to count to 100 without an error, using 3 for BUZZ. The catch? The direction of the count switches from clockwise to counter-clockwise every time a player misses.

NAME THAT TUNE

PLAYERS: 2 or more
EQUIPMENT: None
PREPARATION: None

Here's a game you can play just about anywhere—indoors or out, while riding, sitting or walking. All you need is something to tap with and something to tap against. A knuckle or fingernail will do for the first, while a book, table-top, dashboard or watch crystal will do for the latter. You could clap, too.

One of you taps out the rhythm of a tune, and the other must guess what it is. Start with simple, well-known tunes with a strong, distinctive rhythm, like "Hail, Hail, the Gang's All Here," or "Jingle Bells." As you get used to rhythm separate from melody, you will find that you can recognize more and more tunes when they are tapped out.

At the beginning, it's a good idea to take turns tapping out songs for each other. After you've become old hands at the game, one player taps a tune, and if the other player guesses correctly, he or she becomes the tapper. If the guess is not correct, the first tapper goes again.

HOUSE THAT JACK BUILT

PLAYERS: 2 or more
EQUIPMENT: None
PREPARATION: None

This giggly sort of game is very like the nursery rhyme, the House
that Jack Built. The first player makes a statement and the second player
adds on a phrase. The players continue taking turns, and each one must
repeat accurately all that has been said as well as adding a new phrase.
None of the statements needs to be true, and the funnier the better.

For example:

I have a car.

I have a chauffeur who loves the car.

I have a maid who loves the chauffeur who loves the car.

I have a dish that was cracked by the maid who loves the chauffeur
who loves the car.

I have a boy who smashed the dish that was cracked by the maid
who loves the chauffeur who loves the car.

I have a whip that spanked the boy . . .

And so on. Any player who misses is out.

MY GRANDMOTHER'S TRUNK

PLAYERS: 2 or more
EQUIPMENT: None
PREPARATION: None

Poor Grandma always travelled with the strangest collection of stuff. Once she took a trip, and in her trunk she carried fruit, feathers, foreign cars, fake jewelry, a fountain and some other surprising objects. On another trip her trunk contained pillows, parsley, portraits, penguins, a psychiatrist and, oddly enough, pajamas.

To play the game, the first player starts by mentioning one item which grandmother carried in her trunk. The next player repeats this item and adds another item starting with the same letter.

Each time a new item is added, the player must repeat the whole list, starting with the first item, before adding on a new one. The list must be said in the exact order. First person to make a mistake loses.

For a slightly more difficult game, don't start all Grandma's stuff with the same letter. Let her take anything at all with her! (If you want to win at either of these games, take a look at the memory trick on page 122.)

GRANDMA IS A STRANGE ONE

PLAYERS: 2 or more
EQUIPMENT: None
PREPARATION: None

In this game, each player takes turns having a strange grandmother. The first player—say, Laurie—starts out:

"My grandma is very strange. She loves tennis but she hates games."

Laurie's statement is based on a secret combination that she has thought up.

The next player asks a question, testing:

"Does she like carrots?"

"Yes," says Laurie, and gives them another clue, "but she hates peas."

"Does she like dogs?"

"No, but she's crazy about raccoons."

Laurie's secret combination is that her grandmother likes anything that has a double letter in it, like buttons—but not bows, zoos—but not animals, pepper—but not salt.

As players discover Laurie's grandmother's secret, they join her in giving clues to the other players.

That's the usual way to play this game, and once you discover the formula, the game is over. But actually, this is where the fun begins. Grandma can be strange in different ways: she can hate anything that has a certain letter in it. Or anything that grows (watch out, that's a tricky one—*many* things grow). Or anything with two syllables (she hates flying but she loves jets). Or anything with two legs. Or 4-letter words. Or anything that doesn't have a smell to it.

If your group is studying French, your grandmother could hate any feminine noun (she loves hats but she hates dresses). That is a really rough one, and unless your group is very sharp, they'll never guess it.

You can go on for hours with this game. The last player to "catch on" to the secret is the next one to have a strange grandmother.

FLASH CATEGORIES

PLAYERS: 2
EQUIPMENT: Several dozen small cards or sturdy paper cut down to business card size
PREPARATION: On each card, write a word which designates one classification, such as flower, gem, month, state, country, article of clothing, television program, color, opera, playwright, composer, artist.

The cards are shuffled to start with, and the pack is placed face down between you. The player who goes first calls out a letter of the alphabet. The other player turns up the top card and quickly reads it aloud. Each player tries to name something in the category which starts with the called letter, and the first one to get a correct answer wins the card. If no one can win the card, it goes to the bottom of the pack. Play the game until all the cards are won (if possible) and the player with the greater number of cards wins the game.

Hold onto the cards after you play. Or keep them in the glove compartment of the car. You can use them over and over to play Flash Categories.

EAGLE EYE

PLAYERS: 2 or more
EQUIPMENT: A list you draw up ahead of time. See below.
PREPARATION: See below.

Automobile trips and train trips may seem as fast as jet travel if you play Eagle Eye.

To begin the game, draw up a list of the objects you are likely to see, taking into consideration the part of the country you are in. For example, you assign a higher point value to an Eskimo if you happen to be in Brazil than you would while driving through Alaska. The player who first sights the object gets the points, and every time the same sort of object is sighted again, you can score it again.

Here is a sample scale of points:

Horses (one, a pair, a herd)	2	Golfer	4
Red light	1	Lightning rod	2
Railroad crossing	2	Lake, pond or river	1
Freight train	2	Motor boat or rowboat	2
Red barn	1	Fisherman	3
Farmer in field	2	Pheasant, duck or turkey	4
Farmer in field with plow	4	Hay wagon	5
Cyclist	3	Deer	6
Sheep (one, a pair, or herd)	2	Cows (one, a pair, or herd)	2

Winner is the player who gets the highest score in a given period of time, usually a half-hour.

ALPHABET ON ROAD AND TRACK

PLAYERS: 2 or more
EQUIPMENT: Paper and pencil for each player or team
PREPARATION: None

Contestants may be two individuals or two teams. Each of you looks for the first sign you can find—on a billboard or on a road sign—that contains an A—like "Downtown Augusta—turn right."

The player (or the team) that sees it writes it down and circles the A.

Then you try to find a road sign containing a B. The first player (or team) to complete the alphabet wins. If you spot a phrase containing two desired letters *in order*, such as the D and E in DovEr, you may copy that word and circle both letters.

Hint: The driver had better stay out of this game!

FAMOUS WORDS THAT WERE NEVER SAID

PLAYERS: 2 or more
EQUIPMENT: None
PREPARATION: None

"Of course the shoe didn't fit, but do you think I was going to tell *him* that?"

Who never said it? Cinderella, of course!

Dig out your old books of fairy tales, nursery rhymes and myths of all kinds to bone up for this game. Your job is to find the words that would have ended the story before it started—or, if the story is ended, the secret behind it that would never never have been said. Your opponent's job is to guess who never said it.

Here are a few to start you off. See page 632 for the answers.

1. "Look, what Mother does is her own business. I'm going back to college."
2. "You can't really think I'm going to trade a perfectly good cow for those old dried-up beans!"
3. "What cherry tree, Dad?"
4. "Bake tarts? On a hot day like this?"
5. "No, I'm looking for a *square* table that seats four."
6. "If you think we're taking a bath in public, you've got another think coming!"
7. "I don't care what that old witch says. I'm getting an Afro."
8. "What do you mean, lick the platter clean? We're both vegetarians."
9. "That's very nice of you, but I couldn't possibly live alone in the woods with seven men."
10. "What an actress needs is a nice neat haircut that's easy to take care of."

THE MISSING LETTER

PLAYERS: 2 or more
EQUIPMENT: None
PREPARATION: None

This game seems simple, but it is deceptive.

All you have to do is ask the other player a question and then mention a single letter of the alphabet. Your opponent must answer your question with a sentence which does not use that letter at all! Answers may be serious or silly. Then it is the next player's turn to answer his or her question, leaving out a specified letter. Simple? Wait till you try to express yourself without the letter E or the letter S! Writing instead of speaking makes it easier—but not much!

Here are some sample questions and answers:

What do you think of school this year? S.
I don't like it at all.

What did you do last summer? E.
I don't know—it was dark.

What do you put in your pen to write with? I.
We use pea soup.

What do you live in? H.
I live in a large zoo.

QUICK CONTESTS

7

Contests for Two or More

AMPE (1-2-3 SHOOT — AFRICAN STYLE)

PLAYERS: 2 or more
EQUIPMENT: None
PREPARATION: None

This children's game comes from southern Ghana, but it is also played in other African countries.

You've probably played a similar game when you need to pick someone as the leader or decide who should go first. Two players face each other and make a fist, choose "Odds" or "Evens" and say "1–2–3—Shoot!" and they each shoot out one or two fingers. If they both put out the same number of fingers, "Evens" gains a point. If they put out different fingers, "Odds" gains a point. Three points wins.

In this African game, the players face each other, and clap their hands on "One" and "Two," but on "Three," stick out one foot in front. If they both stick their feet out on the same side (one the left foot and the other the right foot), "Evens" wins the point. If they stick out opposite feet (both right feet or both left feet), "Odds" wins. The game goes on until one person wins by getting 11 points.

Since they have kicked out opposite legs, Odds wins here.

Since they have kicked out legs on the same side, Evens wins here.

After a few rounds, the game gets more complicated. The players jump after the second clap, before extending their feet. As the game goes on, they do tricks after the jump—clap their feet, cross them over and back, click their heels—whatever they decide on. When they land, they pause for a fourth count, see who has won the point, and start again.

LOW DOWN AMPÉ

Two players sit or squat. They clap their hands on their knees for "One" and "Two" and shoot their fingers out on "Three" (as in our version). Sometimes they keep their hands behind their backs. They shoot out one or two fingers from their hand, and even switch from one hand to the other, if they choose.

GROUP AMPÉ

Form a circle with "It" in the middle. "It" walks around and then stops in front of someone, calls "Odds" or "Evens," and "It" plays the game with that player. If "It" loses, the other player becomes the new "It." And the game goes on.

CHINESE CHALLENGE

PLAYERS: 2 or 3
EQUIPMENT: None
PREPARATION: None

This version of 1–2–3 Shoot works well with two or three players, and it's not only a contest, it's a guessing game.

The players count "1–2–" and instead of 3—as they shoot out their fingers—they call off the number of fingers that they think will be out—theirs and the other player's, too. The player whose guess is closest wins a point. If a total of three fingers have been put out, and one player called "one" while the other called "five," they both get a point. Ten points wins the game.

TABLE FOOTBALL

PLAYERS: 2 (more can play in round robin tournaments)
EQUIPMENT: A sheet of paper
    Table (ideal length for beginners is at least 40 inches or 1 meter, but you can play on a table of any length)
    Any flat surface, such as a book or ruler
PREPARATION: Using the sheet of paper, make the football as follows:

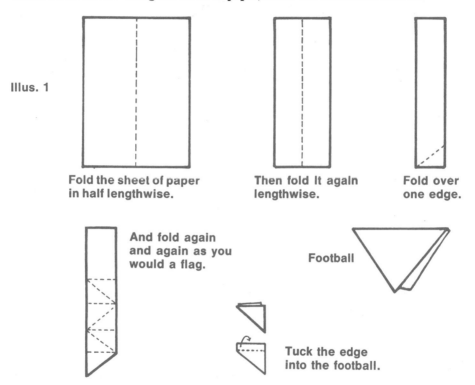

Illus. 1

Fold the sheet of paper in half lengthwise.

Then fold it again lengthwise.

Fold over one edge.

And fold again and again as you would a flag.

Football

Tuck the edge into the football.

Flip a coin or shoot out fingers (page 353) to see who goes first.

THE FIRST MOVE: Set the football on end at the edge of the table as in Illus. 2:

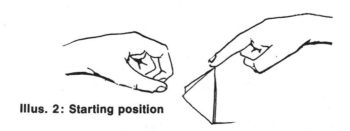

Illus. 2: Starting position

Or lay it flat—part on and part off the table as in Illus. 3.

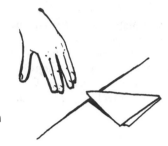

Illus. 3: Alternate starting position

Then flick or shove it across the table. The object is to get the football *just exactly* on the edge of the opponent's side of the table, with one edge of the football sticking over the end of the table—*without going off*. This is a "touchdown" and it is worth six points.

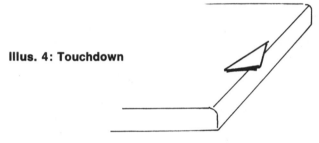

Illus. 4: Touchdown

Your opponent, without moving the football, makes an open fist, and flicks it back with the same idea in mind.

The play continues, with players taking turns.

THE RULES

1. If you hit the ball off the table, you get a "down."

It is up to your opponent then, to put the ball back in play, starting as in Illus. 2 or 3, from his or her end of the table.

2. When you have made four "downs" of your own, your opponent gets a chance for a field goal. (See Rule 6.)

3. Touchdown: When you get a touchdown, it is worth six points and a try at an extra point. This "try" is a chance to make a field goal. (See Rule 6.)

4. You may not hit the football with your thumb or cover the football with your hand at any point during the game.

5. You may not pick up the football in the middle of play, unless you shoot it off the table and get a "down."

6. Field goal procedure: When you get four downs, or when your opponent has a chance at an extra point after a touchdown, you put fingers in goal post position. (See Illus. 5.)

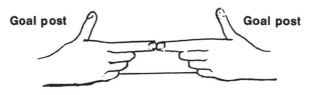

Illus. 5: Goal Post Position

Your opponent sets the football on end (as in starting position, Illus. 2), approximately 3 inches (7.5 cm.) from the edge of table, and tries to finger-kick it between the goal posts. To avoid arguments, you are the one to decide whether the kick is good or not. A field goal is worth three extra points, unless it takes place after a touchdown, in which case it is worth only one extra point.

After a field goal, your opponent starts the ball back in play, beginning at his or her edge of the table (with the ball in position as in Illus. 2 or 3).

BACKWARD ALPHABET

PLAYERS: Unlimited
EQUIPMENT: Watch with a second-hand or a stop watch
PREPARATION: None

Each player in turn recites the alphabet backwards. The one who can do it fastest is the winner. The other players watch for omissions, and anyone skipping a letter is out.

PENNY SOCCER

PLAYERS: 2
EQUIPMENT: 3 or more coins. (You can play with all pennies or any other group of coins. Playing with a variety of coins in the same game is more interesting.)
              A table
              Pen or pencil
PREPARATION: None

You, sitting at one end of the table, are the Defender. You place your index finger and pinky on the edge of the table, with your middle fingers bent underneath (like this):

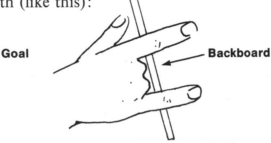

Goal   **Backboard**

Illus. 1

The space between your fingers on the table is the Goal.

Your opponent—the Attacker—sits at the other end of the table, and arranges the pennies in either this order:

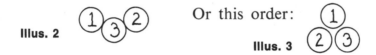

Illus. 2   ①③②   Or this order: ①②③

Illus. 3

THE FIRST MOVE: The Attacker—with four fingers bent—pushes, or flip-pushes the pennies, just enough to break the formation and prepare for the next move.

Illus. 4

THE SECOND MOVE and all the moves after that, are used to manoeuvre a penny into the Defender's goal. The Attacker may use any finger or fingers to shoot the penny through, but *not* his or her thumb. The Attacker gets as many turns as it takes (no one counts them), as long as the Attacker doesn't break any of the rules.

THE RULES

1. The penny that the Attacker shoots must go in a path between the other two pennies.

2. The penny must not touch either of the other two pennies.

3. If the Attacker has a difficult shot to make—a curve, for example—the player may use a pen or pencil to assist the shot. In Illus. 5 you see the problem the Attacker is up against.

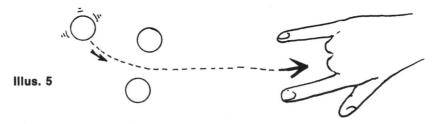

Illus. 5

In Illus. 6 you see how a pen can be used to solve it.

Illus. 6

4. The penny may not go off the table.

5. To be a goal, the penny must hit the backboard.

The players take turns trying to shoot a goal. If the Attacker breaks one of the rules, his or her turn is over and the Defender becomes the Attacker. The next time the opponent's turn comes up, the game begins all over again with the basic penny formation and a fresh start.

The player who makes the most goals, after an equal number of turns, wins.

PLAYING WITH MORE THAN 3 COINS

If you use more than 3 coins (you can use any number), begin with a pyramid formation like this:　　　　　　　　or this:

Illus. 7

The Attacker must always designate the two coins he or she is shooting between. If the coin hits another coin on the table, the turn ends.

PENNY SOCCER FOR EXPERTS

Choose one of the three pennies as the one you will shoot into the goal. Turn it heads up while the other two are tails up, or vice versa. If you score any other penny, your turn continues, but that penny does not count as a goal.

TABLE WRESTLE

PLAYERS: 2 or more
EQUIPMENT: 2 chairs for each 2 contestants
          1 table for each 2 contestants
PREPARATION: None

This is another strength contest.

The players sit down facing each other on two chairs with a small sturdy table in between. The table should be small enough so that when the players sit and reach across, they can easily touch each other's shoulders.

The players place their right elbows squarely on the table with their forearms and wrists straight up. They clasp hands. At a signal, they try to turn each other's wrist down until it touches the table.

As soon as one player forces the other's wrist to the table, the contest is over. Left hands can be used only to grasp the chairs they sit on, not the table.

Left-handers should be matched up with other left-handers.

HAND WRESTLE

PLAYERS: 2 or more
EQUIPMENT: None
PREPARATION: None

You can hand wrestle anywhere. First, two players stand opposite each other, each with right foot forward and legs apart. They stand in the same position as for fencing.

Then the players grasp each other's right hands. (Left-handers can wrestle only against other left-handers.) While holding right hands firmly, both players count to three. At the number "Three," both start to turn, shove, twist and pull with their wrists, trying to throw each other off balance. The first player to move his or her right foot (that's the forward foot) loses.

If you have a large group, several hand wrestling contests can go on at the same time.

OVER THE LINE

PLAYERS: 2 or more
EQUIPMENT: Tape
PREPARATION: None

Two players at a time (or two teams) can test their strength in this pulling contest. You can play it in a gym or outdoors.

Mark on the floor with tape two parallel goal lines 20 feet (6 m) apart. Two players start by facing each other exactly midway between the two goal lines. At a signal, each player grabs the other's wrists and tries to pull the player back across his or her own goal line. The first player to pull the opponent over the goal line two out of three times wins.

If you are playing teams, first choose sides and the score can be kept by teams. A player from one team is matched against a player from the other team. The players should be matched for equal strength. Don't let a little kid try to pull a heavyweight!

If a player pulls his or her hand free, then both must go all the way back to the middle and start again. So hold tight when you get your opponent near your goal line.

HOP WRESTLING

PLAYERS: 2
EQUIPMENT: None
PREPARATION: None

Here is an off-beat wrestling match which is fun for contestants and onlookers, too.

Two players stand facing each other with right hands grasped in a hand-shaking position. Each one also grasps his or her raised left foot in back with the left hand.

At the word "Go," they both start pulling and pushing. They may hop about on their right feet to maintain their balance, but they can't release their left feet. The object is to make the other player go off balance and fall, or merely let go of the left foot in order to prevent falling.

INDIAN WRESTLE

PLAYERS: 2 or more
EQUIPMENT: Gym mat for each 2 contestants
PREPARATION: None

An Indian wrestle should always take place on a rug or a gym mat, or on soft grass, if you do it outdoors.

Two players lie down on their backs side by side. Then they lock arms. When the signal is given, they lock legs and the contest is on.

Each player uses all his or her strength and skill to try to roll the other player over. The one who rolls the opponent over first wins. Sometimes the players' legs may become unlocked. If this happens, they must wait for another signal to lock them again, and the match continues.

Several contests can be held at the same time. Just be sure the matches are far enough away from each other so no one gets kicked.

BLINDMAN'S BUTTON

PLAYERS: 2
EQUIPMENT: Buttons, screws, paper clips, beans, bobby pins, etc.
PREPARATION: None

Blindfold two players and then place each before a different pile of mixed buttons, screws, paper clips, beans and bobby pins. The first player to sort the pile correctly is the winner.

DOUBLE TROUBLE

PLAYERS: 2
EQUIPMENT: Pencils and paper for 2
2 identical jars
A book
A table
20 toothpicks each, in piles
PREPARATION: None

Here is a contest to test your powers of concentration and co-ordination.

Seat yourselves at a table with the book between you in such a position that you can both read it easily. The object of the game is to write with one hand, copying on your paper from the book, while with the other hand you simultaneously pick up from your pile of toothpicks and drop them into your jar, one at a time!

The winner is the one who gets all the toothpicks into the jar first. In the case of a tie, the winner is the one who has copied the most.

TOOTHPICK TEEPEE

PLAYERS: 2
EQUIPMENT: 25 toothpicks for each player
A bottle with a neck smaller than the length of the toothpicks
PREPARATION: None

Place the bottle on the floor between the players and choose for the first turn. The first player places a toothpick across the top of the bottle and then the next player lays another toothpick across it. They continue taking turns, adding one toothpick at a time from their individual piles.

If a player upsets the "teepee," he must add to his pile whatever toothpicks fall off. The game continues until one player wins by getting rid of all his or her toothpicks.

TOOTHPICK
IN THE
BOTTLE

PLAYERS: 2
EQUIPMENT: A narrow-necked bottle or jar
                A handful of toothpicks
PREPARATION: None

Divide the toothpicks equally and set the bottle on the floor between the players. Then you take turns holding your hand about 2 feet (60 cm) above the bottle and trying to drop one toothpick in at a time. Add up your scores of hits and disregard the misses. The one who gets the most toothpicks in the bottle is the winner.

In order to avoid arguments, it's a good idea to place the bottle near a wall or a piece of furniture which acts as a height marker below which you may not place your hand. That way it is fair for both players. Or if both players are exactly the same height, they can simply stand up straight, no bending allowed, and drop the toothpick from the same point.

JUMP-UPS

PLAYERS: 2
EQUIPMENT: None
PREPARATION: None

Players kneel on the floor with arms outstretched and bodies straight. Then, with all the energy they can muster, they leap to a standing position. They must do this twice in a row to score a single point. After one player takes two turns, the other gets two turns to try to score. Then they continue with two more turns, and so on.

The first player to get 10 points wins.

JUMPING JACK

PLAYERS: 2
EQUIPMENT: None
PREPARATION: None

Both players squat and cross arms in front of their bodies. At a signal, they spring up with their feet spread and their weight on their heels. At the same time, they throw their arms up and to the sides, diagonally—like the hands of a clock at 10:10—above the shoulders.

Then they quickly drop down to the original starting position. See which player can repeat this action of jumping up and dropping down the most times within 15 seconds.

BODY HOIST

PLAYERS: 2
EQUIPMENT: None
PREPARATION: None

In this game, the players raise their bodies off the floor with only their hands.

They begin by sitting on the floor with legs straight out in front of them. Then they place their hands on the floor under their thighs, palms down, and at a signal with all their strength, push their bottoms and legs off the floor, keeping their legs out straight and heels up. Whoever can keep off the floor longest wins.

GOING UP THE WALL

PLAYERS: 2
EQUIPMENT: None
PREPARATION: None

Players will need to practice this exercise often before they can master it.

First they sit on the floor with head, shoulders and back against the wall. Then they bend their legs, and put their knees up against their chests. If possible, set up the opponents so that they are sitting against opposite walls. This way they can watch each other without getting in each other's way.

Then without using their hands to support their bodies, they work themselves up along the wall so they finish by standing with their backs against the wall. At a signal they begin and the one who rises to a standing position first, wins.

CHINESE GET-UP

PLAYERS: 2 or more
EQUIPMENT: None
PREPARATION: None

Chinese Get-Up can be played indoors or out. It takes skill and lots of practice and is especially suited for 11 and 12-year-olds. Rubber-soled shoes or sneakers help players get a good grip on the ground.

Two players sit back to back with their arms folded over their chests. Then at a signal, each player tries to stand up while still keeping arms folded. The first player to do this wins. The trick to winning is to push up against the back of the other player. The one who does this first has the advantage. Sometimes a player with a better sense of balance can win over a stronger player.

Several pairs of players in a group can try this stunt at the same time. Then the winners can be matched with each other and a final winner chosen.

CHICKEN FIGHT

PLAYERS: 2
EQUIPMENT: None
PREPARATION: None

Each contestant stands on one foot and folds both arms across his or her chest. At the word "Go," the action starts.

The players hop toward each other and bump into each other. They may butt with folded arms, back or shoulders, trying to make the other player lose his or her balance. The object of the game is to force the other player to go off balance and place both feet down on the ground.

ROOSTER FIGHT

PLAYERS: 8–20
EQUIPMENT: Chalk
PREPARATION: None

Each player squats and grabs his or her ankles using both hands. While in this position the players try to upset each other, but only by using their shoulders and backs. Hands must not be removed from the players' ankles.

The free-for-all takes place inside a marked circle with from 8 to 20 players at a time. If you play in a gym, use chalk to mark a circle about 10 feet (3 m) across.

If anyone moves or is pushed outside of the marked circle, that player is out of the game. And if any players move their hands off their ankles, fall over by themselves, or get pushed off balance, they too are out. Sometimes a whole row of players will fall, one after the other. This is usually very funny.

The last one to remain squatting is the winner.

BROOM PULL-UPS

PLAYERS: 2
EQUIPMENT: A broomstick
PREPARATION: None

Save this game for two players who are fairly evenly matched in size and strength.

The players sit on the floor facing each other, with their legs extended straight in front of them. The soles of their shoes press against each other. They both grasp the broomstick with both hands, holding it horizontally.

At the word "Go," each one starts pulling on the stick in an effort to raise the other person from the floor. The one who first stands, falls over, or lets go of the stick, loses.

TOE TO TOE

PLAYERS: 2
EQUIPMENT: None
PREPARATION: None

Two players sit on the floor facing each other. Their knees are bent and their shoes are touching—sole to sole. They hold each other's hands.

Then they try to raise each other off the floor without lifting themselves. Whoever succeeds in lifting the other player off the floor first wins.

You are not allowed to resist your opponent by raising or twisting arms or by kicking. The only way you can protect yourself is by flexing your muscles.

RUSSIAN HOP

PLAYERS: 2
EQUIPMENT: None
PREPARATION: None

Set up a goal line 20 feet (6 m) from the starting line. Two players drop down in a squatting position at the starting line with their arms folded across their chests.

At a signal, they leap upward and forward off both feet. After the hop, they return to the squat position with their arms still folded across their chests—and hop again. The players should keep at least 3 feet (1 m) apart in case one loses his or her balance.

The player who hops to the goal line this way and returns in the same fashion to the starting line first, wins.

BAG OF AIR

PLAYERS: 2
EQUIPMENT: 2 paper bags
           A supply of books (about a dozen)
PREPARATION: None

Pit two players against one another, arming each with a paper bag and a supply of books. Each player lays the paper bag flat on a table or desk and covers it with a book. The object is to blow up the bag, thus lifting the book. Then a second book is added, and the bag is blown some more. The winner of the contest is the player who can lift the most books with a bag of air.

HAND PUSH

PLAYERS: 2
EQUIPMENT: None
PREPARATION: None

Players stand and face each other so that the toes of their shoes touch. Both of them then bend their arms at the elbows, holding their hands palm outward, as if they are going to clap hands with each other.

At a signal, they press their palms together and hold them there. Then they each try to push the opponent back. Whichever one forces the other player to take one step back, wins.

KNEEL-PUSH

The same game can be played with the contestants down on their knees, but this time they keep their arms outstretched. The object is for one of them to get the other to lose balance and topple over. But remember, they can only push each other's palms; touching any other part of the body is out. The first one to fall over loses. Or the players can keep score and see who can win 10 pushes first.

PAPER TRAINING RACE

PLAYERS: **2 or more**
EQUIPMENT: **2 sheets of newspaper for each player (and a few extras in case they tear)**
PREPARATION: **None**

In this race you're not allowed to take a step that isn't on newspaper! Each player starts by putting down a sheet of newspaper in front and stepping on it. Then the player puts down the second sheet of paper and steps on that—and has to turn around and pick up the first piece of paper and put it down, before another step can be taken. The process is repeated all the way to the finish line.

ANAGRAMS

PLAYERS: 2–4
EQUIPMENT: A set of anagrams, which usually can be purchased inexpensively, or you can make your own from cardboard. Each cut-out should be about an inch (2½ cm), square and you can print a letter on one side. (See note below.)
PREPARATION: Set all the anagram squares face down on the table.

Each person picks up one letter to see who goes first. The one with the lowest letter (A is the best) gets to turn over the letters one by one and set them out on the table so that everyone sees them at the same time. Player #1—Ken—keeps turning up letters until he or another of the players—Verlyn—sees the possibility of making a word of four or more letters. The first player to call out the word—let's say it is Verlyn—gets the word for her own. She places it in her corner of the table.

Verlyn is now the one to turn up the letters, and she continues until another word is seen by one of the players, in which case that player takes the word and gets to turn over the letters.

Players may steal words at any time by adding a letter from the table to any existing words. For example, suppose Ken has the word POOL and an "S" shows up on the table. Verlyn has been waiting for an "S," hoping to steal that word. She says quickly, "Stealing POOL," and makes the word SPOOL, which she puts in her column of words. She couldn't steal POOL with POOLS, because a "steal" really has to change the meaning of a word, not just lengthen it. When she steals, however, she doesn't get a chance to turn up letters; all she gets is the word itself.

Players should keep all their words in full view at all times so that other players can steal them.

The main advantage in being the one to turn up the letters is that you control the game. You can go as rapidly or slowly as you want. Going rapidly sometimes benefits a player who does not know a great many words. When the game is fast, it is likely that many of the letters will go to make simple words; they are easier to see quickly.

To score, count up the number of letters in all your words. The one with the most letters wins.

Note: If you can't find an Anagram set and need to make your own, you may want to follow this guide, more or less in making up the letters: A–13, B–4, C–4, D–8, E–20, F–4, G–6, H–5, I–13, J–2, K–2, L–6, M–4, N–10, O–13, P–3, Q–2, R–10, S–6, T–9, U–8, V–2, W–2, X–1, Y–3, Z–2.

If your Anagram set has number values on the letters, count your score by totalling up those number values. This makes the game much more interesting. Each vowel, for example, is worth only one point, because there are so many of them in the game. The more often-used consonants—N, R, S, and T—are worth only 1 point, too. Worth 2 points each are D, G, H and L; for B, C, F, M and P you get 3; for Y you get 4; for J, K and V, you get 8; for Q, X and Z—10.

It's a good idea to keep a dictionary handy when you play this game, to consult in case of disputes.

CONTEST MARSHMALLOW

PLAYERS: 2
EQUIPMENT: A string about 1½ feet (45 cm) long
A marshmallow
PREPARATION: Pull the string through the marshmallow (you can tie it to a skewer and pull it through that way) so that the marshmallow is exactly in the middle of the string.

This is a very quick contest for two.

Give the players each one end of the same string. They have to chew along the string as rapidly as they can. The one who gets the marshmallow wins and eats it.

WHEELBARROW RACE

PLAYERS: 4 or more
EQUIPMENT: None
PREPARATION: None

First, set up a goal line about 30 feet (9 m) from the starting line. Then divide up into two pairs. In each pair, one is the Wheelbarrow and the other walks him or her. The Wheelbarrows get down on their hands, while the Walkers stand behind them and grab hold of their ankles, lifting them to a comfortable walking position.

When they are ready, both pairs face the goal line. At a signal, they begin hurrying towards the goal, the Wheelbarrows walking on their hands and the Walkers holding up the Wheelbarrows' ankles. The first pair to reach the goal line wins.

Then the players alternate positions, letting the Wheelbarrows switch with the Walkers. After two or three races, the Wheelbarrow of one pair switches positions with the Walker of the other pair, so that each player can see who is really the fastest.

WILLIAM TELL RACE

PLAYERS: 2 or more
EQUIPMENT: An apple for each player or each team
PREPARATION: None

William Tell shot the apple *off* a head—it's your job to keep it on! At a starting signal, players balance an apple on top of their heads and then walk to the finish line. If the apple falls off, it's back to the starting line! Two can play at a time, or you can work the game in teams.

TURNABOUT RACE

PLAYERS: 2
EQUIPMENT: None
PREPARATION: None

Set up a starting line and a goal line about 20 feet (6 m.) away. Two players stand on the starting line facing the goal. At a signal, they both jump straight up, making a complete turn in the air, so that they come down in about the same place, facing the same direction. Then they take three short steps forward and repeat the jump and turn. They do this again and again until one of them reaches the goal line. The first one to get there wins.

MATCHBOX DUEL

PLAYERS: 2
EQUIPMENT: 2 small matchboxes
PREPARATION: None

Two players stand facing each other at hand-shaking distance, each one with one hand behind his or her back. The forward hand is extended, palm downward, with a matchbox on the back of the hand. At the word "Go," each one tries to knock the matchbox off the other's hand without losing his or her own. You may not bring the second arm into play, nor move your feet from their original stance, but otherwise, anything goes.

Winning three matches out of five makes you a winner. Should both players drop their matchboxes simultaneously, it counts as a draw.

EGGS IN A BASKET

PLAYERS: 2
EQUIPMENT: 8–10 hardboiled eggs or pebbles
                 2 baskets or shallow boxes
                 1 soup spoon
PREPARATION: None

You can play this game at Easter with colored hardboiled eggs, or you can use round pebbles to play it at any time.

Mark a starting line, with a goal about 20 feet (6 m) away. Place all the eggs in one basket at the starting line, with the empty basket nearby.

At the word "Go," one player must run from the starting line to the goal, touch it and run back again to the start. While that player is running, the other one starts transferring the eggs from one basket to the other, one at a time, using only the spoon. The egg-player keeps the other hand behind his or her back. When the runner returns to the starting line and touches the basket which the eggs are being placed in, the egg-player can't put in any more eggs. Count up the number of eggs that made it into the basket, and this is the egg-player's score. Now the egg-player becomes the runner, and the runner starts again with one full basket and one empty one, transferring the eggs by spoon.

Keep adding up your scores. The first one to score 100 eggs is the winner.

Note: The faster the runner runs, the less time the other player has to transfer eggs!

BOOK WALK

PLAYERS: 2 or more
EQUIPMENT: 2 books of equal size and weight
PREPARATION: None

Set up a goal line about 20 feet (6 m) away. Before players start racing, let them practice balancing a book on their heads. Once they have mastered it, they are ready to begin the book walk.

At a signal, each one places a book on his or her head and begins walking toward the goal line. The first to reach the line wins. If the book drops off their heads, they must stop and, keeping their bodies erect, bend down (bending knees only), pick up the book and place it back on their heads. Then, keeping the book balanced on their heads, they rise and continue.

They can vary this by walking backwards to the goal line. Also try using side steps!

If you have a large group, you can play this as a relay race.

CHIMP RACE

PLAYERS: 2 or more
EQUIPMENT: None
PREPARATION: None

Players stand side by side. At a signal, they spread their feet apart, bend over and grasp their ankles. In this position, with knees stiff, they both walk to the goal line, about 20 or 25 feet (6 or 8 m) away. The one who gets there first wins.

If either one loses the grip on their ankles, they must return to the starting point and begin again.

You can play this as a relay race, if you have a large group.

RANSOM NOTE

PLAYERS: 2
EQUIPMENT: Old newspapers
      Brown wrapping paper or paper bags
      2 scissors
      2 containers of paste or rubber cement
      Pencil and paper
PREPARATION: None

Have you ever been intrigued by the ransom notes you have read about which are composed of words cut from newspapers? Why not play Ransom Note and try your hand at it?

You both decide on a short note, preferably a funny one. For example: "Place 3 large cabbages in a paper bag and leave them at the lamppost at midnight and we will return your kangaroo unharmed." Or you might use a nursery rhyme such as "Mary Had a Little Lamb," etc.

Write the message down so that both players can refer to it, or make a copy of each and get going. The idea is to write the message using only newspaper clippings pasted onto the wrapping paper. Of course, the letters and words can be of all different sizes, but it's best to try to stick to headlines or large printing from the ads.

Try to find whole words that you need for your message, but sometimes you'll need to put words together from individual letters or combinations of letters. For instance, in forming the word "kangaroo" in the message above, you may find the AN together, and if you find the word ROOT, you can use that to help form your word.

The first one finished is the winner.

BEAUTIFUL BABY CONTEST

PLAYERS: 2 or more
EQUIPMENT: Baby bottles with new nipples, punctured by a straight pin
PREPARATION: Fill the bottles up to the 1-ounce (28 g) mark with water.
Test them to make sure that the water runs out of each bottle at the same speed.

At a signal, each beautiful baby tries to empty its bottle. The one to finish drinking the water first wins.

MANCALA

PLAYERS: 2
EQUIPMENT: 14 cupcake holders—or jar tops—or any other small
      container-like holder
      18 pennies or marbles
PREPARATION: None

    There are many versions of Mancala. It originated in ancient Egypt, and is one of the oldest games in the world. You can play it on a special mancala board, if you have one, or by using any small containers you have at hand. (If you are outdoors, you can play it simply by scooping out little holes in the earth.)

    This is one of the easiest versions, but it is as fascinating as the more complex versions, and just as good today as it was thousands of years ago.

    Set out your "board" like this:

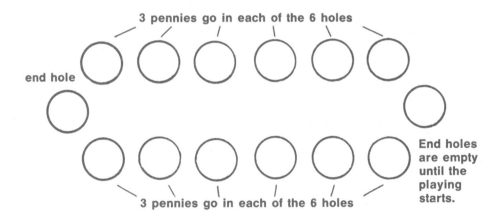

    Put 3 pennies in each "hole" except for the ones on the ends. Those end holes are common property, and belong to both players.

    One player—Scott—starts, scooping up all the pennies from one of the holes on his side of the board and distributing them—one penny to a hole—in each of the next holes moving toward the right, including the holes on the end.

    The object of the game is to be the first player to get rid of all the pennies on your side of the board.

If Scott's last penny falls into the end hole, he goes again. He can choose any hole on his side of the board, scoop out the pennies, and distribute them one by one in the holes to the right.

If his penny lands in a hole which is on the other player's side of the board, and there is no penny at all in that hole, Scott gets to scoop out the opposite hole (on his side of the board) and distribute the pennies in it. If he has no pennies there, his turn is over.

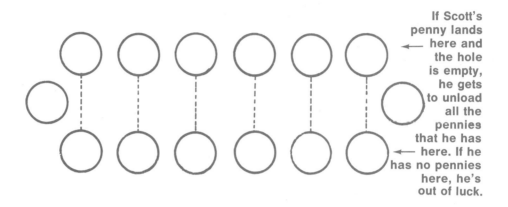

If Scott's penny lands here and ← the hole is empty, he gets to unload all the pennies that he has ← here. If he has no pennies here, he's out of luck.

This is a game of strategy and it can be very tricky. When you think you've almost slaughtered your opponent, you can find suddenly that you've lost. The African experts play it very rapidly (it seems as if they're not even thinking) and we don't understand how they do it!

"NOW" JOUSTING

PLAYERS: 2–30
EQUIPMENT: 2 tablespoons for each player
             1 small potato for each player
PREPARATION: None

In olden days, knights used to joust (pronounced same as "just") with lances on horseback. The object was to knock the knight off the horse. This jousting contest for any number of players can be held indoors or out, and you don't need lances or horses. The object is to knock the potato off the spoon.

Players line up as two teams with the same number on each side. Each player in turn gets two tablespoons and one potato. The spoons should all be the same size, and the potatoes should be small. The players have to carry the potato on the spoon in one hand and the empty spoon in the other. The empty spoon is used to joust with. The way you joust is to try to knock off your opponent's potato with your spoon. At the same time you must protect your own potato.

At the start, one player jousts against a player from the opposing team, or two contests can go on at the same time. The one whose potato falls to the ground first is out. Then the winner from Team A jousts against the winner from Team B, or else a new player jousts with another player from the opposing team. This goes on until one team has no one left to joust. That team is the loser; the other team wins.

If you have five players or fewer, you can have a jousting free-for-all. This is played without teams; you can joust with anyone. The last player left with a potato on the spoon wins.

AUTOBIOGRAPHIES

PLAYERS: 2–8
EQUIPMENT: About 10 sheets of paper for each player, tied together with a string to make a "scrapbook"
Glue (several jars or sticks)
Old magazines and newspapers
Scissors for each player
PREPARATION: Label each page of the "scrapbook" with a heading of your choice, such as:

My First Picture	Where My Money Went
My Proud Parents	My Mate
My First Meal	My Wedding
My Favorite Toy	My Greatest Weakness
My Pet	The Most Fun I Ever Had
My School	My Work
My Favorite Teacher	My Boss
My Best Friend	My Worst Sin
My Ambition	My Family
My First Date	My Last Fling
My Greatest Love	My Retirement
Where I Made My Fortune	My Secret Hobby

There is no time limit on this game and no winners. The job of the players is to cut out photographs from the magazines and newspapers which will illustrate their "lives" and paste them down in their scrapbooks. The funnier the better. And everyone gets to take their book home afterwards. These autobiographies will be kept and laughed over long after all other parties and party games have been forgotten!

THE WOOLLCOTT GAME

PLAYERS: 2 or more
EQUIPMENT: Pencil and paper
 A watch or clock with a sweep second hand
PREPARATION: None

Alexander Woollcott has been credited with inventing this one-minute game for two, which can be played just as well in a small group or as a quick contest.

One person keeps score and does the timing while the player concentrates for 60 seconds. During that minute, the player must think up all the words he or she can which start with a given letter. That's all there is to it!

Sounds easy, doesn't it? Well, try it. The timekeeper says, "Start when I give you the letter—R," and then starts timing. As the player starts calling off words that begin with R, the timekeeper must keep track of the number of words by marking them off in groups of 5, like this: ⊬⊬

Of course, the dictionary is packed with common words beginning with every letter of the alphabet, but you'll be surprised how difficult it is to think of them as you sit there faced by that relentless second hand, not to mention the grinning timekeeper!

When the minute is up, total up the score and then change roles. Give each other letters of similar ease or difficulty (see below). If you get a Z, you're entitled to give a Y, but an S deserves a C.

Order of frequency as a starting letter: S-C-P-A-B-T-M-D-R-H-E-F-L-G-I-W-N-O-U-V-K-J-Q-Y-Z-X.

PARTY GAMES FOR AGES 6-8

8

PARTY TIPS FOR THE
6-TO-8-YEAR-OLD SET

When you're planning a party for 6-to-8-year-olds, vary the games so that a quiet game follows an action game. If you have at least two rooms to party in, move the games back and forth, alternately, from one room to another. This also gives the feeling of action and excitement. And if you keep the party moving rapidly, there won't be time for squabbles and problems to start.

Set aside a place where the guests can keep the things they have already collected—their "loot." Many little ones worry about what is happening to their candy bags or to the prizes they collected. If you can reassure them that the loot is in a safe place, they are free to get involved in the games.

Prizes are important. They don't have to be big ones. A package of chewing gum is a good prize, and so are any of the items listed below. If your budget is really tight, you may get around the prize-press by keeping a large score card, with a gold star pasted down (or a pencilled star written in) for the winner of every game. Then at the end of the party, pass out one prize to each child on the basis of the stars. Or put all the prizes (gift-wrapped) in a large bag and let the one with the most stars grab first, the one with the least grab last. If you see that one child is getting more than his or her share of stars, also give a star to the runner-up in each game as the party progresses. Everyone needs some stars.

PRIZES

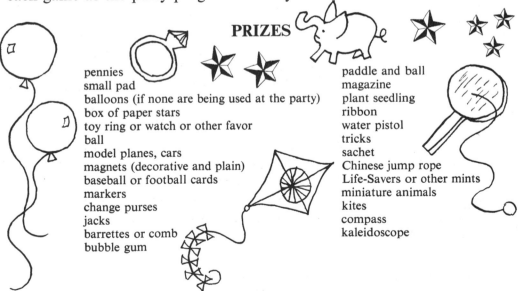

pennies
small pad
balloons (if none are being used at the party)
box of paper stars
toy ring or watch or other favor
ball
model planes, cars
magnets (decorative and plain)
baseball or football cards
markers
change purses
jacks
barrettes or comb
bubble gum

paddle and ball
magazine
plant seedling
ribbon
water pistol
tricks
sachet
Chinese jump rope
Life-Savers or other mints
miniature animals
kites
compass
kaleidoscope

PAT THE LION

PLAYERS: 5 or more
EQUIPMENT: String 6½ feet (2 meters) long
PREPARATION: None

The Lion stands inside a cage which consists of a small circle—just large enough for the lion to stand in comfortably, perhaps about 2 feet (60 cm) across—formed with the string. The Lion Tamer walks around the Lion and tries to keep other players, the Visitors, from patting the Lion. The Lion may be patted on the foot, shoulder or back.

One at a time, the Visitors try to sneak up and pat the Lion without first being patted by the Lion Tamer. A Visitor who succeeds in patting the Lion becomes the Lion Tamer and the previous Lion Tamer becomes the Lion. This continues until everyone has had a chance to become Lion Tamer and Lion.

If the players are very young, take care to see that the Lion receives only a pat, not a whack. If some of the Visitors don't get to pat the Lion the first time, give them another chance after the others have tried.

PENCIL DARTS

PLAYERS: 3–6
EQUIPMENT: Large sheet of paper
  Blindfold
  Pencil
  Sheet of paper for scoring
PREPARATION: Draw a circle on the large sheet of paper. Put a big dot in the middle and draw lines from the dot to the edge of the circle. When it is finished, it should look like a target or a pie with about eight or nine slices. Put a number in each slice.

One by one, each player is blindfolded and takes a turn jabbing at the circle with a pencil. Holding the pencil up in the air, he or she says, "Tit-tat-toe," and then puts the pencil down on the paper, trying to land inside the circle. If the pencil point makes a dot within a section of the circle, the player initials that section. However, if the pencil lands outside the circle, on a line, or in a section which already has someone's initials, there is no score and the next player gets a turn.

Each player keeps a list of the numbers he or she tapped. If there are any arguments about who tapped what, you can check it by taking a look at the circle itself where the initials were written in. Then, when all the numbers have been tapped, add up the players' scores. The player with the highest score wins. And this is important: if a player touches the bull's eye, that is an automatic win!

HIDE AND SEEK

PLAYERS: 3 or more
EQUIPMENT: None
PREPARATION: None

Hide and Seek is one of the all-time most popular games. This is one way to play.

One player is "It." "It" stands at a spot that is chosen as Goal with closed eyes and counts to 100. While "It" is counting, everyone runs to hide. As soon as "It" reaches 100, "It" calls out:

> **Bushel of wheat**
> **Bushel of rye,**
> **All not hid**
> **Holler "I."**

If someone is not yet in a hiding place and calls out, "I," "It" counts to 100 again, but this time by tens. Then "It" calls out:

> **Bushel of wheat,**
> **Bushel of clover,**
> **All not hid**
> **Can't hide over.**
> **All eyes open! Here I come!**

Then "It" goes out to hunt for the players. As soon as "It" sees a player, "It" calls out the name of the player and both start running to the goal. If "It" gets there first, "It" taps the goal three times and calls out:

> **One two three for (player's name)!**

But if the player gets to the goal first, that player tags the goal once and calls out:

> **Home free**
> **One two three!**

In case of a tie, the player is "home free."

The game goes on until all the players have been brought back to the goal. The first player who was caught is "It" when the game is played again.

SARDINES

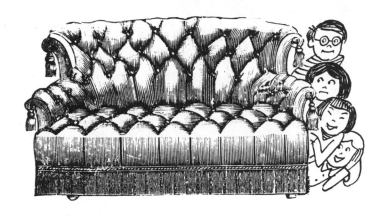

PLAYERS: 5 or more
EQUIPMENT: None
PREPARATION: None

This is "Hide and Seek" backwards. Only one player hides, and the other players go hunting individually. When a hunter finds the hiding place, though, instead of announcing it, that player gets into the hiding place, too. And so it goes. As each hunter finds the hiding place, the hunter joins the hunted until they are crowded—you guessed it—like sardines. The game goes on until the last hunter finds the sardines.

AFRICAN HIDE AND SEEK

PLAYERS: 2
EQUIPMENT: None
PREPARATION: None

In Africa, boys and girls play a game of hide and seek which is similar to our game, except that it is played by only two people. There is another difference, too, which young children delight in.

The player who hides is called the Owl. When hidden the Owl calls "Whoo, whoo," just like an owl. Then the Fox, who has been hiding its eyes, starts to look for the Owl. If the Fox finds the Owl, it pretends to eat it up, while the Owl pretends to cry. Then the Owl becomes the Fox.

If, however, the Owl can leave its hiding place and get back to home base before the Fox sees it, the Owl remains the Owl, and it gets to hide again.

DOG EAT BONE

PLAYERS: 6–20
EQUIPMENT: A bean bag, stone or similar object
PREPARATION: None

The players form a circle. One player, the Master, is blindfolded and sits in the middle with a "bone" (a bean bag, stone or some other easy-to-grab object) placed close by.

One player after another acts as the Dog and tries to capture the "bone" without being heard by the Master. If the Master hears a sound, he or she points in the direction of the sound and says "Doggie!" If the Master is pointing in the right direction, the Dog must go back to the circle. The Master stays in the middle.

If a Dog is able to pick up the bone without being heard by the Master, then the Dog becomes the new Master.

DOG STATUES

You can also play Dog Eat Bone as an elimination game. Instead of a circle, the Master sits at one end of the room with the bone directly behind him or her. The other players stand back at least 10 or 15 feet from the Master, toward the other end of the room, and they take turns tiptoeing up to try to get the bone. The Master turns quickly if there is any sound. If a Dog is caught moving, the Dog is out. If the Dog does a quick enough freeze, it is safe. The Dog who gets the bone is the new Master.

SNEAKY STATUES

PLAYERS: 5 or more
EQUIPMENT: None
PREPARATION: None

Here is Dog Statues without the dogs. All the players line up against one wall of the room except for one ("It"), who stands with his or her back to the other players at the end of the room.

The object of the game is for the players to cross the room and tag "It" without being caught moving.

"It" counts to 10 aloud, facing the blank wall, and then wheels around. The other players freeze in whatever positions they were in at the count of 10. If they sway or shake or move at all, and "It" sees it, they must go back to the wall and start again.

"It" can count at any speed. The first player to tag "It" is "It" for the next game, or gets to choose the new "It."

HOT OR COLD

PLAYERS: Unlimited
EQUIPMENT: None
PREPARATION: None

One player, the Guesser, leaves the room, as the other players choose some object, such as a door, a vase, a picture, a pillow, which is in the room. When the group decides on the object, the Guesser is called in. The Guesser must try to guess which object the group selected. When the Guesser moves toward the object the group says "Warm." As the Guesser gets closer, everyone says "Warmer." When the Guesser gets very near, they say, "Hot!"

If the Guesser is far away from the object, though, everyone says, "Cold." If the Guesser moves farther away, they say, "You're getting colder." The game goes on until the Guesser names the object, and then another player becomes the Guesser.

You can play the same game a little differently. Instead of saying "Hot" or "Cold," everyone hums. The closer the Guesser gets to the object, the louder everyone hums. When the Guesser moves farther away, everyone hums more softly.

THE WAITING GAME

PLAYERS: **2 or more**
EQUIPMENT: None
PREPARATION: None

Suppose you're in a waiting room, at the doctor's office, or in a restaurant. You've run out of conversation, and you really want to kill time. This game needs no moving about, no great concentration, and the only requirement is that you *be* somewhere!

You say, "I see something red," or "I see something black," or you name any characteristic of the object you have secretly decided on.

The other person must guess what you have chosen. If your surroundings are open, you may say "hot" or "luke-warm" or "cold," as the person guesses, depending on whether the object guessed is near or far from the one you picked. If you're in a small room, it shouldn't be necessary to give clues. If you're in a bus or plane, you must choose something inside, since objects in the landscape go by too fast.

WASHERWOMAN

PLAYERS: **2 or more**
EQUIPMENT: None
PREPARATION: None

This a game that all the players will delight in. Even grown-ups, if they are not too tall, can participate, and have fun doing it.

Partners stand facing each other and clasp hands. Without letting go of each other's hands, they start to turn in opposite directions. One set of arms goes over their heads, and then as the turn is completed, the other set of arms goes up.

That's all there is to it! They just keep on turning and turning as long as they want, and when they get tired of going in one direction, they can change and turn in the other direction.

Washerwoman is easiest for two people of the same height, but it's funnier if there is a difference. There's a limit to the difference, though, since the shorter person's arms must be long enough to go over both their heads. Of course, if a tall person (like a mother or father) can stoop way over and turn at the same time, then he or she can play Washerwoman with someone quite small.

A-HUNTING WE WILL GO

PLAYERS: 10 or more
EQUIPMENT: None
PREPARATION: None

One player, the "Fox," picks out two players to be the "Lambs." The rest of the players join hands in a circle around the Fox, with the Lambs outside. The players skip around and around and sing:

A-hunting we will go,
A-hunting we will go,
We'll catch a fox
And put him in a box
And never let him go.

While the singing is going on, the Lambs come close to the circle and try to tease the Fox.

The Fox meanwhile tries to slip out of the circle, under the arms of the players who try to keep the Fox in. When the Fox gets out, it tries to catch the Lambs. When it catches a Lamb, that Lamb becomes a Fox. Another Lamb is selected by the original Fox, and the two Foxes try to catch the two Lambs. The last Lamb wins.

SHADOWS

PLAYERS: 6–30
EQUIPMENT: A sheet
A lamp or a flashlight
Objects such as a carrot, a shoe, scissors, a bottle, etc.
PREPARATION: Hang up the sheet in a doorway (if you have an exercise bar, that's an easy way to hang it up) and put the light behind it, along with the objects, which you conceal from the players.

Darken the room that the players are sitting in. Then turn on the light behind the sheet and hold up the objects so that their shadows fall on the sheet. The players have to guess what each object is. If you divide the guessers into two teams, the team that gets the correct answer first the most times wins.

LINE UP

PLAYERS: 6–30
EQUIPMENT: Same as above, and also a hat, a mop, pillows, etc.
PREPARATION: Same as above

This is an interesting variation on Shadows. You have to guess who each player's shadow belongs to. You can make up disguises for yourselves to change your shapes. For instance, you can stuff pillows under your clothes, put on a false nose, or wear a hat or mop on your head. The person or team that guesses the most players wins.

PASS THE BEANS

PLAYERS: 5–25
EQUIPMENT: 1 bean bag
PREPARATION: None

One player, "It," stands in the middle of a circle. The other players, who form the circle, stand close together so that "It" can't see their hands behind their backs as they pass a bean bag from one to another. They must do this so quietly and carefully that "It" doesn't spot them. "It" tries to guess who has the bean bag, and keeps on guessing until "It" guesses right. Then the person who is caught with the bean bag changes places with "It" and the game begins again.

If you don't have a bean bag, you can play the game with a ball or a coin.

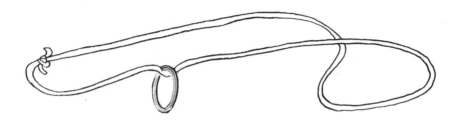

SMUGGLER'S RING

PLAYERS: 8–20
EQUIPMENT: A heavy string long enough to reach around the circle of players
A small ring: a curtain rod ring will do, or the ring from a looseleaf notebook
PREPARATION: Pull the string through the ring and tie the ends of the string together.

The players sit or stand in a circle. They all hold the string in their hands. The object of the game is to pass the ring from one fist to another without revealing who has it.

"It" steps into the middle and watches the others carefully. The players in the circle slide their hands back and forth over the string. They do this all the time, even when they are not passing the ring, so that "It" can't be sure where the ring is. When "It" guesses correctly, he or she joins the circle, and the one who was caught with the ring becomes "It."

BUDDIES

PLAYERS: 20–40
EQUIPMENT: Music—from tape cassette, radio, phonograph, or piano
PREPARATION: None

Pair off all the players, either letting them choose their own "buddies" or through one of the pair-off games on pages 444–449. If there is an extra person, he or she can be the leader.

The "buddies" form two circles, one inside the other, with one buddy in each circle. Make sure that no two buddies are in the same circle, and that the players know who their buddies are.

When the leader plays the music, the outer circle walks in one direction, and the inner circle walks in the other.

When the leader suddenly stops the music, the buddies must run for each other, grab each other's hands and stoop down low. The last pair of buddies to stoop are out of the game. Then they help to spot the next pair who are last-to-stoop, the next time the music stops.

The game continues. Each time the music stops, the last pair of buddies to find each other and stoop are out. The last couple left in the game wins.

FULL OF BEANS

PLAYERS: Unlimited
EQUIPMENT: Dried lima beans or kidney beans or small pebbles
PREPARATION: Before the guests arrive, hide the beans all in one room
    in different places, such as closets, behind books, under ash trays,
    in bottles, on shelves and under sofa cushions. WARNING: Be
    sure to remove anything valuable or breakable in the room,
    because the players will be moving around quickly.

When all the guests have arrived, tell them that you have hidden beans all over that room—and only in that room—and that they have 5 minutes to find them.

When the 5 minutes are up, all the players count their beans, and the player with the most is the winner.

PING PONG HOCKEY

PLAYERS: 4–10
EQUIPMENT: A ping pong ball
**PREPARATION: Move the furniture to the side of the room so that you have
a large playing space.**

Divide the group into two teams. Then mark off the playing space. It should be about 20 feet (6m) long and 6 feet (2m) wide. The goals for each team are at opposite ends of the playing space. Mark them with string or with small stones. Then find the middle of the playing space, and place the ping pong ball there. That is the starting point.

Each team now tries to blow the ball to its own goal, without blowing it offside, and at the same time stop the other team from blowing the ball to the other goal. The players can all blow at the same time, or they can take turns blowing. The ball *may not* be touched by any player —it can only be blown. If the ball goes out of bounds, put it back in the middle of the playing space at whatever point it went out.

A team gets a point every time it blows the ball to its goal. The first team to get 5 points wins the game.

UPSTAIRS, DOWNSTAIRS

PLAYERS: 3–6
EQUIPMENT: A flight of stairs
A stone, button or coin
PREPARATION: None

One person is the leader and holds a stone, button or coin. The other players all sit on the lowest step.

The leader holds out closed fists, and each player has a turn to guess in which hand the object is hidden. When all the players have had a chance to guess, the leader shows which hand holds the object. Those who guessed correctly move one step up. Those who didn't guess right remain sitting where they are.

Then the leader shifts the object about and gives the players another chance to guess which hand it is in. This process repeats as the players move up to the top of the stairs. After they reach the top, they start moving down each time they guess correctly. The first player to get to the top and then back to the bottom of the stairs wins. The winner is the leader in the next game.

SIMON SAYS

PLAYERS: **Unlimited**
EQUIPMENT: **None**
PREPARATION: **None**

No matter how many people are present, you will have fun playing this classic game. Be sure you have enough space, because the game can become very active.

One player, male or female, is chosen to be Simon, the leader, and Simon stands on a box, chair or table so everyone can see and hear the commands. The rest of the players stand about 3 feet apart, if possible, and face Simon. The leader starts by saying, "Simon says *Hands out in front of you.*" Each player must then stretch out their hands. Then the leader might say, "Simon says *Drop hands*." Each player drops hands.

As Simon calls out orders, the players must follow the order BUT only if the leader first says "Simon says." If the leader just says: "*Walk backwards*," then everyone is supposed to disobey and stand still. The group is only to obey the command when it comes from Simon and the leader says "Simon says."

If someone obeys an order that is not supposed to be followed, that person drops out of the game. Or if players do *not* obey an order which should be obeyed, they drop out, too. The last person left in the game is the winner.

In this game, Simon can obey the directions, too, but doesn't *have* to. Simon may even do something entirely different to trick the players. For instance, the leader might say, "Simon says *Put your hands on your hips*," while putting his or her hands on shoulders. If the players watch the leader, they are likely to do what Simon does—instead of what Simon says!

Also the leader may give orders like this: "Simon says, *Take one step forward . . . Now one step to your right*." In this case, the players must only take the one step forward and NOT the step to the right—because the leader did not say "Simon says," before giving the second order.

A skillful leader will call out commands rapidly and should be perfectly fair in judging whether the players followed them correctly. For example, if you are supposed to be marching, and then are supposed to stop, the leader must judge whether you stopped marching immediately or took too long to stop.

Each person should have a turn being Simon.

RING ROPE

PLAYERS: 10–25
EQUIPMENT: A rope long enough to reach around the circle of players
PREPARATION: Tie the ends of the rope together.

All the players stand in a circle, holding the rope with both hands close together. Two are chosen to leave the circle and become tappers.

These two tappers walk around the inside of the circle and try to tap one of the hands of the players holding the rope. If any players think their hands are going to be tapped, they should quickly drop their hands from the rope, because the tappers must tap at least one hand while it is holding the rope. Of course, the tappers may try to trick the players by pretending to tap one hand while actually aiming to tap the hand of the player next door.

If one of the players in the middle taps the hand of someone who is still holding the rope, they change places and the tapped player becomes one of the tappers.

CATCHING THE STICK

PLAYERS: 6 or more
EQUIPMENT: A cane, yardstick, or any straight stick about 3 feet (1 m) high
PREPARATION: None

All the players except one stand around in a circle. The extra player is "It" and stands in the middle. "It" stands the stick up on the floor and holds the top of it with his or her fingers, preventing the stick from falling over.

The players in the circle take numbers by counting off, beginning with "one." Then the game is ready to begin.

"It" calls out a number and takes his or her hand off of the stick. The person whose number is called must run up to the stick and grab it before it falls on the floor.

If the stick hits the floor before the player can get to it, then the player returns to his or her place in the circle. But if the stick is caught before it falls, the player changes places with "It" and calls out the numbers and holds the stick.

BIRDS CAN FLY

PLAYERS: 3–50 (if space permits)
EQUIPMENT: None
PREPARATION: None

The players line up side by side, facing the leader, but not too close together. They need enough space between them so that they can wave their arms up and down.

The leader begins by saying, "Birds can fly," and waves his or her arms to look like wings. The other players imitate this. The leader may say, "Bats can fly," or "Bees can fly," or "Airplanes can fly." Every time the leader mentions anything and says it can fly, he or she waves arms.

Then the leader may suddenly say, "Tigers can fly!" and flap arms like a bird at the same time. Those players who also flap their arms are out! The leader has tricked them. When the leader mentions something that can't fly, the players must keep their hands at their sides. The players must listen carefully, and be wide awake, or they will be out of the game.

The last person left in the game becomes the leader for the next game.

STOP AND LISTEN

PLAYERS: 3–40
EQUIPMENT: None
PREPARATION: None

This game can be played almost any place where there are things to tap. One player does the tapping while the others guess. The tapper stands behind the other players and they must not try to turn around. Then the tapper taps various objects: the window, the floor, or a pot, or a lamp shade, or a newspaper.

The first person to guess what is being tapped has a turn to become the tapper.

HOT POTATO

PLAYERS: 6–30
EQUIPMENT: A small potato, ball, stone, or piece of wood
PREPARATION: None

The players sit around in a circle facing inwards and one is chosen as leader. The leader steps out of the circle. Then an object, such as a small potato, ball, stone or piece of wood, is passed around from player to player. Each player must accept the object and pass it very quickly.

As the object is passed, the leader closes his or her eyes or turns away. When the leader yells "HOT," the player holding the potato is out. The game is played over and over again until every player but one is out. The last one left in the game is the winner.

If more than 30 want to play, you can form two or more circles. Each one must have its own potato to pass around, but there is only one leader. The winner in each circle can then form a final circle, to see who is the grand winner.

You can also play this game with music, like Buddies or Musical Chairs, with the leader stopping the music at intervals.

BARKING DOGS

PLAYERS: 6–20
EQUIPMENT: A ball
          Music, from a tape cassette, radio, phonograph or piano
PREPARATION: None

As in Hot Potato, the players sit in a big circle and pass the ball around to the right. While they do it, the leader or another person who is not in the circle, plays the music. Every once in a while, the music stops. Whichever player has the ball at that moment becomes a dog. The dog must get down on all fours and bark. Then the dog sits back and passes the ball to the right again as the music starts.

The next time the music stops, whichever player has the ball becomes a dog—but so does the player who was the dog the time before! Once a dog, you're a dog for the rest of the game. So every time the music stops, every person who was caught before gets down on hands and knees and barks.

Soon you have a roomful of barking dogs, and it is time to end the game or start again. The first person who became a dog plays the music for the next game.

FOUR UP

PLAYERS: 10 or more
EQUIPMENT: None
PREPARATION: None

This is a good game to play in a classroom or at a party.

Four or more players go up to the front of the room. If there are more than 20 players in all, then more than four can be up. The others put their heads down on their desks, and are not allowed to peek.

The four players tip-toe around the room as quietly as possible. Each one lightly taps a player and whispers, "Someone is tapping you." The player who was tapped does not look up, but remains with head on the desk. He or she puts up one hand, however, so as not to be tapped again. Of course, the tappers try to disguise their voices. Then the four tappers go back to the front of the room.

Now those who have been tapped stand up. They are supposed to guess who tapped them, but each has only one turn to guess. The tappers don't let them know if their guesses are right or not until all have had a chance to guess. Then the tappers tell the players if they were right or not.

Those who guessed correctly change places with the tappers. Those who didn't guess right sit down again, and the tappers who were not caught get to tap again.

OINK OINK

PLAYERS: 8 or more
EQUIPMENT: A blindfold (or scarf or large handkerchief you can tie around
        "It's" eyes)
PREPARATION: None

This is Blindman's Buff made easy. The players walk or run in a circle around "It" who is in the middle and blindfolded. When "It" shouts "STOP," the circle freezes. "It" points to one of the players and says, "Oink Oink." The player pointed to has to reply, "Oink Oink," but may disguise his or her voice. "It" has to guess who it is from voice alone. If "It" is right, the player who got caught is "It." Otherwise, the circle starts moving again and the game continues.

SWAT THY NEIGHBOR

PLAYERS: 10 or more
EQUIPMENT: A rolled-up newspaper
PREPARATION: None

All the players, except "It" stand in a circle. They all hold their hands behind their backs. "It" carries a rolled-up newspaper and walks around the outside of the circle, behind the backs of the players.

"It" walks until he or she puts the newspaper into the hands of one of the players—let's say George. As soon as George feels the newspaper, he grabs it and swats the player to his right with it (Martha), across the back.

Martha runs around the circle with George chasing after. "It," meanwhile, steps into George's place. Martha tries to get back in place before George can catch her. If she gets home safely, George, still carrying the newspaper, is "It" for another turn. If Martha is caught, she becomes "It."

BIRD, BEAST
OR FISH

PLAYERS: 9–33
EQUIPMENT: None
PREPARATION: None

Divide the group into teams of equal number. One person acts as the Judge and doesn't belong to either team.

Each team chooses one player to send to the Judge. The Judge tells them alone what animal, bird or fish they will be, say "Bluejay," or "Lion," or "Monkey," or any other creature. The Judge must tell the same name to each chosen player very quietly so that no players on either team can hear.

Then the chosen players go back to their separate teams and try to act out the animal they are supposed to be. The other members of the team have to guess the name of the animal. They are allowed to ask questions, but the answers to the questions must be *acted out*, not spoken. For example, a player might ask, "How do you eat?" The players acting out the animal must eat the way that particular animal eats.

The first team to guess the animal wins. Then another member of each team is chosen to go up to the Judge, who selects another animal, bird or fish to act out. The team that comes in first 10 times is the grand winner.

For more acting games, see pages 498-514.

FOX AND GANDER

PLAYERS: 4–10
EQUIPMENT: None
PREPARATION: None

Two players are selected out of the group, one to be the Fox and one the Gander. The others are all Geese. The Geese line up behind the Gander, each player holding the shoulders of the goose in front. The Fox faces the Gander, standing 6 feet (2m) away.

Then the Fox says, "Goosey, goosey, gander," which is the signal to begin. The Fox runs over and tries to tag the last player in line.

The Gander spreads arms out wide, trying to protect the flock and keep the Fox from tagging the last goose. The line of geese sways from side to side to prevent the Fox from tagging the last goose.

When the Fox does tag the end goose, the Fox becomes the Gander and stands first in line. The last (tagged) player becomes the Fox. The former Gander is now second in line as everyone else shifts down.

This is a game with lots of action, and everyone should have a chance to be Fox, Gander and Goose.

BEADING THE STRING

PLAYERS: 4–10
EQUIPMENT: Strings, about 2–3 feet (1 m) long, one for each player
                              Beads or macaroni
PREPARATION: Make a large knot on the end of every string.

Here's a bead-stringing race. Put a big bowl of beads on the table and give each player a string. If the players are very young, use large wooden beads with large holes. You can use macaroni, too.

When the signal is given, the players start stringing. After about 5 minutes, the leader calls out, "Stop!" Or you can use an alarm clock. The player with the most beads on the string is the winner.

This game is especially good to play at the end of a party, when young children may be tired and need the quiet time this game provides. (Even more so for the person who is *running* the party.) Sometimes, the bead-stringing goes on past the end of the game, as some parents arrive late to pick up their children.

12 Ways to Play Musical Chairs— With and Without Music— With and Without Chairs

MUSICAL CHAIRS

PLAYERS: 6–40
EQUIPMENT: Chairs, one less than the number of players
           Music, from tape cassette, radio, phonograph, or piano
PREPARATION: Line up a row of chairs with alternate chairs facing in
              opposite directions. If one seat of one chair is facing north, then
              the seat of the chair next to it should face south.

This is an old familiar game, but it is still one of the best party games.

As soon as the music starts, all the players begin to walk single file around and around the chairs. Suddenly, the music stops. There is a big scramble for seats. One player is left without a seat, and that player must leave the game. Then one chair is taken away, so there is still one chair less than the number of players.

The music starts again. The players walk around and then the music stops. All try to grab seats. The player without a chair leaves the game and another chair is removed.

This goes on until there are just two players walking around one chair. It gets pretty exciting at this point. When the music stops, the player lucky enough to get into the chair wins.

MUSICAL BUMPS

PLAYERS: 6 or more
EQUIPMENT: None
PREPARATION: None

This Musical Chairs game has no chairs, just music which the leader plays on a piano, or from a record or tape—or may not play at all as the leader may just clap. The players move to the rhythm. When the leader stops the music or stops clapping, everyone must sit on the floor. The last person to sit is OUT and must go to the sidelines with the leader. For a "sit" to be considered "safe," the contestant's bottom must touch the floor.

Vary the type of music or rhythm so that some is loud, some soft, some fast, some with a jazz beat. Vary the length of each segment, too, so that the players are totally unprepared for the moment the sound stops. Use a few very short segments; they make the game exciting.

If the music is on tape or record, change the volume control suddenly. Many players will sit down at the change in dynamics, without realizing the music is still playing and the game still going on. These players are OUT.

When there are just two players left, they will be busy watching each other and there may be one tie after another, as they both hit the floor at the same time. If this happens, ask them to close their eyes while they move to the music. You'll soon have a winner.

MUSICAL BUMPS BACKWARDS

When you have played the game through once or twice, reverse it. Start everyone on the floor. They can move around—twist, turn, kick and reach—but no one is allowed to get up on his or her knees, because that is a shortcut to standing, which is what everyone must do when the music stops. The last one to stand is OUT.

After you play Musical Bumps Backwards twice or perhaps three times, the winners compete against each other to select a champion.

CHANGE CHAIRS

PLAYERS: 6–20
EQUIPMENT: One sturdy chair for each player
**PREPARATION: Set up 2 lines of chairs, about 15 feet (5 m) apart, facing
each other, but *not* directly opposite each other.**

One player is "It" and doesn't have a chair. "It" stands at least 15 feet (5m) away from the nearest chair, and the other players all sit down on the chairs. When "It" yells "Change chairs," everyone changes chairs. Players can change places only with those whose chairs are in the opposite row. Meanwhile "It" tries to get someone's chair.

If "It" succeeds in getting someone's chair, then the player left without a chair becomes "It." If "It" does not get someone's seat, then "It" continues to be "It" and calls out, "Change chairs," until he or she does get a chair.

STIR THE SOUP

PLAYERS: 8 or more
**EQUIPMENT: A chair for every player
except "It"
A cane, yardstick (meter
rule) or broom handle**
**PREPARATION: Arrange the chairs in
a circle.**

"It" stands in the middle of the circle of chairs with the cane or yardstick (or meter rule), or anything you can tap the floor with.

The players stand and walk around "It." As they walk, they say, "Let's stir the soup. Let's stir the soup." "It" pretends to stir the soup with the stick.

Suddenly "It" taps on the floor three times! As soon as this happens, there is a big scramble for the chairs. "It" drops the stick and also runs for a chair. The player who is left without a chair is "It" the next time.

"It" may try to fool the players by occasionally tapping only once or twice.

CAT AND MICE

PLAYERS: 8 or more
EQUIPMENT: Chairs, one less than the number of players
         Table
PREPARATION: None

All the players, except one, sit on the chairs arranged in a large circle. In the middle of the circle there is a table and the extra player hides under it. That player is the Cat.

As soon as Cat calls out "Ready," two or three players, who are Mice, walk over to the table and tap on it. They stand there and tap until the Cat cries out, "I'm going to catch you!" The Cat tries to take them by surprise as it jumps out from under the table. It jumps out quickly and attempts to catch one of the Mice before it can get back to its chair in the circle.

If the Cat catches a Mouse, it takes that player's chair in the circle and the captured player becomes the next Cat. Otherwise, Cat keeps the same role until it can catch a different Mouse. If Cat is unsuccessful twice, choose another Cat. Choose different Mice, too, each time.

FRUIT BASKET

PLAYERS: 10 or more
EQUIPMENT: Chairs for all—except one
PREPARATION: None

With the chairs in a circle, all the players sit on them, except "It" who stands in the middle.

"It" gives each player the name of a fruit. If the group is large, use the name of one fruit several times. All the players must remember their names.

"It" says, "Apple change places with Orange." And Apple must change places with Orange. If there are several apples and several oranges, then all of them need to get up and change. "It" may also order three fruits to change places with each other. "It" may say, "Bananas, pears and cherries change places." Whenever players change places, "It" tries to get a seat. The one left without a seat is then "It."

The game really gets hilarious when "It" says, "Fruit basket upset!" Then all players must get up and change places.

THE HOT SEAT

PLAYERS: 8 or more
EQUIPMENT: A chair for every player
PREPARATION: Arrange the chairs in a circle.

This is a fast action game. All the players sit in a circle on the chairs. The one left without a chair is "It" and stands in the middle. The chairs must be close together so that the players can quickly slide over from one chair to the next. One chair is left vacant and that one is called "the hot seat."

"It" tries to get into the hot seat. But it isn't so easy, because every time "It" tries to do this, one player next to the hot seat moves into it. In that way another chair becomes empty and when "It" tries to get into the new hot seat, it is quickly occupied by one of the players next to it.

When "It" is fast enough to get into the empty chair, someone else becomes "It."

OCEAN WAVE

PLAYERS: 8 or more
EQUIPMENT: A chair for every player except one
PREPARATION: Place the chairs to form a circle

The players sit in the chairs in a circle, except for "It" who stands in the middle. "It" calls "Shift right" or "Shift left." At the call "Shift right," each player must move to the chair on the right. And at "Shift left," each player moves to the chair to the left.

"It" changes the call fast and often, but must be careful not to call faster than the players can move or there will be a big mixup. Of course, "It" can call several "Shift rights" or "Shift lefts," following each other.

Every once in a while, "It" tries to get a seat. "It" may wait for 3 or 4 calls before running for it. When "It" does manage to steal a seat, the player who is left without a chair becomes "It," and the game continues.

DEEP IN THE JUNGLE

PLAYERS: 12-30
EQUIPMENT: Enough seats for all but 2 of the players
PREPARATION: None

These games have been played and enjoyed at adult parties.

Divide the group into partners. Each set of partners decides that they will be a particular animal. You would have a pair of monkeys, for example, a pair of anteaters, a pair of lions, a pair of leopards.

The partners who don't have chairs ("It") walk about the room together, saying the names of various jungle animals. When their animal is called, the corresponding partners rise and follow the unseated partners around the room. If the "It" partners say, "The jungle is quiet tonight," all the players join the line. If the "It" partners say, "The jungle is noisy," everyone runs for the seats, partners holding hands as they run. Of course, the "It" couple tries to get seats, and the unseated couple becomes "It" next time round.

NOAH'S ARK

In this variation, the players can be any living creatures, and the "It" couple calls "It looks like sunshine" and "It looks like rain."

AROUND THE WORLD

PLAYERS: 8-30
EQUIPMENT: Chairs, one for each player except one
                Paper and pencil for each player
PREPARATION: Arrange the chairs in a circle.

The players sit on the chairs, all except "It" who stands in the middle of the circle. Each player chooses the name of a different city and writes it down on a piece of paper for "It," who makes sure that the same city has not been selected by 2 players. "It" calls out, for example, "I am taking a trip from New York to London." Then the players who have chosen those cities must immediately change places. If "It" calls out, "I am taking a trip *Around the World*," everyone must change seats.

"It" tries to get one of the chairs while the other players are changing places. If "It" succeeds, the player who is left without a chair is "It," and goes into the middle of the circle and calls out the cities.

PARTY GAMES FOR AGES 8-UP

9

Before the Party

What do you do while your guests are arriving? They don't all show up at the same time, and you don't want to start opening presents or eating food or playing anything major when several guests are still expected. The games in this section are all "fooling around" games that are meant to keep the party going when the party isn't quite ready to get going.

FEELIES

PLAYERS: Unlimited
EQUIPMENT: 2 covered baskets or boxes
                 2 dog biscuits, 2 prunes, 2 onions, 2 carrots, 2 bracelets,
                 2 pieces of string, 2 nails, 2 wads of tissues, and any other
                 objects with different feels that you can find, 2 of each so
                 that the baskets are identical
                 Pencils and paper for each 2 contestants
PREPARATION: Put the objects in the covered baskets.

As your guests arrive, two by two, tell them they may slip their hands into the baskets under the cover and feel the objects, without looking at them. Let them feel around under the cover for about a minute, then let another two contestants have a turn. After each couple takes its turn, give them paper and pencil and tell them to list the objects they felt in the basket. The couple with the most complete, correct list wins.

ELBOW-COIN TRICK

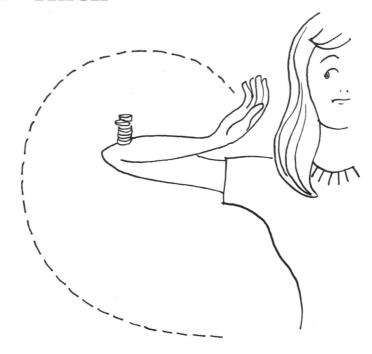

PLAYERS: Unlimited
EQUIPMENT: A few piles of coins
PREPARATION: None

This trick takes a good bit of practice. Few people can do it the first time they attempt it, but it really doesn't take long to get the feel of it. And as a "before the party" game, it's particularly good because more than one person can practice it at a time while you wait for other people to arrive.

Place a pile of coins (start with just one, then 2, and then increase to 4 or 5) on your elbow with your hand bent back near your shoulder and your palm open and facing upward. Now bring your hand forward and down sharply in an arc. The coins will fly off your elbow into such a position that your open hand scoops them in automatically before they fall to the floor.

Winner is, of course, the person who can catch the most coins.

Note: The "Guinness Book of World Records" reports 74 quarters as the record elbow-coin catch. You may not want to tell your guests that!

LOTTERY

PLAYERS: Unlimited
EQUIPMENT: 1. A large glass jar or paper bag of peanuts or dried beans
    2. An orange (not seedless)
    3. Part of a page of a newspaper
    4. A tall glass of water
    5. A large dictionary
    6. A table lamp
    7. A long piece of string
    8. A photograph of a baby
    9. A small stack of writing paper
    10. A head of lettuce
    Paper and pencil for each player
PREPARATION: Count, measure, find out the answers to the questions
    below. If you want, you might attach a card to each object
    with the question on it (see below).

As your guests arrive, give them each a pencil and sheet of paper. Then without touching the objects, each guest is to write down on the page:

1. The number of peanuts or beans in the jar
2. The number of seeds in the orange (divide it and eat it later)
3. The number of words printed on both sides of the newspaper scrap
4. The quantity of water in the glass
5. The number of pages in the dictionary
6. The height of the lamp
7. The length of the string
8. The age of the baby
9. The number of sheets in the stack of paper
10. The weight of the lettuce

The winner is the player who guesses closest in the greatest number of classifications.

ODD BEAN

PLAYERS: Unlimited
EQUIPMENT: 12 beans for every player, plus some extras for beans that get lost
PREPARATION: None (see below)

This game, the 1-2-3 Shoot of beans, is a particularly good one to play before the party starts. People can join it as they arrive, and it can go on as long as you want.

Measure out the beans beforehand in little bags, so you can hand a set of 12 to the players as they arrive. It saves time when many guests arrive at the same moment.

With his 12 beans, one player—let's say Gregory—puts a few beans in one fist, stretches it out toward another player and asks, "Odds or evens?" If the other player—Connie—guesses correctly that Gregory's closed fist has an odd number of beans in it, she collects those beans. If she guesses wrong, she has to turn over that many beans to Gregory. The object, of course, is to collect all the beans. When you want to stop playing, the winner is the one with the most beans.

HUL GUL

PLAYERS: 2 or more
EQUIPMENT: 12 beans for each player (or small stones or nuts or marbles)
PREPARATION: None

This ancient game is something like Odd Bean. One player—let's say David—puts a few beans in one fist and holds it out to Kathy, saying, "Hul gul."

Kathy says, "Hands full."

David says, "How many?"

Then Kathy has to guess the number of beans in David's hand.

Let's say that David has 8 beans in his hand. Kathy guesses that he has 3. David shows Kathy the 8 beans and says, "Three plus 5 makes 8. Give me 5 beans." Kathy has to give him 5 beans from her supply.

If Kathy had guessed 10 beans, David would have said, "Ten minus 2 is 8. Give me 2 beans."

If Kathy had guessed correctly—8 beans—David would have had to give her all of the beans in his hand.

The game goes on until you want to quit. Just have everyone count the beans or nuts or stones or marbles that they have left and the one with the most wins. Or you can go on playing until one player has all the beans.

UMBRELLA BOUNCE

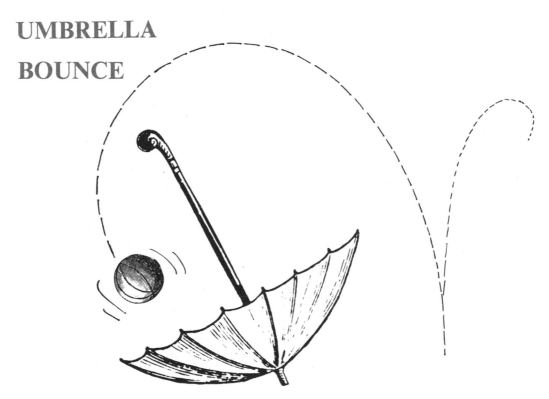

PLAYERS: **Unlimited**
EQUIPMENT: **An umbrella**
  A ball (a rubber ball, a tennis ball, or a ping pong ball will do)
PREPARATION: **None**

Open the umbrella and set it upside down on the ground. Mark a starting line about 10 to 15 feet (3 to 5 m) away and use a "live" ball that bounces well.

The object is to bounce the ball into the umbrella so that it *stays* in. You can't toss it in directly—the ball must bounce once.

Each player gets 5 or 10 turns, depending on how many players you have and how much time you want to spend playing this game. Each ball that stays in the umbrella scores one point.

BALLOON HEAD

PLAYERS: Unlimited—one at a time
EQUIPMENT: Balloons
                   Paper and pencil for recording scores
PREPARATION: None

Simplicity itself: Each player must bounce the balloon off his or her head and see how many times it can be repeated without using hands. The one who hits the balloon with his or her head the most times (no arms, shoulders permitted either) wins.

UP FEATHER!

PLAYERS: Unlimited
EQUIPMENT: A feather for each group
                   Watch with a second hand or a stop watch
PREPARATION: None

How long can you keep a feather up in the air, just by blowing it? Here's your chance to find out. Keep a stop watch or check the second hand of your watch as players try. The one who manages to keep the feather up longest wins.

You can make a full game of this, if you want. Divide the group into 2 or 3 smaller groups. Everyone in each group joins hands while the leaders throw the feathers up in the air. The group that keeps its feather up the longest wins.

BLOW GUN

PLAYERS: 2 or more
EQUIPMENT: A paper straw for each player
           A supply of used wooden matches (a minimum of 20 or 30)
PREPARATION: Cut off the burnt tips from the matches.

Set up a wastebasket 6 feet (2 m) away from an uneven floorboard or some other spot that people can line up at.

Each player gets 10 matches (you can use the same ones over and over again, but have a few extras for ones that get lost).

Then they use the straw as a blowgun and shoot the matches into the wastebasket—or try to. Keep track of each player's score. The one with the most wastebasket "hits" wins.

CARD FLIP

PLAYERS: Unlimited
EQUIPMENT: A shoe box or a man's hat
           An old deck of cards (You can use incomplete decks. Just put
           them together so that each player has the same number of cards.)
PREPARATION: None

Set the hat (or the shoe box) on the floor from 6 to 10 feet (2 to 3 m) from the door. The door sill is the starting line, and each player must stand on the far side of it. You may not step over the door sill, and if you lean so far over that you lose your balance, you automatically lose.

Each player then flips, snaps, tosses or sails five cards, one at a time, trying to get them into the hat. When all the cards have been flipped, count one for each card that got in.

Icebreakers

Some icebreakers are "get acquainted" games. Often played at clubs or groups as a way of welcoming new people, they make it easier for unacquainted guests to become part of the group. Others are games that are meant to loosen up a bunch of people so they are relaxed and laughing and ready to take part enthusiastically in whatever games or activities you have planned.

You'll find both types in this section. Also, take a look at Races for Small Spaces on pages 493–497. Almost every one of these is also a super icebreaker!

ZIP ZAP

PLAYERS: 8 or more
EQUIPMENT: None
PREPARATION: None

One player volunteers to be the leader and stands in the middle. Then everyone in the circle, going clockwise, is given a chance to call out his or her first and last name. Each person tries to remember the name of the player on the right and left.

Then the leader suddenly points a finger at a player—say Stan—and says slowly, "ZIP—one, two, three, four, five." At this Stan must answer by giving the full name of the player to his left.

If the leader said, "ZAP—one, two, three, four, five," Stan's answer would be the name of the person to his right. If Stan doesn't give the answer before the count of five, then he has missed and becomes "It," while the previous "It" takes Stan's place in the circle.

If Stan gives the name before the count of five is reached, then "It" remains where he or she is and points to another player. Make it very clear that "ZIP" means the person to the left and "ZAP" is for the person to the right.

BLOWN-UP FORTUNES

PLAYERS: 5 or more
EQUIPMENT: A balloon for each player, and quite a few extras to substitute for the ones that break ahead of time
A fortune, written on a slip of paper, for each player
PREPARATION: Push 1 fortune into each balloon.
Blow up the balloons and tie them.

The fortunes may be funny or serious or silly—anything you think will add to the fun of the party. Here are a few suggestions:

> If you don't stop eating so much cake, you'll get fat.
> You will get a pleasant surprise before the day is out.
> You will marry a robot and have 14 children.
> You will be the first 7-million-dollar drop-out.
> You will be a prisoner in the zoo.

You get the idea. When everyone has arrived, throw the balloons up in the air and let the players catch them. After they have each captured a balloon, tell them to burst the balloon if they want to find out their fortunes. Your party begins with a BANG.

MUSICAL GRABS

PLAYERS: 12–30
EQUIPMENT: Music (from a tape or record player)
PREPARATION: None

The players select partners and then form two circles—one partner in the outer circle and one in the inner circle. "It" stands in the middle, and someone else takes care of the music.

When the music starts, the circles move in opposite directions. When it stops, the circles stop moving, and "It" calls out a command such as "Head to head!" Then the partners have to find each other quickly and put their foreheads together. If "It" can get his or her head together with a partner who hasn't been found yet, "It" becomes that player's partner when the music starts again. The player left without a partner becomes "It," and issues the next command. The fun is in the many possible commands:

Nose to nose
Eye to eye
Cheek to cheek
Foot to foot
Head to toe
Hand in hand
Back to back
Hand to ear
Back to front
Heel to toe
Shoulder to shoulder
Hand to knee

Make up your own!

BUMPITY-BUMP-BUMP

PLAYERS: 5–25
EQUIPMENT: Name tags for each player
                Safety pins to keep the name tags on
PREPARATION: Make the name tags out of heavy paper
                An index card is fine. Insert the safety pin through the tag
                beforehand so that the players can pin them on quickly

All the players sit in a circle. "It" stands in the middle and suddenly points to a player and says, "Right. Bumpity-bump-bump."

The player who was pointed at must respond with the name of the person to his or her right. But similar to Zip Zap (page 432), the player must do this before "It" finishes saying, "Bumpity-bump-bump."

"It" may say "Left. Bumpity-bump-bump." In that case the player must quickly learn the name of the person to the left. If the player cannot give the name of the person next door, that player becomes "It." After a while, everyone changes places to make the game more interesting. They get to know each other better, too.

AUTOGRAPHS

PLAYERS: 5 or more
EQUIPMENT: Paper and pencil for each player
PREPARATION: Type or write a list of your guests on each page of paper.

This is a good way to get your guests acquainted, when most of them are strangers to each other.

Give each player a copy of the guest list. Each person goes around and tries to find out who everyone is. The printed lists of names give them a start. Then they must learn who belongs to each name.

The next step is for each player to get each guest to autograph the piece of paper. For example, if one of the names on the list is Kay Robbins, the other guests will have to get Kay to sign after the typed KAY ROBBINS.

The first player to get the complete list of names with correct signatures wins.

BEAN SHAKE

PLAYERS: 10–30
EQUIPMENT: 10 dried beans for each player
                A small plastic bag or envelope for each player
PREPARATION: Place the beans in small plastic bags
                or in envelopes, so that you don't need to take the
                time to count them out when the party is on.

Give each player 10 dried beans. Then they are to start shaking hands with each other, over and over, as many times as possible. Why? Because each player gives away a bean to every tenth person he or she shakes hands with. The idea of the game is to get rid of all your beans quickly.

This is a very funny scene, with everyone shaking hands. While you are trying to get rid of your beans, and handing them out to every tenth person you shake with, at the same time you are getting beans back from other shakers!

It's a good idea not to let the players know that they will be your tenth person, because they may try to move away from you. However, no one can refuse to accept a bean if he or she is really the tenth person you shake hands with.

You can also play this game in exactly the opposite way. In the second way, the one who ends up with the *most* beans is the winner. Then everything changes and everyone is anxious and eager to become the tenth player.

First play it one way, then switch to the other. Some of the players will get all mixed up, but it certainly gets everyone acquainted quickly!

INTRODUCTIONS

PLAYERS: 8 or more
EQUIPMENT: A chair for each player, except one
PREPARATION: None

This icebreaker begins with the players seated on chairs in a circle. There can be as many players as you have chairs.

One player—"It"—goes to the middle of the circle. Then everyone counts off, clockwise, calling out his or her name. For example, the players say, "One—Amy Cross," "Two—John Foster," "Three—Liz Hawkins," and so on. Everyone must remember his or her number. "It" does not have a number, and just gives his or her name.

After everyone has counted off, the action starts. "It" calls out two numbers, 5 and 12, for example. Then the players who are numbers 5 and 12 quickly change places. While they are doing this, they must yell their own first names. At the same time, "It" yells out his or her first name, too, and tries to get one of the empty chairs.

If "It" gets to one of the empty chairs first, "It" gets the number of the person who had the chair. The left-out player becomes "It" and calls out the next numbers.

If "It" is not quick enough to get into an empty chair, the game goes on as it was. "It" can also call, "Introductions!" In this case *everyone* must get up and change seats, calling out their first names at the same time.

Make sure the chairs are sturdy.

TALK FEST

PLAYERS: 4–30
EQUIPMENT: Watch with a second hand or a stop watch
PREPARATION: None

Divide the group in half and line them up in two rows. Those in one row stand back to back with those in the other row. The players standing back to back become partners.

At a signal, the players turn around quickly and face their partners. They must talk to each other without stopping. They must both talk at the same time, about anything at all, and it doesn't have to make sense! All players must keep this up for 30 seconds.

Sometimes this game is played with only two players talking at a time. They stand in the middle of the room talking fast and furiously while the others watch and laugh. A contest can be set up, and those receiving the most applause are the winners.

FOLLOW THE LEADER

PLAYERS: 4 or more
EQUIPMENT: None
PREPARATION: Set up a few "hurdles" (see below) in uncrowded places

This is a good warmer-upper, and it can be played with any number of players, but be sure to put away breakables beforehand and to point out to the leader the limits of the game—which rooms or parts of the house are out of bounds.

One person is chosen as the leader and the rest of the group must do everything the leader does. It is a good idea to alert the leader beforehand so that he or she can figure out a number of interesting and unusual ways to lead the group.

Each player follows the other in a line close behind the leader. If you are in a large area, such as a hall or a gym, the leader can start by making a large circle, and then close in to make a smaller one. Leaders can skip, jump, run or hop or take any other kind of steps. When the circle is small, the leader can unwind it and run in a straight line. The leader can jump over a rope or some hurdles that are set up ahead of time (logs or cartons will do). The leader can do running broad jumps, somersaults and cartwheels.

Almost any activities are fun to do this way. Keep in mind that they should be different from each other and not too hard or too easy for the players.

After this icebreaker, the players will be ready for almost any active game. Depending on the leader, they may be ready for a rest.

This is also a good way to end a party. The leader can pick up papers, carry used dishes out to the kitchen, put on overshoes, and so on, and all the players *must* follow.

BAG ON YOUR HEAD

PLAYERS: 8–30
EQUIPMENT: For every player:
     A large paper bag
     A slip of paper with a number on it
     A safety pin
     A small card or pad
     A pencil
PREPARATION: Write numbers on the slips of paper for the players to
     pin to their clothes.

This is another good game to start a party with, if the guests know each other fairly well. As each guest arrives, he or she gets a set of all the equipment listed above. Each player pins the slip with the number to his or her chest, pokes out eye-holes in the paper bag, and slips it on. Then each player tries to guess the names of the other players, who are also wearing bags on their heads. When the players recognize someone, they write that number and name on their card. At the same time, the players try to keep the others from guessing who they are. They try to walk differently or perhaps skip or hop. They may disguise their voices and do many odd things to keep from being recognized.

When all the guests have arrived and the players have finished filling out their cards, ask them to write their own names on the reverse side, and give the card to the person on the right. Read off the correct names and numbers. As the leader reads, the player whose name is called takes off the paper bag. Players total up the correct answers. The one who guessed the most names correctly is, of course, the winner.

WHO AM I?

PLAYERS: 8 or more
EQUIPMENT: Slips of paper with safety pins on them, one for each player
PREPARATION: Write the names of well-known people, living or dead, on
               the slips of paper

As the players arrive, pin the slips of paper on their backs without showing them the name on the front. Of course, they can see the names pinned to everyone else's back, but not their own. Then let them try to find out their own identities from each other by asking any question except "What's my name?" Answers can be given only in the form of "Yes" or "No."

Players cannot ask the same person more than one question at a time. They must go from one person to another. When players think they know who they are, they don't say anything, but go to the leader for confirmation.

For example, a player could ask, "Am I a general?" or "Did I fight against England?" and so on, but not "Am I George Washington?" This type of direct question is saved for the leader, when the player is already fairly sure of the answer. If players guess wrong, they go back to asking questions. After players guess correctly, they rejoin the game as answerers.

The leader can keep a record of the order in which players guess their identity and declare the winner later. The game is noisy and funny, because everyone is busy trying to be the first one to find out who he or she is. Players must also answer questions put to them by others.

A word of caution: Cover or remove all mirrors.

ANIMAL FARM

PLAYERS: 8 or more
EQUIPMENT: None
PREPARATION: None

This icebreaker is noisy, so be prepared for a racket!

It starts off with you saying that you have a farm with pigs on it and you imitate the sounds they make, "Oink, oink, oink."

Another player says, "I have cows on my farm, moo, moo."

Each player in turn mentions an animal on his or her farm, and imitates its sounds. At the same time, all the players who have already announced their animals make their sounds, too. The noise is soon terrific!

Here are some more of the animals around a farm which you can choose: dogs, cats, pigs, crickets, frogs, owls, goats, sheep, horses, crows, katydids, mice, chickens, geese, roosters.

ACT IT OUT

PLAYERS: Up to 20
EQUIPMENT: None
PREPARATION: None

The players sit in a circle. A leader, in the middle, walks around the circle, whispering something to each player.

The leader may whisper: "Make believe you are pitching a ball." To another: "Make believe you are diving into a swimming pool." Other suggestions might be riding a bike, giving a speech, wrestling, tying a knot, climbing a ladder, sitting in the movies in back of a tall person, writing on a blackboard, eating spaghetti, playing tennis.

Each player is given just one activity to act out, and keeps it secret from the others.

Then the leader starts the game by pointing to one of the players. That person stands up, gives his or her full name, and acts out the idea without saying another word. The players try to guess, and the one who is first to guess correctly what is being acted out then stands up, gives his or her name, and acts out another pantomime.

The game continues until everyone has had a turn. A player can have only one turn. If someone guesses correctly twice, the turn passes to the right-hand neighbor, or the guesser can choose someone who hasn't had a turn yet.

WHAT'S YOUR LINE?

PLAYERS: 6 or more
EQUIPMENT: None
PREPARATION: None

The object of this icebreaker is to guess each other's ambitions or major interests. After the players are seated, they take turns standing up and acting out in pantomime what their "line" is. One person may pretend to type. Another may act out being a detective. Players who do not know each other can guess as well as anyone else.

For more acting games, see pages 498-514.

BROOM DANCE

PLAYERS: 7 or more
EQUIPMENT: A broom
                 Music (record player)
PREPARATION: None

The Broom Dance is always a funny mixer. You need an odd number of people to play and an extra person to start and stop the music.

The players all take partners. (For different ways of pairing up, see page 444.) The extra person dances with the broom. When the music suddenly stops, all the players must change partners. The person with the broomstick drops it and grabs a partner.

The player who is left without a partner picks up the broom and dances with it until the music stops again.

MULTIPLICATION DANCE

PLAYERS: 8 or more
EQUIPMENT: Music (record player)
PREPARATION: None

Play any kind of dance music. Two players start off by dancing with each other. Then stop the music. The dancers separate and each one selects another partner. The 2 couples dance until the music stops again. Then each one chooses another partner, and 8 people dance. This goes on until everyone is dancing.

You need an even number of players for this icebreaker. If you have an extra player, he or she can start and stop the music.

Pairing Off Partners

Most of the time when people pick partners for some 2-person game, they pick the people who are their closest friends. Often they do it because their friends will be "mad" at them if they don't. And it makes a party clique-ish and dull.

Here are a few ways to get people paired off with new partners without anyone's losing face or feeling hurt.

LINES

PLAYERS: 8 or more
EQUIPMENT: None
PREPARATION: None

The easiest, fastest way to select partners: ask the players to form two separate lines, next to each other. Then players standing side by side become partners. If you want to pair up boys with girls, ask the boys to form one line, girls the other.

BALLOON BUDDIES

PLAYERS: 8 or more
EQUIPMENT: 1 balloon for each player
          Names of players on small slips
PREPARATION: Put a slip bearing the name of a player in each balloon.
          Blow up the balloons and tie them.

When you're ready for the next paired-up game or dance, let the balloons fly and tell each player to take only one. When they burst the balloon, they will find inside it the name of their next partner.

If you want to make sure that you're pairing up boys with girls, use 2 different colors of balloons. Put only boys' names in one color and girls' in the other, and tell the players which color to reach for.

PROVERBS

PLAYERS: 6–20
EQUIPMENT: A card for each player with half a proverb written on it
PREPARATION: Write half a proverb on each card.

As each player arrives, or when you are ready for a game that requires partners, hand out the proverb cards to the players. They will find their partners by putting the two parts of the proverb together.

You can play this as a game, if you want. Chop up the proverb into four pieces of paper instead of two, mix them up and put four disjointed parts into an envelope. When your guests arrive, hand them each an envelope. The winners are the players who put together a proverb first.

You can use index cards for this game, or scraps of paper, or giant-size cards like these.

DON'T CRY OVER | A ROLLING STONE

For a list of familiar proverbs, see page 584.

SONGS

PLAYERS: 6 or more
EQUIPMENT: A card for each set of partners with the first line of a song written on it
PREPARATION: Write up the song line in two sections. Then cut each card so that each half reveals half the first line of the song.

As the players arrive or when you're ready for the next paired-off game, hand out the song cards to the players. Select songs that are well-known to everyone in the group. The players find their partners by putting the parts of the song together.

SPLIT SIMILES

PLAYERS: 6 or more
EQUIPMENT: A card for each player with half a simile on it
PREPARATION: Write half a simile on each card.

You can use similes exactly as you used song titles on the previous page. Give the first part of the simile to one group and the last word to another. Then they need to find each other.

Here are some similes to work with:

Blind as a bat	Bright as a penny	Busy as a bee
Cold as ice	Crazy as a loon	Dark as night
Dead as a doornail	Fast as greased	Fat as a pig
Flat as a pancake	lightning	Fit as a fiddle
Hard as a rock	Green as grass	Happy as a lark
Mad as a wet hen	Heavy as lead	Light as a feather
Old as the hills	Neat as a pin	Nutty as a fruitcake
Scarce as hen's teeth	Playful as a pup	Proud as a peacock
Sly as a fox	Slippery as an eel	Slow as molasses
Still as a mouse	Snug as a bug in a rug	Sour as vinegar
Thin as a rail	Straight as an arrow	Sweet as honey (sugar)

RIDDLE PAIRS

PLAYERS: 8 or more
EQUIPMENT: A card for each player
PREPARATION: Write one line of a riddle on each card

Before the pairing-off game, distribute the cards to the players. Their job will be to find the answer—or question—to their riddle. You can stick to well-known riddles if the players are very young, such as "Why did the chicken cross the road?" and "Why do firemen wear red suspenders?" and any others which are particularly familiar to the group. But if the players are older, you can use riddles they've never heard before. Then they will have to find a reasonable answer to the question or a reasonable question for the answer.

You'll find a collection of riddles on page 580.

TERRIBLE TWOSOMES

PLAYERS: 8 or more
EQUIPMENT: A card for each player
PREPARATION: Write on the cards the names of
half of a famous team or couple.

Hand out the cards to the players and stand back while they try to find the other half of their twosome. You can use the matching words on page 298 if you prefer, or such pairs as:

Tom and Jerry
Batman and Robin
Popeye and Olive Oil
Superman and Lois Lane
Mickey Mouse and Minnie Mouse (or Pluto)
Abbott and Costello
Sonny and Cher
George Washington and Martha Washington
Marc Antony and Cleopatra
Dean Martin and Jerry Lewis
Jack and Jill
Gilbert and Sullivan
Mutt and Jeff
Napoleon and Josephine
Romeo and Juliet
Ruth and Naomi
The Devil and the Deep Blue Sea
Laurel and Hardy
Edith and Archie Bunker
Shakespeare and Anne Hathaway
Cinderella and Prince Charming
Hansel and Gretel
Starsky and Hutch

CONNECTIONS

PLAYERS: 6 or more
EQUIPMENT: A card for each player
PREPARATION: Write name of the person on one set of cards, the object on the other.

In this system of pairing off, you match up the famous character or person with the object he or she is identified with, such as:

Aladdin	lamp
Goldilocks	porridge
Cinderella	glass slipper
Sleeping Beauty	spindle
Rapunzel	hair
Jason	Golden Fleece
Oliver Twist	"more" food
Orville Wright	plane
Midas	gold
Bo Peep	sheep
Miss Muffet	spider
Eve	apple
Robin Hood	bow and arrow
King Arthur	round table
Lot's wife	salt

If you want to pair up boys and girls, give the boys one list and the girls the other.

CLAY MIXER

PLAYERS: 8–30
EQUIPMENT: Clay or Play-doh, enough to make marble-like balls for half the people at the party
Small strips of paper, like fortune cookie strips, one for every girl or boy at the party
PREPARATION: Write the names of all the girls at the party (or all the boys) on the fortune cookie strips. Then insert one inside each small piece of clay and round off the clay into a marble-like ball.

Place the balls in a basket or bowl and when you're ready to pair off partners, let each boy (or each girl) select a ball which contains the name of a new partner.

FISH POND

PLAYERS: 6 or more—an equal number of boys and girls
EQUIPMENT: A string with a pencil or other light weight tied to the end
for every set of partners
A screen (optional)
PREPARATION: Tie the pencils or the weights to the strings.
Set up the screen, if you have one, in a corner.

This pairing-off game is also an icebreaker. Start with the girls hiding behind the screen—or, if you don't have a screen, behind a door which is open a few inches.

One boy is given the string with the pencil tied to it. He throws the string over the screen, and without knowing who has thrown it, a girl on the other side grabs the end. Then she becomes his partner.

Each boy gets a turn until all the girls are out from behind the screen or door.

Next time, the boys hide in the "pond" and the girls fish for them.

Party Games

MURDER

PLAYERS: 6 or more
EQUIPMENT: A slip of paper for each player (one with an X on it and one with an O), the rest blank
PREPARATION: Fold over the slips so that the markings on them cannot be seen and put them in a bowl

Tell the players that you're going to play Murder and you'll find everyone wildly enthusiastic. This turns out to be the most popular game at many parties, and that in itself is a mystery!

Each player selects a slip of paper from the bowl, looks at it without letting anyone else see it, and then re-folds it carefully and puts it back in the bowl. The player who picked the X is the Murderer and the player who picked the O is the Detective. The Detective leaves the room and waits out in the hall or in the next room. The Murderer does nothing.

If the party is taking place at night, now put out the lights. The Murderer goes to someone in the room and puts *one* hand on his or her neck. The Victim screams and falls down dead. At the scream, put the lights back on.

If the party is taking place in the daytime and you cannot get the room dark, don't try. Just let the Murderer "kill" the Victim in full view as everyone sits around on the floor. No one will tell.

Call back the Detective, who is then going to make inquiries and try to find out who-dun-it.

Players don't have to tell the truth about what they were doing. They can say anything they like: that they were out walking the goldfish or asleep on the chandelier or playing chess with Chevy Chase. But guilt will out! Believe it or not, very often the Detective can really tell who did it because culprits look guiltier than the others and give themselves away! The Detective gets three guesses, and as many questions as needed.

Then it is back to the bowl for another round of this game with a new Murderer and Detective and hopefully a new Victim.

If the group is large, it is good to have two detectives. They can confer about their suspicions and it is less lonely. They each get one guess.

In some versions of this game, all players have to tell the truth, except the Murderer. This is all right when adults play, but most children's parties take place in the afternoon when it's light. Since the kids are just sitting around, watching the murder, they *can't* tell the truth! And making up silly alibis is half the fun.

TIME BOMB

PLAYERS: 4–50
EQUIPMENT: A cordless alarm clock or a kitchen timer
PREPARATION: Send the players into another room and set the alarm clock to go off in 5 minutes. Then hide the clock somewhere in the room—under the couch, behind a curtain, in a wastebasket— or in any other spot.

The "time bomb" is the alarm clock. Once the clock is hidden, the players are called back to look for it. As soon as a player spots the clock, he or she whispers the hiding place to the leader and sits down. The others continue to hunt. If the alarm goes off before *everyone* has found the clock, those players who haven't found it are "blown-up" and out of the game. They help the leader to hide the clock in a trickier place for the next game.

Only those who found the clock can play in the next game, and the time limit is cut down to three minutes. The game goes on with the time limit shortened until only one person is left to find the clock. That person is the winner.

TRUTH OR CONSEQUENCES

PLAYERS: 6–24
EQUIPMENT: A list of questions
                    Supplies for contests (see pages 353–390)
PREPARATION: See above

This game is a great one for young children aged 8 and up—even adults can play it! It starts with quizzes where you don't have to know anything and ends with a series of contests where you don't have to do too much. But it's a lot of fun.

The leader announces that he or she will be asking a series of questions and if you don't tell the truth you must take the consequences. Then the leader explains that if the players answer the questions correctly that's very good, but they get nothing. However, if they answer wrong, they have to take the consequences and do something and that might win them a prize.

Then, taking one person at a time, the leader asks a very simple question, such as:

Who is buried in Grant's Tomb?
What color is the sky?
Where do fish live?
What do pigs say?
What do cows say?
What nationality is the President
   of the United States?
How many legs has a cat?
How big is a horse?
What makes a car go?
How much is two and two?

At first the players answer correctly, but you as the leader explain that nothing happens and give the players another chance. Sometimes they need quite a bit of encouragement to give wrong answers—that Dracula is buried in Grant's Tomb, for example, or that fish live in small huts—but they gradually get the idea. If the answer is wrong, you team them up with another person who gave a wrong answer and select for each twosome a contest from among the ones on pages 353-390. (Be sure that the two contestants both like the contest. Especially with young children it is important for them to feel that they are able to do what you're asking of them and want to do it. The most popular contest is usually The Beautiful Baby Contest on page 385.)

The winner of each contest may then be pitted against another winner, tournament-style, until there is only one grand winner, or you can give prizes to the winners of each separate contest, and to the losers as well.

WHO'S MISSING?

PLAYERS: 10–30
EQUIPMENT: None
PREPARATION: None

All the players sit around the room on chairs or on the floor. One of them is "It" and goes out of the room. While "It" is gone, another player leaves the room by a different door or simply hides. All the other players change places.

Now "It" is called back into the room. "It" must look at the players and see how quickly he or she can find out who's missing. This is a lot harder than it sounds! After "It" finds out, the missing person becomes "It" and a new person hides. Each time, all the players change places.

You can play this game as a contest by letting someone time each player with a watch or clock that has a second-hand.

CAMOUFLAGE

PLAYERS: 5–25
EQUIPMENT: Small objects to hide, such as a leaf, a string, a ring, a strip of tape, a stamp, etc.
Paper and pencil for each player
PREPARATION: Hide the objects all round one room, but place them where they can be seen if you look. The way you hide them is by placing them next to something else of the same color. For example, put a green leaf against a green curtain, or a brown string on a brown rug, a strip of tape on a lamp base. Keep a list of the objects and where you have hidden them.

Give the players paper and pencil and let them walk around the room trying to find and write down the names of all the "hidden" objects. Set a time limit of about 15 minutes. Of course, the time limit will be longer if you have many objects to be found. When the time is up, the player who has found the most objects is the winner.

CATCHING THE SNAKE'S TAIL

PLAYERS: 10 or more
EQUIPMENT: None
PREPARATION: None

Players line up one behind the other with their arms around the waist of the player in front. The first player—let's say, Donna—has arms free. She tries to catch the last player on the line—Alec.

The line or "snake" twists and turns while Donna, the head of the snake, tries to catch Alec, the Tail. Anyone who lets go of the player in front is out. So hang on tight!

When Donna catches Alec, she goes to the end of the line and the second person becomes the head. In that way everyone has a turn to be at the head and tail of the snake.

LOOSE CABOOSE

PLAYERS: 10 or more
EQUIPMENT: None
PREPARATION: None

You need lots of space for this game. Players form groups of three or more. Two people are not in any group, because they will be the loose cabooses.

The groups line up and hold each other's waists. They are the trains which the loose cabooses try to hitch onto. They run around and make sharp turns every time a loose caboose tries to grab hold of the last player and join the train. If the loose caboose does catch onto a train and can't be shaken loose, the first player of the train becomes a loose caboose.

INDIAN CHIEF

PLAYERS: 10–30
EQUIPMENT: None
PREPARATION: None

The players sit around in a circle. One player goes out of the room. While he or she is out, one of the players is chosen to be Indian Chief. Then the person who left the room returns.

The Indian Chief makes all kinds of motions, such as slapping knees, raising arms, shaking head, and the other players watch and do the same thing. When the Indian Chief changes his or her motions from one kind to another, all the other players do the same thing. But the players try not to look at the Indian Chief, because the person who was out of the room has to guess who the Chief is—who it is that is leading and changing the motions.

The guesser watches the players to see where they are looking, so the players have to be especially careful. After the guesser discovers who the Indian Chief is, the Indian Chief becomes the guesser. Or if many people are playing, a new guesser should be chosen. When the guesser leaves the room, someone else is chosen Indian Chief.

RUMOR

PLAYERS: 8–30
EQUIPMENT: Several sheets of paper and pencils
PREPARATION: None

Divide the group into two equal lines or teams. The first players of each team are the captains. They get together and make up a message for both teams. It might be a proverb such as "A bird in the hand is worth two in the bush," or it may be a line from a song, or an original sentence.

They write two copies of the message, fold the papers and give one to the last player on each team, who can't look at it. Then the captains go back to the head of their teams.

At a signal, each captain whispers the message to the next player in line—who whispers it to the third player. The message passes from player to player until the last person in line gets the message.

When both teams are finished, the last player of each team says aloud the message he or she has heard. Then they open up the slips of paper and read what the original message was. They are usually quite different. The team that gets the message correct (or more correct) wins.

Now the last player becomes the captain and the two new captains decide on another message. The game is played over and over again until everyone has had a chance to make up a message, and to prove that rumors can't be believed.

ACTIONS SPEAK LOUDER

You can play this game with actions instead of words.

Three or four players leave the room while the group decides on a scene that one person—say, Dick—will act out. The scene can be something like "Horseback Ride through Chinese Restaurant," or "Murder in the Amusement Park," or "Party in the Haunted House." It should be fairly complex so that the act lasts a couple of minutes.

Then the first player—Meredith—is called in and watches Dick pantomime the agreed-upon scene.

Then the second player—Edward—is brought in. Ed watches Meredith repeat (or try to repeat) the actions which Dick just performed.

Then the third player—Sandy—comes back, and watches Ed's version of Meredith's performance.

When the fourth player—Angelo—is brought in, he sees Sandy's translation of the actions, and announces what he thinks she's doing.

The results are hilarious and prove once and for all that actions do not always speak louder than words.

I TOOK A TRIP

PLAYERS: 4 or more
EQUIPMENT: None
PREPARATION: None

Everyone sits around in a circle. One player, the leader, goes around saying to each player, "I took a trip. What did I take along?" The players name any object they please. One may say, "a suitcase," another says, "a pickle." Other answers might be "a lunch box," "an alarm clock," "a peanut butter sandwich," "your poodle."

After each player has named an object, the leader goes around and asks a different question, any kind of question that will be funny, because the players are not supposed to laugh. The leader asks the same question of each player and they each must give the same answer they gave before.

For example, the leader asks something like, "What did I travel on?" The answers would come out, "a suitcase," "a pickle," "a lunch box," and so on. Since anyone who laughs is out of the game, the leader purposely tries to think of questions that will make their answers seem funny and silly.

After everyone has a chance to answer the first question, the leader asks another, such as "What did I wear around my neck?" and then another, trying to get everyone to laugh. The player who laughs last wins.

HORSE RACE

PLAYERS: 3–13
EQUIPMENT: Score sheet, prepared on a large sheet of paper
                A penny for each player
                A deck of cards
PREPARATION: Prepare the score sheet as in the diagram below, depending
                on how many "horses" are running in the race.

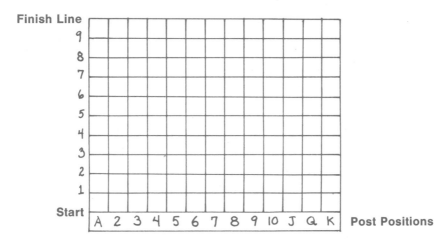

For 13 "horses." If you have fewer players, reduce the number of post positions. For example, for 6 players, use Ace through 6.

Prepare your deck, depending on how many people are playing. If you have 13 players, pull out 13 different cards to give out to them—the Ace through the King. If you have only 10 players, don't use the face cards. The suits of these cards should be varied, with an equal number of cards of different suits, if possible.

Put the score sheet down flat on the table. Pass out the specially selected cards to the players. They hold on to them so they can remember which card they have. Then everyone places his or her pennies in the starting box for the card they picked.

Shuffle the balance of the deck and turn up one card at a time. Let's say the first card is the 4 of Hearts. The person who received a 4 when you gave out the cards moves his or her penny up one box. But so does anyone else who happens to have a card of the same suit—in this case, a Heart.

Turn up the second card and continue the race, until you have a winner.

MAD AD AGENCY

PLAYERS: 5–25
EQUIPMENT: 10 ads, cut from magazines
          10 pieces of cardboard or heavy paper
          Paper and pencil for each player
PREPARATION: Mount the ads on the cardboard or heavy paper and then
          cut each picture into 4 uneven and irregular pieces. Mix them
          all up and place them on a table. Then number each piece
          separately from 1 to 40.

Give each player a pencil and paper. The players are to look at
the pictures, but they may not touch them. They have to decide which
pieces go together to form the various ads. Then they write down the
numbers of the four pieces which together make up a complete ad.

For example, if a picture of a chocolate cake has been cut up into
four pieces, and if the numbers on the pieces are 10, 5, 1, and 8, those
numbers should be written down together.

The first player to get all the ads correct, or the largest number
correct, wins the game.

FORFEITS

PLAYERS: 5–25
EQUIPMENT: None
PREPARATION: None

Forfeits is an old, old game. It has been popular for centuries because it's such fun.

The players each put a piece of clothing, jewelry or some personal belonging into a pile on the floor. These are the "forfeits." One person is chosen to be the judge, and another to hold up the forfeits over the judge's head.

The judge sits in front of the pile and cannot see what is being held overhead. As the sock or necklace or belt is held over the judge's head, the other player says:

> **"Heavy, heavy hangs over thy head.
> What shall the owner do to redeem the forfeit?"**

Then the judge (without looking up) commands the owner to do some act or stunt in order to get back the property.

Some ideas for stunts?

1. Try to stand on your head.
2. Answer yes to every question asked by every player in the group.
3. Sing a song.
4. Tell a ghost story.
5. Make at least 3 people laugh.
6. Dance a jig.
7. Walk across the room on your knees.
8. Tell a joke no one in the room has heard.
9. Give a 1-minute talk about elephants.
10. Say five times rapidly: "Three big blobs of a black bug's blood."
11. Say five times rapidly: "Truly rural."

Of course, the judge and the person who is holding up the forfeit also have articles in the pile, and they must act out a command in order to get them back, too!

THIS IS MY NOSE

PLAYERS: 3–30
EQUIPMENT: None
PREPARATION: None

Everyone lines up facing one of the players, who is "It."

"It" points to a part of its own body, but calls it by some other name. For example, "It" points to a foot and with the other hand points to a player and says, "This is my nose."

Meanwhile, "It" starts counting to 10 and the player who was pointed at must answer before the number 10 is counted. But the player must answer *in reverse*—pointing to his or her own nose and saying, "This is my foot."

If the player does not answer "correctly," he or she is out of the game. If the answer is correct, "It" goes on to another player and tries to get that one confused.

"It" may continue by pointing to its own elbow and saying, "This is my knee," and the person "It" points to must then point to his or her own knee and say, "This is my elbow."

Play the game quickly, so that it is hard to keep from getting mixed up.

TEAKETTLE

PLAYERS: 3–50
EQUIPMENT: None
PREPARATION: None

One of the players—"It"—leaves the room. The rest of the group decides upon some word (a homonym) that has at least two different meanings but sounds the same, such as blue (blew) or tide (tied). Let's say the group uses "tide."

When "It" comes back, the people in the group take turns using a sentence with the chosen word, but instead of "tide" or "tied," they each substitute the word "teakettle." "It" must figure out the correct word.

They could use sentences like these:

**The teakettle (tide) came in so fast we were almost drowned.
The two players teakettle (tied) for first place.
The horse was teakettle (tied) to the post.**

The game goes on until "It" guesses the word. Then the player whose sentence gave the clue becomes "It," and leaves the room while the group decides on some other words.

Note: In some sentences you need to use the word "teakettle*s*," "teakettle*d*" or "teakettl*ing*." You would do this only if the sentence forced you to add a suffix to the original word. For example, if the words are "bear-bare," you would say, "This is the story of the three little teakettles (bear-s)," or "The tiger came through the jungle, teakettling (bare-ing) his teeth at me."

Here are some other homonyms:

air—ere—heir—e'er	foul—fowl	read—reed
aisle—isle—I'll	fur—fir	red—read
ball—bawl	gilt—guilt	right—write
base—bass	hall—haul	road—rowed—rode
bear—bare	kid—kid	role—roll
beau—bow	knead—need—kneed	rough—ruff
board—bored	led—lead	sale—sail
bolder—boulder	loan—lone	scene—seen
bough—bow	mail—male	sea—see
bowl—bowl	missal—missile	seam—seem
bread—bred	mussel—muscle	so—sew—sow
break—brake	new—knew	stair—stare
canopies—can of peas	pail—pale	suede—swayed
ceiling—sealing	pair—pare—pear	sweet—suite
current—currant	pause—paws—pours—pores	tear—tier
dear—deer	peak—peek	there—their—they're
die—dye	pedal—peddle	vain—vein—vane
duck—duck	pennants—penance	vale—veil
fair—fare	plane—plain	wail—whale
father—farther	pole—poll	waist—waste
faun—fawn	pour—pore	watch—watch
flue—flu—flew	quarts—quartz	weather—whether
fly—fly	rapped—rapt—wrapped	

SEE IT!

PLAYERS: 5–20
**EQUIPMENT: 15 objects, such as a pencil, hat, carrot, dish, pin, ribbon,
bracelet, ring, spool of thread, cracker, paper clip, matchbox,
key, golf ball, ticket stub, etc.
Cloth large enough to cover the objects
Paper and pencil for each player
A watch with a second hand**
PREPARATION: Place the objects on the table and cover them with the cloth

Give each player a pencil and paper and ask them to gather round
the covered objects. When you take off the cover, warn them that in exactly
one minute you will cover up the objects again, and then they must write
down as many of the objects as they can remember. They cannot write
anything down until the cover goes back on. The player with the longest
list of correct objects wins.

STEAL THE BACON

PLAYERS: 10–30
EQUIPMENT: An object such as a ball, Indian club or shoe
PREPARATION: None

You need a large space to play this game.

Divide the group in two equal teams. Each team stands behind a goal line, side by side, and faces the other team. The goal lines are about 30 feet (10m) apart. The players on each team count off, each starting at #1. Every player must remember his or her number.

Place the object—the ball, or Indian club, or shoe—in the middle between the two teams. Now the leader calls out a number. The players whose numbers are called (one from each team) run into the middle. They are both trying to "steal" the object and bring it back across their own goal line. When one player snatches it, the other tries to tag him or her before the goal line is reached. If the player with the object succeeds in getting it across the line without being tagged, that team gets one point. If the player is tagged, the other team gets a point.

BOW WOW

PLAYERS: 12–40
EQUIPMENT: None
PREPARATION: None

You can play this game at home or in a gym. If you play it at home, though, make sure to move back the furniture so you have lots of space.

One player is "It" and all the others stand in a circle, about an arm's length apart.

"It" runs around the outside of the circle, taps one of the players, and keeps running. The tapped player runs around the outside of the circle, in the opposite direction from "It."

When "It" and the tapped player meet each other running, they must get down on all fours and bark, "Bow Wow," three times. Then they each must get up quickly and continue running around the circle in the same direction as before. The first one to reach the empty space in the circle gets the place. The one left out becomes "It" in the next round.

If the same person is about to be "It" for a third time, choose another "It."

STALKING BIGFOOT

PLAYERS: 5–20
EQUIPMENT: A large table
               2 blindfolds
PREPARATION: None

Two players are chosen: one is the Hunter, the other is Bigfoot. Both players are blindfolded and stand at opposite ends of the table.

The Hunter tries to catch Bigfoot, but of course, can't see where Bigfoot is. Bigfoot tries to keep away from the Hunter, but can't tell where the Hunter is. Each tries to fool the other by giving false signals. The Hunter may tiptoe to one end of the table and start pounding and then quickly run to the other end because he expects Bigfoot to run away from the noise. The Hunter may whisper, call out, and give all kinds of misleading signals. Bigfoot also may make sounds and then run to a different spot to fool the Hunter.

The others in the group have fun, too, watching Bigfoot try to escape. Sometimes Bigfoot walks right into the surprised Hunter. Those watching should be quiet so as not to give any clues. They should also stop Bigfoot and the Hunter from running into anything. After the Hunter catches Bigfoot, choose two other players to take their places.

UP
JENKINS!

PLAYERS: **12 or more**
EQUIPMENT: **A long table**
Chairs or benches
A coin
PREPARATION: **None**

As many players can take part in this game as there are seats on both sides of the table. Form two teams with an equal number of players and choose a captain for each team. The teams then sit along each side of the table, facing each other. The captains sit at the ends of the table.

The captain of one team gets the coin and passes it under the table to the second person of the team. The players on that team pass the coin under the table back and forth from one player to another. The object of the game is to do it so carefully that the opposing team cannot guess which player has the coin.

At any time, the captain of the opposite team may call out, "Up Jenkins!" At this signal, the players on the team with the coin hold their hands over their heads with their fists clenched. The captain then calls out, "Down Jenkins!" and the players slap their hands with palms flat on the table, keeping the coin hidden under one of the palms. Be careful that there is no clinking sound of the coin when hands are slammed down on the table.

Then the first two players on the opposite teams guess which player has the coin. One of them says "Show Up," to the player he or she thinks has the coin. This player must lift up both hands to show if the coin is on the table. If it isn't, the second player gets to guess.

If one of the guesses was right, the guessing team gets a point, and has a chance to hide the coin. But if the guesses both were wrong, the coin stays with the first team, who gets a point. The team with the most points wins.

NUMBERS LINE-UP

PLAYERS: 8–20
EQUIPMENT: Paper plates or cards for each player
                  Red and blue crayons
                  String or tape
PREPARATION: Write numbers on the back of the plates or the cards.
                  Use different colors for each team.

You need 2 exactly equal teams of 4 to 10 players for this game. It is best with a large group (18 to 20 players) and you need a large room, such as a gym, to play in.

Each person on each team is given a number. If you have 7 players on each team, you will have numbers 0 to 6; if you have 10, use numbers 0 to 9. Give each player a card with his or her number on it.

The teams stand at opposite ends of the room, with a string or tape separating them, drawn across the middle of the area. A leader stands at the line and calls off numbers. The leader might call "Four hundred thirty two!" At this, the players on each team with cards numbered 4, 3 and 2, run to the line. They line up in the right order, holding their cards in front of them. The first team to line up correctly gets one point. The first team to score 15 points wins.

Numbers like 432, 678 and 123 are easy. There's more fun with a difficult number like 481 and 972 and 638. There's even more excitement with a number like 8,462,935. Leaders must remember not to call out a double number like 233, since there is only one of each number on a team.

You can make the game harder and more exciting if you have 20 players who are good in math. The leader can call out, "I'm adding these numbers: 2, 5, 9, and 7 and I will subtract 3. Total?" The players on each team can get into a huddle for this, and the first players to run to the answer line with the correct answer win. In this case, the 2 and the 0 stand together to form 20. You can also multiply and divide for variety.

BALLOON
BASKETBALL

PLAYERS: 11–19
EQUIPMENT: A generous supply of balloons (10 or 20)
         Chairs for every player except one
PREPARATION: None

Set up the chairs in two rows—about 3 feet (1m) apart—facing each other. Place two of the chairs at either end, between the rows.

**"Baskets"
stand here** ◯ ▢ ▢ ▢ ▢ ▢ ◯ **and here**
                ▢ ▢ ▢ ▢ ▢

Divide the players into teams. Each team picks a "Basket"—a player who *stands* on the chair at the end of the row. The "Baskets" resemble baskets in shape by making a circle of their arms, with hands clasped together. The other players sit on the chairs.

The referee tosses a balloon into the air in the middle of the rows. The object of the game is for each team to get the balloon through its own Basket, but no one can get up from his or her chair.

The Basket can weave around on the chair and try to capture the balloon, as long as it doesn't move its feet or open its hands.

Each balloon batted through a Basket is worth two points. If the balloon goes out of bounds, the referee tosses another one up from whatever point the balloon went out. After a Basket is scored, the referee starts the play going again by tossing up the balloon at the middle of the rows.

Twenty points wins—or play for a set period of time.

CATEGORIES

PLAYERS: 3 or more
EQUIPMENT: None
PREPARATION: None

The players sit in a circle and they set up a rhythm by tapping their thighs twice, clapping hands twice in front of them, and snapping their fingers at about shoulder level—in that order. The first player begins by saying "Category" on one set of finger snaps, and then giving the name of the category on the next set of snaps. The category should be a broad one, such as trees, fruits, or flowers, television shows, desserts or breeds of dogs.

All the players keep up the tap-tap, clap-clap, snap-snap rhythm straight through as the player to the left names something in the category on the next snap, ending the name by the second snap. The next player to the left must give another name on the next snaps, and so on until somebody misses—like this:

#1 (tap-tap, clap-clap) Category (as they snap).
　　(tap-tap, clap-clap) Countries (as they snap).
#2 (tap-tap, clap-clap) England (as they snap).
#3 (tap-tap, clap-clap) Fiji (as they snap).
#4 (tap-tap, clap-clap) United States (as they snap).
#5 (tap-tap, clap-clap) Er— (as they snap).

Player #5 is out. Player #6 starts the whole process again, naming a new category. Play on until there is only one person left, the winner.

Easy? There's one more requirement. You can't repeat a name. Wait till you're all set to say your word and the player before you says it! You have about three seconds to come up with another name that hasn't been said before. Remember, the name of the object must be given in rhythm. And if your tongue gets tangled up, that's a miss, too!

HOT POTATO SPUDS

PLAYERS: 6 or more
EQUIPMENT: Potato, ball, stone or piece of wood—anything grabbable or passable
PREPARATION: None

This hilarious game is played just like Hot Potato (page 410), but in this game you are not eliminated when you're caught with the potato. Instead, the next time you get the potato, you have to pass it in a "fancy" way. The leader sets the order.

Here are a few fancy ways to pass potatoes:

1. Over your head
2. Standing
3. Standing and turning around and sitting down
4. Under your left leg
5. Under you right leg
6. Around your neck
7. Behind your back
8. Shaking hands with the next player
9. Winking at the next player
10. Whistling or singing
11. Holding your nose
12. Bouncing up and down

Of course, if you're caught again and again, you gather up your penalties. You have to do the fancy thing you did the first time and then add a new one along with it! When you've been caught several times, it takes you longer to pass the potato than anyone else, naturally, so you're more likely to be caught again! The person who is running the music or the clapping may or may not want to take advantage of you!

THE MYSTERY VOICE

PLAYERS: 8–30
EQUIPMENT: Blindfolds for half the players
PREPARATION: None

This voice-guessing game can be enjoyed only by players who know each other well.

Half of the players sit, on chairs or on the floor, and blindfold themselves. Then the other players walk over and each one stands beside a seated player.

The game starts when one of the standing players sings part of a song to the sitter. The blindfolded player must guess who the singer is. As soon as the player guesses correctly, he or she takes off the blindfold.

Then the next standing player sings part of a song, and the seated one must guess who is singing. As soon as all the sitting players guess who the mystery voices are, the players switch sides. The singers now sit and blindfold themselves and the others stand and sing.

It's perfectly fair to disguise your voice so that your friend has a difficult time guessing who you are. If you want to find out which side has the best guessers, let someone keep track of the time it takes each team to do its guessing.

If you play this in a classroom, seated players don't need blindfolds. They just put their heads down on their desks.

THE CIRCLE TEST

PLAYERS: 12 or more
EQUIPMENT: None
PREPARATION: None

The players form a circle, linking elbows. Then all the players step back and pull as hard as they can. The object is to break the circle without your elbows giving way. When it finally breaks, the two players whose arms unlinked are out, and the circle forms again, smaller this time, but just as tight. No stopping is allowed, except when the break occurs. If the circle seems invincible, and it doesn't look as if anyone is going to break arms, tell everyone to take three steps into the middle of the circle (which relaxes it) and then *quickly* to take three steps back. This snap will often create another break.

MONKEY SEE MONKEY DO

PLAYERS: 10–30
EQUIPMENT: None
PREPARATION: None

This is a very funny game, but it is hard on the players because they aren't allowed to laugh. Here's how it goes:

All the players sit close together in a circle. One of them starts the game by turning to the right-hand neighbor and doing something to him or her. The player may squeeze an arm, muss up hair, straighten clothes, make a face, whatever. Whatever that player does, the neighbor must do it to the next player to the right, and that player must do the same thing to the next neighbor.

This goes on all around the circle until it gets back to the first player.

Anyone who laughs is out of the game. Or instead that person can pay a forfeit to stay in the game. (*See Forfeits on page 460*).

The player to the right of the first person then has a chance to do something to the next person, and the game goes on.

CAT AND RAT

PLAYERS: 10–20
EQUIPMENT: None
PREPARATION: None

One player is chosen to be "Rat," and stands in the middle of a circle formed by the other players. Another player is chosen to be "Cat," and stands outside the circle. Cat must try to catch Rat.

The players in the circle hold hands very tightly to keep Cat from breaking through and catching Rat. Rat makes faces at Cat, howls, and teases. Cat tries to break through the circle, sneak underneath the locked arms, or even climb over the arms. Cat must trick the players in the circle so as to get in and chase Rat.

When Rat is caught, Cat and Rat join the circle. The two players who broke the circle to let Cat through become the next Cat and Rat.

If Cat has a very hard time breaking through, after a while he or she can ask for another Cat to help.

SHERLOCK AND WATSON

PLAYERS: 10–30
EQUIPMENT: Blindfold
PREPARATION: None

Everyone joins hands in a circle, except for two players who are inside the circle. One is blindfolded and is called "Sherlock." Sherlock must try to catch the other player, who is called "Watson."

The blindfolded player calls out "Watson!" Then Watson must answer, "Sherlock!" In this way, Sherlock can tell what part of the circle Watson is in. Watson must stay within the circle, and whenever Sherlock says "Watson!" the other must answer "Sherlock!"

When Watson is caught, he or she becomes the blindfolded Sherlock. The previous Sherlock chooses a new Watson and joins the circle. The game continues until everyone has had a turn being Sherlock and Watson.

SCARS

PLAYERS: 4–10
EQUIPMENT: Make-up crayons
           Tissues
           Eyebrow pencils
           Cleansing cream
           An index card for each player
           Pencil for each player
           Mirror
PREPARATION: None

Each player invents a horror story about an imaginary scar on some (exposed) part of the body. But they don't tell the story to anyone. Instead they write down the three most important words in the story on an index card. For example, suppose you received your scar in a haunted house when a chandelier broke free and crashed down on you. The key words that you write might be: haunted house—chandelier—crash.

Or maybe you got your scar in hand-to-hand combat with a vicious robot who had a "contract" to murder you. Your key words might be: robot—fight—murder.

When you finish your cards, put them face-down in a pile.

Now you choose partners (see "Pairing Off Partners" on page 444) and, in teams of two, apply scars to each other's bodies or faces. (Make sure, whatever part of you is getting the scar, that you rub in some cleansing cream first. Otherwise, you may have the scar for longer than you want it.)

When you're ready to begin, shuffle the cards. The person with the shortest fingers begins. He or she pulls a card from the pile on the table, and looking in a mirror at the scar, tells how it came to be—using the key words on the index card.

Then the next person (to the right) pulls the next card, and tells his or her story.

Continue until everyone has had a turn.

More ideas for horror stories:

dark	masked intruder	shrubbery
blizzard	hitchhiker	knife
jungle	rattlesnake	sleeping bag
Christmas tree	ornament	Santa Claus burglar
pingpong paddle	brother	anger

Two Kinds of Scars

You can place a scar anywhere—on your face, neck, hand—anywhere that it will show. Draw the scar itself with the eyebrow pencil. Then draw in the stitches. They can be small dots along each side of the scar (the girl) or actual stitches that cross the scar line (the boy).

THE PRISONER'S SCAR

In this version of the game, you need a blindfold. Blindfold the person with the biggest feet. Then all the other players walk past the "Bigfoot," who has to catch one of them.

Then off come the blindfolds. Bigfoot takes a good look at the captive's scar and pulls a card. Then Bigfoot tells how the prisoner's scar came to be, using the words on the card as the key elements in the story.

Blindfold the prisoner next time, and the game repeats, until everyone has had a turn.

HILARIOUS HANDKERCHIEF

PLAYERS: 6 or more
EQUIPMENT: A handkerchief
PREPARATION: None

The players form a circle. One of them stands in the middle, throws a handkerchief up in the air, and starts laughing. Everyone in the circle laughs, too, until the handkerchief hits the floor. At that moment there is complete silence. Anyone who laughs is out.

DICTIONARY

PLAYERS: 4–8
EQUIPMENT: An unabridged dictionary
            Paper and pencil for scorekeeping
PREPARATION: None

One player is "It" and looks through the dictionary for a word whose meaning is likely to be unknown to the other players.

Let's say that Keith selects the word "paronymous." He goes on to give a definition of it to the other players. However, he must define it in his own words—not just read it from the dictionary—and the definition he gives them does *not necessarily have to be right.*

Keith might say that "paronymous" means "similar to," for example, and add that it comes from the root, "para," which means "related to." Keith made that up.

The other players have to decide whether or not they believe that Keith has given them a correct definition of the word. Keith gets one point for every player who guesses wrong.

The player to Keith's right goes next.

Note: "Paronymous" is an adjective which refers to words "containing the same root or stem." "Lively" and "life" are "paronymous" words.

PHONIES

PLAYERS: 4–12
EQUIPMENT: Paper and pencil for each player
            Small cards or sturdy slips of paper with "difficult" words
            written on them
PREPARATION: Go through an unabridged dictionary and select a few
            dozen words that no one in the group is likely to know the
            meaning of. Write the words, one to a card.

Pass one card among the players, let them each look at it and figure out for themselves what it means—no looking in dictionaries! Then it is up to them to convince the other players. One by one, each player gives a definition of the word. A good Phonies player may even give a short talk about the word, where it comes from and how he or she just happens to know what it means—such as:

"It's an odd coincidence, I know this word because my Aunt Hannah used to . . ."

It doesn't matter if they're wrong and if they have no idea what the word means. The object of the game is to convince the other players that they know what they're talking about.

Of course, one of them may actually know what the word means but will he or she be as convincing as a talented Phony?

Each player writes the mystery word on the sheet of paper with the definition he or she thinks is correct and the name of the person who gave it. Every time a player's name appears on one of these sheets, it is a point for him or her. Most points wins.

Pass out another card and go through the same process, and another, until you've gone through 10 or so words. The fun comes when you look up the words in the dictionary and find out that all your friends are Phonies. Or are they?

Some words to use:

agnate	fipple	leptorrhine	thaumaturgy
aeromancy	galangal	muticous	urticate
bornan	hospodar	otiose	vorant
deodar	irade	rumal	yerk
epistemic	jussive	subfuscous	zarf

Your dictionary has lots more.

UMMM

PLAYERS: 10 or more
EQUIPMENT: A chair for each player except one
           A blindfold
PREPARATION: Arrange the chairs in a close circle

    This game creates great hilarity at teen-age parties. It is actually a more grown-up version of Blindman's Buff.

    Blindfold one player, who is "It." After the blindfold is in place, all the other players take seats in the circle.

    "It" walks around the circle and sits down on the lap of one of the seated players—without touching the seated player in any other way at all.

    "It" says "Ummm."

    The seated player says "Ummm" (in a disguised voice, of course).

    "It" has to try to guess the identity of the seated player. If "It" isn't sure and wants to say "Ummm" again, the seated player must reply with "Ummm" a second time.

    "It" gets one more "Ummm" and a reply, and then one guess. If the guess is correct, the seated player is "It," gets blindfolded, and then everyone changes seats for the next round. If the guess is wrong, "It" goes back into the middle and the game starts again.

    Note: Warn the players to disguise their laughter, too.

END OF PARTY

PLAYERS: Unlimited
EQUIPMENT: Sheet of paper for every player
              Pencil for every player
PREPARATION: Draw a series of numbered boxes on each sheet of paper.
              It should look like this:

1	2	3	4	5	6	7	8	9	10	11	12	13	14	15	16	17	18

Have you ever had a party drag on and on because you didn't want to be rude and tell everyone please to go home? Here is a game that tells them.

Give each guest a sheet of paper with the heading on it and tell them you are about to test their concentration. Then read off the following directions:

1. If the letter X appears in the newspaper more than the letter E, put the letter X in space 17. Otherwise, put E there.

2. If the sky sometimes is gray, put an R in spaces 2, 7 and 13, unless people sometimes go for long walks, in which case put R in spaces 8 and 18.

3. If Pat and Pamela are girls' names, put a P in space 7, unless Pat is sometimes a boys' name, in which case do nothing.

4. If the River Seine is in Bulgaria, put an I in space 3, unless Perth is an Australian city, in which case put a P in space 6.

5. Put an H in space 1, unless lettuce is edible, in which case put it in space 2.

6. If Shakespeare wrote "Cymbeline," put a B in space 16, unless George Bernard Shaw wrote "Pygmalion," in which case put a V in space 16.

7. If stockings are worn on one leg, put an S in space 13. If they are worn on 2 legs, put an S in space 4 as well.

8. If 9 and 8 are 16, put an A in space 1. If they are not 16, put an A in space 9, unless Cinderella went to the ball, in which case put an A in space 7.

9. If a collie is a dog, put an I in space 12, unless carrots are sold by the ear, in which case put an O in space 12.

10. If Jack Horner pulled a prune out of his pie, put a Q in space 10. If it was a peach, put an X in space 10. If it was a plum, put a Y in space 10.

11. If pigs get sunburned, put an I in space 3, unless people talk French in Fiji, in which case put a P in space 3.

12. If a manatee is a mammal, put an O in space 15 unless a whale lays eggs, in which case put an E in space 15.

13. If the moon is closer to us than the sun, darken spaces 5, 11 and 14, unless giraffes can sing, in which case put an O in these spaces.

14. If Ernest Hemingway wrote "Islands in the Stream" put a T in space 1. If Joseph Conrad wrote "Lord Jim" put a T in space 9 also. If Charles Dickens wrote "Hamlet" destroy this puzzle.

If you haven't already figured it out, you can find the de-coded message on page 632.

SPECIAL PARTY GAMES

10

Relay Races

PEANUT RACE

PLAYERS: **2 or more**
EQUIPMENT: **2 large bowls of peanuts (in the shell)**
2 smaller empty bowls
PREPARATION: **None**

This racing stunt tests steadiness of hand. Two players can enjoy it and so can a group divided into two teams. Just two players race at a time.

Before you start, place one of the bowls of peanuts at each end of the racing space about 20 feet (6 m) long. Take two smaller empty bowls and place them about 3 feet (1 m) to the side of the peanut bowls at each end.

The object of the game is to carry as many peanuts as possible on the back of your hand from a filled bowl to the empty one at the other end of the course. One player starts from each end, and at a starting signal runs across the room, passing the opponent, who is running from the other end. The player digs one hand into the bowl of peanuts and tries to get as many to stay put on the back of that hand as possible. Since the player can use only one hand, it is not possible to pile up the peanuts or rescue any that fall off.

When the player is loaded up, he or she starts across the room, balancing the peanuts until they can be poured into the empty small bowl. The player who gets the most peanuts in the small bowl safely wins the round.

Repeat the race if you have teams until everyone has had a turn.

You can also play this game with dry beans instead of peanuts. Let the loser of each round pick up the spilled beans.

KANGAROO RACE

PLAYERS: 6–50
EQUIPMENT: A ball for each team. The balls can be identical or they can vary in size from a tennis ball to a basketball. If they do vary, play the game again so that each team gets a turn with each ball.
PREPARATION: None

Divide the players into even teams, with not more than about 6 players to a team. Give each team a ball.

The first player on each team places the ball between his or her knees and jumps to a goal line about 30 feet (9 m) away, keeping the ball between the knees. Crossing the goal line, the player grabs the ball and runs back to the team with it in hand, giving it to the next player, who places it between knees and jumps toward the goal line. And so on until everyone on the team has run.

If the "Kangaroo" loses the ball on the way, he or she must retrieve it and begin to jump from where it was lost. The first team to finish wins.

COWBOY RACE

This game is played in the same way as the Kangaroo Race, but instead of jumping, each player has to run (or try to) while holding the ball between his or her knees. For this game, the ball should be large—a basketball or beach ball. The ball may not be touched with the hands while the player is in motion, and of course, valuable seconds are lost every time the player has to stop, pick up the ball and start running again.

To do it successfully, you should press the ball gently between your legs, holding your legs in a bow-legged position. You will find running with the ball easiest when you roll the upper part of your body from side to side, shifting the weight on your feet as you do it. This way, you will make progress forward, and the ball will stay between your legs.

BALL AND ANKLE RACE

PLAYERS: 2 or more
EQUIPMENT: A ball for each player, any size from tennis ball to football or basketball. But they should be the same size for players who are competing.
PREPARATION: None

Mark a starting line and a goal line any distance apart that seems convenient. The object is to race with the ball held between your ankles. It's up to you whether you jump, or inch along in a kind of shuffle. Do whichever seems to get you there the fastest without dropping the ball! If you drop it, you have to go back to the starting line and begin all over.

BLOW-THE-CUP RELAY

PLAYERS: 6 or more
EQUIPMENT: A paper cup for each team (cone-shaped cups are best)
A piece of string for each paper cup—about 15 feet (5 m) long
PREPARATION: Pull the string through the bottom of the paper cup

Tie the strings to furniture, doorknobs or nails so that they are stretched tight. Try to get them shoulder-height or a little lower.

Now line up the teams behind each string, players one behind the other. Put all the cups at the end of the string which is closest to the players and have the open ends of the cups face the players.

At a signal, the first player on each team starts blowing into the cup to move it along the string, and follows the cup to the other end of the string as it is blown along. As soon as the cup reaches the end of the string, the blower pushes it back by hand to the starting position for the next player to blow. This relay really leaves you breathless!

The first team to finish wins.

BALLOON RACES

PLAYERS: 2 or more
EQUIPMENT: A balloon for each player plus extra balloons in case of accident
PREPARATION: None

Give each player a balloon which he or she blows up and ties securely. When the contestants are ready, ask them to stand against the wall. At a signal, they are to cross the room, keeping the balloons in the air by hitting them only with their heads. No hands! The one who crosses the room and comes back to the starting point without touching the balloon (except by head) wins the game.

In another kind of contest, the balloons do the racing. Each player blows up a balloon of a different color, but instead of tying them, they just hold them shut. Then the players line up in a row and, at a signal, let their balloons fly. The balloons swerve and swiggle, and the one that travels farthest wins.

Make sure first that all the players are capable of blowing up their own balloons.

PILLOWCASE RELAY

PLAYERS: 8 or more
EQUIPMENT: A pillow and a pillowcase for each team
PREPARATION: None

Divide the group into two or more equal teams. The players on each team line up about 20 feet (6 m) from the goal line. Place the pillows on the goal line, one opposite each team. The first player on each team holds a pillowcase.

At the starting signal, the first player on each team runs to the goal line, puts the pillowcase on the team's pillow and runs back, carrying the pillow, handing it to the second person on line.

The second player runs to the goal line and takes the pillowcase off the pillow, leaving the pillow on the goal line, and runs back to the third player with the empty pillowcase.

The third player does what the first player did, and the fourth player does what the second player did. Each one has a turn either putting on or taking off the pillowcase. The first team to finish wins.

If you play the game again, let the players change places so they do different things the second time.

SUITCASE RELAY

PLAYERS: 8–24
EQUIPMENT: 2 suitcases of old clothes (one for each team)
PREPARATION: None

Two teams of equal size line up behind the starting line. About 15 feet (5 m) away stand two suitcases full of clothing. The suitcases must contain similar articles of clothing. For instance, if you have a hat, a skirt, a jacket, a tie, a scarf, a belt and a necklace in one suitcase, you must have the same items in the other.

At a signal, the first person on each team runs to the team's suitcase and opens it up. The player dresses in all the clothes in the suitcase, closes the suitcase and runs back to the starting line, carrying the suitcase.

There he or she takes off all the clothes and puts them back in the suitcase, closes it, and runs back to leave it in its original position. Then this player runs back to the team and tags off the second player in line, who goes through the same actions. This continues until every player has had a turn. The team to finish first wins.

PIG ROLL

PLAYERS: 6 or more
EQUIPMENT: None
PREPARATION: None

Line up the group in teams, but between lines leave plenty of room for you need lots of space for this race. The players are Pigs and they are going to *roll* to the pigpen. The first Pigs on each line lie on the floor, parallel to the opposite wall. Their arms rest on the floor, too, but stretch overhead.

At a signal, the Pigs start rolling across the room to the pigpen. Rolling one way is enough for very young players, but older ones can roll back, too. The trick is to roll straight; generally, as you roll, your body turns and you go off course. Each Pig must touch the opposite wall with its entire body (which means its body must be straight), before it can start rolling back.

If the Pigs are rolling both ways, the returning Pig must roll into and *touch* the next one who is waiting (in rolling position) on line. Then the first Pig jumps up to make way as the newly-bumped Pig starts rolling to the pigpen.

DOG DASH

PLAYERS: 8 or more
EQUIPMENT: None
PREPARATION: None

Divide the group into two or more teams. Explain that now they are Dogs and have four legs, so they must use all four of them to run with. Make sure they understand that dogs run on their *feet* and not on their *knees*.

At your signal, the first Dog from each team runs to the opposite wall. There it must turn its back to the wall and wag its tail three times while counting aloud "One—Two—Three!" to make sure it gets all the wags in. The Dog can get up on its hind legs to do the wag, which provides a needed breather. Then, on all fours, the Dog races back to its team, faces the next Dog on line, wags another "One—Two—Three" count, and goes to the end of the line. On count "Three" the next Dog starts running.

It is tiring to run on four legs for a long distance so don't make the dash-track more than 20 feet (6 m) long.

THOUGHT FOR THE DAY

PLAYERS: 6–40
EQUIPMENT: A large blackboard (as in a classroom) or a large sheet of
  paper stuck up on the wall
  Chalk—or pencils
PREPARATION: None

Divide the group into two or more teams. Line up a distance away, facing the blackboard or paper, and give the first player in each line a piece of chalk—or pencil.

At a signal, the first player of each team runs to the board, writes down a word, returns to the line, and gives the chalk to the second player, without talking.

The second player runs to the board, writes down another word, either in front of or after the first word.

Then the third player does the same thing, and so on, until each player has had a turn. The team must end up with a complete sentence in order to win. And you can't write words in between.

Be sure to have a clear space between teams and the blackboards or paper, so remove all chairs and desks that may be in the way. Another important thing to watch is that your writing is legible. Then the other members of your team won't have to take precious time to figure out what your word is.

Whatever sentence you come up with is your thought for the day.

ART RELAY

This game is played in much the same way as Thought for the Day. Divide the group into even teams and line them up about 10 feet (3 m) from the blackboard or a sheet of paper on the wall. At a signal, the first player runs up to the team's section and starts to draw the figure of a person, or part of a person. Each player gets only 10 seconds at the board. Have someone keep time carefully. When time is called, the first player runs back and the second player runs up and adds to the drawing.

The game continues until everyone has had a chance to add to the drawing. The team that has the most "finished" drawing wins.

There may be some arguments as to what makes one drawing more "finished" than another. To avoid this, have the teams decide in advance just what they want the drawing to show. Write out a list such as head, body, arms, legs, eyes, nose, mouth. Extra things, like shoes, socks, skirts, pants, eyelashes, etc., make the drawings more finished.

FAST LEMON

PLAYERS: **8 or more**
EQUIPMENT: **2 pencils and 2 lemons**
PREPARATION: **None**

No, this is not a game with used cars but with real lemons!

Divide the group into two or more equal lines. Give the leader of each line a full-length pencil and a full-grown lemon. As the teams line up single file, mark a starting line and a finish line along the floor (about 20 feet or 6 meters away at the most).

The object of the game is to push the lemon with the pencil along the floor in a straight line—if you can. Each player must push it to the finish line and back to the next teammate in line. The team to finish first wins.

What you discover is that the lemon always keeps rolling, despite a slight wobble. You'll have trouble keeping it in your lane, so be sure the furniture is pushed back.

A hint from experienced lemon-rollers: don't push too fast. This generally causes the lemon to roll the wrong way.

FANCY DUDE RELAY

PLAYERS: 6–30
EQUIPMENT: 2 assortments of old clothes, with similar articles in them
        (one for each team)
PREPARATION: None

Divide the group into equal teams. Each team chooses a captain who stands about 20 or 25 feet (6 or 8 meters) away. At a signal, the first player on each team runs up to the captain and puts a piece of clothing on him or her, such as a hat, shoe, scarf, handbag, umbrella, etc. Then this player runs back and tags the second player on the team.

The second player runs to the captain, adds another article of clothing and runs back to tag the next player. The third player dresses the captain some more and so on, until each member of the team has added an item of clothing. You can imagine what the captain looks like after everyone on the team has had a chance to dress him or her up!

The team that finishes first wins.

Races for Small Spaces

SALTY WHISTLE RACE

PLAYERS: 2 or more
EQUIPMENT: 1 salty soda cracker (biscuit) for each player
PREPARATION: None

Have you ever tried to whistle with your mouth full? Here is a whistle race which is lots of fun.

Any number can take part in the race, but only two people play at one time.

Choose two teams, line them up side by side with the teams facing each other. At a signal, the first member of each team starts eating a salty cracker. When finished eating, that player must whistle the first few notes of a song. Then the next player on the team eats a cracker and whistles a tune.

This goes on until all the players on a team have had a chance to eat a cracker and whistle. The first team to finish wins.

Warning: It's a good idea to have a judge watching to make sure everyone has whistled.

HAIR RIBBON RELAY

PLAYERS: 8–48
EQUIPMENT: One hair ribbon for each team
PREPARATION: None

Two equal teams line up single file. The first player in each line has a long hair ribbon.

At a signal, the first player in each line turns around and ties the ribbon, making a bow, on the head of the next player. Then that player takes it off, turns and ties the hair ribbon on the head of Player #3. This goes on until the last player unties the ribbon. The first team to finish wins.

A hair ribbon is the funniest object to play this relay with, but you can use other objects of clothing for variety. Try gloves, or a sweater that buttons down the back!

ALL TIED UP

PLAYERS: 8 or more
EQUIPMENT: A ball of soft string for each team (with the same length of string on each)
PREPARATION: None

This funny relay calls for two teams of 4 or more players. The teams line up side by side and face each other. The first player on each team is given the ball of string. Then at a starting signal, the first player holds onto the end of the string and hands the ball to the next player. The next one holds onto the string and unwinds enough so that he or she can pass the ball along to Player #3. The ball is handed along the line, unrolling as it goes.

When the ball of string gets to the person at the far end of the line, that player hands the ball behind his or her back to the player it just came from. That player passes it back, with each player holding on as well as possible, till it gets to the front of the line. Then Player #1 pulls the string around and starts handing the ball along towards the end of the line again.

You see what's happening? The teams are getting wrapped up by the string. The first team to get wrapped up and use all the string wins.

Now you can have an untying relay with the same rules, as each team tries to untie itself first.

PINOCCHIO RACE

PLAYERS: 10–20
EQUIPMENT: 2 matchbox tops
PREPARATION: None

Divide the group into two teams. The object of the game is to pass the matchbox top from player to player, but you're not allowed to touch it. You have to pass it on your nose. If the matchbox drops, the player who last had the matchbox may pick it up; otherwise, no touching. First team to get the matchbox all the way to the back of the line and forward again wins.

ORANGE RACE

PLAYERS: 8 or more
EQUIPMENT: An orange for each team
PREPARATION: None

This wonderful ice-breaker never fails to win laughs and sometimes develops a contortionist or two.

Start by dividing the group into equal teams, males and females alternating, if possible. The idea is to pass an ordinary orange from one member of the team to the next, right down the line, using your chin and neck alone.

The first person in line tucks the orange under the chin. The next player must remove the orange with his or her own chin and be ready to surrender it to a third chin. First team to pass the orange down the whole line wins.

If the orange falls to the floor, the player with the clumsy chin must pick it up *by chin alone!*

CANDY GRAM

PLAYERS: 8 or more
EQUIPMENT: Candy with holes in the middle, such as Lifesavers
     A toothpick for each player (plus a few extras in case of breakage)
PREPARATION: None

Divide the group into teams of equal number and line them up single file. Arm each player with a toothpick and give each of the leaders a Lifesaver. The leader spears the candy with the toothpick in his or her mouth and tries to pass it to the toothpick of the next player. No hands allowed.

When the Lifesaver has been passed down the line, toothpick-to-toothpick, and reaches the last player, that player runs with toothpick and candy to the head of the line, taking the first position in the file. Everybody moves back a step. The Lifesaver is passed again. Each of the players must carry it, and the first team to finish the whole sequence wins.

If the candy should fall from the toothpick, it must be picked up with the toothpick alone, with no hands touching. You'll find toothpicks are somewhat fragile and can't withstand much pressure.

DOUGHNUT DESPAIR

This is played exactly the same way as Candy Gram, but it uses doughnuts instead. Pass them on ice-cream sticks.

BLOW-ME-DOWN RACE

PLAYERS: 2
EQUIPMENT: 2 (dry) medicine droppers (the kind that comes with nose
        drops)
        2 small downy feathers (the kind in some sofa pillows)
        or see below
PREPARATION: None

If you can't get feathers, take 2 rounds of tissue paper about an inch (2.5 cm) in diameter, and pleat them into cones.

Place the feathers or paper puff cones on a smooth-topped table near one edge. The object is to blow them across the table solely by means of air pumped from the medicine droppers. You may not actually touch the droppers to the feathers, but need to use the tiny puffs of air to blow them across. First one to blow his or her feather or paper puff off the opposite side of the table is the winner.

MAGNETISM

PLAYERS: 8 or more
EQUIPMENT: A paper straw for each player
        A couple of pieces of cleansing tissue, such as Kleenex
PREPARATION: None

This relay produces many laughs. Divide the group into two or more teams. Each player is given a straw. The lead player on each team is also given a small piece of Kleenex or other tissue. By drawing in his or her breath, the leader holds the tissue on the end of the straw and passes it on to the next teammate. The idea is to pass it to each member of the team. If the tissue falls on the floor, it must be picked up the same way, by drawing breath through the straw, and then passed to the next player.

The team that finishes first wins. If only a few people are playing, pass the paper back in reverse order.

Acting Games

CHARADES

Charades is a fast and exciting guessing game that you can play in many different ways—with just a few players, with partners, with teams. One player (or more, depending on what version you play) tries to act out in pantomime for the others some word or group of words, without using the word itself. In most games of charades the acting-out must be done silently—without any words. You can use code movements that you've agreed on beforehand, but you're not allowed to speak at all. Some games permit you to speak, but when they do you cannot use the words you're trying to get across.

In this section you'll find many different types of charade games to suit all kinds of groups of all ages.

THE GAME

PLAYERS: 10–30
EQUIPMENT: Scraps of paper (one for each player)
        Pencils for all
PREPARATION: None

Divide the group into two teams, each team with a captain. Pass out paper and pencils. The team members are each to write out on their scraps of paper one of the toughest, most un-actable words or quotations or names of movies, plays, books—whatever—they can think of. Then they fold up the scraps of paper, the captain collects them, and puts them into a hat or bowl or bag. The captains now trade the scraps of paper, and the race is on.

Each captain rushes back to his or her team and lets the first "actor" select a scrap of paper and proceed to act it out. Both teams can play at the same time, and the first team to guess all the words on the scraps of paper wins. Also, the teams can take turns. (See page 503.)

Let's say that Gordon is the first actor on his team. He dips into the bag and pulls out the proverb, "A stitch in time saves nine." First he lets his team know that it is a proverb by a pre-arranged signal. You can make up your own signals, but usually a proverb or saying is indicated by wiggling two fingers on each hand to indicate quotation marks.

"Saying!" shouts Sally, one of the players on the team. Gordon nods and points to her.

Then he lets his team know there are six words in the saying by holding up six fingers in a definite motion.

"Six words!" yells Rick, another player on the team.

Gordon nods again. His next decision is which word to act out first. He decides on "stitch." He holds up two fingers.

"Second word," Sally says.

Gordon nods again. He makes believe he is sewing.

"Sewing," Kris says.

Gordon indicates the material in his hand.

"Fabric," says Sally, "cloth—material—"

Gordon tries to indicate a very little stitch on the imaginary material.

"Hole," says Rick, "tear, rip—"

Gordon isn't getting anywhere. He waves his hands back and forth in front of him to stop them and show them that he's going on to something else. He holds up two fingers again.

"Second word, still," says Sally.

Gordon nods. Then he cups his hand to his ear.

"Sounds like," says Anne.

Gordon nods. Then he starts to scratch himself.

"Scratch," yells Kris, "itch—"

Gordon points to her and nods vigorously.

"Itch," says Kris, "sounds like itch—"

"Stitch," yells Rick. Gordon looks insanely happy, points to him and nods. Now Gordon holds up four fingers.

"Fourth word," says Sally.

Gordon points to his watch.

"Watch," says Anne, "clock, wrist-watch, what time is it—"

Gordon leaps toward her and points.

"What time is it?" Anne asks.

Gordon points and waves her on.

"Time," shouts Sally.

Gordon swerves and points to her and nods.

"Uh—stitch—uh—time," Sally sums up what they know so far.

At this point, the team will probably guess what Gordon's message is. If they don't, he'll probably go ahead to the last word, "nine," which is also easy to act out.

As soon as the team guesses Gordon's charade, the next team member rushes up to collect a charade and act it out.

CHARADE SIGNALS

Here are some other signals you can work out ahead of time with your team. Most of them are classic signals which are used all over the world by charades players:

BOOK TITLE: Holding hands up in front of you, as if a book is lying in them.

MOVIE: Put one fist up to your eyes so you can look through it like a camera lens and rotate the other fist in circles as if winding up a handle (like an organ grinder).

TV SHOW: With one finger of each hand draw a rectangle in the air to indicate a screen.

PLAY: Indicate an actor by placing one hand on your chest and the other out to the side as if declaiming a speech.

SONG TITLE: Starting at your open mouth, wiggle the fingers of one hand from there out to the side as if a trill is coming out of your mouth.

Indicate small words (articles, conjunctions and prepositions) such as "the," "an," "at," "a," "if," "but," "with," "for," "so" (any small thing) by holding up your thumb and forefinger about an inch or two apart. Then the team starts running through all the small words and won't stop until you point to one of them.

Indicate the number of syllables in a word by holding out your left arm and placing fingers of your right hand on your forearm. However many fingers you place on it is the number of syllables in the word.

Indicate which syllable you are going to act out by following this movement with another of the same kind—only this time, if you're acting out the first syllable, only put one finger on your arm—two for the second syllable, and so on.

To show the group that the word they guessed was correct, Gordon, in the example, nodded vigorously and pointed. Some people tap the side of the nose instead. Nodding is a more natural thing to do, though, and speeds up the game.

WAYS TO PLAY

You don't have to have both teams playing at the same time, though it is a very exciting game if you do. What you miss is being able to see your opponent struggling with the charade you thought up.

If you want, you can let the teams take turns, each player taking as long as necessary to act out the charade, holding a watch on the actor and jotting down the time on the team's score pad.

Or you can give each player a time limit and they either get it or they don't. Three minutes is long enough. Use a stop-watch—or a kitchen timer.

For ideas for charade sayings, see the Proverbs section on page 584.

WHERE AM I?

PLAYERS: 2–30
EQUIPMENT: 30 scraps of paper
PREPARATION: Write a place, such as those listed below, on each scrap of paper.

This game is excellent for beginners, but just as much fun for experienced charades players. You can play it with just one other person, dividing the cards between you and acting them out one at a time. Or you can make it into team play, just as you do with a regular Charades game.

A player selects one of the listed locations and tries to reveal where he or she is through pantomime. The act may be serious or comic or both.

But in this game "sounds like" and "syllable" play is not allowed. Here you really have to act out the whole thing, with no signals or tricks.

1. in a submarine	26. in a shoe shop
2. on a roof	27. in a taxi
3. in a gold mine	28. behind a ticket booth
4. on parade	29. in a canoe
5. in a jewelry store	30. on a mountaintop
6. in a bank	31. on a plane
7. in a zoo	32. on a bus
8. in a printing shop	33. in the jungle
9. in a lighthouse	34. at a football game
10. in a theatre	35. on a rollercoaster
11. on a train	36. in a pet shop
12. in a cafe	37. in a gymnasium
13. in a museum	38. in a garden
14. in a library	39. in church
15. in a fire station	40. in a final examination
16. on shipboard	41. in a fashion show
17. up an apple tree	42. on an iceberg
18. in a kitchen	43. at a switchboard
19. in a courtyard	44. in an office
20. in the hospital	45. in a supermarket
21. on a picnic	46. on a farm
22. in the desert	47. in a band
23. on a space ship	48. in a chorus line
24. in an aquarium	49. in jail
25. in a closet	50. on the moon

OPEN IT

PLAYERS: 2–30
EQUIPMENT: Scraps of paper
PREPARATION: Write names of items, such as those listed below,
            on the scraps of paper.

In this game, the players act out the opening of something, such as the objects listed below. The idea is to reveal the imaginary object you are opening. For instance, you could pick up a package of flower seeds by tearing off a corner, sprinkling the seeds onto the ground and watering them. You could open a safety pin and use it to fasten parts of your clothing.

You can play this with just two people, or with teams.

1. package of flower seeds
2. safety pin
3. wallet
4. candy bar
5. can of paint
6. Chinese fortune cookie
7. watermelon
8. photo album
9. bottle of ketchup
10. walnut
11. "Dear John (or Jean)" letter
12. jar of glue
13. umbrella
14. box of crackers
15. package of cough drops
16. woman's purse
17. can of shoe polish
18. safe
19. jar of vitamins
20. package of butter
21. cupboard
22. box of stationery
23. jar of peanut butter
24. tool box
25. first aid kit
26. filing cabinet
27. package of cheese
28. sewing kit
29. doctor's bag
30. box of laundry soap
31. make-up kit
32. Pandora's box
33. jack-in-the-box
34. package of panty hose
35. birthday present
36. telegram with bad news
37. a can of sardines
38. a jeweler's box with a diamond bracelet in it
39. a music box
40. a banana
41. an alligator's mouth
42. a "forbidden" book
43. a vampire's coffin
44. the refrigerator
45. the window of a burning building
46. an overcrowded closet
47. the door to the lion cage
48. a pill box
49. a poison ring
50. a compact

SCREAMS

PLAYERS: 10–30
EQUIPMENT: Whistle, pans, paper bags, newspapers, washtub, bells,
          musical instruments, noise-makers, a sound-effects record, if you
          have one
PREPARATION: None

This is a hilarious act for the performers as well as the audience. Clever sound effects help to put it over with a bang.

Announce to the players that they are about to discover a savage lion in the living room. Of course, anyone who comes upon a savage lion in the living room is bound to scream. *But,* you tell them, the scream must be done in pantomime. No actual sound should be uttered. Players may open their mouths, throw up their arms, perhaps, as if to scream but the actual sounds will be supplied by a crew handling the sound effects.

One by one each player comes into the middle of the room, walks a few steps, opens an imaginary door and pretends to see the savage lion. Then he or she must pantomime the act of screaming wildly.

The funny part happens when the person pretends to scream. The "sound crew" adds the sound effects, but instead of a scream, all kinds of peculiar noises come out. Here are examples:

Blow a whistle
Crash pans together
Pop a paper bag filled with air
Rip a newspaper
Ring a bell
Play briefly on a musical instrument
   (trumpet is best if you can get one)

The sound crew members can also use their own voices by shrieking and howling or even roaring.

Performers can take turns being part of the sound crew. Everyone should have a turn doing each thing.

If you don't want to use a sound crew on the spot, you can work out the sounds ahead of time and record them on tape. Allow about 5 seconds for each sound.

It's a good idea to have one "sound engineer," who coordinates the sound to the scream. Correct timing is vital. At the instant the player pantomimes the scream, the sound should pour forth.

SILLY SIGHTS

PLAYERS: 2 or more
EQUIPMENT: None
PREPARATION: None

Everyone thinks up a silly sight which he or she might have seen, such as those listed below. One after another, the actors act them out, while the others try to guess what they are. The audience keeps guessing as the act is going on, while the performer nods either *yes* or *no* to the guesses.

1. A laughing rabbit
2. A motorcycle with six wheels
3. A cat that walks backwards
4. A wet sun
5. A swimming camel
6. A rubber dollar bill
7. A crying ostrich
8. A talking scarecrow
9. A book that can be eaten
10. A man as tall as a tree
11. A flying dog
12. A square football
13. A dancing spoon
14. A cloud in a closet
15. A walking pencil
16. A whale in a goldfish bowl
17. A rowboat on the desert
18. A horse only 5 inches tall
19. A pompous pig
20. A railway track made of sugar

STRANGE SPEECHES

PLAYERS: 2 or more
EQUIPMENT: None
PREPARATION: None

Here are speeches with no speech! The player merely pantomimes the act of giving a rousing speech. The more bounce and enthusiasm that goes into it, the better. The player should make all sorts of wild gestures with exaggerated facial expressions.

Each performer should be given a brief spoken introduction, such as, "And here is Jerry Wilson who will speak on the topic, *How to Fly a Kite in a Closet*."

The pantomimed actions need have little or nothing to do with the announced topic. A prize might be awarded to the most enthusiastic performer. Players may think up their own topics or may select one from a list you make up in advance.

Some ideas:

1. My Cold Trip to the North Pole
2. What I Think about Spaghetti
3. How to Stand on Your Head
4. Famous Cowboys of the East
5. Washing Dishes Can Be Fun
6. Fun with Taxidermy
7. How to Blow Soap Bubbles
8. Why I Like to Climb Trees
9. Why I Don't Like to Climb Trees
10. Build Your Own Airplane
11. Strange Facts about Alligators
12. How to Make a Cabbage Salad
13. The Funniest Story I Ever Heard
14. What Happened on My Last Birthday
15. What I Did Last Summer
16. Keep an Elephant for a Pet
17. How to Carry Peanut Butter in Your Pocket
18. The Men in My Life
19. The Women in My Life
20. How to Be Very Very Popular
21. I Fought Monsters in Transylvania
22. King Kong is My Best Friend
23. What We Can Learn from Babies
24. Karate is Really a Safe Sport
25. Insects Don't Bite, You Just Think They Do

Another way to play this game: Write each topic on a slip of paper, fold it, and put it in a bowl. Then let the players pull out their speech topics by chance. Give them just 10 seconds to plan and prepare the speech.

SLOW MOTION

PLAYERS: 4 or more
EQUIPMENT: None
PREPARATION: None

There is something particularly amusing about a charade that is performed in slow motion. It may be difficult sometimes for the players to keep from laughing during the act, but that is all part of the fun. Two or more players can act at the same time.

Select an act that offers plenty of opportunity for physical movements. It should consist of a scene that is familiar to the audience, such as playing tennis or checking out groceries at the supermarket or perhaps a classroom activity.

Once the act has been more or less worked out, the performers should rehearse it at normal speed to get acquainted with the basic movements. The players then repeat the act more and more slowly, until they have it down clearly in slow motion.

There are two special ways to make slow motion acts funny. First choose funny physical movements, such as:

1. A golfer spins slowly around several times after giving the ball a terrific whack and then sinks to the ground in exhaustion.

2. A waiter tries desperately to balance several imaginary dishes in his hand. As they spill, he desperately grabs the air, trying to catch them before they smash to the floor.

3. A fist fight in which the players react violently to each blow, careening across the room. Note: when you work this out, be very specific about where each blow lands, so that each player can react appropriately. (Of course, the blows don't *actually* land; there would be nothing funny in that.)

4. Two people doing the latest dance step.

The other important thing is to build the expression on your face slowly. Whenever something happens, build up your facial expression a little at a time until it is quite exaggerated. For instance, the waiter would grow more and more terrified as he grabs at his imaginary dishes.

Keep the slow-motion acts short and punchy.

IT TAKES TWO

PLAYERS: 4 or more
EQUIPMENT: None
PREPARATION: None

Pairs of players act out these skits, which may range in length from a few seconds to 3 or 4 minutes. Performers should take as much time as they need to work out a skit in which the actions are both clear and funny. The audience needs to guess who the characters are and what they are doing.

1. Barber as he tries to cut the hair of a wriggling child
2. Doctor and patient
3. Mailman and lady-of-the-house
4. Grocery clerk and customer
5. Cowboy roping a wild horse
6. Carpenter and assistant
7. Taxi driver and passenger
8. Dancer and awkward partner
9. Swimming instructor and student
10. Pedestrian asks directions of policeman
11. Sprinter and track coach
12. Lion tamer and ferocious lion
13. Parent teaches child to cook
14. Pianist and singer
15. Bank teller and customer
16. Person tries to escape determined bee
17. Tightrope walker and spectator
18. Baseball pitcher and catcher
19. Boss dictates letter to secretary
20. Parent tries to soothe crying baby
21. Driving teacher and student driver
22. Fisherman tries to catch fish
23. Play director shows actor how to act
24. Person tries to teach dog to shake hands
25. Parent trying to get baby to eat strained rhubarb

These are just a few situations that the actors can develop. Point out that in order for the skit to be funny each character must need something very urgently from the other person. For example, when the pedestrian asks directions of the policeman, the pedestrian might be on the way to de-activate a time-bomb, if only he or she could find the right house. Meanwhile, the policeman could be trying to catch Public Enemy No. 1, who just walked down the street!

The doctor may be trying to perform a vital operation on the wrong patient—who won't be anesthetized and is desperate to get out of there because his or her house is on fire.

Make the situations as far out as you want. The more ridiculous, the better!

PAPER BAG PLAYWRIGHTS

PLAYERS: 10 or more
EQUIPMENT: One paper bag for every 5 players
About 5 or 6 items for each bag, such as are indicated in the following description
PREPARATION: None

You don't have to be a playwright to play this game. All you need is paper bags full of assorted items and a good imagination.

Here's how it goes: Divide the group into teams with about five players on each team. Then take several paper bags—one for each team —and fill them, but put different objects in each bag. Then each team has 10 minutes to prepare a skit using the objects in the bag.

For example, Team A has a bag containing a banana peel, a handbag, a detective's badge, a moustache, a razor, and a handkerchief. The group may decide to act out a skit that can go like this:

Two underworld characters (one with a *moustache*) are planning a robbery. They are sitting on a park bench and the thug with the moustache is eating a *banana*. He throws the *peel* on the ground for an unsuspecting victim to slip on and wipes off his fingers with a *handkerchief*. A victim comes along, carrying the *handbag,* and slips on the peel. As one of the thugs helps her up, the other character darts out and grabs her handbag.

She and the first thug run after the robber, but he escapes. A detective appears, wearing the *badge*. He sees the banana peel, and upon examining it, finds a hair on it.

"Aha," he wisely proclaims, "the man who was eating this had a moustache." The thug pulls out a *razor* from his pocket and begins to shave off the moustache, but is caught just in time, etc.

A terrible plot? What can you expect from a paper bag? Besides, it doesn't matter. No one is going to see it but the other people who are holding a bag. And they'll create plots just as terrible as yours.

MIRROR ACT

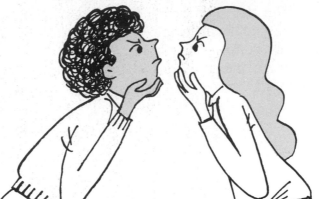

PLAYERS: 2 or more
EQUIPMENT: None
PREPARATION: None

    With a bit of practice, this mirror act can be highly entertaining. The idea is for two players to coordinate pantomime movements so as to give the appearance of one player looking at his or her reflection in a full-length mirror. This means that both players comb their hair or brush their teeth in unison, just as if one player performed these movements in front of a mirror.

    Here are notes and suggestions for building a superior performance.

1. Face each other sideways to the audience.
2. You should be approximately the same height.
3. Practice a single movement until you can do it at precisely the same moment and then go on to the next.
4. Practice all movements in slow motion at first, and then speed up slightly. It is best to do all movements with only moderate speed.
5. Choose broad sweeping movements that can be seen clearly by the audience.
6. Keep your feet planted in one place except when you make definite foot movements.
7. Do not smile or laugh (that makes it even funnier).
8. Some ideas for mirror movements:

- Lean forward and touch noses, as if peering closely into mirror.
- Gaze in fond admiration, passing hand over hair and tilting head in a dramatic pose.
- Push palms together and rotate arms, as if polishing the mirror.
- Twist face into comical expressions.
- Smile broadly.

9. The act may be given a funny finish by unexpectedly breaking the synchronization. You, for example, might wave good-bye while your mirror image beckons "Come here." Or you beckon "Come here" as your mirror image waves good-bye. You would stare briefly in surprise at each other, shrug, face the audience, bow in unison and exit.

IN THE MANNER OF THE WORD

PLAYERS: **4 or more**
EQUIPMENT: None
PREPARATION: None

While one player, say George, is sent out of the room, the others decide on an adverb which he will have to guess. The clues will be acted out—silently—by the other players.

Let's say the adverb is "sweetly." When George comes back into the room, he asks Susie to do a dance step, for example, "in the manner of the word." Or to walk with a book on her head "in the manner of the word." Or to polish the table—or comb her hair or eat a chocolate or read a magazine—whatever he asks her to do, she must do it "in the manner of the word."

When Susie has executed a dance step reeking with sweetness, George asks another player to do the same thing, or a different action. There is no limit to the number of guesses George gets, and the game goes on until the adverb is discovered. Then George selects a new guesser (preferably the one whose act helped him to guess) and the game goes on.

Be sure to pick adverbs that are easy to act out, like:

aggressively	hotly	shame-facedly
angrily	hypnotically	sharply
anxiously	impatiently	significantly
bitterly	indifferently	sleepily
brilliantly	jokingly	sneakily
brutally	languorously	softly
charmingly	laughingly	stonily
childishly	lethargically	teasingly
cleverly	lightly	tenderly
clumsily	lovingly	tentatively
coolly	masterfully	timidly
cruelly	mischievously	toughly
daintily	miserably	tremblingly
demurely	murderously	uncomfortably
desperately	nastily	unctuously
eagerly	obsequiously	untidily
flirtatiously	powerfully	venomously
gently	prettily	viciously
gingerly	rambunctiously	wickedly
gratefully	roughly	wisely
hatefully	rudely	wistfully
heavily	sadly	zestfully

IN THE MANNER OF THE WORD WITH WORDS

PLAYERS: 4 or more
EQUIPMENT: None
PREPARATION: None

This game is played just like the last one, but this time, instead of pantomiming something "in the manner of the word," you give a short speech—on any subject that the guesser selects.

For example, let's say the word is "violently." You might be asked to describe your math class "in the manner of the word," or tell about a popular television program, or discuss world peace. The guesser would have no way of knowing, of course, what the word is, and some of the combinations you get can be hilarious!

Another way to play this game is to write the adverbs on scraps of paper and subjects for speeches on other scraps. Put the scraps in separate bowls and let each player take one from bowl A (adverbs) and one from bowl B (speeches). Then, as each person delivers a speech, the others try to guess the adverb which is being acted out.

For ideas for speeches, see page 508.

Carnival Games

The games in this section are adaptations of the ones you'll find at fairs and bazaars, amusement parks and carnivals. You can use them in a couple of ways.

If you make the games (most of them just need to be set up—not actually *made*) yourself, for your own amusement, you can play them in competition with a friend—or friends.

If you want to use a carnival theme for your party, you set them up before the party starts. As people arrive, they experiment with them and play them in organized games later. You'll want to do a bit of work on the painting and decorating of the games, because shine and glitter is an important part of the fun of a carnival.

BUCKET BALL

PLAYERS: **Unlimited**
EQUIPMENT: **Bucket**
        Ball
        A couple of books
        Gift wrapping paper (optional)
PREPARATION: **If you are presenting this game in a real carnival atmosphere, put brightly colored gift wrapping paper around the outside of the bucket. If you want to go further, you can paint a face on the bottom of the bucket, or paste on one from a magazine.**

Place the bucket on its side at a slight angle. You can use a book or two to prop it up. A medium-sized ball is about right for this game (see the illustration), and the best distance for throwing is 6 to 10 feet (2 to 3 m). Experiment with this so that the game is not too easy.

When contestants throw the ball, it will bounce right out again if it hits the bottom of the bucket. You can avoid this, though, if you discover the right spots to hit. For example, if you toss the ball to the left or right side of the bucket at an angle, it will stay in unless you throw it too hard. You will get the same result if the ball hits the lower side of the bucket just beneath the rim. Naturally, no matter where the ball hits, it will bounce, but when it hits a side first it will only bounce around inside the bucket. But don't tell your guests that!

Don't use wooden balls. They don't bounce around so much and are much too easy to keep in the bucket.

CANDLE SHOOT-OUT

PLAYERS: Unlimited
EQUIPMENT: 3 candles
            2 or 3 water pistols
            Matches (you'll need plenty of them)
            Plastic sheeting and tarpaulins (plastic tablecloths are good)
PREPARATICN: Set up the candles in low holders on a table in a corner.
            Protect the wall behind them (and to the sides) with plastic
            tablecloths to catch the spray. Put a tarpaulin underneath the table
            and around it.

This is one of the most delightful carnival games ever, though it has two serious drawbacks. You can't really play it outdoors, because the candles blow out. And it's difficult to set it up indoors, because everything in sight gets soaking wet. So—if you still want to try it—gather up all the tarpaulins and plastic protection you can find for your home, and cover the walls and floor.

Experiment with your water pistols to see how far away you can get from the candles and still blow them out. About 15 feet (5m) away is a good spot to start testing. Contestants will toe whatever line you set up as they aim their water pistols and shoot out the candles. Don't make the game too easy, but it shouldn't be impossible, either. Allow each player ten squirts to shoot out all three candles.

RING THE BOTTLE

PLAYERS: Unlimited
EQUIPMENT: An unbreakable soda bottle (empty)
      Aluminum foil (optional)
      Cardboard or old clothes hangers. (You can also use curtain rings, rubber jar rings or plain bracelets as rings.)
PREPARATION: If you want to decorate the bottle, wrap foil around it to give it a festive look. If you want to make your own rings, you can cut small flat hoops out of stiff cardboard, or bend them out of soft, thick wire. If you use clothes hangers, after you have made them into rings be sure that you twist the ends together securely. Then put some vinyl tape over them, so that no one can get hurt on the edges.

Set up the bottle on the floor or on a chair some distance away. Put some pebbles in the bottom of it, so that it stands securely. First test yourself throwing the rings at the bottle. You might start this testing at 10 steps away. The object is to toss the ring horizontally in such a way that it comes to rest over the neck of the bottle.

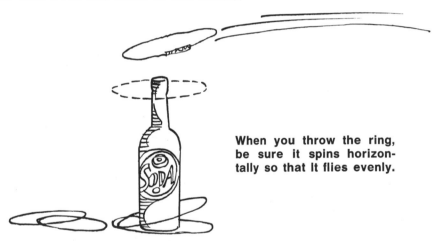

When you throw the ring, be sure it spins horizontally so that It flies evenly.

This looks easier than it actually is. There will be a great many misses before a ring finally falls over the neck of the bottle. You can make the game easier or more difficult by changing the size of the rings you use. You can obviously snare your bottle easier with a large ring than with a small one.

You can play with several different sets of rules. If you give 5 rings to each contestant, you can insist that the winner get all 5 of them on in order to get a prize. Or perhaps only 3 out of 5. Or, if you have enough rings, you might ask your guests to stand in a big circle and let everyone take turns throwing at the bottle.

RING THE PRIZES

PLAYERS: Unlimited
EQUIPMENT: Small prizes that you wrap in gift paper
     Small scraps of plywood to set the prizes on
     Rings (as used in the last game)
PREPARATION: Set up the prizes, each on a plywood block in a separate
     area of the house

     This game is very much like Ring the Bottle, only instead of the bottle, the contestants throw their rings for the prizes. If the ring falls over the prize and down around the plywood base, the prize is theirs.

Note: Once a player has won a prize, his or her turn is over!

     See page 393 for a few ideas for prizes.

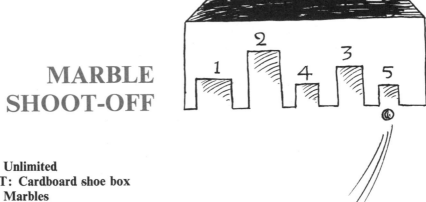

MARBLE SHOOT-OFF

PLAYERS: Unlimited
EQUIPMENT: Cardboard shoe box
     Marbles
     Gift wrapping paper (optional)
     Paint
PREPARATION: Turn the shoe box upside down and cut about 5 notches
     on the long side of the box. The notches should be approximately
     1 to $1\frac{1}{2}$ inches (2.5–3.5 cm) wide and different heights from 2 to 4
     inches (5 to 10 cm). Cover the box with gift wrapping paper, if
     you want to make it glamorous, and then paint large numbers
     above each hole.

     Place the box on the floor against a wall and pace off 5 steps. Give each player 10 marbles and keep score. They take turns rolling their marbles toward the shoe box, aiming for one of the numbered holes, and they score according to the number on top. The first player to get 100 points wins.

INDOOR GOLF

PLAYERS: 1–4 at a time
EQUIPMENT: 9 boxes
          Wrapping paper, foil or paint
          Tape, paint, or contrasting paper
          2–4 beanbags of different colors, if possible
          Index cards
PREPARATION: Decorate the boxes as much as you want with the
          wrapping paper, foil or paint. Then number them from 1 to 9
          with some kind of tape or paint or contrasting paper.

Set up the boxes at various places around the room or rooms that you will be using. Put some in open places, others behind furniture, under chairs, at a slant in spots that are difficult to reach.

As you set the boxes in place, keep in mind that each player will start from a place you select (0) and throw a beanbag at Box 1. You will keep count of the number of shots it takes him or her to get the beanbag (the golf ball) into the box (the hole). The player will move to Box 1 and throw from there at Box 2, and then move to Box 2 and throw to Box 3. So place the boxes in order, making it possible to reach each one from the preceding number.

After the boxes are ready, go over the course yourself with your family and friends to see what "par" is. Par will be the number of shots it should normally take a good player to go from one box to the next. Then print out some score sheets (on index cards) that look like this:

Players' names go here.

On the left, list the number of the "hole," and at the right list the number of throws that are "par" for that hole. Leave room at the top for the names of the players.

Holes					Par
1					2
2					2
3					3
4					3
5					3
6					4
7					4
8					4
9					4
Total					29

Score the game as you would a golf match of 9 holes. Two players can play a match against each other, or four can play, if you have enough beanbags. If you'd rather make this a game for prizes, you could give a prize to anyone who breaks par (gets a lower score than par), or to the player who gets the lowest score of the game—or the day.

THE DING-A-LING GAME

PLAYERS: **Unlimited**
EQUIPMENT: A small embroidery hoop (or see below)
           A bell
           A ball or beanbag
           Mounting tape
PREPARATION: Suspend the hoop from the top of a doorway with
           mounting tape, and suspend the bell within the hoop. Mark a
           starting line about 10 feet (3 m) away.

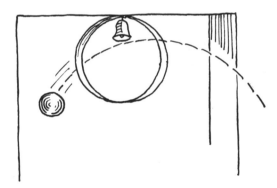

This is a real amusement park game. You stand behind the starting line and try to throw the ball through the hoop, aiming to hit the bell, if possible. Get another player to stand in back of the hoop to catch the ball and return it to you.

Each player gets 5 consecutive turns. Score as follows:

        Touch the hoop—2 points
        Through the hoop—5 points
        Ring the bell—10 points

If you don't have an embroidery hoop, you can make a substitute which will do as well from the lid of a gift box about 6 inches (15 cm) square—or even rectangular. With a scissors cut out the flat top of the lid, leaving the frame intact.

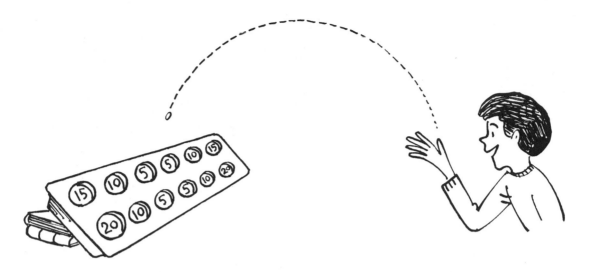

PENNY TOSS

PLAYERS: Unlimited
EQUIPMENT: A muffin tin
           10 pennies
           A couple of books
           Construction paper in different colors (optional)
           Shiny paper with gummed back (optional)
PREPARATION: Cut out 12 rounds of paper to fit into the holes of the
           muffin tin. Then cut numbers out of shiny paper and glue them
           onto the rounds in contrasting colors so that they show up well.
           Mark the muffin cups as follows:
                     15 10 5 5 10 15
                     20 10 5 5 10 20
           Tilt the muffin tin against some books and mark a starting line
           about 6 feet (2 m) away.

The object of the game is to throw your penny into a high-scoring muffin cup or any muffin cup. First test the distance and tilt of the muffin tin to make sure that the game is not too easy.

Give players 5 pennies each which they try to throw into the holes. When they have tossed all the pennies, they remove them themselves and add up their scores.

Take turns tossing until one player reaches a score of 100 points.

MORE
CARNIVAL
IDEAS

If you're setting up your party as a carnival, you may want to have a fortune-telling booth. See pages 553 to 571 for fortune-telling games you can use. All you really need for your "booth" is a table with a brightly colored piece of fabric thrown over it. If you can get a large scarf with fringed edges, so much the better! Behind the table, on the wall you can put up a zodiac poster or draw your own "mystic symbols" on a sheet of paper.

Another interesting booth is one where guests can get "made up" with complete disguises or just a design on one cheek. (Be sure to put cleansing cream on your customers' faces first so that whatever you design is removable!)

You can even set up refreshments as if they are for sale on a gaily decorated table, and then let people help themselves.

If you are going to set up "booths," it is a good idea to get someone to help run them. Perhaps a parent or a brother or sister would be willing to take over the fortune-telling and make-up chores, so that you can keep the party rolling.

Music is important, too. It should be going in the background continuously while people are milling around and playing the games. If you don't have happy, honky-tonk circus or carnival music records or tapes at home, check in your local library. They often have records they lend out, and they may have just what you want.

Check the Before the Party games (pages 425–431); some of those are excellent carnival competitions.

Look around in your collection of manufactured games and see if you have others that you can lay out on tables for immediate contests. You can use marble shooting galleries, bagatelle or pinball-type games, hockey sets, skittles, and many others for this purpose. You may have more carnival material right at hand than you have room for!

Ghost Stories

Are you planning a slumber party? A Halloween party? A spine-tingling ghost story may be just the ticket! If you have some that you can get your hands on, read them over so that they're fresh in your mind and you will be able to spread a bit of fear around the fire.

Take a look at the stories here, too. All of them are supposed to be true. Whether they are or not, they are all terrifying, especially if you tell them in a quiet, matter-of-fact way, and, when it is appropriate, say that your Grandmother was there when . . .

THE VANISHING OLIVER LARCH

It happened in 1889 on Christmas Eve.

The setting was a farm near South Bend, Indiana. It had snowed, and four or five inches of the white mantle covered the yards and the hen-house roof. Eleven-year-old Oliver Larch lived on the farm with his parents who were giving a Christmas party for some old friends of the family, a minister and his wife and an attorney from Chicago.

After dinner they gathered around a pump organ, and Mrs. Larch played carols while the others sang. She played "Silent Night" and "The Twelve Days of Christmas." Warm voices filled the cozy room, and laughter. After a while Oliver went to the kitchen to pop corn on the wood-burning range.

At this point his father noticed that the gray granite bucket used for drinking water was almost empty. He asked Oliver to run out to the well in the yard and refill it. The boy set aside his corn-popper and put on his overshoes. He picked up the bucket and opened the door to the yard. It was just a few minutes before 11 o'clock. It would soon be Christmas, and he wanted to get back to the party quickly.

His father returned to the living room to add his voice to the chorale, as Oliver stepped out into the night—and eternity. About a dozen seconds after he had left the doorway the adults around the organ were stunned by screams from the yard.

They rushed out the same door Oliver had used. Mrs. Larch grabbed up a kerosene lamp to light the way. Outside, the dark, starless night was filled with scream after scream of, "Help! Help! They've got me! They've got me!"

What made the adults recoil in horror was that Oliver's screams were coming from high *above* them in the blackened sky. The piercing cries grew fainter and fainter and finally faded away completely as the stunned group stared at each other in speechless disbelief.

The men sprang to life, seized the lamp, and followed the youngster's tracks toward the well. They did not get far. Halfway to the well, roughly 30 feet (10 m) from the house, the tracks abruptly ended. No signs of a scuffle or struggle, just the end of the tracks. They found the heavy stone bucket about 15 feet (5 m) to the left of the end of the tracks, dropped in the snow as though from above. That was all. Oliver had started straight for the well, and then had been carried away by—what? He was a big boy, weighing about 75 pounds (35 kg), too heavy for a big bird or even several birds to lift. Airplanes had not been invented yet, and no balloons were aloft that night. Who or what seized Oliver Larch? The mystery has not been solved to this day, and probably never will be.

NIGHT RIDE

This story was told by an old doctor who lived a hermit's life in a small New England village. It happened when he was a young boy, but he told it and retold it in exactly the same way until his death.

When the doctor was fifteen years old, his father had a bay colt which he let his son ride. One evening the boy started riding to a nearby town. On the way he had to pass a cottage where a woman by the name of Dolly Spokesfield lived. She was rumored to have unusual powers, skill in the black arts and the ability to turn herself into almost anything she wished. She was, it was whispered, a genuine witch of the inner circle—certainly a person to be avoided by anyone out at night alone.

As the lad approached Dolly Spokesfield's cottage he kept to the middle of the road and urged the colt to a faster trot. But his precautions were in vain.

As the colt and rider came abreast of the cottage, a coal black cat suddenly leaped out of the darkness and landed on the colt's neck. The frightened horse stopped short, almost throwing the boy over his head. The boy tried desperately to get rid of the cat and urged his mount on, beating him with his whip, but the cat held on and the colt refused to move with the black cat hissing upon his neck.

The boy was afraid to leave his horse and run, and in panic he dismounted and began to beat the cat with the whip, holding the colt by the bridle rein as he reared and plunged, trying to shake off the cat.

At last the boy dislodged the cat and he hurriedly rode home. The poor colt was bruised and clawed by the cat, and apparently exhausted by his ordeal. So injured and frightened was he that the boy was afraid the animal would die before morning. He turned him loose in the barn instead of putting him in the stall, and went to bed trembling and fearful that the colt wouldn't last the night.

At dawn, the boy hurried to the barn to inspect the battered and clawed animal. To his amazement, the young horse was in perfect condition. He showed no sign of exhaustion, and nowhere on his body could the boy find a trace of bruises from the whip, a claw mark or a single reminder of the frantic events of the previous night.

The story had an even stranger ending. A neighbor soon stopped by to report that Dolly Spokesfield had just been found almost dead, her body bruised and beaten as though by a whip. And under two of her fingernails were some short bay hairs, such as you'd find, perhaps, on the neck of a young colt ridden by a frightened boy alone in the night.

THE DOCTOR'S VISITOR

Dr. S. Weir Mitchell of Philadelphia was one of the nation's foremost neurologists during the latter part of the 19th century. One snowy evening after a particularly hard day he retired early, and was just falling asleep when his doorbell rang loudly. He hoped it had been a trick of his ears, or that his caller would go away, but the bell rang again even more insistently. Struggling awake, he snatched a robe and stumbled down to see who it was. He muttered in annoyance as he slid the bolt to unlock the door, completely unprepared for the shivering child who stood in the swirling snow.

The small pale girl trembled on the doorstep, for a thin frock and a ragged shawl were her only protection against the blustering snow-filled wind. She said in a tiny, plaintive voice, "My mother is very sick—won't you come, please?"

Dr. Mitchell explained that he had retired for the night and suggested that the child call another doctor in the vicinity. But she wouldn't leave, and looking up at him with tear-filled eyes, pleaded again, "Won't *you* come, please?" No one—and certainly no doctor—could refuse this pitiful appeal.

With a resigned sigh, thinking longingly of his warm bed, the physician asked the child to step inside while he dressed and picked up his bag. Then he followed her out into the storm.

In a house several streets away he found a woman desperately sick with pneumonia. He recognized her immediately as someone who had once worked for him as a servant, and he bent over the bed, determined to save her. As he worked, the doctor complimented her on her daughter's fortitude and persistence in getting him there.

The woman stared unbelievingly at the doctor and said in a weak whisper, "That is impossible. My little girl died more than a month ago. Her dress is still hanging in that cupboard over there!"

With strange emotions Dr. Mitchell strode to the cupboard and opened it. Inside hung the little dress and the tattered shawl that his caller had worn. They were warm and dry and could never have been out in the storm!

THE FRIGHTENED DOG

Tom grew up in North Carolina, where he, two of his friends and his dog often went on hunting trips into the woods and swamps.

One day they set forth with their guns, planning to be gone only a few hours. Late that afternoon it began to rain very hard. Since they were far from home, they decided to spend the night in an abandoned shack they had stumbled upon, rather than try to find their way home in the dark. The shack was empty except for some rubbish, a few old clothes and a lantern which still had some kerosene in it. Eventually the boys fell asleep on the floor, with the dog curled up beside them, while the rain splattered upon the roof overhead.

Some time during the night the boys were awakened by the dog whining and scratching at the door. He was trembling violently, and the hair on his back was raised as though he were either frightened or angry.

Rather sleepily, one of the boys started for the door to let the pup out. Then he froze in his tracks. From the black woods outside the shack came a weird, startling sound. A combination of whine, low moan, and rising and falling wail, it was like nothing the boys had heard before anywhere. They stared at each other, and reached for their light rifles as the dog raced around the room, barking and whining and showing his teeth. One boy quickly lit the lantern.

The window openings of the shack contained no glass but were covered with mosquito netting. Suddenly the dog hurled himself through one of these openings and ran off into the woods, snarling and barking.

The three boys waited with hearts pounding and .22's clutched in their hands. At last the strange sound faded away in the distance and they heard nothing but the patter of the rain on the tin roof.

A few minutes later the dog leaped back through the broken netting and came toward them, whining and shaking, with his tail tucked between his legs. He was a very frightened white dog. That was the most amazing part of the adventure, for when he had left the shack to run into the woods after the "thing," he had been black!

THE STRANGE DEATH OF MRS. REESER

Fire, a great blessing from the days of the cave man on, occasionally sets off mysteries which man finds as difficult to believe as he does to solve. This was the case in the 1951 death by burning of Mrs. Mary Reeser of St. Petersburg, Florida.

This elderly lady lived alone and was last seen alive by a friend the night before her unusual death. Her friend went to call on her again at about eight o'clock on the morning of July 2, 1951, to take her some coffee and a telegram. To her astonishment she found the handle of the door too hot to hold. In alarm she ran for help. Some carpenters who were working nearby returned with her and forced open the door to Mrs. Reeser's room.

The room was almost unbearably hot although the windows were open, and a ghastly sight greeted them. Close to one of the open windows were the charred remains of a chair—and of Mrs. Reeser herself. All that was left of either was a small pile of blackened wood and a skull. A pile of charred wood on the floor contained several coil springs and a few bits of bone.

Nearby another small pile of charred wood marked where a small end table had stood, and a burned floor lamp lay some distance away. The room itself was strangely affected by the fire. Above a line three or four feet from the floor, the walls and curtains were heavily coated with black soot, as were the screens of the open windows.

A base plug in the wall had melted, short-circuiting a lamp and clock which had stopped at 4:20. A small wall-type gas heater was turned off and unaffected by the fire. There had been such terrific heat in the room that candles on another table had melted and run out of their holders onto the table itself. Under the pile of charred wood and bones there was a burned spot on the rug. But nothing else had caught fire.

What happened in that room may never be known. Neither arson experts from the police department and Board of Fire Underwriters, nor doctors could determine what had caused such terrific heat and such strange reactions to it. It was estimated that temperatures up to 3,000° F (1650° C) would be required for such complete destruction of a body and a chair, and not even a burning body, clothing, and wood could generate that temperature, even for a short time.

There had been no lightning that night. Experts determined that no explosive fluids or inflammable chemicals had been present that could raise the ordinary temperature of a fire (such as a cigarette-started fire) to the degree at which such complete cremation could take place. A mirror on the wall was cracked and distant candles melted. Why hadn't other things in the room caught fire? Why wasn't the house destroyed as it would have been in an ordinary fire? Why did it stay so unbearably hot in that room until eight in the morning, even with the windows open?

This was no ordinary fire and no ordinary event. But what was it?

LORD DUFFERIN'S STORY

Lord Dufferin, a British diplomat, was the central figure of this story, which has become one of England's classic tales of the supernatural.

One night during a stay at a friend's country house in Ireland, Lord Dufferin was unusually restless and could not sleep. He had an inexplicable feeling of dread, and so, to calm his nerves, he arose and walked across the room to the window.

A full moon illuminated the garden below so that it was almost as bright as morning as Lord Dufferin stood by the window. Suddenly he was conscious of a movement in the shadows and a man appeared, carrying a long box on his back. The silent and sinister figure walked slowly across the moonlit yard. As he passed the window from which Lord Dufferin intently watched, he stopped and looked directly into the diplomat's eyes.

Lord Dufferin recoiled, for the face of the man carrying the burden was so ugly that he could not even describe it later. For a moment their eyes met, and then the man moved off into the shadows. The box on his back was clearly seen to be a casket.

The next morning Dufferin asked his host and the other guests about the man in the garden, but no one knew anything about him. They even accused him of having had a nightmare, but he knew better.

Many years later in Paris, when Lord Dufferin was serving as the English ambassador to France, he was about to walk into an elevator on his way to a meeting. For some inexplicable reason he glanced at the elevator operator. With a violent start he recognized the man he had seen carrying the coffin across the moonlit garden. Involuntarily, he stepped back from the elevator and stood there as the door closed and it started up without him.

His agitation was so great that he remained motionless for several minutes. Then a terrific crash startled him. The cable had parted, and the elevator had fallen three floors to the basement. Several passengers were killed in the tragedy and the operator himself died.

Investigation revealed that the operator had been hired for just that day. No one ever found out who he was or where he came from.

THE TERRIBLE HAND

Over 50 years ago a Mrs. Roy Jackson, now of Harrison, New York, went to live in Paterson, New Jersey with her young husband. They were poor but eventually stumbled on an extremely inexpensive house, even for those days. Yet, Mrs. Jackson felt uneasy about the house and at first wanted no part of it, even at $12 a month.

Still, the Jacksons moved in. Even her brother, a lawyer who checked the lease, remarked on the house's vaguely sinister atmosphere.

He said he felt a "presence" there that was "not good," but the rent was so low. . . .

The months went by and Mrs. Jackson's apprehension grew. Then one day she learned from neighbors that the reason the house was so cheap was that it was supposed to be haunted. A mother had killed herself and two children in the house several years before and since then no one had stayed there longer than a few days. There were rumors of lone women renting the place and being found dead a day later after shrieking "Someone has me by the throat."

Roy Jackson scoffed at these yarns and insisted they stay on, in spite of his wife's feeling that she was constantly being peered at, followed, and warned to move. Then came the First World War, and Roy began to talk of enlisting. It was on an October night that the young wife came face to face with terror and almost lost her life.

She was lying on a sofa in the living room, thinking about the changes the war would make in her life and looking at a bright spot on the ceiling made by the gas fixture on the table. Suddenly she was aware of a second bright spot on the ceiling. Perhaps another light from outside, a reflection from a mirror? But there was no other light or mirror.

The spot grew and grew, writhing like "thousands of cobwebs turning and twisting into a mass about three feet long and two feet wide," she said later. A point protruded from the whirling mass, then another and another until she recognized it as a hand with five long pointed fingers. Suddenly the mass stopped whirling.

The mass then grew a long wispy arm behind the fingers, and the entire shape darted down from the ceiling, seizing Mrs. Jackson by the throat. With an agonized lurch, she hurled herself to the floor and lay on the rug, face down and gasping for breath. Moments later she forced herself out of the room to the stairs. Shaken but unhurt, she finally convinced her husband they should move. One encounter with the gray whirling terror had been enough.

Out of curiosity the Jacksons returned to Paterson in 1930 and visited their ex-landlady. She was in great pain from an old injury. It seems that after the Jacksons had left, the house had been rented to a single woman. One night the landlady heard screaming and had run up to help. The spinster lay face down on the floor, dying, but grabbed the landlady in her terror, tearing ligaments which had never healed.

Mrs. Jackson, who recalls her experience vividly, has not recorded the Paterson house number, only that it stood on North Third Street. . . .

PSYCHO LOGICAL GAMES

II

Personality Games

LIKES AND DISLIKES

PLAYERS: 6–12
EQUIPMENT: Paper and pencil for each player
PREPARATION: None

This is a game only for friends who know each other fairly well. Everyone is given a sheet of paper and pencil and asked to list five likes and five dislikes and sign his or her name. Likes and dislikes can include hats, short hair, television, big cars, olives, homework, false teeth, blind dates—anything the players want to write—except people's names.

The lists are collected and each one is read aloud by the leader, who doesn't tell which player created it. Then everyone tries to guess who wrote each set of likes and dislikes. It's fun to see if you really know your friends!

REVELATIONS

PLAYERS: 6–10

EQUIPMENT: Questionnaires that you prepare ahead of time
　　　　　　Score sheets that you prepare ahead of time
　　　　　　Pencil for each player

PREPARATION: This game calls for a great deal of work before the party, but it's worth it. The questionnaires can contain as many items as you want, depending on how long you want to play and how many people are taking part. Twelve is a good number to start with. You'll find ideas for questions in the sample questionnaire which appears on the next page. After you type up or write up the questionnaire, photocopy it, one for each player.
　　　　　　You also need to make up a score sheet that looks like this:

	DAN	PETER	MARIA	IAN	LINCOLN	CAROLE
1			EINSTEIN			
2						
3						
4						
5						
6						
7						
8						
9						
10						
11						
12						

This game is a more complex version of Likes and Dislikes. Play it for a while and you'll start to wonder if you really know anybody! The point is to ask off-beat questions, the kind you and your friends probably have never talked about—and to see whether you can tell how each person will answer. Only use this game in a group where the players know each other well. Or *think* they do.

Pass out the questionnaires and ask everyone to fill one out. You can do this days before the party, if you have a chance to collect the sheets in advance. But if you ask your friends to bring the sheets along, they'll probably forget.

SAMPLE QUESTIONNAIRE

Name...

SPECIAL INSTRUCTIONS: In no case may you use the name of any person in the room in answer to any of these questions. Do not show your answers to this questionnaire to anyone in the room.

1. You have been convicted of a crime and will be in prison for the next 20 years. There is no use appealing the judge's decision. You are in a private cell. The only person you can talk with is the person in the next cell. Anyone you want, living or dead, can be in the next cell. Whom do you want?

2. You can have anything in the world that you want for Christmas, but it has to come from one shop and it will be non-returnable. From what shop do you want your gift certificate?

3. You have just won a contest. You will be sent on a two-week trip, all expenses paid, to any place you want to go. Where do you want to go?

4. You can spend Monday, Tuesday and Wednesday afternoons next week with any people you want, living or dead. Whom do you select for Monday? Tuesday? Wednesday?

5. Write down your worst fault. (Don't write what people *tell* you your worst fault is. Write down what *you* think it is.)

6. Write down your best quality. (See note above.)

7. Write the name of the funniest comedian you ever saw.

8. Write the name of the most moving play or film you ever saw.

9. Write the name of the most moving book you ever read.

10. If you had a previous life, where was it? In what year?

11. You have to eat the same thing for your evening meal every night for a year. What will you have?

12. You are going to be given a pet and you can choose what it will be. But it won't be a dog, cat, bird or horse. What pet do you want?

These are just a few ideas for questions. Here are some others:

> If you were in a circus, what job would you like to do?
> What is the most beautiful place you ever saw?
> Who is the most attractive woman you ever saw?
> Who is the most attractive man you ever saw?
> Name your favorite fairy tale.
> What is the strongest part of your body?
> What time are you at your best? (Name the hour of day, a.m. or p.m.)
> What do you like to do best at an amusement park?
> If you were a jungle animal, what animal would you like to be?
> If you were a bird, what bird would you like to be?
> If you could take all your favorite people with you, where would you choose to live?

When all the questionnaires are filled out, gather them up and pass out score sheets and pencils to the players.

Then, without revealing the identity of the players, you read Question 1 and the answers to it. Each player is to indicate on the score sheet which response belonged to Carole, which to Dan, which to Ian, etc.

Let's say that the questionnaire you have on the top of the heap belongs to Maria, who said that she would like to spend the next 20 years in prison talking with Albert Einstein. If Carole thinks that Maria said it, she'd write "Einstein" in the Maria box for Question 1. If she thinks Brian said it, she'd write Einstein in his box.

When you've read all the answers to Question 1, go on to Question 2. Don't worry about keeping the questionnaires in order.

After you've finished reading the answers to all the questions comes the fun part—finding out the right answers—which you can do in any number of ways. Working with one question at a time, you can go around the room, each person telling what he or she wrote. The players "mark" their own papers, crossing out the ones they have wrong. Or you can have each player read off the answers from his or her own sheet. Do what comes naturally to your group.

The person with the most right answers, of course, wins.

If you didn't know your friends very well before this game, you may, by the end of it.

ESSENCES

PLAYERS: 2 or more
EQUIPMENT: None
PREPARATION: None

The most fascinating of all the guessing games, Essences calls on your imagination and perception as well as logic.

Before the game begins, the players agree on what kind of subject will be used—whether it will be a famous person or fictional character, or someone that everyone in the group knows (it could be someone in the room), which is the most fun. Then one player thinks of a person and it is up to the others to identify him or her by finding out the "essence" of the person. There is no limit on number of questions.

Here is a sample game:

JIM: I am thinking of a fictional character who is male. (His subject is Ebenezer Scrooge from Dickens' *A Christmas Carol*.)

ANNE: What music is this person?

JIM: Discordant modern music.

BILL: What kind of animal is this person?

JIM: A skinny anteater.

CAROL: What color is this person?

JIM: Grey.

ANNE: What article of wearing apparel?

JIM: An old sweater. (Jim resisted the impulse to say an old dressing gown, which is what is *associated* with Scrooge, but not what his *essence* is.)

BILL: What kind of tree?

JIM: An old gnarled oak with most of its branches gone.

As you can see, no one can say whether your answers are right or wrong; they are just your impression of what the character is like. At some point in the questions, the guessers will want to summarize what they feel about the character you've described, and you can set them more on the right track if you think you've led them astray with some of your impressions. Generally, it's amazing how accurately they describe your character! They can take any number of guesses to identify it, too. And you're as happy as they are when they get it right.

Other categories you can ask about:

what recreational event	what time of day
what restaurant	what dessert
what kind of dog	what country
what piece of furniture	what book
what fruit	what kind of film
what flower	(western, horror film, war movie, etc.)
what mineral	what sport
what kind of house	what facial feature
what part of the body	what car

TWO-FACED TEST

PLAYERS: 2–20
EQUIPMENT: Paper and pencil for each player
PREPARATION: None

You can present this as a test of your friends' psychic abilities. Or as a "free association" test. But it isn't either one. It's a hilarious way to tell silly fortunes.

Ask your friends to concentrate. You will announce a category, and they are to write down the first thought that comes into their minds.

1. **Name of person in the room (or movie or rock star)**
2. **Peculiar human quality**
3. **Odd place**
4. **Embarrassing activity**
5. **Item of apparel you wear under your clothes**
6. **Your least favorite song**
7. **Length of time**
8. **Something it takes two to do**
9. **Bad habit**
10. **Destructive act**

When your friends have finished writing down their lists, read off the real questions, which are:

1. **What is the name of your secret lover?**
2. **What does he/she see in you?**
3. **Where did you meet?**
4. **What were you doing?**
5. **What were you wearing?**
6. **What was the orchestra playing?**
7. **How long has this been going on?**
8. **What do you do most of the time when you're alone?**
9. **What is likely to break it up?**
10. **What are you going to do next?**

PARTY PSYCHOANALYSIS

By the way you answer the questions in the following "tests," supposedly the psychologist will be able to tell you all about yourself. The tests are silly, and have nothing to do with real psychology, but they are fun at parties and get people laughing and talking. Ask all the questions before you tell people what they "revealed" about themselves.

WALKING IN THE WOODS

You are walking through the woods when you come to a clearing. In the clearing, there is a lake. Beside the lake, there is a cup. You are thirsty.

1. What do you do:
   a. Use the cup to take a drink from the lake?
   b. Leave the cup where it is?
   c. Examine the cup in order to decide what to do?
2. Then do you—
   a. Put the cup back where it was?
   b. Leave it where it is?
   c. Take the cup away with you?

The water in the lake looks inviting. You are warm.

3. Do you—
   a. Wash your face and hands in it?
   b. Go swimming in it?
   c. Stay out of it?

You see a bear approaching as you stand by the lake. He is walking slowly and evidently doesn't see you.

4. Do you—
   a. Run as fast as you can?
   b. Stand very still?
   c. Try to make friends with the bear?

(SEE PAGES 632–633 FOR YOUR ANALYSIS.)

IN A DREAM GARDEN

1. Describe your dream garden.
2. Where is your house in relation to the garden?
3. What is the house like?
4. What is the key to your house like?
5. What would you do if you lost your key and wanted to get into your house?
6. You are standing alone holding something. What is it?
7. Near your garden is a house that belongs to someone else. It has a wall around it. There is a gate in the wall and a lock on the gate and you have no key for this lock. You want to get in. What would you do?

(SEE PAGE 633 FOR YOUR ANALYSIS.)

ARE YOU AN EXTRAVERT OR AN INTROVERT?

An extravert, according to the psychologists, is a person who is outgoing and sociable. They say that extraverts like people (though they usually don't have many really close friends), express themselves easily, enjoy parties and other social gatherings, and adjust to new situations readily. Their personalities are more on the outside, easy to get to know and understand.

The introvert's personality, on the other hand, is more on the inside. Introverts withdraw from social situations and live more with books and ideas than with fun and frolic. They are often sensitive and easily hurt, and generally it is harder for them to talk about their feelings. They have fewer friends than the extraverts, but the few they have are often close.

Very few people are completely one way or the other. "Extravert" and "introvert" are actually ideas taken to extremes—not people. Most people fall somewhere in between, having characteristics of both types.

Which is it better to be? It doesn't matter. Either one can be creative, brilliant, kind, constructive, lovable and fun. Sometimes, though, it's more convenient to be one type than another. If you have to go to a lot of parties, you'd enjoy it more if you were an extravert. If you have to do a lot of reading, you'd be happier being an introvert.

But this kind of problem takes care of itself as you get older and you can choose the things you like to do. If you're an introvert, for example, you'd never take a job where you had to entertain people all the time and try to sell them things. If you're an extravert, you'd never try for a job that "made a hermit out of you." The question would just never come up.

Do extraverts have more fun? It depends on what you call fun. What is fun for the extravert may be a bore to the introvert. An extravert may have a splendid time making small talk all evening with a dozen people, when that could put an introvert to sleep. An introvert might have a perfectly marvelous time sitting with one close friend and listening to music, which might have an extravert pacing the floor.

So now that you see that it makes absolutely no difference which you are—you'll see that it makes no sense at all to take the following test and find out.

ARE YOU AN EXTRAVERT OR AN INTROVERT?

1. Do you always keep your promises, even when it's really difficult or unpleasant to keep them?
2. Do you get bored easily?
3. Do you often laugh out loud at funny movies?
4. Do you make up your mind about people quickly when you meet them for the first time?
5. Do you usually climb stairs two at a time?
6. Do you like to do puzzles?
7. Do you pick your friends very carefully?
8. Do you like to ride on rollercoasters?
9. Do you shout or move around when you're watching a race or an important game?
10. Have you ever bought anything expensive that you had to save up for over a long period of time?
11. Do you have a bad temper?
12. Do you often leave things to the last minute?
13. Are you a dreamer?
14. Do you (or did you) occasionally play hookey from school?

15. Do you often rush to get somewhere, even if you have plenty of time?
16. Do you talk a lot when you're with a group of friends or at a party?
17. Will you take almost any dare?
18. Do you like to dance?
19. Do you often exaggerate when you're telling your friends about something that happened to you?
20. Do you get very embarrassed if you have to make a speech?
21. Do you have to make a real effort to stay out of trouble?
22. Is it easy for you to talk about your feelings with members of your family?
23. Have you ever pretended to be sick in order to avoid a bad day at school or work?
24. Do you like to organize parties and get-togethers with your friends?
25. Do you have an easy time making friends with girls (if you're a girl) or boys (if you're a boy)?
26. Do you avoid crowds?
27. Do you often think about something so hard that you forget what's going on around you?
28. Are you shy?
29. Can you keep a secret?
30. Are you easily moved by a sad movie?
31. Do you often spend an evening just reading a book that has nothing to do with your school work?
32. Do you often get into trouble because you do things without thinking them through?
33. Do you usually eat faster than your friends, even when you're not in a hurry?
34. Do you walk faster than your friends?
35. Do you enjoy spending long periods of time alone?
36. Do you like to be doing something with your hands all the time, even when you're watching television?
37. Are you usually early for appointments?
38. Do you enjoy planning ahead?
39. Do you often think about God or why human beings were created?
40. Are you involved in many extra-curricular activities?

(SEE PAGE 633 FOR YOUR SCORE.)

Testing Your Senses

All the following games test your senses—your senses of smell, taste and touch and your ESP, as well. You can play two of them as party games, with a large group; the others are better for just you and a friend to experiment with on a rainy afternoon.

PSYCHO NOSE

PLAYERS: 2
EQUIPMENT: A blindfold
                A clamp clothespin
                An apple
                An onion
                A raw potato
                A sharp knife for cutting the vegetables and fruit
PREPARATION: None

Did you know that you taste with your nose? This is psychologically true, and you can prove it by playing this game.

The object of Psycho Nose is to distinguish, by taste alone, between apple, onion and potato. Sound easy? Blindfold one player. Then clamp his or her nose gently but firmly with the clothespin, or let him or her hold the nose closed tightly (no cheating!) so breathing is done through the mouth. Now the blindfolded player has to eat a piece of each of the foods, or any two of them, and tell which is which. The nose remains clamped (or pinched) until the test is over. After that, it's your turn.

Don't think something has gone wrong with your sense of taste if you can't tell an apple from an onion under these conditions. Taste is achieved by both the olfactory nerves, which cause the sensation of smell, and the taste buds of the tongue. The olfactory nerves function only when you breathe through your nose, and taste buds alone will not do the trick!

TEST YOUR TASTE

PLAYERS: 2
EQUIPMENT: 10 different liquids, such as water, fruit juices, milk, soup,
           tea, coffee, vinegar, root beer
           A blindfold
           Score sheet
PREPARATION: Label any of the liquids that need identifying.

This is a much simpler game than Psycho Nose. You don't have to hold your nose; only your eyes are shielded.

One of you puts on a blindfold, and the other arranges the liquids in any order.

The tester gives the taster a teaspoonful of liquid #1. The taster may sip or drink the spoonful, and then must state what it is. The tester writes down the answer, but doesn't say whether it's right or wrong. Continue as quickly as possible until the taster has tasted all the liquids. Try not to let more than a few seconds—just long enough to write down the answer—elapse between one liquid and the next. That is what makes the test tricky. Even though you can taste with all your tasting faculties, it's the fast change from one to the other that lends confusion to the game.

For the second half of the game, switch sides. The ex-taster rearranges the liquids into any order he or she prefers, and then gives the test. The one with the highest score of correct answers is the winner.

SMELL IT

PLAYERS: 3–20

EQUIPMENT: 10 to 15 objects that have a strong smell, such as soap, onion, banana, cloves, garlic, cinnamon stick, powder, orange, peanuts, peppermint, chocolate, perfume, sachet, etc.
Tissue paper
Pencil and paper for each player
Small cards with numbers on them

PREPARATION: Wrap the objects in a few layers of tissue paper so that the players cannot see the object or recognize its shape. Put pinholes through the paper to help the smell come through.

If you have a bad cold, you won't do too well at this game. But those who can use their noses will enjoy playing Smell It.

Put the wrapped objects on a table and place a number beside each one. The players each have pencil and paper on which they will write the correct object after the number. No one may touch the objects—all they can do is sniff and smell them! The player with the greatest number of correct objects wins.

FEEL IT

PLAYERS: 5 or more

EQUIPMENT: 10 or 15 small objects, such as an apple, plum, peach, carrot, grape (peeled perhaps), a glove, a fork, a shoelace, a paper clip, an eraser, a leaf, a handkerchief, piece of macaroni, a bead, a salt shaker, part of a roll of paper towels, a dog's bone, a beanbag
A cloth or bag to keep them in
Paper and pencil for each player

PREPARATION: None

You play this game as you sit around a table. Everyone needs a pencil and sheet of paper. The leader has a cloth or bag of objects, and passes each object around *under the table* so that no one can see it.

Each person feels the object and then passes it under the table to the next person. The leader takes it back from the last player without letting anyone see it.

After the players have held and felt each object, they write down what they think it is. The player with the largest number of correct answers wins.

SO YOU THINK YOU HAVE ESP . . .

PLAYERS: 2
EQUIPMENT: A book with full-page illustrations or a magazine
PREPARATION: None

Maybe you do have ESP!

Choose a quiet time and a quiet mood and put your psychic powers to a test that may—as the ads say—amaze you with its results. One of you should select a book with illustrations in it, preferably full-page illustrations, but don't say what book it is that you have chosen. You could use a magazine, too, with full-page ads.

Open the book to an illustration and ask your partner a specific question concerning it, such as, "How many people (or animals or houses) are in the picture I'm looking at?"

Now concentrate as hard as you can on the number of people in the picture while your partner concentrates on trying to read your mind. The answer may be right or wrong, but in either case, go on to the next question. Don't make a guessing game of it. If the answer is wrong, just say, "No, there are two people. I am now going to concentrate on what one of them is doing. Try to tell me what that is."

The results may truly astound you, especially if the first answer should happen to be correct. That will give you both a feeling of self-confidence which adds a tremendous impetus to your psychic powers. If you don't seem to get anywhere, change roles and let your partner choose another book and "send" a picture to you by thought transference.

MIND OVER MONEY

PLAYERS: 2
EQUIPMENT: A coin
              Score sheet
PREPARATION: None

There is a theory that the mind can influence inanimate objects and cause them to conform to one's will. This isn't the same as ESP, but there's a connection.

Take a coin. If you flip it a great many times, you should come out with an average of 50 heads and 50 tails in every 100 flips, according to the Law of Averages. The more trials you make, the closer to an exact 50–50 you will come.

However, the order in which the heads and tails will come follows no pattern, and if you are clairvoyant—or possess ESP—you should be able to predict the result of each successive flip with an accuracy which is greater than the expected 50 per cent.

Now let's go a step further and say you possess the power to influence objects. If you do, you may be able to influence the flip of the coin and cause it to turn up heads, or tails if you prefer, a disproportionate number of times. In short, you will upset the Law of Averages.

To try your powers, let one person decide to concentrate on either heads or tails. The other keeps track of the number of tosses, and the number of times the coin turns up right. You may decide for yourself, when you are the "influencer," whether you prefer to have the other person flip the coin or whether you wish to flip it yourself, and perhaps influence it more directly.

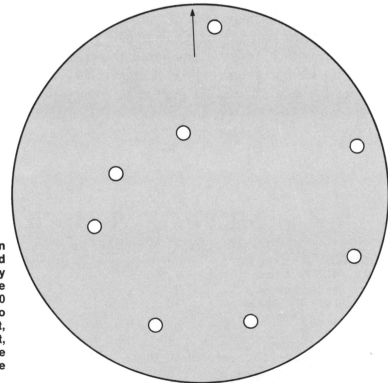

Grille Pattern

This circle is a pattern for the grille you need for the Personality Grille and the Love Grille on pages 570 and 571. Trace it onto cardboard, cut it out, and punch holes in it, as indicated in the pattern. Draw in the arrow.

Fortune-Telling Games

How many ways are there to tell fortunes? Literally, thousands, maybe tens of thousands! People have been trying to find out what life has in store for them ever since they were able to think about the future. Would they be safe? Would they have enough to eat? Would the people they loved love them back?

No one can ever be completely sure about the answers to these questions. Any answer is temporary. You may be safe in today's tornado, but will tomorrow's tiger get you? You may have a job and savings today, but be fired next week. The one you love may leave or may change.

And because people want to know the answers so intensely, they'll try anything to find out, with anything they have at hand! A daisy? Pull the petals out one by one to find if he/she loves you or loves you not. A buttercup? Put it under your chin. If your chin shines yellow, you're in love. A coin? Flip it. Heads you do/will/are, tails you don't/won't/aren't.

Then there are marvelously complex systems—like the *I Ching* from China, which is based on the fact that everything is always changing. Like the African *Ifa*, so difficult to learn that its priests train for the task from childhood, memorizing thousands of verses and cryptic and beautiful poetry. Like *geomantics*, a deep and earthy system that probably had its origins in ancient Egypt. There is astrology and the Tarot and numerology. The Africans throw cola nuts, the island people throw cowrie shells. The gypsies read your palm and your tea leaves. Others read the lumps on your head, the way you write, even your dreams. People throw names in a hat, stab a list of "magic" symbols with a pencil, count the letters in their questions or the numbers in their names. They bounce a ball or jump rope to come up with a significant initial.

Is there anything to it? Do any of the systems work?

According to occult thought, they almost *all* work. The psychics and the seers tell us that there is no such thing as coincidence. Nothing happens by accident. Everything is connected to everything else by a sort of "synchronization" in time. When you ask your question—whether you consult an oracle, go to an astrologer, pull the petals off a daisy or flip a coin—the *time* is related to your question. It has the same "character," the same feeling. And you will be guided automatically to an answer that is in the same tone or key.

That doesn't mean that you can't change your life or change the future. The answer you got is only a reflection of the time. Change yourself a bit, change the situation and ask again. It doesn't mean that dire predictions are going to come true, either. You can tell a great deal about the authenticity of a system by the kinds of answers it gives you. If it predicts disaster or death, get rid of it! Somebody's doing something wrong! No system can predict a thing like that. If it tells you what to do, instead of describing a situation and letting you decide for yourself, it probably isn't worthwhile. If it recommends action or thinking that hurts somebody else, it's something to ignore.

In any case, the seers tell us, your inner self knows the answer to every question. When you're ready to pick up the information, it provides it willingly through whatever means you allow. So any fortune-telling system may work. Even one you make up—for fun—yourself.

That's what they tell us. Whether you believe it is up to you.

Here is an assortment of easy, quick, fortune-telling games, *just* for having fun. Believe them or not!

WILL I GET MY WISH?

EQUIPMENT: A deck of cards

For a quick "yes" or "no" answer to a question, take an ordinary deck of cards and pick out every card under the rank of 7. Use only the higher value cards (including the Aces) of which there will be 32.

Then go through the following process three times:
1. **Shuffle the cards thoroughly.**
2. **Cut them with your left hand.**
3. **Deal out 13 cards, face up.**
4. **As you go through the cards, pick out the Aces and set them aside.**
5. **Return the cards (except for the Aces) to the deck.**

Your answer depends on the number of Aces you have set aside. If you have all 4 of them, the answer is "yes." (If all 4 came up in the first deal, it is a resounding "yes.") Chances are less good with fewer Aces.

FORTUNE TELLING WITH DOMINOES

This ancient method of telling fortunes is limited. You can only do it once a month, and never on Friday or Monday. When you can do it, you may only draw 3 dominoes at a sitting. Break the rules and the answers will be "wrong."

Shuffle the dominoes around the table—face down—before selecting one. Before you select a second domino, shuffle them around again.

If you select

6-6: You will marry someone rich and have many children.

6-5: Don't be discouraged. Even if the person you love rejects you, you will eventually succeed.

6-4: Early marriage and much happiness.

6-3: Love. Happiness. Riches. Honors.

6-2: Happy marriage. Luck in business. Bad luck for thieves.

6-1: Two marriages. The second one will be happier.

6-Blank: Loss of a friend.

5-5: Luck. Success, but not necessarily money.

5-4: Not good for money matters. You will marry someone poor or someone who has expensive tastes.

5-3: Comfortable marriage. You will never be poor.

5-2: Misfortune in love. If you marry the one you love, it may not work out in the long run. For a female: a good life, if you stay single.

5-1: You will receive an invitation and you will enjoy yourself very much. Not good for money matters.

5-Blank: For a female: sorrow through the affections. For a male: difficult financial conditions.

4-4: An invitation (to a party?) at which you will have a wonderful time.

4-3: You will marry young and live happily.

4-2: A big change in your life. If you quarrelled with a friend, you will make up and be better friends than before.

4-1: Happy marriage.

4-Blank: Bad for love affairs. This foretells quarrels and separations. Don't tell your secret; it won't be kept.

3-3: Riches.

3-2: Good for love and travel.

3-1: Secret love affairs.

3-Blank: Invitation (to a party?) at which you will meet someone new. If you marry, difficult mate.

2-2: Success in love. Happiness in marriage. Success, but not necessarily money.

2-1: For a female: you will marry young and live a life of luxury. For a male: lucky in love.

2-Blank: Bad luck. For females: good luck if you live alone. Safe voyage. Possible accident, but protection against physical injury.

1-1: Affection and happiness in love and marriage.

1-Blank: Loss of money. Sorrow in love.

Blank-Blank: Sorrow in love. Disappointment.

HOW TO TELL FORTUNES WITH DICE

EQUIPMENT: 3 dice
    A dice cup or box
    A board
    A piece of chalk
PREPARATION: Draw a chalk circle on the board

This method of telling fortunes is less restricted than the domino method on page 555, but it also has its limitations. You may not use it on days which are unlucky for dice—Mondays and Wednesdays.

Put the dice in the dice cup and shake it with your left hand. Then throw the dice into the chalk circle. You read the message by counting the number of spots on the top of the three dice and checking the total in the following list.

If you get the same number twice, you will get news from someone far away.

If you throw the dice out of the chalk circle, don't bother to count the totals. It means you will have a quarrel.

If the dice fall on the floor, it will be a violent quarrel.

If one die lands on top of the other, the answer is negative.

If you throw

- 3: **Success in love. Many lovers.**
- 4: **Many lovers, but you will not be perfectly pleased with any of them.**
- 5: **Obstacles or quarrels in love. If you're going on a trip, some disagreeable incident will take place, but it won't be serious.**
- 6: **Many lovers, exciting life.**
- 7: **Luck in money matters.**
- 8: **Stinginess. Whoever throws it will never be poor, but may live poorly through miserliness.**
- 9: **Good luck in everything—except games of chance.**
- 10: **Good luck. If a young girl throws it, she will not marry soon. She will have good luck in other matters. If a married woman throws it, she may get a legacy. If a man throws it, good luck in love.**
- 11: **Extravagance. Waste of money.**
- 12: **An event of some kind, happy or unhappy. Has nothing to do with matters of love.**
- 13: **Be suspicious. People around you may not be trustworthy.**
- 14: **If a female throws it: unhappy marriage. Good life if she stays single. For a man: dishonesty, lack of principles.**
- 15: **Bad luck in speculation. Good luck in marriage.**
- 16: **Bad luck in business. Good luck in marriage.**
- 17: **You won't find the property you lost. Good luck in your work. Disappointment, otherwise.**
- 18: **Riches, honors, a happy life. Good luck in love and in your work. Bad luck for thieves.**

APPLE TWIST

For this "Who Loves Me?" game, you need an apple with a stem.

Twist the stem once for each letter of the alphabet. Where the stem falls off is the initial of your true love.

FOUR KINGS/FOUR QUEENS

EQUIPMENT: An ordinary deck of playing cards

Here is another "he-loves-me-he-loves-me-not" game. Or maybe you could call it a "they-love-me-they-love-me-not" game, for people with four strings to their beaux.

Set up four playing cards—all Kings, if you want to find out about men, all Queens, if you want to know about women—in a row horizontally.

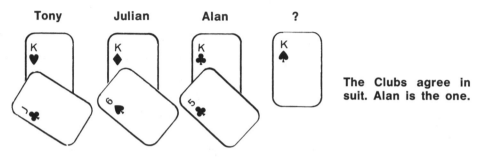

The Clubs agree in suit. Alan is the one.

Assign them names, so that each King or Queen represents a different person. The King of Hearts, for example, might be Tony; the King of Diamonds, Julian; the King of Clubs, Alan; and the King of Spades—someone you don't know yet—or a specific name, if you want.

Then the questions start. The first question might be, "Which one is in love with me?" You start dealing out the deck, laying the cards face up, starting on the King of Hearts, placing each card halfway up on each King. The first card which agrees in suit with the King it is placed upon, indicates the answer to your question.

If, for instance, you deal a Jack of Clubs onto the King of Hearts, you go on to the next card. A 6 of Spades on the King of Diamonds? On to the next card. A 5 of Clubs on the King of Clubs—there is your answer. Alan is in love with you.

If you don't have a match-up after dealing four cards out, go on to deal another card on the King of Hearts, another on the King of Diamonds, and another, or however many it takes.

Continue to ask questions, all of them beginning with "Which one . . ." and each question is answered as soon as the suits agree.

MY FORTUNE

PLAYERS: 2 or more
EQUIPMENT: Paper and pencil
PREPARATION: See below

You make up this game yourself to suit the players. It's great slumber party fare, but you can also design it for parties by using different questions and answers.

Write down the questions you and your group would be most interested in, or would laugh at the most. You could have:

1. What will I be when I grow up?
2. Who will I work with?
3. What will they call me?
4. Where will I live?
5. What is the most exciting thing I'll ever do?
6. Who will I marry?
7. How old will I be?
8. Where will we go for our honeymoon?
9. What will we do for fun?
10. What will be my greatest achievement?

The list, of course, is endless. Take a large sheet of paper, divide it into boxes about 3 inches (7.5 cm) square and write one question at the top of each box. (Even better is a notebook in which you use a new page instead of a box for each question.) Below each question, write a list of answers, appropriate, humorous and just plain crazy—and number them. For example, some answers to question 10 might be:

1. Staying awake.
2. Remembering your address.
3. Getting the bubble gum off your face.
4. Learning to belly dance.

Once you've got at least six answers for every question, you'll be equipped to tell anyone's (well, almost anyone's) fortune. Simply ask the first question and say, "Choose a number from 1 to 6." When the player says a number, read the corresponding answer.

If you have more than six answers for a question, say, "Take a number from 1 to 9," on that particular item.

BIRTHDAY PROPHESIES

EQUIPMENT: A ruler

Here is a birthday message for you, though it might not be your birthday:

Q C N M D W E S U R X H J

To read it, use the table on page 561. This contains 31 lines to allow for every day in a month. Take the date in the month on which you were born (the 6th, for instance) and lay a ruler just below that line on the table. Find each letter of the message in the alphabet across the top, and read down the column to the letter just above the ruler.

Using the 6th as your birth date, you would find Q in the top row above the line and trace down to line 6, to find B as the first true letter. Doing the same thing with C, the second code letter, you would find U, etc.

The message may not be clear and may need some thought. If it does not seem to apply to you right now, it may apply at any time up until a year after your next birthday. If you are curious, you can find out the code message for any of your friends by tracing out their birth dates.

If you are a skeptic, you may wonder how the same message could apply to all people born on the same day of the month. Here is the secret: Every person has a different personality, and interprets the message in the light of individual knowledge and ambitions. Thus, the same message has a different meaning for different people.

How can the same message apply to every birthday you have? The prophesy only works once for each person.

BIRTHDAY ANAGRAMS

When you finish finding your prophesy, there's another message waiting for you in the table on the next page. After you eliminate the letters in your prophesy, an anagram is left with an answer to your question. What question? The one that's burning inside you. If you're in doubt, the Mystic Spirit knows.

If you have trouble figuring out the message, you'll find the anagram decoded on page 633.

BIRTHDAY PROPHESIES
AND ANAGRAMS

	A	B	C	D	E	F	G	H	I	J	K	L	M	N	O	P	Q	R	S	T	U	V	W	X	Y	Z
1	M	A	R	E	H	X	E	T	O	E	E	M	T	I	E	V	W	N	A	T	T	I	T	O	N	I
2	M	T	H	I	E	I	T	H	O	T	T	S	T	E	N	I	T	I	S	T	R	A	M	G	H	E
3	D	O	I	T	P	E	A	R	O	E	K	B	E	M	Y	N	T	P	R	E	E	D	O	A	T	N
4	E	F	E	Y	I	F	D	S	O	S	G	O	A	P	R	T	R	N	N	N	D	N	K	E	T	U
5	G	R	E	W	Y	S	T	R	I	D	E	T	T	S	I	E	B	H	I	T	S	B	A	A	V	Y
6	I	S	O	F	R	N	I	T	O	Y	O	S	K	O	M	P	L	A	B	E	E	L	O	U	T	B
7	E	T	I	D	Y	A	L	A	N	D	E	H	E	N	O	S	F	H	S	P	A	C	A	E	M	D
8	A	D	A	P	N	E	H	I	N	M	N	A	O	Y	O	N	W	T	B	L	U	S	E	D	O	D
9	D	S	E	I	A	M	D	T	R	Q	A	O	P	L	E	A	H	E	S	O	K	G	F	D	R	E
10	V	K	R	N	T	E	M	A	P	Y	C	R	A	Y	A	I	T	R	H	Q	E	Y	O	W	U	L
11	T	S	E	R	O	C	E	R	H	S	E	P	A	W	T	E	B	I	F	E	L	R	E	A	K	E
12	T	W	E	R	E	B	R	F	I	E	D	P	E	V	U	H	N	L	A	E	R	O	F	I	L	Y
13	U	S	A	H	A	C	G	U	S	M	O	N	E	K	P	O	T	C	R	I	T	R	E	H	E	M
14	S	U	I	T	P	O	V	A	I	Y	H	R	H	G	A	Y	L	E	T	T	H	E	U	W	I	P
15	S	E	G	R	S	D	W	T	R	S	A	P	O	N	E	H	I	G	L	O	I	T	E	H	D	R
16	D	O	O	R	S	A	N	S	T	S	D	E	O	M	K	A	N	N	A	E	D	R	E	E	T	S
17	H	O	O	D	S	W	K	O	N	K	N	I	T	N	I	T	D	I	P	U	A	T	E	R	O	T
18	W	O	O	B	U	K	E	R	U	E	N	A	T	N	O	N	D	W	N	W	A	Y	E	A	R	S
19	S	D	O	O	B	H	O	P	O	Y	E	L	E	M	T	A	C	A	E	N	H	R	N	P	E	T
20	U	Y	U	Y	U	I	O	E	O	K	C	N	N	R	A	D	T	H	R	O	C	T	O	E	W	N
21	A	Y	A	H	O	O	O	C	U	E	S	E	G	U	N	K	L	E	R	C	P	I	F	A	R	T
22	E	S	P	A	T	A	C	O	R	N	B	U	Y	A	W	K	O	T	E	F	N	E	T	I	O	D
23	N	O	M	E	N	O	S	L	E	E	D	B	L	I	K	K	S	M	D	I	S	T	A	I	O	K
24	O	M	O	T	B	I	D	E	Y	T	R	D	E	M	O	R	C	Q	A	U	N	S	O	U	W	N
25	C	L	I	E	T	U	O	I	N	C	L	G	T	S	H	A	L	U	O	E	M	I	N	S	Y	W
26	R	H	U	O	Y	S	P	I	A	P	S	E	T	T	U	I	B	R	O	E	U	D	N	L	A	R
27	T	E	X	A	N	S	U	E	R	M	F	U	L	P	U	N	E	T	T	L	O	U	I	H	A	U
28	I	P	I	N	W	B	G	N	O	D	E	N	D	N	N	A	F	I	F	E	R	M	E	E	T	S
29	C	E	L	A	R	H	T	V	P	E	U	O	F	L	A	T	A	L	I	R	N	W	I	O	S	Y
30	E	L	E	T	E	O	U	T	O	H	C	O	L	L	Y	E	T	R	M	R	T	M	H	U	L	V
31	O	N	I	F	R	O	T	E	A	R	O	T	G	N	I	T	S	P	S	T	U	L	O	P	E	S

LOVE FRIENDSHIP MARRIAGE HATE

To test your compatibility with another person, match up your names like this:

CLARISSA BEDLINGTON
ROBERT HUGH MERIVALE

Then strike out the letters that are the same in each name, like this:

C̷L̷A̷R̷I̷S̷S̷A̷ ̷B̷E̷D̷L̷I̷N̷G̷T̷O̷N
R̷O̷B̷E̷R̷T̷ HU̷G̷H MER̷I̷V̷A̷L̷E

Now start reading off "Love Friendship Marriage Hate," one relationship for each letter which is left, as follows:

"Love (C), Friendship (A), Marriage (I), Hate (S). Love (S), Friendship (D), Marriage (L), Hate (N). Love (N)." Therefore, Clarissa loves Robert.

Let's see how he feels about her:

"Love (R), Friendship (H), Marriage (U), Hate (H). Love (M), Friendship (E), Marriage (R), Hate (V). Love (E)."

Isn't that convenient?

DAISY, DAISY

EQUIPMENT: A daisy

When you're plucking the petals off a daisy, try it with this ancient rhyme. Just start again (if you need to) when you finish plucking off the 12th petal.

"One I love
Two I love
Three I love I say.
Four I love with all my heart
And five I cast away.
Six he loves
Seven she loves
Eight they both love.
Nine he comes
Ten he tarries
Eleven he courts
And twelve he marries."

MATCH OR MISMATCH?

EQUIPMENT: A ruler (optional)

To break the ice at a party, use the table on page 564 and on page 565 and see if a couple is matched or mismatched.

Let's say that the boy was born April (the fourth month) 1, 1955, and the girl was born September (the ninth month) 27, 1957. You find their key numbers by adding across the dates until only 1 digit is left:

$$\text{BOY: } 4 + 1 + 1 + 9 + 5 + 5 = 25 = 2 + 5 = \qquad 7$$
$$\text{GIRL: } 9 + 2 + 7 + 1 + 9 + 5 + 7 = 40 = 4 + 0 = 4$$
$$7 + 4 = 11 = 1 + 1 = 2$$

The total of their key numbers is 2, so look at No. 2 section on the Boy-Girl table. Because the boy's key number (7) is odd, he selects the odd message under "boy." The girl's number (4) is even, so she selects the even message under "girl." Copy one message right below the other:

O X Y G Q K Y U H M G D S HS F N
W U T S X Q K N G G S S E L Y T L

Now use Rogues' Gallery for combining every pair of letters. A ruler is helpful for following the chart. Find O in the column at the side and W in the line across the top (or vice versa). Follow the lines across and down until they intersect (at T), the first letter. X and U intersect at H; Y and T intersect at I, and so on:

T H I S I S F U N . . .

The message may turn out to be enthusiastic, warm, cool—or a jumble (zero, nothing).

If you don't like your message, try it again—using phone numbers instead of birth dates!

BOY-GIRL TABLE

	Boy					Girl			
1. Odd	HUJJK	OEWUA	CUZBZ	RP	1. Odd	DVCQT	QMOVF	LQWUE	YO
Even	XVXOE	OEBYG	KEOXR	RC	Even	VZOXM	NTINT	CCOQT	AH
2. Odd	OXYGQ	KYUHM	GDSHS	FN	2. Odd	WVNOK	HOFVQ	EBMGJ	SD
Even	MEFWQ	PBXHA	NZLVH	WJ	Even	WUTSX	QKNGG	SSELY	TL
3. Odd	FFTGV	VPXHY	SUPTZ	IT	3. Odd	CMVRH	CGYTI	FVDEM	LC
Even	RVGEB	WCXRD	ABTQN	MZ	Even	ERMSB	VKSND	CSFHV	GM
4. Odd	YAVRR	VXQDI	AQJOK	NK	4. Odd	ARHKI	ZPOLB	EMAPH	IW
Even	DFEKO	SGPPI	CMAHV	PS	Even	DGURW	HFEVR	WELXB	FA
5. Odd	XYGVD	WHPSJ	GDOXW	AB	5. Odd	UZWOJ	HTSPQ	EGETX	PI
Even	WJANL	ZMJSE	LVXGQ	QK	Even	SHXDJ	YQQYP	MMAAB	EK
6. Odd	WYZNA	UMCGM	IAEMK	DL	6. Odd	WHPYG	NBIFX	JHZFJ	JQ
Even	AJOWJ	PMHGF	BCMKI	IN	Even	YOGOG	SLAMT	QKZRL	JY
7. Odd	FTSLV	RRZNA	TEXKM	QR	7. Odd	BWNLN	AIHLQ	DVYRF	GG
Even	FYTNM	GNVAG	FEAZU	SF	Even	LYXVK	AYHSA	RNBSE	GY
8. Odd	NAOQH	JSYLE	IFXNR	KY	8. Odd	DWFEQ	JYPSJ	CPNLN	CP
Even	YCSPZ	HIHPI	XSLMY	IU	Even	WKZXG	YZOCL	GKULH	RI
9. Odd	VZLFU	NUQTD	TKLUG	CR	9. Odd	NWCTI	FDHIY	BOTPX	SN
Even	GCMML	MNVZY	KGTKV	HL	Even	JKZCP	LNDIN	BOKOO	CN

This table provides the key to the Match or Mismatch game on page 563.

The Rogues' Gallery is a device for obtaining a message. You'll find the instructions for using it on page 563.

ROGUES' GALLERY

	A	B	C	D	E	F	G	H	I	J	K	L	M	N	O	P	Q	R	S	T	U	V	W	X	Y	Z
A	Q	D	S	B	U	N	O	R	J	I	P	M	L	F	G	K	A	H	C	X	E	Z	Y	T	W	V
B	D	M	G	A	K	H	C	F	O	X	E	Z	B	P	I	N	Y	W	V	U	T	S	R	J	Q	L
C	S	G	U	F	W	D	B	T	L	N	O	I	R	J	K	Q	P	M	A	H	C	X	E	V	Z	Y
D	B	A	F	H	J	C	X	D	I	E	Z	Y	N	M	P	O	W	V	U	T	S	R	Q	G	L	K
E	U	K	W	J	Z	G	F	V	R	D	B	N	T	L	Q	S	O	I	P	M	A	H	C	Y	X	E
F	N	H	D	C	G	X	E	B	P	Z	Y	W	O	A	M	I	V	U	T	S	R	Q	L	F	K	J
G	O	C	B	X	F	E	Z	N	M	Y	W	V	I	H	A	P	U	T	S	R	Q	L	K	D	J	G
H	R	F	T	D	V	B	N	S	K	O	I	P	Q	G	J	L	M	A	H	C	X	E	Z	U	Y	W
I	J	O	L	I	R	P	M	K	D	A	H	C	G	N	B	F	X	E	Z	Y	W	V	U	Q	T	S
J	I	X	N	E	D	Z	Y	O	A	W	V	U	P	C	H	M	T	S	R	Q	L	K	J	B	G	F
K	P	E	O	Z	B	Y	W!	H	V	U	T	M	X	C	A	S	R	Q	L	K	J	G	N	F	D	
L	M	Z	I	Y	N	W	V	P	C	U	T	S	A	E	X	H	R	Q	L	K	J	G	F	O	D	B
M	L	B	R	N	T	O	I	Q	G	P	M	A	K	D	F	J	H	C	X	E	Z	Y	W	S	V	U
N	F	P	J	M	L	A	H	G	N	C	X	E	D	I	O	B	Z	Y	W	V	U	T	S	K	R	Q
O	G	I	K	P	Q	M	A	J	B	H	C	X	F	O	N	D	E	Z	Y	W	V	U	T	L	S	R
P	K	N	Q	O	S	I	P	L	F	M	A	H	J	B	D	G	C	X	E	Z	Y	W	V	R	U	T
Q	A	Y	P	W	O	V	U	M	X	T	S	R	H	Z	E	C	Q	L	K	J	G	F	D	I	B	N
R	H	W	M	V	I	U	T	A	E	S	R	Q	C	Y	Z	X	L	K	J	G	F	D	B	P	N	O
S	C	V	A	U	P	T	S	H	Z	R	Q	L	X	W	Y	E	K	J	G	F	D	B	N	M	O	I
T	X	U	H	T	M	S	R	C	Y	Q	L	K	E	V	W	Z	J	G	F	D	B	N	O	A	I	P
U	E	T	C	S	A	R	Q	X	W	L	K	J	Z	U	V	Y	G	F	D	B	N	O	I	H	P	M
V	Z	S	X	R	H	Q	L	E	V	K	J	G	Y	T	U	W	F	D	B	N	O	I	P	C	M	A
W	Y	R	E	Q	C	L	K	Z	U	J	G	F	W	S	T	V	D	B	N	O	I	P	M	X	A	H
X	T	J	V	G	Y	F	D	U	Q	B	N	O	S	K	L	R	I	P	M	A	H	C	X	W	E	Z
Y	W	Q	Z	L	X	K	J	Y	T	G	F	D	V	R	S	U	B	N	O	I	P	M	A	E	H	C
Z	V	L	Y	K	E	J	G	W	S	F	D	B	U	Q	R	T	N	O	I	P	M	A	H	Z	C	X

FAME-FORTUNE-FUTURE BOARD

PLAYERS: 1 or more
EQUIPMENT: A marker for each player
A pair of dice
Pencil and paper
A large sheet of paper
Ruler
PREPARATION: If you're playing this alone, you don't need to use anything but the chart on the next page. But if you're playing with it as a party game, enlarge the chart on the next page, transferring it to a larger sheet of paper. Make it large enough so that there is room for each person's marker to rest on a letter.

You use the Fame-Fortune-Future Board to spell out messages from the Mystic Spirit. Place your marker on the middle E. Then throw the dice. If the numbers that appear are 5 and 2, for example, move 7 letters in any direction—up or down, right or left (not diagonal). Or you may move 5 letters in one direction or 2 in another, including backwards. Or 2 spaces in one direction and 5 in another. Only the final letter you land on counts.

You must be very quiet and seek the guidance of the Mystic Spirit to tell you in what direction to take your moves. Write down each letter you finally land on for that turn. At first you will probably accumulate a meaningless string of letters, but sooner or later a word or phrase will be spelled out. Regard messages of 3 letters as unimportant, 4-letter messages as doubtful; but messages of 5 or more letters are probably significant. Think hard about the meaning of the message.

Take turns making your moves, if you're playing this as a party game. When your turn comes around again, move from the point where you left off—*unless the minute hand on the clock has passed 12*. In this case, you must start from the middle again. No player's turn may run past the 12 on the clock, or the Mystic Spirit may be offended. If you lose your place and are not sure where you belong, rely on the Mystic Spirit to guide you correctly.

If you don't believe in Mystic Spirits, have fun anyway.

FAME-FORTUNE-FUTURE BOARD

```
E S F L Y A N E R W O T K H I D E B G R A O N H T
T N A R C S E H G A E M T I O D B E S F L Y A N E
U H C L I T M O W N A S E R I N Z P T F E D O E S
L E L E H V S T A N C O D Y E R U I F O Q H L R A
O S G B E S F L Y A N E R W O T K H I D E A U W P
D X N D N R E I D X S E H C L I T M O W B U T O T
E D A O J E R W O T K H I D E B G R A N G T N T I
F I M I T N F O Q H A U T J N R E I O A R J A K W
T E O T U A I T N A R C S E H G A D N S A N R H E
P R R M A Y U U G E X L M O D A E X H E O R C I R
Z N E E H L R L A I D H E T U K M S T R N E S D O
N J W A Q F E O E Z I G F Y A M T E E I H I E E M
I T I G O S Y D O B A W E C P N I H S N T D H B A
R U T H F E D E R Y S I L Q B U O C A Z E X G G N
E A P E I B O F A F N Q R W O I D L P P S S A R G
S H A S U D C T P V C J U K V S B I T T A E E A L
A Q S C R O N P I O X U T E H O J T I F P H M O E
N O E R E I A Z N I R E S A N W O M W E T C T N H
W F T A Y T T S V H E L G N A M O R E D I L I H V
O I H N D M E A G H E S C R A N T U L O W I O T S
M U N T O C N A T S V H E L G N A M O R E T D E T
T R O U L O D E F T P Z N I R E S A N W O M B S A
I E A R G B E D I H K T O W R E N A Y L F S E A N
L Y D O C N A T S V H E L G N A M O R E W I T P C
C H E S X D I E R N J T U A H Q O F I U R E Y D O
```

READING TEA LEAVES

EQUIPMENT: A cup of tea which has been brewed from real tea (not a tea bag)
PREPARATION: None

You have to use your imagination when you read tea leaves! If you see a pattern that reminds you of a mask, for example, you might announce that the person is going to get a part in a play, or be invited to a costume party (especially if you know that one is coming up). You could get very psychological and say the person is hiding his or her real self. If you see a door, you could say there will be a change—old doors closing and new ones opening up. If the specks remind you of a kangaroo, you might advise looking before leaping—or moving rapidly (in leaps and bounds) to a goal. Don't be afraid to make up vague nonsense. It may sound silly to you, but your friends will take it very seriously. Because of that, you need to be careful not to go around scaring people. Keep your predictions happy ones.

Here are a few symbols which you can keep in mind for the times when you really don't see much in the cup:

Anchor: Good results from your plan.

Clover Leaf: Good luck. If it is at the top of the cup as you look at it, it is coming soon. If it is at the bottom, there will be a delay.

Clouds: If they are thick, delay. If they are light, good results.

Cross: If it is at the top of the cup, without clouds around it, good luck is coming soon. If at the bottom, troubles over which you will triumph.

Dog: At the top, faithful friends. If surrounded with clouds and dashes, a false friend. At the bottom: be careful not to make anyone jealous or you'll be sorry.

Flower: If at the top or in the middle of the cup, you have or will have a good marriage. If it is at the bottom, anger.

Letter: In the clear, you'll have good news soon. With dots around it, money is coming. Hemmed in by clouds, bad news.

Moon: If it is clear, high honors; if it is clouded over, disappointment which will pass. If at the bottom of the cup, good fortune.

Mountains: One mountain signifies powerful friends. More than one—powerful enemies. If they are clear, friends who have authority.

Snake: At the top or in the middle: if you act honorably, your enemies will not triumph over you. If surrounded by clouds, watch your temper and your actions carefully to avoid trouble.

Star: Happiness. With dots around it: good fortune.

Sun: Luck and happiness. Surrounded by dots, a great change in your life.

Tree: Good health. A group of trees wide apart: you will get your wish. With dashes around them: your good luck has already begun. With dots: riches.

PERSONALITY GRILLE

EQUIPMENT: Cardboard
               Scissors
               Pencil
               Hole punch (optional)

PREPARATION: Trace the grille on page 552 onto your cardboard.
Cut it out and punch the holes that are shown in the
diagram into it. Draw in the arrow.

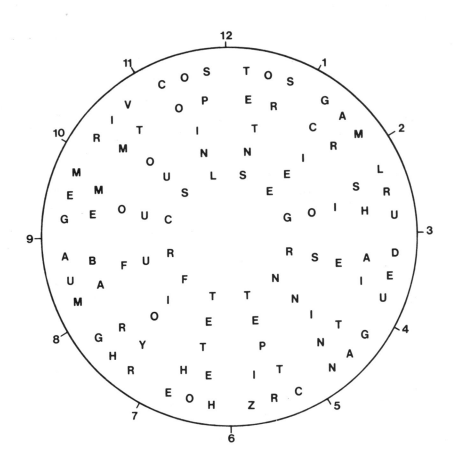

The Personality Grille will give you a one-word message which describes the essence of your character.

Find out your exact hour of birth. Disregard the minutes. Even if you were born at 3:59, your hour is still 3. Lay the grille that you just made on the circle of letters shown here, with the arrow pointing to your hour. Read the message clockwise around the circle.

LOVE GRILLE

EQUIPMENT: Same as for Personality Grille (page 570)
PREPARATION: Same as for Personality Grille

If you've already made the grille that you need for the Personality Grille, you can use it to get an 8-letter message in this game. The 8-letter message will tell you about how your relationship will work out with any person you want to name.

Use a deck of cards for this one. First remove all the 2's from the deck. Then shuffle the cards and pick one of them. Place the grille with the arrow pointing to the number or name that gives the card's rank. Read the message clockwise around the circle.

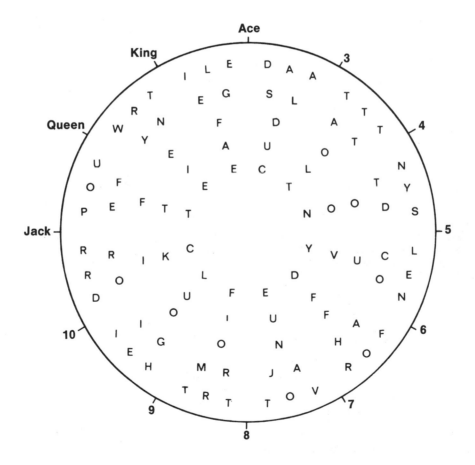

Biorhythm

Can you tell when you're going to be at your best—next week or next month? The Biorhythm experts say that you probably can, if you are among the 85 per cent of the population for whom Biorhythm seems to work.

Biorhythm is based on the idea that all human beings operate on three basic cycles. All three of them start the moment that you are born.

The first is a "physical" cycle. It lasts 23 days, and when you chart it, it looks like this:

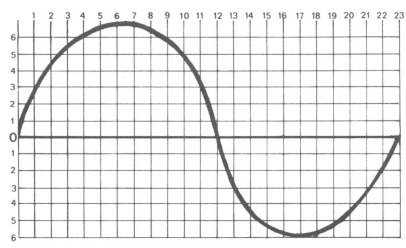

Physical Cycle—23 days

Starting at the base-line, the physical cycle goes up for about 6 days. Then it peaks and starts down. It crosses the base-line on about the 11th or 12th day and goes into the low phase. It continues downward for about 6 days, starts up on about the 18th day and crosses the base-line on the 23rd day. Then the whole cycle starts again.

When the cycle is above the base-line, say the experts, you have lots of energy. You're stronger, your coordination is better, and you're faster than at other times in the cycle.

When the cycle is below the base-line, you're apt to tire more easily. Your reflexes won't work as quickly, and you won't feel quite up to par.

But the really "critical" days take place when the line crosses the base-line. Then, supposedly, you are accident-prone, your judgment may be poor, and you may be more susceptible to colds or viruses or whatever is going around.

That doesn't mean that you are going to have an accident or going to get sick on a critical day. Not at all! If you got wrecked or sick every time you had a critical day, you wouldn't be around very long! But the experts say that you are more *likely* to have a problem on these days. If you know that, and you're a bit more careful than usual, they say you can probably avoid the "human errors" that don't need to happen at all.

The emotional cycle is based on a 28-day time-span. It looks like this:

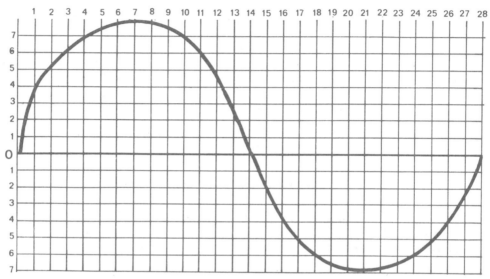

Emotional Cycle—28 days

The cycle starts up for the first 7 days and crosses the base-line at the 2-week mark. It moves down for another week and then starts up again, crossing the base-line on the 28th day. This means that every 2 weeks, you have a "critical" emotional day, the same day of the week that you were born. For example, if you were born on a Wednesday at noon, every other Wednesday will be a critical day. If you were born close to midnight, Thursday might be the critical day.

When your emotional cycle is up, you're likely to be more stable, more creative, more perceptive and better able to deal with yourself and other people than at other times in the cycle.

When it is low, you tend to be negative or moody and depressed.

On a critical day in the emotional cycle, you're more likely to lose your temper and become emotionally upset about minor matters than on other days of the cycle. Of course, if you flunked a test or got fired, or your house exploded, you'd feel terrible no matter what day it happens, but on a critical day, you'd feel worse.

The intellectual cycle is based on a 33-day time-span:

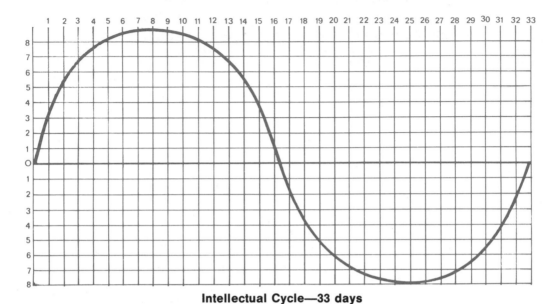

Intellectual Cycle—33 days

The cycle goes up for the first 8 or 9 days. Then it starts down, crossing the base-line on about the 17th day. It stays below the base-line for another 16 days and crosses again on day # 33.

When your intellectual cycle is up, you're likely to be more alert, to learn more easily and express what you know more clearly.

When it is low, you won't think so fast. You're apt to shut out new information and overlook important facts.

On an intellectual critical day, experts say, you are apt to make errors in judgment, if you're not careful. *It is very important to remember that biorhythm doesn't tell you what's going to happen or what you'll do.* It doesn't forecast anything, except your own inclination. You don't *know* any less when the intellectual cycle is low or critical than you do when it's high. If you don't study much for a test, and you take it when your intellectual cycle is up, you'll probably get a better mark than you would if you took it when the cycle was low. But if you knew that your cycle was low, and studied particularly hard for that test, and checked over your work more carefully than usual, you'd do just as well or better. If you really know your stuff, your worst may not be very far away from your best.

Some sports figures baffle the biorhythm experts, who try to predict whether the athletes will win or lose, based on their biorhythm cycles. A few of these athletes are just so good that even in a low period, they far out-distance the competition. There is nothing magical about the biorhythm cycles. They don't change you. You are always yourself— for better or worse. If you know that your cycles are critical or down, you can try a little harder, and be a lot more careful.

Cycles are seldom all down or all up. Usually, it's a mixed bag, and when one cycle is up, that can compensate for the low cycles.

HOW TO FIGURE OUT YOUR BIORHYTHM

First you have to figure out how many days you have been alive. That is easy, especially with a pocket calculator. You do it in 3 steps:

1. Multiply your age by 365.
Example: If you are 15, multiply $15 \times 365 = 5475$.

2. Count the number of leap years since you were born. The table on the next page lists all the leap years since 1896. Find the first one after your day of birth and count up to the present.

Add this figure to the total you arrived at in Step 1.
Example: For a person of 15, there would be 3 or 4 leap years. If you were born March 1, of a leap year, don't count the leap year you were born in. You hadn't been born when the "leap year day" took place.   3

3. Now add the number of days that have elapsed since your last birthday. The easiest way to do this is to count off months. Let's say that your birthday was April 15 and it is now November 23. Count as follows:

April 15 to May 15:	30
May 15 to June 15:	31
June 15 to July 15:	30
July 15 to August 15:	31
August 15 to September 15:	31
September 15 to October 15:	30
October 15 to 31:	16 days
October 31 to November 3:	3 days

for a total of   202 days.
Add this total to the other two figures: 202

Add the three figures together: 5680 days since you were born.

Leap Years (February 29)			
1896	1920	1944	1968
1900	1924	1948	1972
1904	1928	1952	1976
1908	1932	1956	1980
1912	1936	1960	1984
1916	1940	1964	1988

The number that you have is the total number of days since you were born. Write it down on a separate sheet of paper. It is the *key number* for your biorhythm today. If you want to figure out a day in the future or in the past, you work the same way, adding the years, leap year days and months until you get to the date you want.

FINDING YOUR PHYSICAL CYCLE

1. Divide the key number by 23.
Example: If the key number is 5680, divided by 23, the total would be 246.95652. The numbers before the decimal point represent the number of complete physical cycles you have lived through from the time you were born. The numbers after the decimal point tell you what percentage of your current physical cycle you're into.

2. Write down the numbers which appear after the decimal point (.95652) and clear your calculator.

3. Multiply the numbers you just wrote down by 23. *Don't forget to include the decimal point.*
Example: .95652 × 23 equals 21.99996

4. Look at the numbers which appear to the left of the decimal point this time, and the first one to the right of it. This is the point at which you are in your physical cycle.
Example: In the example, you are at Day # 21.9, or the 22nd day of your physical cycle.

5. Look at the physical cycle graph on page 572. Day #22 is the last day of the cycle. Your biorhythm curve is just below the base-line. Tomorrow will be a critical day.

FINDING YOUR EMOTIONAL CYCLE

1. Divide the key number by 28.
Example: Using the key number 5680, divided by 28, the total is 202.85714.

2. Write down the numbers which appear after the decimal point (.85714) and clear your calculator.

3. Multiply the number you just wrote down by 28.
Example: .85714 × 28 equals 23.99992. You are at Day #23.9 of the emotional cycle, or the 24th day. Look at the chart for the emotional cycle page 573. Day 24 is below the line, but on the way up.

FINDING YOUR INTELLECTUAL CYCLE

1. Divide the key number by 33.
Example: Using the key number 5680, divided by 33, the total is 172.12121.

2. Write down the numbers which appear after the decimal point (.12121) and clear your calculator.

3. Multiply the number you just wrote down by 33.
Example: .12121 × 33 equals 3.99993. This would be Day #4 of your intellectual cycle. Look at the intellectual chart on page 574 to see where this is in the cycle.

After a while, you won't have to refer to the charts on the previous pages to see where you are in your cycle. As long as you remember how long each cycle is, it is easy to figure out where in the cycle it comes.

TESTING BIORHYTHM

Are you one of the 85 per cent for whom Biorhythm works? Test it yourself. Start keeping a record of how you seem to be operating every day. Did you keep hitting your head all day Monday? Did you have a hard time concentrating on Wednesday? Did someone really get on your nerves for no reason on Saturday? Jot down notes about how you feel and the things you do and keep the record for a few weeks—without checking your Biorhythm chart at all. After that time, look back at the biorhythm cycles for those days and see if you find any correlation.

Don't write out the cycles first. That way you might psych yourself into acting the way the chart suggested, and it wouldn't be a valid test.

Another way to test your own Biorhythm is to spot check it.

Figure out:

    1. Where your cycles were on days when you had silly accidents that were your own fault (especially the Physical Cycle).

    2. Or look up the chart to see how it looked when you went to that party where you had such a great—or terrible—time (especially the Emotional Cycle).

    3. Or check back to the last exams you took and see what your chart shows for that day, and whether it seems to have any relationship to your grades (especially the Intellectual Cycle).

If it doesn't seem right, check to see if your cycles are working in reverse. For some people, Biorhythm works backwards.

A great deal of research into Biorhythm has been done in recent years and is being done now. Many corporations are testing it all over the world. Several companies in Europe and Japan claim that when they warn their employees about critical days, they cut the accident rate.

One trucking company won't let employees drive on double critical days (when 2 lines are crossing the base-line), but doesn't worry much about one critical day.

A pilots' association is trying to get the airlines to re-assign pilots so that those who have double or triple critical days don't have to fly on those days. Or at the very least, they feel the airlines should make sure that both pilot and co-pilot are not having critical days at the same time!

SOME BIORHYTHM PUZZLES

Scott's Exam

Scott, who was born on December 14, 1962, has to take a difficult exam on June 13, 1977. If he studies well for the test and comes in well prepared, how do you think he'll do?

Rod's Race

Rod is a racing car driver who has to decide whether or not to drive in a race that will be held on February 14, 1976. What would you advise? His birthday is January 29, 1932.

Sara's Try-Out

Sara, an actress, could try out for a marvelous part on March 26, 1977. If she doesn't try out on that day, she'll have to wait for the director to get back from Europe on May 5, 1977. Her agent wants to know what to tell the director. Sara's birthday is December 30, 1957. What should she say?

(ANSWERS ON PAGE 633)

Riddles

What did the spaniel say to the parrot?
"I'm a cocker, too." (cockatoo)

What makes the Tower of Pisa lean?
It never eats.

Why did the postman get the sack?
To carry the mail in, of course.

How do you make a Maltese cross?
Pull his tail.

Why do birds fly south in the winter?
It's too far to walk.

What is the difference between a miser and a canoe?
The canoe tips and the miser doesn't.

How can you tell a friend, in 2 letters, that you dislike him?
Write to him twice.

How do you make a bandstand?
Take away their seats.

Why did the little inkspots cry?
Their mother was in the pen doing a long sentence.

Why did the girl give her strapless dress pep pills?
She wanted it to stay up all night.

What does someone always take before you get it?
Your picture.

What does a spendthrift save and a miser spend?
Nothing.

One man made it but didn't use it. One man bought it, but didn't need it. One man needed it, but didn't see it. What is it?
A coffin.

Why doesn't the U.S. government have to import dudes from any other country?
Because a Yankee Doodle Doo.

What is the difference between a stag, a Rolls Royce and a donkey?
A stag is a deer, a Rolls Royce is too dear and a donkey is you, dear.

In what month do people talk least?
February, because it's the shortest month.

What is yellow, long, and seldom rings?
An unlisted banana.

Why did the boy eat chicken soup with his knife?
His fork leaked.

If your nose runs and your feet smell, what's wrong with you?
You're built upside down.

What did the cannibal say when he saw the missionary sleeping?
Ah! Breakfast in bed!

Why did the elephant cross the road?
It was the chicken's day off.

What should you feed elephants on?
Tuesdays.

Four pusher-uppers
Four puller-downers
Two hookers, two crookers
And a swishy wishy.
What am I?
A cow.

What's purple and wrinkled and races around at 75 miles per hour?
A raisin in a sportscar.

What's white and yellow and zooms past at 60 miles per hour?
An egg sandwich on its way to the airport.

What is yellow and black and has wheels on top?
A dead school bus.

Why did Custer die with his boots on?
He had holes in his socks.

What happens to ducks that fly upside down?
They quack up.

Why did Moses cross the Red Sea?
To get to the other side.

If an Apache hitches a ride on the thruway, what season is it?
Indian thumber.

What is a naval destroyer?
A hula hoop with a nail in it.

What is the hardest part of milking a mouse?
Getting the bucket underneath it.

What speaks every language?
An echo.

What gets broken every time you say its name?
Silence.

How many peas go into one pot?
None. You have to put them in the pot.

What did the Martian say to the gas pump?
Take your finger out of your ear and listen to me.

How do you keep an elephant from going through the eye of a needle?
Tie a knot in its tail.

What did the man get when he stole the calendar?
Thirty days.

What does a man with good eyesight usually see less of than a man with bad eyesight?
  The eye doctor.

Why couldn't Eve get the measles?
  Because she'd Adam.

What did the cat say just before the ark landed?
  Is that Ararat?

What is the largest room in the world?
  Room for improvement.

Why is March the shortest month?
  Because the wind blows 2 or 3 days out of every week.

How do you drive a baby buggy?
  Take away its rattle.

What does a 500-pound parrot say?
  Polly wants a cracker NOW!

Why was the cannibal kid sent home from school?
  He tried to butter up the teacher.

What did the cannibal emcee say on the television program?
  Give that little lady a hand.

Why did they call the Louisiana cowboy Tex?
  He didn't want to be called Louise.

Do you shrink from kissing?
  If I did, how do you think I got this big?

What is being "absolutely sure?"
  Being wrong at the top of your voice.

Why did all the covered wagons stop?
  They had Injun trouble.

Proverbs, Sayings and Maxims

**Walk softly
and carry
a big stick . . .**

There are over 160 familiar proverbs, sayings and maxims in the following list. You can use them for several of the games in this book, such as "Charades" (page 498), "Proverbs" in the "Pairing Off Partners" section (page 445), and with "Hangman Grows Up" (page 308).

A barking dog never bites.
A bird in the hand is worth two in the bush.
Absence makes the heart grow fonder.
A cat can look at a king.
A cat has 9 lives.
Actions speak louder than words.
A fool and his money are soon parted.
A friend in need is a friend indeed.
All's fair in love and war.
All's well that ends well.
All that glitters is not gold.
All things come to him who waits.
All work and no play makes Jack a dull boy.
A man's home is his castle.
A miss is as good as a mile.
An apple a day keeps the doctor away.
Any port in a storm.
A penny saved is a penny earned.
April showers bring May flowers.

A rolling stone gathers no moss.
A squeaky wheel gets the most grease.
A stitch in time saves nine.
As ye sow, so shall ye reap.
A watched pot never boils.
A word to the wise is sufficient.
Bad news travels fast.
Beauty is in the eye of the beholder.

Beauty is only skin deep.
Beggars can't be choosers.
Be it ever so humble,
    there's no place like home.
Better late than never;
    better still, never late.
Better safe than sorry.
Better to bow than to break.
Birds of a feather flock together.
Blood is thicker than water.
Brevity is the soul of wit.
Business before pleasure.

Cast not your pearls before swine.
Charity begins at home.
Children should be seen and not heard.
Cleanliness is next to godliness.
Clothes make the man.
Cold hand, warm heart.
Crime does not pay.
Curiosity killed the cat.
Dead men tell no tales.
Don't count your chickens before they're hatched.
Don't cross your bridges until you come to them.
Don't cry over spilt milk.
Don't give up the ship.
Don't put all your eggs in one basket.
Don't put off for tomorrow what you can do today.
Do unto others as you would have them do unto you.
Early to bed and early to rise, makes a man healthy, wealthy and wise.
Easier said than done.
East, west, home's best.

Easy come, easy go.
Every cloud has a silver lining.
Every dog has his day.
Experience is the best teacher.
Faint heart ne'er won fair lady.
Familiarity breeds contempt.
Fifty million Frenchmen can't be wrong.
Fools rush in where angels fear to tread.
Forewarned is forearmed.
For want of a nail, a shoe was lost.
Get thee behind me, Satan!

PERFECT!

Give a man enough rope
   and he'll hang himself.
Great oaks from little acorns grow.
Half a loaf is better than none.
Handsome is as handsome does.
Haste makes waste.
He also serves who only stands and waits.
Heaven helps those who help themselves.
He travels fastest who travels alone.
He who hesitates is lost.
He who laughs last laughs best.
Home is where the heart is.
Home is where you hang your hat.
Honesty is the best policy.
If at first you don't succeed, try, try again.

If the shoe fits, wear it.

If wishes were horses, beggars would ride.
It is always darkest before the dawn.
It is an ill wind that blows no man good.
It is better to light one candle than to curse the darkness.
It's all in a day's work.
It takes two to make a quarrel.
It takes two to tango.
Jack of all trades, master of none.
Keep a civil tongue in your head.
Laugh and the world laughs with you; cry and you cry alone.
Laugh before breakfast, cry before dinner.

Leave well enough alone.
Let him who is without sin cast the first stone.
Let sleeping dogs lie.
Like father, like son.

Little pitchers have big ears.

Little strokes fell great oaks.
Look before you leap.
Lost time is never found again.
Love thy neighbor as thyself.
Make hay while the sun shines.
Man cannot live by bread alone.
Many hands make light work.
Marry in haste, repent at leisure.
Misery loves company.
Monkey see, monkey do.
Music hath charms to soothe the savage beast.
Necessity is the mother of invention.
Neither a borrower nor a lender be.
No man can serve two masters.
No man is an island.
No man is a prophet in his own country.
Nothing ventured, nothing gained.
One hand washes the other.
One man's meat is another man's poison.
Out of sight, out of mind.
Out of the frying pan, into the fire.
People who live in glass houses shouldn't throw stones.
Possession is nine-tenths of the law.
Practice makes perfect.
Practice what you preach.
Rome wasn't built in a day.
Seeing is believing.
Seek and ye shall find.
Silence is golden.
Spare the rod and spoil the child.
Sticks and stones may break my bones,
    but words will never hurt me.
Still waters run deep.
Strike while the iron is hot.
The child is father to the man.

The devil finds work for idle hands.
The early bird catches the worm.
The fat is in the fire.
The grass is always greener in the other fellow's yard.
The love of money is the root of all evil.
The morning is wiser than the evening.
The pen is mightier than the sword.
The pot calls the kettle black.
The proof of the pudding is in the eating.
There is an exception to every rule.
There is many a slip twixt the cup and the lip.
There is method in his madness.
There is nothing new under the sun.
There's no fool like an old fool.
There's no fury like a woman scorned.
There's no place like home.
There's safety in numbers.
The road to hell is paved with good intentions.
The thought is father to the deed.
The truth will out.

Time and tide wait for no man.
Time heals all wounds.
Time is money.
'Tis better to have loved and lost than never to have loved at all.
To err is human, to forgive divine.
Tomorrow is another day.
Too many cooks spoil the broth.

Turn-about's fair play.
Turn the other cheek.
Two heads are better than one.
Two's company, and three's a crowd.
Variety is the spice of life.
Virtue is its own reward.
Walk softly and carry a big stick.
We are all in the gutter, but some of us are
     looking at the stars.
When poverty comes in the door,
     love flies out the window.
When the cat's away, the mice will play.

Where there's smoke, there's fire.
While there's life, there's hope.
Woman's work is never done.
You can lead a horse to water, but you can't make him drink.
You cannot make an omelet without breaking eggs.
You can't have your cake and eat it, too.
You can't judge a book by its cover.
You can't make a silken purse out of a sow's ear.
You can't take it with you.
You can't teach an old dog new tricks.
You made your bed, now lie in it.
You must learn to crawl before you can run.

**Two heads are
better than one . . .**

The Big List Game–Lists

BOYS' NAMES

Aahmes 10
Aaron 2
Abbas 10
Abbotson 7
Abbott 3
Abel 1
Abiezer 10
Abijah 10
Abirah 10
Abishur 10
Abner 3
Abric 10
Abros 10
Absalom 4
Ace 1
Achilles 5
Achsel 10
Ackerley 10
Adair 6
Adal 10
Adalric 10
Adam 1
Adamson 8
Adar 10
Addis 10
Addison 3
Addo 10
Adel 10
Adelbert 8
Adelgar 10
Adelhart 10
Adelmo 10
Adelwin 10
Adlai 4
Adlar 10
Adlo 10
Admetus 8
Adolf 2
Adolph 1
Adolphus 4
Adon 10
Adonis 4
Adrian 4
Adriel 10
Aeneas 7
Agar 9
Agilo 10
Agnar 10
Agnus 10
Agur 10
Ahanu 10

Ahmik 10
Ahrens 7
Aidan 10
Aiken 10
Ainsley 8
Ainsworth 8
Airell 10
Airlie 10
Ajax 5
Alain 5
Alair 7
Alan 1
Aland 10
Alanson 9
Alanus 10
Alard 10
Alaric 8
Alastair 4
Alayne 8
Alban 7
Alber 10
Alberic 10
Albern 10
Albert 1
Albin 6
Albion 8
Albright 8
Alcides 10
Alcott 8
Alda 10
Alden 3
Alder 10
Alderley 10
Aldith 10
Aldo 4
Aldous 4
Aldred 10
Aldric 10
Aldrich 10
Aldwin 10
Alec 1
Aleron 10
Alexander 1
Alexis 3
Aleyn 4
Alf 7
Alford 10
Alfred 1
Algar 8
Alger 9
Algernon 5

Alison 4
Allain 9
Allan 1
Allard 9
Allen 1
Alleyn 3
Allison 7
Allister 10
Almaric 10
Alois 10
Alonzo 4
Aloysius 3
Alpheus 10
Alphonso 3
Alred 10
Alric 8
Alroy 10
Alston 8
Altair 10
Alton 9
Alvan 10
Alver 10
Alvernon 10
Alvin 1
Alvis 5
Alvord 10
Alwin 3
Alworth 10
Alwyn 4
Amadeus 8
Amadis 10
Amaldo 10
Amalric 10
Amasa 10
Ambert 10
Ambler 10
Ambrose 4
Amery 6
Amiel 10
Amin 10
Amon 10
Amory 3
Amos 1
Amparo 10
Amsden 10
Anastasius 7
Anatole 6
Ancel 5
Anders 10
Anderson 6
Andre 3

Andrew 1
Andros 10
Angel 7
Angelo 2
Angus 4
Anis 10
Annibal 10
Anoki 10
Ansel 6
Anselm 8
Anson 8
Anthony 1
Antol 10
Anton 6
Antoniades 7
Antonio 3
Antony 1
Apollo 7
Ara 10
Arad 10
Arber 10
Archer 8
Archibald 4
Ardel 10
Arden 10
Ardeth 10
Ardmore 8
Ardolph 10
Arend 10
Argyle 10
Ari 8
Arian 10
Aric 10
Ariel 7
Aristides 10
Aristo 10
Aristocles 10
Aristotle 10
Arius 10
Arkwright 10
Arlen 5
Arles 7
Arlet 10
Arleth 10
Arley 9
Arlin 7
Arlo 6
Arlyn 10
Armand 6
Armando 5
Armen 10

Armstrong 10
Arnold 1
Aron 10
Arrigo 10
Arsen 8
Artemid 10
Artemus 10
Arthur 1
Arturo 3
Arundel 9
Arvel 10
Arvin 10
Asa 6
Ashbrook 10
Ashburne 10
Ashby 8
Ashcroft 10
Asher 10
Ashford 10
Ashley 4
Athel 10
Athelstan 10
Athmore 10
Attwood 8
Atwater 10
Atwell 10
Atwood 10
Aubert 10
Aubin 10
Aubrey 3
Audley 10
Audrey 4
Audric 10
Audwin 10
August 6
Augustine 8
Augustus 7
Aurelio 8
Aurelius 8
Aurick 10
Austin 3
Avalon 10
Averil 8
Avery 5
Avin 10
Axel 4
Aylett 10
Aylmar 8
Aylsworth 10
Aylward 10
Aylwin 10

Aymon 10
Azar 10
Azel 10

Bailey 10
Bainbridge 8
Baird 10
Baldric 10
Baldur 10
Baldwin 7
Balfour 8
Ballard 8
Bancroft 7
Banning 9
Bannister 7
Barbour 10
Barclay 4
Bardo 10
Barker 7
Barkham 6
Barlow 5
Barnabas 4
Barnaby 3
Barnard 8
Barnett 6
Barney 3
Barnum 8
Barrett 7
Barron 8
Barry 1
Barstow 7
Bart 6
Barthold 10
Bartholomew 2
Bartlett 8
Bartolo 10
Barton 7
Bartram 10
Basil 3
Bassett 10
Bateman 9
Baxter 8
Bayard 10
Bayley 10
Bayliss 10
Baylor 10
Beau 5
Beauford 10
Beaufort 10
Beaumont 10
Beauregard 10

Bela 6	Boswell 6	Burnett 5	Cavendish 8	Conger 8	Daryl 3
Belcher 10	Bothwell 8	Burney 6	Cecil 3	Connell 6	David 1
Belden 10	Bourke 6	Burton 2	Cedric 4	Connor 5	Davis 5
Bellamy 8	Bourne 10	Byram 4	Cesaro 5	Conover 6	Dawes 7
Belmont 8	Bowden 10	Bryan 4	Chad 6	Conrad 3	Dean 6
Ben 1	Bowen 4	Byrne 5	Chancellor 8	Conroy 6	Delano 9
Benedict 3	Bowie 8	Byron 7	Chandler 6	Constantine 7	Delavan 7
Benito 5	Boyce 9		Chapin 7	Conway 5	Delbert 4
Benjamin 1	Boyd 7	Cadell 10	Chapman 9	Copeland 8	Delmar 8
Bennett 6	Boyle 7	Cadman 10	Charles 1	Corbett 6	Delwin 9
Benno 10	Boynton 8	Cadmar 10	Charlton 6	Corcoran 5	Demosthenes 8
Bentley 6	Bradburn 9	Cadmus 10	Chauncey 4	Corey 6	Dempsey 6
Benton 8	Bradbury 7	Cadoc 10	Chelsea 8	Cornelius 3	Denham 9
Benvenuto 5	Braden 9	Cadwallader 10	Cheney 9	Cornell 6	Denis 3
Beppo 7	Bradfield 8	Caesar 2	Chesley 7	Corydon 10	Denison 5
Beresford 8	Bradford 6	Cain 4	Chester 2	Cosgrove 9	Denman 9
Berg 10	Bradley 5	Calbert 6	Chet 2	Cosmo 3	Dennis 1
Berger 5	Bradshaw 8	Caldwell 5	Chris 1	Cotton 8	Denys 1
Berkeley 8	Brady 6	Caleb 6	Christian 4	Courtland 7	Derby 8
Berman 8	Brainard 10	Callahan 8	Christopher 1	Courtney 4	Derek 4
Bernaldo 6	Brand 10	Calvert 6	Cicero 6	Cowan 6	Dermot 4
Bernard 1	Brandon 5	Calvin 5	Clair 5	Craig 1	Derrick 5
Bernardo 2	Brant 6	Camden 7	Clarence 1	Crandall 10	Derward 7
Bernhard 3	Brendan 5	Cameron 5	Clark 1	Crawford 4	Derwin 9
Bernold 10	Brent 7	Campbell 4	Claude 3	Creon 5	Desmond 3
Bert 2	Brett 4	Canfield 7	Claudius 4	Crispin 8	Devereaux 7
Berton 5	Brewster 4	Carew 10	Claus 6	Cromwell 7	Devin 2
Bertram 1	Brian 2	Carey 6	Clay 8	Culbert 5	Devlin 4
Bertrand 10	Brice 8	Carl 1	Clayborne 10	Cullen 8	Dewar 8
Bertwin 10	Brien 5	Carleton 3	Clayton 4	Culver 3	De Witt 7
Berward 10	Brigham 4	Carlisle 7	Clem 1	Curt 4	Dexter 3
Berwick 10	Brion 6	Carlo 3	Clemence 4	Curtis 4	Dick 1
Berwin 10	Brisbane 8	Carlos 2	Clement 3	Cuthbert 4	Digby 6
Bevan 8	Bristow 9	Carlton 2	Cleon 10	Cutler 5	Dillard 4
Beverley 3	Brisbane 8	Carlyle 7	Cleve 10	Cyrano 5	Dillon 9
Bevis 10	Britton 8	Carmichael 4	Cliff 3	Cyril 4	Dilwin 6
Bill 1	Brock 6	Carmody 10	Clifford 2	Cyrus 3	Dion 5
Billy 1	Broderick 3	Carney 10	Clifton 4		Dirk 7
Blaine 6	Brodie 7	Carol 6	Clinton 5	Dale 5	Dixon 5
Blair 8	Bromfield 8	Carroll 5	Clive 4	Dallas 9	Dmitri 5
Blake 8	Brooke 5	Carter 6	Clovis 6	Dalton 8	Domingo 7
Blakeman 10	Bruce 1	Cartwright 8	Clyde 2	Daly 6	Dominic 4
Blanchard 5	Bruno 5	Carvel 9	Clymer 9	Damien 5	Don 1
Blanco 10	Brutus 7	Carver 6	Colbert 6	Damon 4	Donaghan 5
Blandon 8	Bryan 4	Cary 5	Colburn 8	Dan 1	Donahue 7
Bliss 8	Bryce 6	Caryl 8	Colby 3	Dana 4	Donald 1
Boaz 3	Bryon 8	Casey 3	Cole 4	Dane 3	Donaldson 5
Bob 1	Buchanan 4	Casimir 5	Coleman 7	Danforth 9	Donato 6
Boden 10	Budd 5	Caspar 3	Coley 5	Daniel 1	Donegal 5
Bolton 8	Buddy 5	Cass 4	Colin 7	Darby 5	Donnelly 6
Boniface 8	Burbank 6	Cassidy 8	Collier 8	Darcy 4	Donovan 3
Bonner 10	Burden 7	Cassius 6	Collins 6	Darian 5	Doran 7
Booth 7	Burgess 2	Castor 8	Compton 7	Darius 6	Dorian 4
Borden 7	Burke 3	Caswell 8	Conan 6	Darnell 8	Douglas 1
Boris 2	Burley 8	Cato 7	Conant 5	Darrell 4	Doyle 4
Bostwick 10	Burnell 7	Cavanagh 6	Condon 7	Darwin 8	Drew 5

Driscoll 3
Drummond 6
Drury 8
Dryden 6
Duane 4
Dudley 3
Duff 7
Duke 1
Dunbar 4
Duncan 3
Dunham 4
Dunlap 7
Dunstan 9
Durand 8
Durant 8
Durham 6
Durward 8
Durwin 10
Dustin 4
Dwayne 3
Dwight 3
Dyre 9

Earl 2
Eben 5
Ebenezer 4
Eberhart 8
Ebert 7
Ed 1
Edan 8
Edelbert 10
Edgar 3
Edmond 1
Edmund 1
Edsel 7
Edward 1
Edwardo 5
Edwin 2
Egan 5
Egbert 3
Egerton 9
Egmont 8
Ehrman 10
Elbert 4
Eldon 7
Eldred 10
Eldridge 10
Elgin 8
Eli 3
Elia 7
Elias 4
Eliezer 10
Elihu 9
Elijah 5
Eliot 3
Elisha 10
Ellery 2

Elliott 3
Ellis 6
Ellsworth 8
Elmer 1
Elmo 1
Elroy 2
Elton 10
Elvin 5
Elvis 4
Elwin 4
Elwood 6
Elwyn 4
Ely 2
Emeric 9
Emerson 4
Emery 3
Emil 2
Emlyn 8
Emmanuel 5
Emmet 6
Emory 3
Endicott 7
Engelbert 4
Ennis 8
Enoch 4
Enos 5
Enrico 4
Ensign 5
Ephriam 3
Erasmus 7
Erastus 8
Erbert 7
Erhard 6
Eric 1
Erland 7
Erle 6
Ernest 5
Errol 4
Erskine 7
Erwin 3
Esau 7
Esmond 9
Estevan 8
Ethan 3
Ethelbert 7
Eugene 1
Eustace 3
Evan 4
Evar 10
Evel 6
Evelyn 7
Everard 10
Everett 3
Evers 7
Evert 10
Ewan 7
Ewart 8

Ewell 6
Ewing 8
Ezekiel 4
Ezra 2

Fabian 7
Fairchild 7
Fairfax 8
Farley 4
Farmer 9
Farnham 7
Federico 5
Fedor 6
Felipe 4
Felix 3
Fenwick 9
Ferdinand 3
Fergus 6
Fernando 4
Ferrand 8
Ferris 9
Fidel 5
Fielding 7
Findlay 8
Fitzgerald 5
Fleming 9
Fletcher 3
Florentz 6
Florian 7
Floris 8
Floyd 4
Follett 8
Ford 6
Forrest 5
Forrester 9
Fortescue 10
Foster 4
Fowler 6
Franchot 5
Francis 1
Frank 1
Franklin 1
Fraser 5
Fred 1
Frederic 1
Freeman 5
Fremont 7
Fritz 4

Gabriel 5
Gaines 4
Galahad 7
Gale 7
Galen 10
Gallagher 9
Galvin 8
Garcia 3

Gardner 4
Garfield 8
Garland 10
Garret 9
Garrick 7
Garrison 8
Garth 5
Garver 7
Garvin 6
Garwood 8
Gary 1
Gaston 4
Gavin 5
Gawain 7
Gaye 8
Gayle 6
Gaylord 8
Gene 1
Geoffrey 1
Geordie 3
George 1
Gerald 1
Gerard 1
Gerold 4
Gideon 5
Gifford 4
Gilbert 2
Giles 5
Gilford 8
Gillian 7
Gilmore 7
Gilroy 9
Giovanni 3
Girard 5
Gladwin 9
Glen 6
Goddard 7
Godfrey 4
Godwin 7
Gomer 6
Goodwin 8
Gordon 1
Gouvenor 7
Graham 3
Grant 2
Grantham 8
Granville 7
Grayson 9
Gregg 3
Gregory 1
Grenville 7
Gresham 9
Griswold 3
Grosvenor 6
Grover 5
Guido 4
Guilford 7

Gunther 4
Gus 1
Gustave 3
Guthrie 6
Guy 4
Gwyn 9

Hadley 7
Haines 8
Hal 1
Hale 5
Hallam 10
Halstead 10
Hamilton 5
Hamlet 5
Hamlyn 8
Hamnet 10
Hamon 8
Hank 1
Hanley 9
Hannibal 8
Hans 3
Hansel 4
Harald 4
Harcourt 7
Harding 5
Hardy 7
Hargrave 8
Harlan 6
Harley 5
Harmon 8
Harold 1
Harper 4
Harris 5
Harrison 6
Harry 1
Hart 5
Harvey 1
Hastings 8
Havelock 6
Hayden 5
Hayes 8
Hayward 6
Heath 9
Hebert 10
Hector 4
Hedley 9
Heinrich 4
Henderson 8
Hendrik 3
Henley 7
Henri 3
Henry 1
Herald 9
Herbert 3
Hercules 7

Hereward 9
Herman 2
Hermes 7
Hernan 5
Herndon 7
Herod 8
Herschel 9
Hervey 8
Herwin 10
Heywood 6
Hezekiah 10
Hiawatha 10
Hieronymous 10
Hilary 8
Hilliard 10
Hillyer 10
Hiram 4
Hobart 8
Hoffman 7
Hogan 5
Holbrook 8
Holden 6
Hollis 4
Holman 6
Holmes 7
Homer 3
Honore 8
Horace 3
Horatio 4
Hortensio 9
Hosea 10
Howard 1
Howe 9
Howell 7
Howland 6
Hubbard 6
Hubert 3
Hugh 2
Hugo 4
Humphrey 4
Hunter 7
Huntley 9
Hutchins 5
Hyman 7

Iago 10
Ian 5
Ichabod 8
Ignace 8
Ignatius 10
Igor 5
Ike 2
Immanuel 9
Inglebert 9
Ingram 7
Innis 10
Ira 3

Irvin 7	Joyce 8	Laird 4	Logan 6	Marlow 5	Morell 8
Irving 3	Juan 1	Lambert 6	Lombard 8	Marmaduke 7	Morgan 4
Irwin 3	Judah 9	Lamont 7	Lon 3	Marmion 10	Morley 7
Isaac 2	Judd 3	Lance 7	Loren 8	Marquand 8	Morris 3
Isadore 5	Judson 8	Lancelot 4	Lorenz 4	Marsden 7	Mortimer 3
Isaiah 8	Jules 6	Landis 7	Lorenzo 2	Marshall 3	Morton 2
Ishmael 10	Julian 3	Landon 8	Lorillard 8	Marston 8	Moses 3
Israel 5	Julius 4	Lane 8	Lorimer 7	Martin 1	Munro 7
Ivan 5	Junior 8	Langdon 7	Lorin 5	Marvin 1	Murdock 5
Iver 10	Junius 9	Langley 10	Loring 7	Mason 8	Murphy 6
Ivor 10	Justin 5	Langston 5	Lorne 4	Mathias 7	Murray 3
	Justus 10	Larry 1	Lothario 6	Matthew 2	Murtagh 7
Jabez 10		Lars 4	Louis 1	Maurice 2	Myron 4
Jack 1	Kane 10	Latham 8	Lovell 7	Maury 4	
Jackson 4	Karl 1	Lathrop 7	Lowell 6	Max 1	Napoleon 7
Jacob 1	Karsten 8	Latimer 9	Lucas 3	Maxim 8	Narcissus 9
Jacopo 9	Keane 8	Launcelot 7	Lucian 5	Maximilian 7	Nat 2
Jacques 5	Kearney 8	Lauren 7	Ludwig 4	Maxwell 5	Nate 3
Jake 3	Keating 7	Laurence 1	Luis 3	Maynard 8	Nathan 2
James 1	Keenan 6	Laurent 5	Luke 3	Mead 7	Nathaniel 4
Jared 10	Keene 4	Lauritz 9	Luther 6	Medwin 7	Neal 7
Jarrett 10	Keir 8	Lawlor 8	Lyle 4	Mel 2	Ned 1
Jarvis 7	Keith 4	Lawrence 1	Lyman 8	Meldon 9	Needham 6
Jason 4	Keller 6	Lazarus 5	Lyndon 5	Melford 7	Nehemiah 7
Jasper 7	Kelly 5	Leal 10	Lynn 3	Melville 5	Neil 5
Jay 5	Kelsey 10	Leander 8	Lysander 9	Melvin 1	Nemo 8
Jed 4	Kelvin 8	Lee 5		Mercer 8	Neriah 10
Jedediah 10	Kelwin 10	Lehman 5	Mac 2	Meredith 7	Nero 7
Jefferson 6	Kendall 3	Leigh 7	Macauley 8	Merivale 6	Nestor 10
Jeffrey 1	Kendrick 8	Leighton 8	Mack 3	Merle 8	Neville 7
Jeremiah 6	Kennedy 7	Leith 7	MacLeod 4	Merlin 9	Nevin 6
Jeremy 4	Kenneth 2	Leland 7	Maddox 7	Merrell 5	Newcomb 6
Jerold 5	Kenrick 10	Lemuel 8	Madison 8	Merrick 7	Newell 7
Jerome 4	Kent 5	Lennox 9	Magan 7	Merritt 9	Newlin 8
Jerry 1	Kenton 7	Leo 1	Magellan 9	Merton 5	Newman 5
Jervis 6	Kenyon 4	Leon 1	Magnus 7	Mervin 4	Newton 6
Jess 3	Kermit 6	Leonard 1	Maitland 8	Mervyn 6	Nicholas 2
Jesse 5	Kerry 4	Leonardo 3	Malcolm 4	Meryl 9	Nick 1
Jesus 6	Kerwin 5	Leonidas 8	Mallory 5	Meyer 7	Nicodemus 7
Jethro 8	Kevin 3	Leopold 4	Malone 7	Michael 1	Nigel 3
Jim 1	Kilburn 7	Leroy 2	Malvin 6	Mickey 1	Nimrod 9
Job 10	Kilroy 4	Leslie 4	Mandel 8	Miguel 3	Noah 2
Jocelin 8	Kim 8	Lester 4	Manfred 6	Mike 1	Noel 3
Jock 6	Kimball 9	Lew 4	Manley 4	Milbank 8	Nolan 9
Joe 1	Kingdon 8	Lewis 2	Manly 9	Milburn 7	Noland 7
Joel 5	Kingsley 10	Lincoln 7	Manny 1	Miles 3	Norbert 6
John 1	Kingston 7	Linden 8	Mansfield 7	Milford 5	Norman 3
Johnson 5	Kirby 5	Lindsay 8	Manuel 5	Millard 7	Norris 5
Jon 7	Kirk 4	Linn 9	Marc 1	Milo 4	Norton 3
Jonah 5	Kirkland 8	Linus 7	Marcel 3	Milton 2	Norval 7
Jonas 8	Kirkwood 5	Lionel 2	Marco 3	Mitchell 5	Norvin 8
Jonathan 3	Kit 6	Lisle 5	Marcus 7	Moe 3	Norwood 6
Jordan 6	Knight 10	Livingston 7	Mario 3	Monroe 6	Nugent 7
Jose 1	Konrad 6	Llewellyn 6	Marion 5	Montague 7	Oakes 10
Joseph 1	Kramer 8	Lloyd 4	Marius 8	Monte 5	Oakley 10
Joshua 4	Kurt 5	Lochinvar 8	Mark 1	Montgomery 8	Obadiah 10
Josiah 7	Kyle 5	Lockwood 5	Markham 6	Moreland 6	Octavius 6

Odell 8
Ogden 6
Olaf 7
Oleg 8
Olin 8
Oliver 3
Olney 6
Omar 4
Oral 8
Oran 10
Ordway 7
Oren 4
Orestes 9
Orin 6
Orion 7
Orlando 4
Orlin 7
Ormond 8
Orpheus 7
Orrin 5
Orsino 7
Orson 5
Orville 6
Osbert 7
Osborn 9
Oscar 2
Osgood 5
Osman 8
Osmond 7
Osric 8
Oswald 3
Othello 5
Otis 4
Otto 3
Owen 5

Pablo 5
Paddy 3
Page 8
Paige 4
Paine 8
Palmer 3
Pandro 8
Paolo 2
Parke 8
Parker 5
Parnell 4
Pascal 9
Pat 1
Patrice 5
Patrick 1
Paul 1
Paxton 9
Pedro 2
Pembroke 4
Pendleton 5
Penn 6

Percival 4
Percy 4
Pericles 7
Pernell 9
Perry 5
Peter 1
Phelan 8
Phil 1
Philander 10
Philbert 8
Philemon 9
Philip 1
Philo 5
Phineas 5
Pierce 6
Pierpont 5
Pierre 2
Pierson 8
Porter 7
Powell 7
Prentice 6
Prescott 7
Preston 5
Primus 9
Prince 7
Proctor 9
Prospero 8
Proteus 10
Putnam 7
Pythias 8

Quentin 6
Quinby 9
Quincy 5
Quinn 6

Radburn 10
Radcliffe 8
Radford 9
Rafael 7
Rafe 8
Rainer 6
Raleigh 5
Ralph 1
Ralston 7
Ramiro 5
Ramon 7
Ramsay 6
Randall 5
Randolph 2
Ranger 8
Raoul 5
Raphael 8
Rastus 6
Rathbun 9
Rawlins 7
Ray 1

Raymond 1
Reade 8
Redern 9
Redmond 8
Reed 4
Reese 5
Reeves 7
Reginald 4
Regis 8
Regnard 7
Reid 3
Reinhart 6
Remus 9
Renard 7
Renato 5
Rene 5
Renfred 8
Reuben 3
Rex 3
Reynold 6
Rhett 5
Rhodes 5
Ricardo 3
Richard 1
Richmond 7
Riddell 8
Ridgely 9
Ridgeway 6
Riley 5
Rinaldo 7
Riordan 8
Ritchie 5
Roald 6
Roark 6
Rob 1
Robert 1
Robin 3
Rochester 6
Rod 2
Roderick 5
Rodman 8
Rodney 3
Rodrigo 3
Roger 1
Roland 4
Rolfe 7
Rollin 8
Rollo 8
Roman 7
Romeo 7
Romulo 6
Romulus 5
Ronald 1
Ronan 9
Roric 8
Rory 5
Roscoe 3

Rosmer 10
Ross 3
Rossiter 6
Rosslyn 10
Roswell 9
Rouald 6
Rover 8
Rowan 6
Rowland 7
Roy 1
Royce 6
Ruben 5
Rudolf 5
Rudyard 7
Ruford 9
Rufus 4
Rupert 3
Russell 4
Rutherford 8
Ryan 3

Salvador 3
Sam 1
Samson 6
Samuel 1
Sanborn 8
Sancho 3
Sanders 6
Sandor 7
Sandy 5
Sanford 8
Santiago 7
Sargent 7
Saul 2
Saunders 6
Sawyer 7
Schuyler 5
Scott 3
Sean 3
Searle 8
Seaton 8
Sebastian 4
Sedgwick 8
Selby 9
Selden 7
Selig 8
Selwyn 9
Serge 6
Sergius 9
Seth 2
Seward 7
Seymour 3
Shaw 9
Shawn 4
Sheffield 9
Shelby 7
Sheldon 4

Shelley 5
Shep 1
Shepherd 4
Sheridan 6
Sherlock 4
Sherman 3
Sherry 5
Sherwin 9
Sherwood 7
Shirley 10
Sid 1
Sidney 1
Siebert 8
Sigfried 9
Sigmund 7
Silas 6
Silvester 5
Simeon 6
Simon 4
Sinbad 7
Sinclair 6
Sloane 7
Snyder 6
Sol 4
Solomon 3
Sonny 3
Spencer 4
Stacey 5
Stafford 8
Standish 7
Stanford 6
Stanhope 8
Stanislaus 5
Stanley 1
Stanton 4
Stefan 5
Stefano 7
Stephen 1
Sterling 5
Steven 1
Steward 8
Stewart 2
Stillman 5
Stilwell 7
Stoddard 6
Stuart 2
Sturges 5
Sumner 4
Sutton 9
Sydney 3
Sylvan 7
Sylvester 2
Sylvius 8

Talbot 7
Tate 8
Taylor 6

Ted 1
Telly 6
Terence 3
Terrill 8
Terry 2
Thad 4
Thaddeus 5
Thatcher 8
Thayer 6
Thelonius 10
Theobald 7
Theodore 1
Theron 10
Thomas 1
Thornton 6
Thorpe 8
Thurman 8
Thurston 10
Tiernan 10
Tilden 7
Tilford 10
Tim 1
Timon 7
Timothy 2
Tito 8
Titus 4
Tobias 6
Toby 5
Todd 4
Tom 1
Toma 6
Tomas 7
Tomaso 8
Tonio 8
Tony 1
Torrance 8
Townsend 5
Tracy 4
Traherne 10
Travis 7
Trelawney 8
Tremayne 6
Tremont 7
Trent 8
Trevelyan 7
Trevor 5
Tristan 4
Tristram 7
Truman 8
Tully 7
Tunstan 9
Turner 7
Tybalt 9
Tyler 5
Tyndall 6
Tyrone 3
Tyson 10

Ubert 10	Verlin 10	Walford 10	Wendell 4	Wilson 5	Wynne 6
Udall 5	Vern 6	Walker 5	Werner 6	Wilton 10	Wythe 10
Ulric 8	Vernon 2	Wallace 3	Wescott 6	Winchell 6	
Ulysses 5	Verrill 9	Walt 3	Wesley 5	Winfield 9	Xavier 3
Upton 6	Victor 1	Walter 1	Weston 7	Winfred 5	Xenos 10
Urban 7	Vincent 1	Walton 7	Whitman 8	Winslow 5	Xerxes 10
Uriah 8	Virgil 8	Ward 5	Whitney 3	Winston 2	
Ursino 7	Vito 3	Wareham 7	Wickham 10	Winthrop 2	Yardley 8
	Vivien 6	Warfield 10	Wilbert 10	Wolcott 7	Ymir 10
Val 7		Waring 10	Wilbur 3	Wolfe 10	York 10
Valentine 7	Vladimir 5	Warner 2	Wilder 10	Wolfgang 9	Yul 4
Valery 8		Warren 1	Wiley 9	Wood 6	Yuri 10
Van 6	Wade 8	Warrick 5	Wilfred 7	Woodruff 7	
Vance 5	Wadsworth 6	Warwick 6	Wilhelm 4	Woodward 6	Zaccheus 10
VanDyke 10	Wainwright 9	Washington 7	Will 1	Worcester 8	Zachariah 10
Vanya 5	Wakefield 7	Watson 8	Willard 4	Wright 5	Zachary 6
Varick 10	Walbert 10	Wayne 4	Willett 9	Wyatt 8	Zed 10
Vasily 8	Walcott 8	Webster 8	William 1	Wylie 8	Zeno 10
Vaughan 3	Waldemar 10	Weldon 7	Willis 4	Wyman 9	Zoroaster 8
Vergil 8	Walden 6	Welford 8	Willoughby 3	Wyndham 10	
	Waldo 4				

GIRLS' NAMES

Abellona 10	Agustina 10	Alita 4	Amalina 10	Andromeda 7	Ardelia 10
Abigail 5	Aida 5	Alix 6	Amanda 3	Aneta 9	Ardelis 10
Acacia 10	Aileen 5	Aliza 6	Amandine 10	Angel 7	Ardella 10
Ada 2	Aimee 5	Allegra 4	Amapola 10	Angela 1	Ardene 8
Adabel 7	Aina 8	Allene 4	Amara 10	Angelica 5	Ardetha 10
Adah 10	Alameda 7	Alletta 6	Amarantha 10	Angelina 3	Ardetta 10
Adalia 8	Alanna 8	Alleyne 7	Amaris 9	Anita 1	Ardis 10
Adaline 4	Alarice 7	Alline 5	Amaryllis 8	Anitra 8	Ardith 9
Adamina 9	Alatea 8	Allison 5	Amber 6	Ann 1	Areta 10
Adara 10	Alba 8	Allyce 3	Ambrosine 10	Anna 1	Aretina 10
Adela 6	Alberta 2	Allyn 5	Amelia 1	Annabella 1	Aretta 10
Adelaide 3	Albina 7	Alma 2	Amelie 5	Annabelle 1	Ariadne 4
Adele 1	Alcena 8	Almedea 10	Amethyst 9	Anne 1	Ariana 7
Adelene 5	Alcyone 10	Almira 10	Amina 10	Annetta 1	Ariella 10
Adelia 5	Alda 10	Alona 8	Aminta 10	Annette 1	Arietta 10
Adelicia 8	Aldabelle 10	Aloys 9	Amity 8	Annora 7	Arita 10
Adelina 4	Aldora 8	Aloysia 9	Amoret 10	Annys 10	Arleen 3
Adelinda 9	Aleda 6	Alphena 10	Amorita 10	Anona 10	Arlena 5
Adella 7	Alethea 9	Alphonsina 10	Ampara 10	Anselma 10	Arlene 1
Adicia 9	Aletta 8	Althea 2	Amy 1	Anthea 10	Arleta 7
Adina 10	Alexandra 3	Alva 10	Amybelle 4	Antoinette 5	Arletta 7
Adione 10	Alexis 4	Alvina 8	Amyntas 10	Antonia 7	Arleyne 10
Adolpha 10	Alfonsine 10	Alvira 9	Ana 7	Antonina 7	Arlina 8
Adrena 10	Alfreda 5	Alwyn 10	Anah 10	Apolonia 10	Arline 8
Adriana 7	Alhena 10	Alyce 2	Anais 8	April 4	Arlis 8
Adrienne 4	Alianna 7	Alys 7	Anastasia 8	Ara 10	Arlissa 7
Agatha 2	Alice 1	Alyssa 6	Anatola 8	Arabella 5	Armanda 10
Agna 10	Alicia 2	Ama 10	Ancelin 10	Araminta 7	Armantine 10
Agnella 9	Alida 5	Amabelle 10	Andrea 3	Arbutus 8	Armeda 10
Agnes 1	Alina 6	Amadis 10	Andreana 10	Ardeen 9	Armilla 10
Agola 3	Alison 5	Amala 10	Andrita 10	Ardel 10	Arminta 10

Arnoldine 10
Artemis 10
Aselma 10
Asgard 10
Asta 10
Astarte 10
Astred 10
Astrid 10
Atalanta 10
Atalie 7
Athene 8
Atilia 10
Aubertine 10
Audrey 1
Augusta 2
Augustina 4
Aurelia 5
Aurora 8
Ava 3
Aveline 10
Averil 8
Ayleen 4
Aylene 4
Azalea 10

Babette 4
Barbara 1
Barbette 8
Barbra 1
Bathilda 10
Bathsheba 8
Batista 10
Bea 1
Beatrice 1
Beatrix 1
Becky 2
Belinda 3
Bella 3
Bellanca 10
Belle 2
Benedicta 10
Benetta 10
Benita 7
Bernadette 5
Bernardina 7
Bernetta 6
Bernice 1
Berta 3
Bertha 1
Bertina 7
Beryl 4
Bess 1
Beth 1
Bethana 9
Bethany 10
Betsy 1
Bette 1

Bettina 3
Betty 1
Beulah 3
Bianca 7
Biddy 6
Billie 5
Bina 10
Birdie 5
Birgit 10
Blanche 1
Bliss 6
Blondina 10
Blossom 6
Blythe 3
Bonita 6
Bonnie 1
Brenda 1
Brenna 10
Bride 10
Bridget 1
Brigette 5
Brigit 1
Bronwen 10
Brunella 10
Brunhilda 4
Burdette 8
Burnetta 10

Caia 10
Calandra 10
Calantha 10
Calla 10
Calliope 10
Callista 10
Calpurnia 10
Camellia 7
Camilla 4
Camille 3
Candace 5
Candida 7
Candy 1
Cara 6
Carin 8
Carisa 8
Carita 9
Carla 1
Carletta 7
Carlotta 3
Carlyn 9
Carmela 8
Carmelita 8
Carmen 1
Carmencita 3
Carmina 7
Carol 1
Carolina 1
Caroline 1

Carolyn 1
Carrie 5
Caryl 4
Cassandra 8
Cassia 10
Cassiopeia 8
Catalina 7
Catherine 1
Cathleen 2
Cathlin 4
Cecelia 5
Cecil 7
Cecilia 4
Cecily 1
Celeste 1
Celestine 1
Celia 1
Celina 4
Charis 10
Charity 3
Charlene 5
Charlotte 1
Charmion 9
Cherry 4
Cheryl 3
Chiquita 3
Chita 4
Chloe 2
Chloris 4
Christabel 5
Christel 7
Christie 5
Christina 2
Christine 1
Cicily 1
Cindy 1
Circe 6
Claire 1
Clara 1
Clarabelle 1
Clarice 6
Clarissa 5
Claudette 4
Claudia 1
Claudine 3
Clematis 8
Clementine 1
Cleo 1
Cleopatra 3
Clio 4
Clorinda 8
Clothilde 10
Clover 10
Clytemnestra 9
Clytie 7
Colette 2
Colleen 2

Columbine 6
Comfort 7
Conception 8
Concetta 4
Connie 1
Constance 2
Consuela 3
Cora 1
Coral 3
Coralie 3
Cordelia 6
Corella 4
Coretta 3
Corinne 3
Cornelia 2
Corolla 3
Cosette 5
Crispina 9
Cristina 1
Crystal 3
Crystine 5
Cybele 5
Cymbaline 8
Cynara 7
Cynthia 2

Daffodil 5
Dagmar 4
Dahlia 3
Daina 10
Daisy 1
Dale 1
Dallas 10
Damalis 10
Damara 10
Damaris 10
Danella 10
Danielle 1
Danila 10
Danita 9
Daphne 3
Dara 10
Darcy 10
Darlene 1
Daryl 4
Davida 10
Davita 10
Dawn 3
Day 5
Debby 1
Deborah 1
Deirdre 3
Delia 2
Delicia 10
Delilah 3
Della 1
Delora 10

Deloris 6
Delphina 10
Demeter 8
Denice 2
Denise 2
Desdemona 4
Desire 6
Desiree 3
Desmonda 10
Devi 10
Diana 1
Diane 1
Dina 5
Dinah 1
Dione 5
Dionne 3
Dixie 2
Doll 7
Dolly 2
Dolores 1
Donalda 6
Donalee 5
Donella 8
Donna 1
Dora 1
Dorcas 8
Doreen 3
Doretta 3
Dorinda 8
Doris 1
Dorita 4
Dorothea 1
Dorothy 1
Drucilla 3
Duana 10
Dulcinea 7
Dulcy 6
Duretta 5

Earlene 10
Easter 10
Eberta 8
Echo 6
Eda 10
Edana 8
Edeline 6
Edina 8
Edith 1
Edmonda 8
Edna 1
Edris 9
Edwardine 9
Edwina 4
Edythe 2
Effie 3
Egbertine 10
Eileen 1

Eilene 2
Elaine 1
Elane 3
Elberta 8
Eldora 6
Eldoris 7
Eleana 8
Eleanor 1
Electra 5
Elena 3
Eleonora 1
Eleta 6
Eletha 7
Elfreda 10
Elida 10
Elinor 1
Elisa 2
Elisabeth 1
Elise 2
Elissa 3
Eliza 1
Elizabeth 1
Ella 1
Elladora 10
Ellamae 3
Ellen 1
Ellora 7
Elly 1
Ellyn 1
Eloisa 3
Eloise 1
Elsa 1
Elsbet 3
Elsbeth 2
Else 2
Elsie 1
Elspeth 2
Elthea 10
Elvina 10
Elvira 2
Emanuela 8
Emeline 6
Emerald 7
Emilia 1
Emilie 1
Emily 1
Emma 1
Emmaline 4
Emmylou 4
Emogene 7
Emryss 10
Enid 2
Enrica 6
Enys 10
Erianthe 10
Erica 2
Erina 10

Erlina 8	Fern 7	Gertrude 1	Hedda 6	Irene 1	Josephine 1
Erlinda 6	Fernanda 10	Gianina 10	Hedwig 10	Irina 3	Joy 3
Erline 8	Fidelia 10	Gidget 3	Heide 4	Iris 1	Joyce 1
Erma 3	Fidelity 10	Gigi 5	Helen 1	Irma 1	Juana 4
Ermelinda 10	Fidonia 10	Gilberta 10	Helena 1	Irmadel 10	Juanita 2
Ermengarde 8	Fifi 3	Gilda 5	Helene 1	Irmalee 10	Judith 1
Ernestine 5	Filippa 5	Gillian 7	Helenka 10	Isabel 1	Judy 1
Ernette 10	Filmena 7	Gina 1	Helga 6	Isabella 1	Julia 1
Esmeralda 5	Finella 8	Ginger 5	Heloise 2	Isadora 2	Juliana 5
Esperanze 7	Finna 10	Giorgina 5	Hendrika 7	Isis 10	Julie 1
Essa 10	Fiona 6	Giovanna 10	Henrietta 1	Isobel 2	Juliet 2
Essie 3	Flamina 10	Gipsy 7	Hephzibah 6	Isolde 10	June 1
Estella 5	Flavia 5	Giselle 7	Hera 8	Ivy 1	Juno 6
Estelle 1	Fleur 8	Gladine 10	Hermia 10	Izolda 8	Justine 3
Esther 1	Flo 2	Gladiol 10	Hermione 5		
Estrella 10	Flora 1	Gladys 1	Hero 7	Jacinta 10	Kaia 10
Ethel 1	Florence 1	Glenda 1	Hester 5	Jacobina 10	Kara 10
Etheljean 3	Floret 10	Glendora 10	Hetty 3	Jacqueline 1	Karen 1
Ethyl 5	Florimel 10	Glenna 10	Hilary 3	Jana 10	Karla 2
Etienette 9	Floris 8	Gloria 1	Hilda 1	Jane 1	Katarina 2
Etta 3	Florrie 1	Gloriana 5	Hildegarde 3	Janella 10	Kate 1
Eudora 5	Forestina 10	Glory 7	Holly 5	Janet 1	Katharine 1
Eugenia 4	Fortuna 10	Glyda 10	Honora 9	Janetta 7	Katherine 1
Eugenie 5	Francena 5	Glynnis 9	Hope 3	Janice 4	Kathie 1
Eulalie 10	Frances 1	Golda 4	Hortense 2	Janina 10	Kathleen 1
Eumenida 10	Francesca 3	Goldie 2	Hyacinth 10	Janna 10	Kathryn 1
Eunice 1	Francie 1	Goneril 8	Hypatia 10	Jasmine 4	Katie 1
Euphemie 10	Francine 2	Grace 1		Jayne 3	Katrina 5
Eurydice 8	Freda 3	Gratiana 10	Ianthe 10	Jean 1	Kay 2
Eustacia 9	Frederica 5	Greer 8	Ida 1	Jeanne 1	Kaya 10
Eva 1	Fredonia 6	Greta 2	Idalah 10	Jeanette 1	Kelda 10
Evadne 10	Freya 10	Gretchen 2	Idalia 10	Jehanara 10	Kelvina 10
Evalina 2	Frieda 2	Gretel 2	Idaline 10	Jelena 10	Kendra 10
Evaline 2	Fritzi 6	Griselda 6	Idelle 10	Jemima 2	Kerry 5
Evangeline 3	Fulvia 10	Grizel 10	Ilene 10	Jennet 7	Kina 10
Evanthe 10		Grushenka 8	Ilka 7	Jennifer 1	Kit 4
Eve 1	Gabriella 5	Guencvere 5	Ilona 5	Jenny 1	Kitty 1
Eveleen 4	Gabrielle 5	Guenna 8	Ilse 6	Jessamine 8	Kleantha 10
Eveline 4	Gail 3	Guinevere 2	Imelda 10	Jessamy 5	Komala 10
Evelyn 1	Galatea 6	Gunhild 10	Imogen 9	Jesse 2	Kristin 5
Eyleen 3	Gale 3	Gussie 3	Imogene 5	Jessica 1	Kuni 10
	Gardenia 7	Gustava 10	Ina 5	Jessie 1	
Fae 2	Garnet 10	Gwen 4	Ines 6	Jewel 5	Lael 8
Faith 5	Gavrila 10	Gwendolen 4	Inez 4	Jill 1	Laetitia 8
Fannie 1	Gay 7	Gweneth 10	Inga 5	Jo 4	Laila 10
Fanny 1	Gazella 10	Gypsy 7	Ingeborg 6	Joan 1	Laina 10
Faustine 10	Gemma 10		Inger 7	Joanna 1	Lala 10
Fawn 8	Geneva 10	Hagar 9	Ingrid 4	Joanne 1	Lalita 8
Fay 1	Genevieve 2	Haida 10	Inis 10	Jocasta 10	Lambertine 10
Faye 1	Georgette 1	Hali 10	Innocent 7	Jocelin 4	Lana 5
Fayette 8	Georgia 3	Hallie 1	Ino 10	Jocelyn 3	Lanessa 10
Fedora 10	Georgiana 5	Hanna 10	Io 10	Joelle 9	Lanette 10
Felice 5	Georgina 4	Hannah 1	Iola 10	Joette 6	Lara 10
Felicia 6	Geraldine 1	Harriet 1	Iolanthe 6	Johanna 3	Laraine 1
Felicity 5	Gerardine 10	Hattie 1	Iona 8	Josefa 7	Larissa 7
Felipa 7	Gerda 10	Hazel 3	Ionia 10	Josefina 9	Laura 1
Fenella 9	Germaine 10	Heather 3	Iphigenia 7	Josepha 5	Laureen 3

Laurel 4
Lauretta 3
Laurette 3
Laverne 1
Lavinia 6
Lea 2
Leah 2
Leanna 8
Leda 10
Lee 1
Leigh 5
Leila 3
Lelia 7
Lena 1
Lenora 1
Lenore 1
Leodora 10
Leola 7
Leona 1
Leonie 9
Leonora 3
Leslie 1
Leta 10
Leticia 3
Letty 1
Liana 7
Liane 8
Libby 1
Lida 6
Lila 3
Lilac 4
Lilian 1
Lilianne 4
Lilith 6
Lillian 1
Lily 1
Lilybelle 3
Lina 2
Linda 1
Linnet 8
Lisa 2
Lisabet 4
Lise 5
Lisette 8
Lisle 5
Livia 7
Liza 3
Lizzie 1
Lois 1
Lola 1
Lolanda 10
Lolita 3
Loraine 1
Lorelei 4
Loretta 2
Lori 8
Lorinda 10

Lorita 7
Lorna 2
Lorraine 1
Lotta 4
Lotte 2
Lottie 1
Lotus 7
Lou 1
Louanne 7
Louella 2
Louisa 1
Louise 1
Luanna 10
Lucasta 8
Lucerne 4
Lucia 4
Lucie 1
Lucilla 7
Lucille 1
Lucinda 5
Lucretia 6
Lucy 1
Ludmila 10
Luisa 2
Lulabel 5
Lulu 1
Lurline 10
Lydia 1
Lynette 6
Lynn 3

Mabel 1
Madalyn 1
Madeleine 1
Madeline 1
Madge 2
Mae 2
Magdalen 3
Maggie 1
Mai 5
Maia 7
Maida 6
Maisie 3
Mala 9
Malina 7
Malvina 8
Mame 3
Mamie 3
Manon 8
Manuela 4
Mara 5
Marcelina 8
Marcella 6
March 7
Marcia 2
Margalo 8
Margaret 1

Marge 1
Margery 1
Margo 2
Margot 3
Margret 1
Marguerite 1
Maria 1
Marian 1
Marianna 1
Marie 1
Marietta 2
Marigold 6
Marijean 10
Marilyn 1
Marina 4
Marion 2
Marjorie 1
Marlene 1
Marna 10
Marta 9
Martha 1
Martine 7
Mary 1
Mary Ann 1
Maryann 1
Marylin 4
Marylou 2
Mathilda 1
Matty 1
Maude 2
Maureen 1
Mavis 3
Maxine 2
May 1
Maya 6
Maybelle 3
Medea 7
Meg 1
Megan 7
Mehitabel 8
Melanie 4
Melicent 6
Melissa 3
Melvina 8
Mercedes 8
Mercy 2
Meredith 6
Merle 6
Merry 1
Meryl 5
Metis 10
Midge 1
Mignon 10
Mignonette 10
Miguela 10
Mila 10
Mildred 1

Millicent 1
Millie 1
Mimi 4
Minerva 5
Minetta 7
Minna 4
Minnie 1
Mione 10
Mira 5
Mirabel 6
Miranda 2
Miriam 1
Miriamne 3
Moina 10
Moira 5
Mollie 1
Molly 1
Mona 3
Monica 2
Mora 9
Morgana 10
Moria 8
Muriel 1
Myra 1
Myrna 1
Myrrh 10
Myrtle 2

Nada 10
Nadia 7
Nadine 5
Naida 9
Nan 1
Nana 3
Nancy 1
Nanette 3
Nanine 8
Naomi 1
Nara 10
Narcissa 10
Natalia 7
Natalie 2
Natasha 8
Nell 1
Nella 6
Nellie 1
Nelly 1
Nerice 10
Nerine 10
Nerissa 7
Nerita 10
Neroli 10
Netta 10
Nettie 1
Neva 8
Nicole 2
Nicolette 3

Nieta 10
Nina 1
Ninon 6
Nita 5
Noelle 5
Nola 10
Nona 8
Nora 1
Norah 1
Norberta 9
Nordica 10
Noria 10
Norine 10
Norma 1
Nydia 6
Nyssa 10

Octavia 10
Odaris 10
Odelette 10
Odelia 6
Odella 8
Odessa 10
Odette 6
Odile 10
Odina 10
Olga 1
Olinda 10
Olita 10
Olive 2
Olivia 1
Olympia 7
Omphale 10
Ona 5
Ondine 10
Onida 10
Onora 10
Oonagh 10
Opal 4
Ophelia 1
Orabelle 10
Oralia 10
Ordelle 10
Orela 10
Orette 10
Oriana 10
Orinda 10
Orita 10
Ottilie 3
Ouida 10
Oya 10

Pamela 1
Pandora 1
Pansy 1
Paola 7
Parmelia 10

Parthenia 10
Pat 1
Patience 7
Patricia 1
Patsy 1
Patty 1
Paula 2
Paulette 3
Pauline 1
Pavita 10
Peace 10
Pearl 1
Peg 1
Peggy 1
Penelope 4
Peony 7
Pepita 10
Perdita 10
Petra 10
Petronella 10
Petrova 10
Petunia 10
Phebe 5
Phedre 10
Philemena 7
Philippa 4
Phoebe 5
Phyllis 1
Pierrette 7
Pilar 10
Pippa 8
Polly 1
Pollyanna 1
Poppy 3
Portia 5
Priscilla 1
Prudence 1
Prunella 8
Psyche 10

Queena 5
Queenie 2

Rachel 4
Rae 2
Raina 8
Ramona 5
Rana 10
Raymonda 3
Reba 3
Rebecca 1
Regan 7
Regina 3
Reina 10
Renata 10
Renee 4
Reva 10

Rhea 1	Sally 1	Suni 10	Trixie 1	Veva 10	Xylopala 10
Rheta 10	Salome 4	Susan 1	Trudie 1	Vevila 10	Xylophila 10
Rhoda 1	Samantha 3	Susanna 1		Vickie 2	Xylota 10
Rina 10	Samara 10	Susanne 1	Ula 10	Victoria 1	
Rita 1	Sandra 1	Susette 1	Una 5	Vida 3	Yarmilla 10
Roberta 1	Santa 7	Susie 1	Undine 10	Vidette 5	Yolanda 1
Robin 5	Sara 1	Suzette 1	Urania 10	Villa 10	Ysolde 10
Robina 10	Sarah 1	Swanhilda 10	Uriana 10	Villette 10	Yvette 1
Romelda 10	Sarai 10	Sybil 1	Ursa 7	Vilma 10	Yvonne 1
Rona 10	Sari 10	Sylvia 1	Ursula 1	Vina 10	
Ronalda 10	Sarita 10			Vincentia 10	Zada 10
Ronnie 2	Sascha 6	Tabitha 4	Valentina 9	Viola 1	Zaidee 10
Rosa 2	Scarlett 5	Taffy 5	Valerie 6	Violet 1	Zamora 10
Rosabel 2	Selena 7	Tallulah 6	Valora 10	Violetta 1	Zara 10
Rosalie 1	Selina 4	Tamar 10	Vanessa 1	Virgilia 1	Zelda 2
Rosalind 2	Selma 2	Tamara 4	Varenka 10	Virginia 1	Zelina 10
Rosamond 2	Semele 10	Tammy 1	Varina 10	Vita 10	Zella 10
Rosanne 6	Serafina 10	Tara 5	Varinka 10	Vivian 1	Zelma 10
Rose 1	Serena 10	Teresa 1	Varvara 10	Viviana 8	Zelota 10
Rosemarie 1	Shan 10	Terese 1	Vasilia 10	Vivianne 3	Zena 4
Rosemary 1	Sharon 3	Tess 1	Veda 6		Zenia 10
Rosetta 6	Sheelagh 4	Tessa 1	Veleda 10	Wanda 1	Zenobia 10
Rosina 10	Sheila 1	Thea 2	Veleva 10	Wannetta 8	Zeora 10
Rosita 2	Sherrill 10	Thelma 1	Velia 10	Wendy 10	Zepha 10
Roslyn 1	Shirley 1	Theodora 1	Velika 10	Wilhelmina 3	Zilia 10
Rowena 5	Sibyl 5	Theodosia 8	Velma 1	Willa 5	Zinnia 7
Roxanne 4	Sidonia 3	Theresa 1	Venetia 10	Winifred 1	Ziona 10
Roxie 5	Signe 4	Thetis 10	Venita 10	Winnie 1	Zoe 5
Rozelle 10	Sigrid 5	Thisbe 6	Vera 1	Winona 6	Zohra 10
Ruana 10	Silene 10	Thomasina 10	Verbena 10	Wynette 10	Zola 10
Ruby 4	Silvia 1	Tilda 10	Verena 10	Wynne 5	Zona 10
Rucita 5	Siobhan 7	Till 1	Vergilia 10		Zora 10
Ruella 10	Sofia 4	Tillie 1	Verla 10	Xanthe 10	Zorabel 10
Ruth 1	Sonia 1	Timothea 7	Verlyn 10	Xanthippe 10	Zorah 10
	Sonja 1	Tina 6	Verna 10	Xene 10	Zorana 10
Sabina 6	Sonya 1	Titania 5	Vernadine 10	Xenia 10	Zorna 10
Sabrina 5	Sophie 1	Toni 4	Verne 10	Xenisma 10	Zula 10
Sacha 10	Stacy 1	Tonia 8	Vernette 10	Ximena 10	Zuleika 10
Sada 6	Star 10	Tracy 6	Verona 6	Xylia 10	Zulena 10
Sadie 1	Stella 1	Tricia 5	Veronica 1	Xylina 10	Zulota 10
Saida 10	Stephanie 1	Trilby 10	Veronique 5	Xylona 10	Zyma 10
Sal 1	Sue 1	Trina 5	Vesta 10		

LAND ANIMALS (MAMMALS)

Aardvark 4	Ant Bear 7	Armadillo 4	Bamboo Bat 10	Bharal 10
Aardwolf 10	Anteater 3	Ass 1	Bamboo Rat 10	Bighorn 8
Addax 7	Antelope 2	Axis Deer 9	Bandicoot 9	Binturong 10
Agouti 9	Aoudad 10	Aye-Aye 10	Barbary Ape 3	Bison 3
Ai 9	Ape 1		Bat 1	Blackbuck 7
Alpaca 7	Arctic Fox 9	Babirussa 10	Bear 1	Blesbok 7
Ammon 10	Argali 10	Baboon 1	Beaver 2	Blue Bull 10
Anoa 10	Ariel 10	Badger 5	Beisa Oryx 10	Boar 3

Bobac 10
Bobcat 2
Bohor Reedbuck 10
Bongo 10
Bontebok 10
Brocket 10
Buck 4
Buffalo 1
Bull 1
Burro 4
Bush Baby 8
Bushbuck 9
Bush Pig 8

Cacomistle 10
Camel 1
Capybara 7
Carabao 10
Caracal 10
Caribou 6
Castor 10
Cat 1
Catamount 10
Cavy 10
Cayuse 10
Chacma 10
Chamois 10
Cheetah 5
Chevrotain 10
Chickaree 10
Chimpanzee 1
Chinchilla 6
Chipmunk 3
Chital 10
Civet 8
Coati 8
Colugo 10
Cony 10
Cottontail 3
Cougar 4
Cow 1
Coyote 1
Coypu 10
Cus-Cus 10

Daman 10
Deer 1
Desman 10
Dhole 10
Dik-Dik 10
Dingo 5
Dog 1
Donkey 1
Dormouse 6
Douc 10
Drill 10

Dromedary 4
Duikerbok 10

Echidna 10
Eland 8
Elephant 1
Elephant Seal 8
Elephant Shrew 10
Elk 2
Ermine 5
Eyra 10

Fennec 9
Ferret 6
Fisher 8
Fitch 10
Flying Fox 10
Flying Lemur 8
Flying Squirrel 6
Foussa 10
Foumart 10
Fox 1
Fox Squirrel 8

Galago 10
Gaur 10
Gayal 10
Gazelle 5
Gemsbok 10
Genet 10
Gerbil 2
Gibbon 3
Giraffe 1
Glutton 10
Gnu 3
Goat 1
Goat Antelope 10
Gopher 3
Goral 10
Gorilla 1
Grison 10
Grivet 10
Ground Hog 2
Ground Squirrel 10
Guanaco 10
Guenon 10
Guereza 10
Guinea Pig 2

Hamadryad 10
Hamster 3
Hamster Mole 8
Hare 1
Hart 7
Hartebeest 9
Hedgehog 7

Hinny 10
Hippopotamus 1
Hog 1
Hog Badger 10
Hog Deer 9
Honey Bear 4
Honey Dog 8
Hoolock 10
Horse 1
Hound 1
Howler Monkey 7
Huanaco 10
Hutia 10
Hyena 2
Hyrax 10

Ibex 6
Ichneumon 10
Impala 6

Jackal 4
Jackass 2
Jack Rabbit 3
Jaguar 2
Jaguarundi 10
Javali 10
Jerboa 10

Kalong 10
Kangaroo 1
Kangaroo Mouse 8
Kangaroo Rat 8
Karakul 8
Kiang 10
Kinkajou 9
Klipspringer 10
Koala 5
Kob 10
Kudu 10

Lamb 1
Langur 10
Leaf Monkey 9
Lemming 6
Lemming Mouse 10
Lemur 5
Leopard 1
Leopard Seal 7
Linsang 10
Lion 1
Llama 2
Loris 10
Lynx 4

Macaque 10
Man 3

Mandrill 6
Mangabey 9
Manul 10
Maral Stag 10
Mare 5
Margay 7
Markhor 10
Marmoset 7
Marmot 8
Marsh Buck 7
Marsh Deer 7
Marten 5
Meerkat 8
Mink 2
Mole 3
Mole Lemming 10
Money Mouse 10
Mongoose 6
Monkey 1
Moonrat 10
Moose 1
Mouflon 10
Mountain Beaver 10
Mountain Goat 3
Mountain Lion 2
Mouse 1
Mule 1
Mule Deer 10
Muntjak 10
Musk Ox 6
Muskrat 3
Musquash 10
Mustang 2

Nilgai 10
Noctule 10
Nutria 6
Nyala 10

Ocelot 2
Okapi 7
Onager 10
Opossum 2
Orangutan 2
Oribi 10
Oryx 10
Otter 2
Ounce 10
Owl Monkey 10
Ox 1

Paca 10
Painter 10
Pallah 10
Pampas Deer 10
Panda 1

Pangolin 9
Panolia Deer 10
Panther 1
Peba 10
Peccary 8
Pekan 10
Phalanger 10
Pichiciago 10
Pig 1
Pig Deer 10
Pika 10
Platypus 6
Pocket Gopher 10
Pocket Mouse 10
Polar Bear 2
Polecat 3
Pongo 10
Pony 1
Porcupine 1
Possum 2
Potto 10
Prairie Dog 5
Pronghorn 10
Puma 2
Pygmy Buffalo 10

Rabbit 1
Rabbit Rat 10
Raccoon 1
Raccoon Dog 10
Ram 5
Rasse 10
Rat 1
Rat Kangaroo 10
Ratel 10
Red Deer 6
Reedbuck 10
Reindeer 1
Rhesus Monkey 10
Rhinoceros 2
Rice Rat 10
Roan Antelope 10
Rocky Mountain
  Goat 6
Roe Deer 10

Sable 2
Saiga 10
Saki 10
Sambar 10
Sapajou 10
Sassaby 10
Sea Lion 5
Seal 2
Seladang 10

Serow 10
Serval 10
Sewellel 10
Sheep 1
Sheep Cow 10
Sheep Deer 10
Shetland Pony 3
Shrew 4
Shrew Mole 10
Shrew Mouse 10
Siamang 7
Skunk 1
Sloth 5
Sow 7
Spider Monkey 6
Spiny Anteater 7
Springbok 9
Springhaas 10

Squirrel 1
Squirrel Monkey 10
Stag 1
Steer 1
Steinbok 8
Stoat 7
Suni 10
Suricate 10
Suslik 10
Swine 3

Tahr 10
Takin 10
Talapoin 10
Tamandua 10
Tamarau 10
Tamarin 10
Tapir 5

Tarpan 10
Tarsier 10
Tasmanian Devil 7
Tayra 10
Tenrec 8
Thylacine 10
Tiger 1
Titi 10
Tree Shrew 10
Tuco Tuco 10

Unau 10
Urial 10

Vampire Bat 5
Vervet 10
Vicuña 7
Viscacha 10

Vole 8

Wallaby 4
Wallaroo 10
Walrus 1
Wanderoo 10
Wapiti 8
Warrigal 10
Warthog 5
Waterbuck 8
Water Buffalo 4
Water Hog 7
Water Rat 5
Weasel 2
Weasel Cat 5
Wild Ass 5
Wild Boar 3
Wildcat 2

Wildebeest 8
Wisent 10
Wolf 1
Wolverine 5
Wombat 5
Woodchuck 2

Yak 2
Yapok 10

Zebra 2
Zebra Duiker 10
Zebra Mongoose 10
Zebu 10
Zibet 10
Zoril 10

FOOD PLANTS

Acorn squash 6
Akee 10
Alecost 10
Alligator pear 6
Allspice 7
Almond 2
Alpine
    strawberry 10
Amarelle 10
Angelica 9
Anise 7
Apple 1
Apricot 2
Arrowroot 8
Artichoke 3
Asparagus 1
Asparagus pea 9
Aubergine 10
Avocado 2

Balm 10
Balsam pear 10
Bambarra
    groundnut 10
Bamboo shoots 8
Banana 1
Baobab 10
Barberry 8
Barley 1
Basil 2

Bayberry 5
Bay leaf 3
Beach plum 8
Bean 1
Beet 1
Bilberry 5
Blackberry 2
Black-eyed pea 6
Black gram 10
Black mustard 10
Black salsify 10
Blackthorn 10
Black walnut 10
Bladder cherry 10
Blewits 10
Blood orange 7
Blueberry 1
Borage 9
Boysenberry 6
Brazil nut 3
Breadfruit 7
Broad bean 7
Broccoli 2
Brussels sprouts 2
Buckwheat 4
Bullace 10
Burnet 10
Butter bean 8
Butternut 6
Butternut squash 7

Cabbage 1
Cabbage
    palmetto 10
Cacao 4
Calamondin 10
Caltrop 10
Camomile 6
Cantaloupe 1
Cape
    gooseberry 10
Capers 7
Carambola 10
Caraway 5
Cardamom 9
Cardoon 10
Carrageen 10
Carrot 1
Cashew nut 3
Cassava 8
Cauliflower 2
Celeriac 10
Celery 2
Celtuce 9
Cep 10
Ceriman 10
Chanterelle 10
Chard 4
Cherimoya 10
Cherry 1
Cherry plum 4

Cherry tomato 3
Chervil 6
Chestnut 3
Chick pea 7
Chicory 6
Chili pepper 5
Chinese cabbage 10
Chinese chives 10
Chinese lantern
    plant 10
Chinese water
    chestnut 5
Chives 5
Cicely 10
Cinnamon 3
Cintrange 10
Citron 7
Clementine 9
Cloudberry 9
Cloves 3
Coconut 1
Coffee 1
Collard 8
Comfrey 10
Coralberry 9
Coriander 7
Corn 1
Costmary 10
Courgette 10
Cowberry 8

Cowpea 10
Crabapple 5
Cranberry 2
Cranshaw melon 6
Cress 6
Crookneck
    squash 9
Cucumber 2
Currant 4
Cuscus 10
Cushaw 10
Custard apple 7

Damson 10
Dandelion 2
Dasheen 10
Date 3
Dewberry 8
Dill 6
Dulse 10
Durian 10
Durra 8

Eddoes 10
Eggplant 3
Elderberry 5
Endive 5
Escarole 6

Fennel 9
Fenugreek 10
Fig 4
Filbert 4
Finocchio 8
Florence fennel 10

Garlic 3
Gean 10
Gherkin 7
Ginger 2
Goa bean 10
Good King
    Henry 10
Gooseberry 6
Granadilla 8
Grape 1
Grapefruit 2
Great nettle 10
Green gram 10
Ground cherry 8
Guava 5
Guinea corn 8
Gumbo 8

Hackberry 8
Haw 10

Hazelnut 5
Honeydew
    melon 3
Hop 8
Horehound 7
Horse-radish 7
Huckleberry 3
Husk tomato 8
Hyacinth bean 10
Hyssop 10

Ilama 10
Indian corn 6
Indian cress 8
Indian currant 9
Indian fig 10
Indian lettuce 10
Indian rice 10

Jack bean 8
Jack-fruit 7
Japanese
    persimmon 10
Japanese
    quince 10
Japan pepper 10
Jersualem
    artichoke 9
Juniper berry 8

Kale 9
Kava 8
Kidney bean 2
Kiwi 7
Kohlrabi 10
Kumquat 6

Lablab 10
Laver 10
Leek 6
Lemon 1
Lentil 3
Lettuce 1
Lichee nut 8
Licorice 4
Lima bean 1
Lime 3
Loganberry 7
Loquat 10
Lotus 10
Lovage 10

Macadamia nut 10
Mace 7
Maize 1
Malabar spinach 10

Mandarin
    orange 7
Mangel-wurzel 10
Mango 5
Mangosteen 10
Manioc 10
Marjoram 5
Marrow 10
Marshmallow 6
Mat bean 10
Maté 10
Maypop 8
Medlar 10
Melon 1
Mercury 10
Mexican apple 10
Mexican black
    bean 10
Mexican ground
    cherry 10
Millet 9
Mint 1
Morel 10
Morello 10
Moreton Bay
    chestnut 10
Moth bean 10
Mulberry 4
Mung bean 10
Mushroom 2
Muskmelon 4
Mustard 1

Navy bean 7
Nectarine 5
New Zealand
    spinach 10
Niger seed 10
Nutmeg 5

Oats 3
Oca 10
Oil palm 10
Okra 5
Olive 2
Onion 1
Orache 10
Orange 1
Oyster plant 10

Palmyra palm 10
Papaya 6
Parsley 3
Parsnip 6
Passion fruit 10
Pawpaw 9

Pea 1
Peach 1
Peanut 3
Pear 1
Pecan 4
Pepper 4
Peppermint 5
Persimmon 6
Pillepesara 10
Pimento 8
Pineapple 1
Pine kernels 8
Pistachio 5
Plantain 9
Plum 1
Plum tomato 6
Pomegranate 7
Pomelo 10
Popcorn 1
Potato 1
Prune 1
Pumpkin 1

Quandong 10
Queensland
    nut 10
Quince 5

Radish 1
Raisin 1
Rambutan 10
Rape 10
Raspberry 2
Red currant 8
Rhubarb 4
Rice 1
Rocambole 10
Rocket 10
Romaine 5
Rose hips 6
Rosemary 5
Rowan 10
Rutabaga 10
Rye 2

Saber bean 9
Safflower 7
Saffron 8
Sage 5
Sago 10
Salsify 10
Samphire 10
Sand leek 10
Sapodilla
    plum 10
Sarsaparilla 9

Savory 8
Scallion 5
Scorzonera 10
Scotch lovage 10
Sea grape 10
Sea kale 10
Serviceberry 10
Sesame 5
Shaddock 10
Shallot 7
Shea-butter
    nut 10
Sloe 10
Sorghum 8
Sorrel 9
Soursop 10
Southernwood 10
Soya 7
Soybean 4
Spearmint 3
Spinach 1

Squash 3
Stinging nettle 6
Strawberry 1
Strawberry
    tomato 10
Stringbean 1
Sugar apple 7
Sugar beet 6
Sugarberry 8
Sugar cane 5
Sunflower 3
Swedish
    turnip 10
Sweet potato 1
Sweetsop 10
Sword bean 9

Tamarind 8
Tangelo 5
Tangerine 2

Tansy 10
Tapioca 5
Taro 7
Tarragon 6
Tea 3
Teff 9
Tepary bean 10
Thyme 3
Tomatillo 10
Tomato 1
Truffle 10
Turmeric 10
Turnip 2

Ugli 10

Vanilla 1
Vegetable
    marrow 10
Vetch 10

Walnut 1
Water chestnut 7
Watercress 5
Watermelon 1
Wheat 1
Whortleberry 10
Wild date
    palm 10
Wild rice 5
Wild spikenard 10
Wineberry 10
Winter cherry 10
Winter cress 8
Winter melon 10
Winter
    purslane 10
Witloof 9
Wormwood 9

Yam 3

Zucchini 6

COUNTRIES AND DEPENDENCIES
OF THE WORLD

Afghanistan 3
Albania 5
Aleutian Islands 4
Algeria 5
American Samoa 7
Andaman Islands 9
Andorra 6
Angola 3
Anguilla 7
Antigua 5
Argentina 3
Armenia (USSR) 7
Aruba 7
Australia 1
Austria 1
Azerbaijan
    (USSR) 10
Azores Islands 7

Baden 6
Bahama Islands 2
Bahrain 9
Balearic Islands 7
Bali (Indonesia) 5
Bangladesh 4
Barbados 6
Bavaria 6
Belgian Congo 7
Belgium 1
Belize 8

Bermuda 3
Bhutan 8
Bimini Islands 7
Bolivia 2
Bonaire 10
Borneo 7
Bosnia
    (Yugoslavia) 8
Botswana 8
Brazil 1
British Solomon
    Islands 9
Brunei 10
Bulgaria 4
Burma 3
Burundi 9
Byelorussia
    (USSR) 10

Cambodia 2
Cameroon 8
Canada 1
Canary Islands 3
Cape Breton
    Island 7
Cape of Good
    Hope (S.A.) 7
Cape Verde
    Islands 8

Caroline Islands 9
Cayman Islands 8
Celebes 10
Central African
    Republic 10
Ceylon 6
Chad 8
Channel Islands 6
Chile 1
China 1
Christmas Island 9
Colombia 3
Comoro Islands 10
Congo 5
Cook Islands 6
Corfu 6
Corsica 4
Costa Rica 5
Crete 5
Croatia
    (Yugoslavia) 8
Cuba 1
Curacao 5
Cyprus 8
Czechoslovakia 5

Denmark 1
Djibouti 10
Dominica Island 10
Dominican Republic 4

Easter Island 5
Ecuador 3
Egypt 1
Elba 4
El Salvador 3
England (UK) 1
Equatorial
    Guinea 9
Estonia (USSR) 6
Ethiopia 4

Faeroe Islands 10
Falkland Islands 8
Fernando Poo 10
Fiji Islands 3
Finland 2
Formentera 10
France 1
French Guiana 5
French Polynesia 9

Gabon 9
Galapagos
    Islands 7
Gambia 4
Georgia (USSR) 7
Germany, East 1
Germany, West 1
Ghana 3
Gibraltar 5

Gilbert and Ellice
    Islands 8
Goa (India) 9
Grand Bahama 6
Great Britain 1
Greece 1
Greenland 2
Grenada 7
Guadalcanal 5
Guadeloupe 6
Guam 7
Guatemala 5
Guernsey Island 3
Guinea 4
Guinea-Bissau 10
Guyana 4

Haiti 3
Hebrides 5
Hispaniola 7
Honduras 4
Hong Kong 2
Honshu 7
Hungary 4

Ibiza 4
Iceland 3
India 1
Indonesia 2
Iran 1
Iraq 1
Ireland 1
Israel 1
Italy 1
Ivory Coast 4
Iwo Jima 5

Jamaica 3
Japan 1
Java 5
Jersey 13
Johore
    (Malaysia) 10
Jordan 2

Kashmir 6
Kauai 6
Kenya 2
Kodiak 10
Kuwait 4
Kyushu 7

Laos 3
Latvia 6
Lebanon 3
Lesotho (formerly
    Basutoland) 9

Liberia 4
Libya 4
Liechtenstein 6
Lithuania (USSR) 6
Luxembourg 5

Macao 8
Madagascar 3
Madeira 7
Majorca 3
Malagasy
    Republic 4
Malawi 6
Malaysia 4
Maldive Islands 10
Mali 8
Malta 7
Man, Isle of 7
Mariana Islands 7
Marquesas Islands 9
Marshall Islands 6
Martinique 5
Mauritania 9
Mauritius 9
Mexico 1
Midway Island 5
Minorca 8
Molokai 6
Monaco 5
Mongolia 2
Montenegro
    (Yugoslavia) 9
Montserrat 8
Morocco 3
Mozambique 7
Muscat 10

Namibia 10
Natal (SA) 10
Nauru 10
Nepal 2
Netherlands 1
Netherlands
    Antilles 7
Nevis 10
New Britain (Papua
    New Guinea) 10
New Brunswick
    (Canada) 8
New Caledonia 6
Newfoundland
    (Canada) 5
New Guinea 2
New Hebrides 7
New Zealand 1

Nicaragua 4
Niger 7
Nigeria 3
Norfolk Island 8
Northern Ireland 1
North Korea 3
Norway 1
Nova Scotia
    (Canada) 3

Okinawa 5
Oman 9
Orange Free State
    (S. Africa) 9
Orkney Islands 3

Pakistan 2
Panama 4
Panama Canal
    Zone 5
Papua New
    Guinea 4
Paraguay 4
Peru 2
Philippines 2
Pitcairn Island 8
Poland 1
Portugal 2
Prince Edward
    Island (Canada) 6
Puerto Rico 1

Qatar 10
Quemoy
    (Taiwan) 5

Reunion 9
Rhodes 5
Rhodesia 1
Rumania 3
Russia (RSFSR) 1
Rwanda 10
Ryukyu Islands 7

St. Christopher 8
St. Croix 5
St. Eustatius 9
St. Helena 7
St. John 5
St. Lucia 6
St. Martin 5
St. Pierre and
    Miquelon Islands 8
St. Thomas 4
St. Vincent 8

Sakhalin Island
    (USSR) 10
Samoa 5
San Marino 8
San Salvador 7
Sao Tome
    & Principe 10
Sarawak
    (Malaysia) 8
Sardinia 4
Sark Island 6
Saudi Arabia 1
Scilly Islands 3
Scotland (UK) 1
Senegal 4
Serbia 6
Seychelles 10
Shetland Islands 7
Shikoku 8
Sicily 3
Sierre Leone 7
Sikkim 7
Singapore 5
Skye Island 8
Solomon Islands 6
Somalia 8
South Africa 2
South Korea 3
Southern
    Rhodesia 8
Southern Yemen 9
South-West Africa
    (see Namibia)
Spain 1
Sri Lanka
    (formerly Ceylon) 4
Sudan 5
Sumatra 6
Surinam 6
Swaziland 8
Sweden 1
Switzerland 1
Syria 2

Tahiti 4
Taiwan 3
Tanganyika 5
Tanzania 4
Tasmania 3
Thailand 2
Tibet 3
Tierra del Fuego 6
Timor 10
Tobago 5
Togo 7
Tonga Island 8
Tortola Island 9

Transkei
    (S. Africa) 10
Transvaal 5
Trinidad 5
Tristan da
    Cunha 10
Tunisia 5
Turkey 1
Turks Island 10

Uganda 5
Ukraine 5

USSR 1
United Arab
    Emirates 8
United Kingdom 1
United States
    of America 1
Upper Volta 9
Uruguay 4

Vatican City 3
Venezuela 4

Vietnam 1
Virgin Islands
    (UK) 5
Virgin Islands
    (US) 5
Viti Levu 9

Wake Island 5
Wales (UK) 2
Wallis and
    Futuna Islands 8

Western Samoa 7
West Irian
    (Indonesia) 8
Wight, Isle of 5

Yemen 7
Yugoslavia 3

Zaire 5
Zambia 5
Zanzibar
    (Tanzania) 6

IMPORTANT CITIES OF THE WORLD

Aarhus, Denmark 10
Aberdeen, Scotland 4
Accra, Ghana 10
Addis Ababa, Ethiopia 7
Adelaide, Australia 6
Agra, India 9
Akron, Ohio 3
Albany, New York 2
Alexandria, Egypt 6
Algiers, Algeria 5
Amman, Jordan 8
Amsterdam, Netherlands 1
Ankara (Angora), Turkey 7
Antwerp, Belgium 10
Arequipa, Peru 10
Asuncion, Paraguay 9
Athens-Piraeus, Greece 1
Atlanta, Georgia 1
Auckland, New Zealand 4

Baghdad, Iraq 6
Baltimore, Maryland 1
Bandung, Indonesia 9
Bangkok, Thailand 2
Barcelona, Spain 1
Bari, Italy 9
Barranquilla, Colombia 10
Basel, Switzerland 4
Beirut, Lebanon 3
Belfast, No. Ireland 2
Belgrade, Yugoslavia 3
Belize, Belize 10
Bengazi, Libya 6
Bergen, Norway 5
Berlin, East Germany 1
Berlin, West Germany 1
Berne, Switzerland 3
Bilbao, Spain 8
Birmingham, Alabama 2
Birmingham, England 2
Bogota, Colombia 4

Bologna, Italy 7
Bombay, India 1
Bonn, West Germany 2
Bordeaux, France 5
Boston, Massachusetts 1
Brasilia, Brazil 5
Brazzaville, Congo 5
Bremen, West Germany 3
Breslau, Poland 10
Bridgetown, Barbados 9
Brisbane, Australia 4
Bristol, England 2
Brussels, Belgium 2
Bucharest, Rumania 5
Budapest, Hungary 5
Buenos Aires, Argentina 1
Buffalo, New York 6

Cairo, Egypt 1
Calcutta, India 2
Canberra, Australia 3
Canton, China 2
Capetown, South Africa 2
Caracas, Venezuela 5
Cardiff, Wales 2
Cartagena, Colombia 10
Casablanca, Morocco 1
Chicago, Illinois 1
Chihuahua, Mexico 8
Christchurch, New
    Zealand 5
Chungking, China 10
Cincinnati, Ohio 4
Cleveland, Ohio 2
Cologne, West Germany 4
Colombo, Sri Lanka 7
Columbus, Ohio 3
Conakry, Guinea 10
Copenhagen, Denmark 1
Cordoba, Argentina 8
Cork, Ireland 5

Coventry, England 7

Dacca, Bangladesh 8
Dakar, Senegal 7
Dallas, Texas 1
Damascus, Syria 5
Danang, South Vietnam 7
Dar es Salaam, Tanzania 9
Dayton, Ohio 4
Delhi, India 2
Denver, Colorado 1
Detroit, Michigan 1
Djakarta (Batavia),
    Indonesia 7
Dortmund, West
    Germany 10
Dresden, East Germany 6
Dublin, Ireland 1
Dundee, Scotland 8
Durban, South Africa 5
Dusseldorf, West Germany 4

Edinburgh, Scotland 1
El Paso, Texas 5
Fez, Morocco 8
Florence, Italy 1
Frankfurt am Main,
    West Germany 3
Freetown, Sierra Leone 6
Fuchou (Foochow), China 9

Gdansk (Danzig), Poland 8
Geneva, Switzerland 1
Genoa, Italy 4
Georgetown, Guyana 10
Ghent, Belgium 8
Giza, Egypt 8
Glasgow, Scotland 1
Goteborg, Sweden 8
Graz, Austria 8
Grenoble, France 7

Guadalajara, Mexico 8
Guatemala City, Guatemala 6
Guayaquil, Ecuador 10

Haifa, Israel 3
Haiphong, South Vietnam 7
Hamburg, West Germany 4
Hamilton, Bermuda 3
Hangchou, China 8
Hannover, West Germany 7
Hanoi, North Vietnam 1
Harbin (Haerhpin), China 10
Hartford, Connecticut 4
Havana, Cuba 1
Helsinki, Finland 3
Hiroshima, Japan 1
Hobart, Tasmania, Australia 10
Hong Kong, Hong Kong 1
Honolulu, Hawaii 1
Houston, Texas 3
Hue, South Vietnam 10
Hyderabad, India 8

Idaban, Nigeria 10
Inchon, South Korea 8
Indianapolis, Indiana 3
Irkutsk, USSR 9
Islamabad, Pakistan 10
Istanbul, Turkey 5
Izmir, Turkey 10

Jacksonville, Florida 7
Jaipore, India 10
Jakarta, Indonesia 6
Jerusalem, Israel 2
Jidda, Saudi Arabia 10
Johannesburg, South Africa 3
Juarez, Mexico 7

Kabul, Afghanistan 7
Kampala, Uganda 9
Kananga, Zaire 9
Kandy, Sri Lanka 10
Kansas City, Missouri 3
Karachi, Pakistan 7
Katmandu, Nepal 3
Kharkov, USSR 10
Khartoum, Sudan 7
Kiev, USSR 5
Kingston, Jamaica 7
Kinshasa, Zaire 10
Kobe, Japan 8
Kowloon, Hong Kong 8
Krakow, Poland 6

Kuala Lumpur, Malaysia 7
Kuwait, Kuwait 6
Kyoto, Japan 9

Lagos, Nigeria 8
Lahore, Pakistan 9
La Paz, Bolivia 8
La Plata, Argentina 9
Leeds, England 3
Leicester, England 8
Leipzig, Germany 4
Leningrad, USSR 1
Leon, Mexico 9
Libreville, Gabon 10
Liege, Belgium 9
Lille, France 9
Lima, Peru 1
Linz, Austria 8
Lisbon, Portugal 1
Liverpool, England 2
Lodz, Poland 9
Londonderry, Northern Ireland 5
London, England 1
Los Angeles, California 1
Louisville, Kentucky 3
Luanda, Angola 10
Lucknow, India 8
Luxembourg, Luxembourg 3
Lvov, USSR 7
Lyon, France 6

Macao, Macao 8
Madras, India 7
Madrid, Spain 1
Malaga, Spain 7
Malmo, Sweden 10
Managua, Nicaragua 6
Manchester, England 2
Mandalay, Burma 6
Manila, Philippines 5
Mannheim, West Germany 7
Maracaibo, Venezuela 8
Marrakech, Morocco 5
Marseille, France 6
Mecca, Saudi Arabia 2
Medellin, Colombia 10
Melbourne, Australia 1
Memphis, Tennessee 4
Mendoza, Argentina 9
Mexico City, Mexico 1
Miami, Florida 3
Milan, Italy 1
Milwaukee, Wisconsin 3
Minneapolis, Minnesota 3
Minsk, USSR 3

Mombasa, Kenya 9
Monrovia, Liberia 8
Monterrey, Mexico 6
Montevideo, Uruguay 7
Montreal, Canada 1
Moscow, USSR 1
Mukden (Shenyang), China 10
Munich, West Germany 3
Muscat, Oman 10

Nagoya, Japan 10
Nairobi, Kenya 5
Nanking, China 9
Nantes, France 8
Naples, Italy 1
Nassau, Bahamas 4
Newark, New Jersey 1
Newcastle, Australia 3
Newcastle-upon-Tyne, England 3
New Delhi, India 1
New Orleans, Louisiana 1
New York, New York 1
Nice, France 4
Nicosia, Cyprus 10
Norfolk, Virginia 5
Nottingham, England 4
Novosibirsk, USSR 10
Nuremberg, West Germany 3

Oakland, California 6
Odessa, USSR 7
Oklahoma City, Oklahoma 7
Omaha, Nebraska 8
Omsk, USSR 9
Oran, Algeria 10
Osaka, Japan 5
Oslo, Norway 1
Ottawa, Canada 3

Palembang, Indonesia 10
Palermo, Italy 6
Panama, Panama 6
Paramaribo, Surinam 9
Paris, France 1
Peking, China 1
Perth, Australia 1
Philadelphia, Pennsylvania 1
Phnom Penh, Cambodia 3
Phoenix, Arizona 5
Pinang, Malaysia 8
Pittsburgh, Pennsylvania 2
Port Arthur, Dairen, China 10

Port-au-Prince, Haiti 8
Portland, Oregon 3
Port Louis, Mauritius 10
Port Moresby, Papua,
    New Guinea 6
Port of Spain, Trinidad-
    Tobago 8
Porto (Oporto), Portugal 9
Poznan, Poland 10
Prague, Czechoslovakia 2
Pretoria, South Africa 7
Providence, Rhode Island 5
Puebla, Mexico 9
Pusan, South Korea 10
P'yongyang, North
    Korea 10

Quebec, Canada 1
Quezon City, Philippines 9
Quito, Ecuador 9

Rabat, Morocco 9
Rangoon, Burma 4
Rawalpindi, Pakistan 10
Recife, Brazil 10
Reykjavik, Iceland 6
Riga, USSR 9
Rio de Janeiro, Brazil 1
Riyadh, Saudi Arabia 10
Rochester, New York 5
Rome, Italy 1
Rostov, USSR 10
Rotterdam, Netherlands 1

Sacramento, California 4
Saigon, South Vietnam 1
St. Louis, Missouri 4
St. Paul, Minnesota 6
Sakai, Japan 10
Salisbury, Rhodesia 8
Salt Lake City, Utah 2
San Antonio, Texas 5

San Bernardino, California 7
San Diego, California 6
San Francisco, California 1
San Jose, California 5
San Jose, Costa Rica 8
San Juan, Puerto Rico 2
San Salvador, Salvador 7
Santiago, Chile 5
Santiago de Cuba, Cuba 10
Santo Domingo, Dominican
    Republic 6
Santos, Brazil 10
Sao Paulo, Brazil 7
Sapporo, Japan 10
Seattle, Washington 1
Seoul, South Korea 3
Seville, Spain 5
Shanghai, China 1
Sheffield, England 4
Singapore, Singapore 2
Skopje, Yugoslavia 10
Sofia, Bulgaria 6
Soochow, China 9
Stockholm, Sweden 1
Strasbourg, France 7
Stuttgart, West Germany 4
Suchow (Hsuchou),
    China 10
Sucre, Bolivia 10
Suez, Egypt 5
Suva, Fiji 8
Swansea, Wales 7
Sydney, Australia 1

Tabriz, Iran 10
Taipei, Taiwan 7
Tananarive, Madagascar 10
Tangier, Morocco 5
Tashkent, USSR 10
Tegucigalpa, Honduras 8
Teheran, Iran 4
Tel Aviv, Jaffa, Israel 3

Tenerife, Canary Islands 10
The Hague, Netherlands 5
Thessaloniki (Salonika),
    Greece 9
Tientsin, China 7
Tijuana, Mexico 7
Tokyo, Japan 1
Toronto, Canada 1
Toulouse, France 9
Trieste, Italy 7
Tripoli, Libya 8
Tunis, Tunisia 8
Turin, Italy 6

Ulan Bator, Mongolia 10
Utrecht, Netherlands 7

Valencia, Spain 5
Valletta, Malta 10
Valparaiso, Chile 6
Vancouver, Canada 1
Venice, Italy 1
Victoria, Canada 2
Vienna, Austria 1
Vientiane, Laos 9
Vladivostok, USSR 5
Volgograd (Stalingrad),
    USSR 6

Warsaw, Poland 1
Washington, DC 1
Wellington, New Zealand 1
Winnipeg, Canada 3

Yalta, USSR 2
Yokohama, Japan 2
Yonkers, New York 5
York, England 3

Zagreb, Yugoslavia 9
Zurich, Switzerland 2

Answers

New Year's Resolution
You would have saved 1,073,741,824 pennies (or $10,737,418.24)!

The Travellers' Dinner
The judge was correct. There were 8 loaves in all, and to divide them equally, each loaf was cut into thirds, giving a total of 24 parts. Each man then ate 8 parts, and the stranger paid with 8 coins of equal value. The Arab who had had 5 loaves (15 parts) consumed 8 himself and the other 7 went to the stranger. The Arab with 3 loaves (9 parts) ate 8 himself and so he contributed only 1 to the stranger. Accordingly, the coins should be divided 7 and 1, as the judge proclaimed.

Which Ones Are Garbles?
Melissa is a Garble.
Celestine is not a Garble.
Stephanie is a Garble.
Duke is not a Garble.
(All Garbles have a circle as part of their equipment.)

Divide the Camels
Since 17 is a quantity which you cannot divide into halves, thirds, or ninths, and 18 *is* divisible by 2, 3 and 9, the Pharaoh's solution was to lend the brothers one camel. Then the eldest son received 9, the second son 6, and the third 2. Since this added up to only 17 anyway, the Pharaoh immediately took back the camel he had lent them. (It happens that the father had made provision for only 17/18 of his estate—1/2 plus 1/3 plus 1/9 equals 17/18!)

Magic Fifteen

2	9	4
7	5	3
6	1	8

Send More Money
The letter M, because of its position in the bottom line, can only be a 1.

M also appears in the second line. That means that the letter S must be a large one, so that you have the 1 to carry over. S must be either 8 or 9; no other number would be large enough to work.

If S is 8 or 9, the letter O must be a 0; no other number would be small enough to work.

Looking at the next column, where O appears again, you know that 1 must be carried over—otherwise, E plus O would equal E. You can write this as E + 1 = N.

Looking at the next column, where N appears again, you can construct an equation:

N plus R—plus 1 (assuming* that a 1 is carried over)—equals E plus 10 (plus 10 because you know that 1 is carried over into the next column). So the equation becomes:

$$N + R + 1 = E + 10$$
$$N + R + 1 = N - 1 + 10$$
$$N + R = N - 2 + 10$$
$$N + R = N + 8$$
$$R = 8$$

*You are making only one assumption: that D and E in the first column add up to 10 or more, so that a 1 carries over into the next column. Assuming you are right, R is 8 (it is 9 if your assumption is wrong).

So, going along with this assumption, you know that D and E can't add up to 10 exactly because you have used up the 0. You know they can't add up to 11, because you've used up the 1. You have also used up the 8 (R) and the 9 (S). What is left?

D and E could be 7 and 6. They could be 7 and 5. But no other combinations are possible.

One of them is definitely 7. Can it be E? No, because then N would have to be 8, and you have already used up 8. Therefore D must be 7.

E must be 5. If E was 6, N would have to be 7, which is impossible because D is 7.

Y becomes 2, N becomes 6, and the sum works:

```
  9567
  1085
------
 10652
```

Cross-Country Tour

It looks as if you'll need a whole new set of four tires, doesn't it? But there's no reason to waste all that trunk space. Actually, you need only two spares. After 4,000 (6,400 km) miles you can remove the front tires and put on the two new spares. Then after 8,000 (12,800 km) miles, you remove the rear tires and replace them with the two taken off the front, and continue for the remaining 4,000 miles. But don't make any side trips!

Who Is the Avon Lady?

From (3) you know that Jill is the model. Therefore she cannot be the Avon lady (2) or the actress (5). You also know she cannot be the sculptor or the race car driver (1). Therefore she must be the private detective; it is the only possibility left.

You know that Tracy is not the race car driver (6). Therefore, she must be the sculptor, since the sculptor and the race car driver are different people (1). Since Tracy is the sculptor, she cannot be the actress, since the two are roommates (4).

Therefore, Liz is the actress and the race car driver, and Tracy must be the Avon lady.

What Is the Name of the Largest Rabbit in the World?

If Jim's leg has been in a cast for 2 months (2) he cannot be the owner of the baboon (3) or the rabbit (1) who just played soccer with his owner yesterday. Therefore, Jim is the owner of the penguin, whose name is Jarvis.

Since the baboon bit Marvin (4), the baboon must be Spot—and therefore Marvin is the largest rabbit in the world.

Which Ones Are Farfels?

Belinda is a Farfel.
Flo is a Farfel.
Dmitri is a Farfel.
Beauford is not a Farfel.
(All Farfels have hair on head or face.)

Russian Tunnel

Malenkov was *not* guessing. He reasoned this way: "I know the other two are smudged because I can see them. Either I am smudged or I am not smudged. If I am not smudged, then Molotov and Vishinsky raised their hands because each saw the other was smudged. So, if I am not smudged, each of the other two would know that he himself was smudged, and each would be able to drop his hand. They haven't done this, so I *must* be smudged."

Because of this incident, it is said, Stalin chose Malenkov as his successor.

Famous 45

8, 12, 5, 20. The result in each case is 10.

The Mailbox Mystery

The vice-president *mailed* the mailbox key, so the envelope containing it was deposited in the locked mailbox. It certainly was not the housekeeper's fault.

African Thinking Game

Every member of the Elephant tribe always tells the truth. Agassu, who says he is *not* an Elephant, cannot be an Elephant, whether he is telling the truth or lying.

Since every member of the Leopard tribe always lies, Agassu, who says he is not an Elephant, cannot be a Leopard. Agassu must therefore be a Crocodile.

We know that Coffi cannot be a Crocodile, because Agassu is a Crocodile. Therefore Coffi, who says he is not a Crocodile, is telling the truth. He cannot be a lying Leopard. He must be a truthful Elephant. And Diamala must be an Elephant, too, because truthful Coffi says so.

The Two Brothers

The brother simply said, "Let's swap horses!" The king's will stated that the son whose *horse* arrived second would get the fortune. Therefore, by riding the other one's horse, the winner of the race could be sure his own horse would be second at the castle gate. So they swapped and sped off.

The Wise King

The king provided that one son was to divide the possessions, while the other son was to have first choice!

Death Meets the Squire
If the squire died without waking, no one could possibly know what he had been dreaming.

Getting a Raise
Bob was smarter. Tom had actually asked for *less* money. Here's how it works: Tom would have received $10,000 the first year, $11,000 the second year, $12,000 the third year. On the other hand, Bob chose the $250 raise every six months, so he received $5000 for the first six months (half of the $10,000 salary) and $5250 for the second half year. Thus, in his first year, he received $250 more than Tom. In Bob's second year, he received $5,500 for the first six months and $5750 for the second half, a total of $11,250—again, more than Tom in the second year. In the third year, Bob made $6000 in the first half, and $6,250 in the second half—again $250 more than Tom. It is obvious why Bob became the boss' choice for his daughter's hand. Meanwhile, Susie eloped with a fellow named Rock.

Which Ones Are Nifties?
The Oaks is not a Niftie.
Leffanoe's Castle is a Niftie.
Charlie's Garage is not a Niftie.
The Church Tower is not a Niftie.
(All Nifties have 5 rectangular windows.)

Revolution in Platonia
The king was imprisoned; the prime minister was executed; the treasurer was freed.

Since all three men received different sentences, the king was not executed and the prime minister was not imprisoned.

The treasurer was freed because the other two men received different sentences.

Thus the king could not have been executed or freed, so he was imprisoned.

The prime minister must have received the remaining sentence and was therefore executed.

Who Wants to Work for King Sadim?
If the minister puts on the scale one nugget from the first province, two from the second, three from the third, four from the fourth, five from the fifth, and none from the sixth province, he can determine which province is guilty.

If the sixth province is guilty, the nuggets will weigh 240 ounces (6720 g), because each nugget on the scale will weigh 16 ounces (448 g).

If the fifth province is guilty, the scale will show 235 ounces (6580 g), for it will hold 10 16-ounce (448-g) nuggets and 5 15-ounce (420-g) nuggets. If the fourth province is guilty, the scale will show a weight of 236 ounces (6608 g), for it will hold 11 16-ounce (448-g) nuggets and 4 15-ounce (420-g) nuggets.

And so on. So if the minister observes the weight given by the scale, he will be able to identify the guilty province immediately and save his life.

In any case, he'd be wise to look for a new job.

Cannibals and Missionaries
In order not to have the cannibals outnumber the missionaries at any time, first the king rowed one cannibal across and then returned for a second cannibal. The cannibal king returned and two missionaries took the boat. One missionary returned, bringing a cannibal with him. All safe so far. Now a missionary went across with the king and brought back a cannibal. Then two missionaries rowed across, and the cannibal king took the boat. He went back for the other two cannibals, whom he ferried across in two round trips. Altogether, 13 trips were required.

The Casket and the Basket
The king began correctly. When the prince got into the basket, he caused the basket with the casket to rise. The casket was taken out, and the queen got into the basket, causing the prince to rise as she descended. Then both the queen and prince stepped out, and the casket was lowered again. The queen got in with the casket (110 plus 80 pounds (55 + 40 kg)) and rose as the king descended. The

king stayed on the ground; the queen stepped out and lowered the casket again. The prince went down, bringing up the casket once more. The queen removed the casket, got into the basket herself and descended, bringing up the prince. Both queen and prince stepped out. Then the prince lowered the casket, stepped into the other basket and descended, bringing up the casket to the empty tower. When the prince stepped out, the basket with the casket fell to the ground, and the royal family escaped with all its jewels!

The Tennis Nut
This problem contains extraneous information. Rodney has played 46 matches since July 1st, 26 of them on weekdays. Therefore, 20 weekend matches have been played. On the weekends two matches a day were played, so a total of ten weekend days has elapsed. In all, 26 + 10 = 36 days which have elapsed since July 1st. So yesterday was August 5th, today is the 6th, and when Rodney sees his boss today he's going to get the axe. He has no time at all.

Which are Krippies?
June is a Krippie.
The Watch is not a Krippie.
The Pansy is a Krippie.
The Dragonfly is not a Krippie.
(All Krippies are girls' names.)

Coffee, Tea for Three
If Abigail orders coffee, then Bridget's and Claudia's orders must be the same. So there are four possibilities:

	Abigail orders	Bridget orders	Claudia orders
1.	coffee	coffee	coffee
2.	coffee	tea	tea
3.	tea	coffee	coffee
4.	tea	tea	tea

If Bridget orders coffee, then Abigail's order must be different from Claudia's. In case 1, it isn't. So you can eliminate that possibility.

If Claudia orders tea, then Abigail's order must be the same as Bridget's. In case 2 it isn't, so you can eliminate that possibility.

Which leaves only 3 and 4 as possibilities, and Abigail is the only one who orders the same drink in each case.

Therefore, Abigail always orders the same drink (tea) after dinner.

The Dressing Room Murder

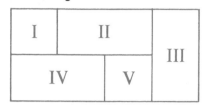

From (4) we know that neither Babe nor Clay occupies dressing room II.

From (1) we know Vera does not occupy dressing room II.

Suppose Adam occupies dressing room II: then, from (3) we have the following possibilities (A represents Adam, C represents Clay and D represents Dawn):

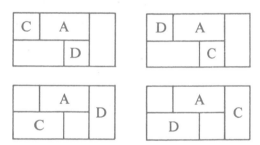

But we can see from (2) that every one of these cases is impossible.

Therefore Dawn occupies dressing room II.

Then, from (3), one of the following situations must exist:

But, from (2), the first of these situations is impossible. Therefore, the second situation is the correct one, and, from (2), Vera occupies dressing room IV.

Then, from (4), Babe occupies dressing room I. Therefore, Adam occupies dressing room V, and, from (1), Adam killed Vera.

The Mutilated Dictionary

Each page has 25 entries, 11 of which have been mutilated. This leaves 14 entries intact and lying between the first five and last six entries on each page.

In every group of 14 entries there are exactly two illustrations, for three illustrations occupy at least 15 entries, while one illustration occupies at most 13 entries.

Since there are two illustrations remaining on each of the book's 632 pages, there must be 2 × 632 or 1,264 illustrations left.

Madness at the Bike Shop

Since each vehicle has two pedals, there are altogether 136 ÷ 2 or 68 vehicles. If X is the number of bicycles and Y is the number of tricycles, then:

$$X + Y = 68$$

Since each bicycle has two wheels and each tricycle has three wheels, the total number of wheels must be

$$2X + 3Y$$

But this number equals 153.

We know that 2X and 2Y equals 2 × 68 or 136. Therefore the 3rd Y must be 153 − 136 or 17. And X is 51.

There are 51 bicycles and 17 tricycles.

Which Ones Are Paraglops?

Ralph is a Paraglop.
Rapunzel is a Paraglop.
Leonard is not a Paraglop.
Judy is a Paraglop.
(All Paraglops wear some kind of decoration.)

Not Comin' Through the Rye

			4	5 E
1W				
2E	3S		W	6 S
W			east	
west		E		10W
	south			
7 S	8 E	9 W	S	11 E	12 S

From (3):

No two of the L-shaped fields are the same kind of field. These can be assigned letters, such as east—E, west—W, and south—S, to represent either corn, wheat or rye. Then E, W and S can be assigned to the fields surrounding them by alternating W and S around the east L-shaped field; alternating E and S around the west L-shaped field; and alternating E and W around the south L-shaped field. Then 1 is a W field, 5 is an E field, and 12 is an S field.

From (1) and (2) and inspection of the plan, the only possible route involves fields 6–S, 4–W, 3–S, west L-shaped, south L-shaped, 10–W and 12–S.

So, from (2), each E field is a rye field, and the east L-shaped field is a rye field.

The Terrible Tic-Tac-Toe Players

1	2	3
4	5	6
7	8	9

The square above has been numbered for convenience' sake in solving the puzzle.

We know, from (3), that the seventh mark must be placed in square 5. So the sixth mark must have been placed in a line already containing two of the opponent's marks—in either square 7 or square 9. Otherwise, either X or O would have been placed in square 5.

But we know from (3) that the sixth mark could not have been placed in square 7. If it had been, square 5 would have been filled with an O. So the sixth mark was placed in square 9 and was X.

Then we know from (1) that the seventh mark will be O in square 5 and, from (2), that O wins the game.

Which are Ribbles?

Ivan is a Ribble.
Lynn is not a Ribble.
The Baron is a Ribble.
Mrs. Hyde is not a Ribble.
(All Ribbles keep their mouths shut.)

The Cat Disappears
You have just found your blind spot. Everyone has one. It is the spot where the optic nerve cord leaves your eye, and there are no nerve cells to register an image. If you use both eyes as you look at the dog, you won't have a blind spot. The image from your left eye will make up for the blank in your right.

Count the Cubes
Both. There are 8 cubes with black tops or 7 cubes with white bottoms. It depends on how you look at it.

Changing Images
It depends upon whether you place your attention on the dark or light color. Either one can be the background.

The Three Movie Buffs
They are all the same height. The man at the right looks tallest. We expect things to look smaller when they are farther away. The man at the right is farthest away and we would expect him to look the smallest. Since he doesn't, we assume he's really larger than the others.

Goofy Geometry
a. Nothing. It is an exact circle, but when it is broken by other lines, our eyes are distracted and follow the new lines instead of the original circle.

b. No. Our eyes cannot separate the figure from the intercepting arcs. Nevertheless, it is a perfect square.

What's on White?
Grey dots appear at the point where white meets white. The white lines look brightest when they contrast with the black areas. When white meets white, therefore, they are less bright, and the grey dots show up.

The Fence
Inside the black squares, you see an even blacker lattice design! Why?

After you concentrate on a picture for a while, your eyes get tired. The most tired parts are certain spots on the "retina," the part of the eye which contains light-sensitive cells. The brightest tones cause the greatest stress to these cells, which gradually become less sensitive to light. When you look away from the white lines, the nerve-ends which are *less* tired lightly reproduce the darker sections of the picture. Your eye transforms a negative into a positive. Here you have become tired of seeing the white lines. Your eyes record the black instead, when you shift your attention.

The Warped Bars
They are perfectly straight.

Nightmare Forest
They are straight. Tilt the book all the way back and you'll have proof!

The Mad Hat
They are the same. Usually we overestimate vertical distances, whether it's the distance from a house roof to a plane or just the drawing on the page.

Cut-Outs
"A" seems larger, but they are both the same size. Our tendency is to compare the base of "B" with the top arch of "A".

Your Hidden Hosts
There are two. One is on top, in the drapes; his wife is in the leaves of the potted palm.

The Unsure Lines
a. Yes, but when you break a straight line with a solid bar, the straight line seems displaced.

b. "B" is the continuation of "A." "C" looks as though it connects with "A" because the solid bar "displaces" the line.

Find the Hidden Shapes

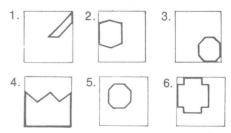

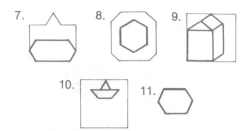

7. 8. 9.

10. 11.

Upside-Down Displays
1. HI
2. OBOE
3. EEL
4. HE IS BOSS
5. SHELL OIL
6. ESSO OIL
7. SILO
8. SOS
9. LOBO
10. BELLE
11. HISSES
12. HILL
13. HELLO
14. LOLLI (POP)
15. HOHOHO

The Calculator Murders
Most of the names can be read upside down on the calculator.

Lise Bell—77383517
Hi Bishel—73451814
Max Carty—none
Lil Ellis—51773717
Bill Hess—55347718
Bobo Hill—77140808
Elsie Lee—33731573
Eli Shill—77145173
Bob Sobel—73805808
Ollie Sol—70531770

This list suggests that Max Carty is the culprit, and his motive is that his name cannot be read on a calculator, which makes him feel rejected. Since the first victim had the lowest number, and the second victim the next lowest number, it would seem that Bill Hess is the next person in line.

More Upside-Down Displays
1. ISLE
2. BLISS
3. BILLS
4. HEEL, SOLE
5. HE SOBS
6. BLESSES
7. BIBLE
8. HOSE
9. ILL
10. SHE LIES
11. BOIL
12. EBBS
13. BEES
14. HOBBIES

Treasure Hunt by Calculator
1. DOORBELL
2. 3507 = CLOSET
3. 708451 = FISHBOWL
4. 114 = HI-FI
5. 700500 = FOOTSTOOL
6. 771501 = WINDOWSILL
7. 371800 = AUTOMOBILE
8. 407378 = TABLECLOTH
9. 3807 = GLOBE
10. 378330 = COFFEE TABLE
11. 53557 = GLASSES
12. 345451 = DISHWASHER
13. 35008 = BOOKCASE
14. 45105 = SOAPDISH
15. 5571007 = LOOKING GLASS

Test Your Visual Memory—#1
There are 64 possible points in each test. For each omitted word, deduct 2 points. For each word out of original order, deduct 1 point.

54 or better   Excellent
48 to 54   Good
40 to 48   Fair
Less   You can improve your memory with practice. Take a look at the memory system on page 122.

Test Your Visual Memory—#2
Some—but not all—of the forms you studied on page 141 are repeated below. On a separate sheet of paper list by number those you think are repeated, then confirm your selection by consulting page 141 and score yourself.

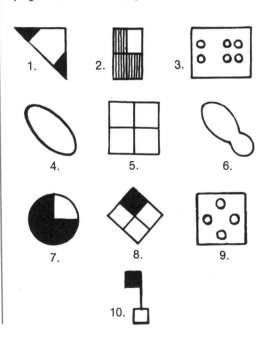

0 or 1 mistake	Excellent visual memory
2 or 3	Good
4	Fair
5 or more	Poor

Test Your Visual Memory—#3

If top and bottom lines are symmetrical and parallel ...... 2 credits

If your drawing follows the same design, a spread-formed letter M .... 2 credits

If you placed the 2 small circles correctly .... 2 credits

If you had the 2 small circles but placed them incorrectly ... 1 credit

If you used double lines in making the form of the letter M 2 credits

If you placed the 2 long dashes correctly .... 2 credits

If you have the 2 dashes but placed incorrectly................. 1 credit

10 credits	Excellent
9 credits	Good
8 credits	Fair
Less	Your memory needs training.

Test Your Visual Memory—#4

For carefully drawn oblong... 1 credit

For circle symmetrically placed within oblong .... 1 credit

For symmetrically drawn square within the circle, four corners *touching* the circle...... 2 credits

For crisscross lines within the square .... 1 credit

For straight line bisecting the square and touching the circle top and bottom .... 2 credits

7 credits	Excellent
6 credits	Good
5 credits	Fair
Less	Poor

Test Your Observation—#1

Allow yourself 4 minutes to answer the following questions about the scene of the accident. Then check your answers with the picture on page 143 and allow yourself 1 point for each answer that is essentially correct.

1. What was the date?
2. The approximate time?
3. Bus number?
4. What was the name of the taxi company?
5. Describe damage to taxi.
6. Could bus damage be described from your vantage point?
7. Did bus driver appear injured?
8. Describe apparent injuries to taxi driver.
9. Name on the ambulance?
10. In which direction was the taxi going?
11. In which direction was the bus going?
12. Describe the apparent point of impact.
13. Which vehicle struck the other?
14. What local news event was posted?
15. Name the newspaper building in the scene.
16. Name the hotel.
17. Describe the vehicle stopped behind the taxi.
18. Name the two streets at the intersection.
19. Name the shop at the intersection.
20. Give the bus's license number.

15 to 20	Good
12 to 14	Fair
Less	Poor

Test Your Observation—#2

Score one point for each correct item. Deduct one point for any item you included which is not actually in the scene. The picture contains 33 items.

boy	clock	vase
girl	mantel	barometer
kitten	small table	lamp
dog	large table	book
tricycle	rug	drapes
doll	picture	curtains
candlestick	birdcage	guitar
mirror	door	ashtray
window	television set	shade
fireplace	flowers	electric outlet
chairs	cushion	dish

25 or more	Excellent
21 to 24	Good
18 to 20	Fair
Less	Poor

Test Your Knowledge of Word Meanings—#1

1. Gradual........ sudden (opposite)

2. Vapid .... insipid (same)
3. Querulous...... uncomplaining
(opposite)
4. Devout .... impious (opposite)
5. Contemptible.. despicable (same)
6. Energetic ...... apathetic (opposite)
7. Gaunt............ haggard (same)
8. Eternal .... temporary (opposite)
   7 or 8 correct   Excellent
   6   Good
   Less   Poor vocabulary power

Test Your Knowledge of Word Meanings—#2

1. Envious ... covetous (same)
2. Reserved... reticent (same)
3. Identical ... heterogeneous (opposite)
4. Moderate... extreme (opposite)
5. Romantic... prosaic (opposite)
6. Liberal...... generous (same)
7. Round ...... circular (same)
8. Cruel ...... vicious (same)
   Scoring is the same as before.

Test Your Reasoning—#1

1. 12.
2. The early bird catches the worm.
3. 2 5 3 6 5 8 1 4 6 9.
4. The sun, since the earth revolves around the sun.
5. 3.
6. (c).
7. (c).
8. It is usually very *difficult* to become *acquainted* with people who are *very* timid. (Note: any similar words, such as *excessively* instead of *very*, are acceptable, if they make the same general sense.)
9. First line calls for 2 and 1. Next line calls for 1 and 1/3.
   8 or 9 correct   Excellent
   7   Good
   6   Satisfactory
   5 or less   Poor

Test Your Reasoning—#2

1. Change 65 to 64, since the series is being raised by multiplying each number by 2.
2. Change 15 to 16, since the series is the successive squares of 2.
3. (c).
4. (c).
5. While the cat's away, the mice will play.

6. (d).
7. (a).
8. A reasonable *amount* of sleep is usually *required* if a person is to *maintain* a high *degree* of efficiency. (Note: any similar words, such as *needed* instead of *required*, are acceptable, if they make the same general sense.)
9. (d).
   Scoring is the same as before.

Are You Thorough?—#1

1. 1 and 16   5. 2 and 20
2. 5 and 7 and 18 6. 8
3. 9   7. 10
4. 3 and 19
For each *exactly* correct answer allow yourself a credit of 2 points.
   12 or more credits Excellent
   10 or 11 credits   Good
   9   Fair
   Less   You worked either too quickly or too carelessly.

Are You Thorough?—#2

1. 15   5. 11
2. 4 and 17   6. none
3. 14 and 21   7. 12
4. 6 and 13
Scoring is the same as before.

Test Your Artistic Perception

1. mouth
2. eye
3. nose
4. spoon in right hand
5. chimney through roof (no credit for smoke)
6. ear
7. filament wires
8. stamp
9. strings
10. rivet at other end of knife
11. trigger
12. tail
13. leg on left side (not a claw)
14. one cat's shadow
15. a bowling ball for the man, placed in his hand
16. net
17. left arm
18. knob on television set
19. hand and powder puff in mirror
20. diamond in upper left of card

16–20 right	Excellent
14 or 15 right	Good
12 or 13 right	Fair
Less	Poor

Test Your Sense of Word Relationships—#1

The following words have the least association with the word groups of the test. If you're in doubt about them, consult the dictionary. Vocabulary as well as general knowledge was involved in this test.

1. grapefruit (not a meal)
2. tiger (not domestic)
3. letter (not printed)
4. recline (the least in degree toward slumber)
5. tree (a single thing)
6. hen (other three are more closely related)
7. New York (not a country)
8. whimper (a subdued sound)
9. stockings (not in the shoe family)
10. picture (smallest, most limited in size)
11. Sun (not a planet)
12. dawn (the others are P.M.)

12 correct	Excellent
10 or 11	Good
8 or 9	Fair
Under 8	Poor

Test Your Sense of Word Relationships—#2

The following words have the least association with the word groupings of the test:

1. atoll (the others are wet grounds)
2. current (the others are necessarily wind manifestations)
3. grudging (unwilling)
4. superfluous (unnecessary)
5. curare (a poison)
6. water (not an element)
7. Tauri (a constellation, not a single star)
8. civet (a carnivorous cat, not cattle)
9. ulna (a bone, not a muscle of the body)
10. pelvis (not a bone of the leg)
11. Darwin (not a religious leader)
12. parishioner (not of the priesthood)

10 or more	Excellent
8 or 9	Good
6 or 7	Fair
Less	Try to improve your word power.

Test Your Sense of Word Relationships—#3

1. suitcase
2. see
3. statue
4. cars
5. climax
6. quantity
7. cows
8. prediction

7 or 8 correct	Excellent
6	Good
Less	Poor word power

Test Your Sense of Word Relationships—#4

1. rose
2. duet
3. caution
4. orchestra
5. suffocation
6. time
7. originate
8. knee

Scoring is the same as before.

Test Your Comprehension

1. (j) and (l)
2. (f) and (k)
3. (b) and (h)
4. (e) and (g)
5. (c) and (i)
6. (d) and (m)
7. (a) and (n)

13 or 14 right	Excellent
11 or 12	Good
10	Fair
Less	Insufficient grasp of what you read

Test Your Mathematical Judgment

1. $30,000
2. 30
3. $3.25
4. $0.40
5. 28

All 5 correct	Excellent
4 correct	Good
Less than 4	Poor mathematical judgment

Test Your Sense of Number Relationships—#1

A. 31 (Rule: add 2, deduct 2; add 3, deduct 3; add 4, etc.).
B. 1 (Rule: repeat twice, deduct 2; repeat twice, deduct 2).
C. 7 (Rule: add 2, add 2, add 2; then deduct 2, deduct 2, etc.).

D. 27 (Rule: multiply by 3, divide by 2, multiply by 1; repeat).

E. 18 (Rule: add 1, deduct 2, add 3, deduct 4, etc.).

F. 39 (Rule: add 3, add 6, add 9, etc.).

All correct	Excellent
5 right	Good
4 right	Fair
Less	Poor mathematical comprehension

Test Your Sense of Number Relationships—#2

A. 1 (Rule: add 1, add 1, deduct 2; repeat).

B. 20 (Rule: divide by 2, add 5; repeat).

C. 40 (Rule: add 3 each time).

D. 8 (Rule: divide by 2, add 4; repeat).

E. 38 (Rule: multiply by 2, subtract 3; repeat).

F. 2 (Rule: deduct 3, divide by 2; deduct 4, divide by 2; deduct 5, divide by 2, etc.).

Scoring is the same as for the previous test.

Test Your Sense of Number Relationships—#3

A. 17 (Rule: add 3, divide by 3, multiply by 2; repeat).

B. 0 (Rule: deduct 4, add 2, divide by 3; repeat).

C. 10 (Rule: add 3, deduct 1, add zero; repeat).

D. 22 (Rule: add 1, add 3, add 6; repeat).

E. 19 (Rule: add 2, deduct 3, add 4, deduct 5, etc.).

F. 15 (Rule: add 1, deduct 2, multiply by 3, divide by 4; repeat).

Scoring is the same as for the previous tests.

Test Your Sense of Number Relationships—#4

A. 3 (Rule: divide by 2, deduct 2; repeat).

B. 8 (Rule: divide by 3, multiply by 2; repeat).

C. 34 (Rule: deduct 8's).

D. 20 (Rule: deduct 1, add 2; deduct 2, add 3; deduct 3, add 4, etc.).

E. 12 (Rule: add 3, deduct 2; repeat).

F. 14 (Rule: add 2, add 2, deduct 2; repeat).

Scoring is the same as for the previous tests.

Are You a Good Organizer?—#1

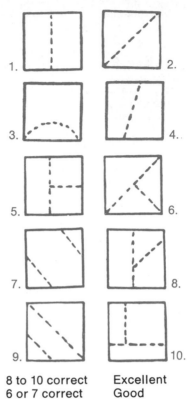

8 to 10 correct	Excellent
6 or 7 correct	Good
5 correct	Fair
Less	Poor

Are You a Good Organizer?—#2

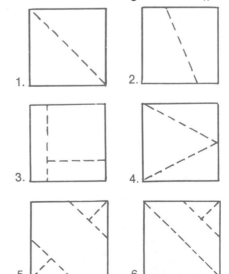

5 or 6 right	Excellent
4 right	Good
3 right	Fair
Less	Poor

Scoring for Visual Analysis Tests 1 Through 5

5 correct	Excellent
4	Good
Less	You need to analyze your problems more carefully.

Visual Analysis Test—#1
Line 1. Figure 2
Line 2. Figure 2
Line 3. Figure 5
Line 4. Figure 4
Line 5. Figure 1
For scoring, see previous page.

Visual Analysis Test—#2
Line 1. Figure 3
Line 2. Figure 5
Line 3. Figure 1
Line 4. Figure 2
Line 5. Figure 4

Visual Analysis Test—#3
Line 1. Figure 4
Line 2. Figure 4
Line 3. Figure 4
Line 4. Figure 2
Line 5. Figure 2

Visual Analysis Test—#4
Line 1. Figure 4
Line 2. Figure 3
Line 3. Figure 3
Line 4. Figure 3
Line 5. Figure 1

Visual Analysis Test—#5
Line 1. Figure 5
Line 2. Figure 3
Line 3. Figure 4
Line 4. Figure 4
Line 5. Figure 5

How Wide-Ranging Is Your Knowledge?—#1
1. biology
2. canoeing
3. dancing
4. furniture
5. singing
6. painting
7. architecture
8. economics
9. rope making
10. electricity
11. television
12. measuring earth tremors
13. gasoline production
14. steel industry
15. physics
16. algebra
17. literature

16 or more	Excellent
14 or 15	Good
12 or 13	Fair
Less	Unsatisfactory (start reading!)

How Wide-Ranging Is Your Knowledge?—#2
1. music (instruments)
2. grammar
3. stamp collecting
4. literature or poetry
5. mythology
6. religion
7. history
8. philosophy
9. gold mining
10. explorations
11. bridge building
12. medicine
13. dentistry
14. sailing, boating
15. music
16. zoology (fish life)
17. racing

16 or more	Excellent
14 or 15	Good
12 or 13	Fair
Less	Try a more varied reading diet.

Test Your Concentration #1
There were 24 pairs of numbers to be circled:

				Total
(a) (9 1)	(2 8)	(3 7)		3
(b) (6 4)	(8 2)			2
(c) (3 7)	(2 8)			2
(d) (5 5)	(2 8)	(7 3)	(9 1)	4
(e) (2 8)	(3 7)			2
(f) (3 7)				1
(g) (3 7)	(8 2)	(4 6)	(5 5)	4
(h) (8 2)	(3 7)	(4 6)		3

(i) (5 5) (9 1)   2
(j) (1 9)   1
     20 or more   Excellent
     18 or 19   Good
     16 or 17   Fair
     Less   Poor concentration

Test Your Concentration—#2
93 — 86 — 79 — 72 — 65 — 58 — 51
44 — 37 — 30 — 23 — 16 — 9 — 2

Test Your Concentration—#3
49 — 47 — 46 — 44 — 43 — 41 — 40 —
38 — 37 — 35 — 34 — 32 — 31 — 29 —
28 — 26 — 25 — 23 — 22 — 20 — 19 —
17 — 16 — 14 — 13 — 11 — 10 — 8 —
7 — 5 — 4 — 2 — 1

Test Your Concentration—#4
1. IF YOU
2. DO WELL THE
3. MINOR TASKS
4. WHICH YOU
5. ARE CALLED
6. UPON
7. TO PERFORM YOU
8. WILL HAVE BUT LITTLE
9. DIFFICULTY WITH
10. THE BIGGER ONES
     20 or more   Excellent
     18 or 19   Good
     16 or 17   Fair
     Less   Try harder to disregard
                   extraneous disturbances.

Test Your Imagination—#1
A: Three men in a tub.
B: The owl and the pussycat getting
   ready to set out to sea.
C: Humpty Dumpty in the act of taking his
   great fall.
D: Little Bo Peep's sheep coming home,
   dragging their tails behind them.
   All 4 correct, Excellent.
   Anything different, good.
   "I don't know" answers, read Mother
Goose.

Test Your Imagination—#2
A: Dog (or cat) entering a room.
B: Ocean as seen from a porthole.
C: Three blind mice.
D: Small garage; long car.

All 4 correct, Excellent.
Anything different, good.
"I don't know" answers, relax your
   imagination.

Test Your Mechanical Comprehension—#1
1. A, transmitting its energy to B, will
   tend to come to rest.
2. The greater absorption of the radiant
   energy of the sunlight by the black
   jacket will cause the snow under it to
   melt faster.
3. The far smaller square footage of
   parachute B will cause it to descend
   faster, despite the lighter weight.
4. Shaft B will turn faster.
5. Gear C will move in direction B.
   Scoring: anything less than 4 correct
shows poor mechanical understanding.

Test Your Mechanical Comprehension—#2
1. Bottle A is the colder.
2. The ball will move in direction C.
3. Gear C.
4. The job is easier for B.
5. Windlass A.

Are You Accurate?—#1
The following pairs are the correct
answers (the same):
1, 3, 4, 6, 10, 11, 13, 16, 17, 18, 20, 24, 25.
For unfinished numbers count $\frac{1}{2}$. For
errors count 1 point.
     Debit of 0 to 3   Excellent
     Debit of 4 to 6   Good
     Debit of 7 or 8   Fair
     Debit over 8   Too careless

Are You Accurate?—#2
The following pairs are the correct answers (the same):
1, 4, 7, 8, 9, 12, 16, 18, 19, 20, 23, 24.
Scoring is the same as before.

Are You Precise?—#1
1 5 4 2 7 6 3 5 7 2 8 5 4 6 3 7 2 8 1
⌐ ∪ ⌐ ⋀ ∧ ○ ⌐ ∪ ∧ ⋀ ⨯ ∪ ⌐ ○ ⊐ ∧ ⋀ ⨯ ⌐
              9 5 8 4 7 3
            = ∪ ⨯ ⌐ ∧ ⊐
6 2 5 1 9 2 8 3 7 4 6 5 9 4 8 3 7 2 6
○ ⋀ ∪ ⌐ = ⋀ ⨯ ⊐ ∧ ⌐ ○ ∪ = ⌐ ⨯ ⊐ ∧ ⋀ ○
              1 5 4 6 3 7
            ⌐ ∪ ⌐ ○ ⊐ ∧

45 to 50   Excellent
40 to 45   Good
35 to 40   Satisfactory
Less   You need to concentrate more when you do detail work.

Are You Precise?—#2

3 1 2 1 3 2 1 4 2 3 5 2 9 1 4
ꓱ - И - ꓱИ - L И ꓱ U И = - L

6 3 1 5 4 2 7 6 3 8 7 2 9 5 4
O ꓱ - U L И ∧ O ꓱ X ∧ И = U L

6 3 7 2 8 1 9 5 8 4 7 3 6 9 5
O ꓱ ∧ И X - = U X L ∧ ꓱ O = U

Score yourself on the number of seconds it took you, but add 2 seconds for each incorrect symbol.

Under 90 seconds   Excellent
90 to 100 seconds   Good
100 to 120 seconds   Fair
120 or more   You need to concentrate more on detail work.

Are You Precise?—#3

1 9 2 8 3 7 4 6 5 9 4 8 5 7 6
- = И X ꓱ ∧ L O U = L X U ∧ O

9 3 8 6 4 1 5 7 2 6 2 4 8 1 3
= ꓱ X O L - U ∧ И O И L X ꓵ ꓱ

4 9 5 1 7 5 2 6 9 3 7 8 4 1 8
L = U - ∧ U И O = ꓱ ∧ X L - X

Scoring is the same as before.

Test Your Space Perception

1. **124** (⊕ ⊊ ꓘ)   4. 4
2. 9 o'clock   5. 1 : 15
3. 4   6. **"ℰ" ("℈")**

5 or 6   Excellent
4   Good
3   Fair
Less   Poor

How Is Your Manual Dexterity?

Count 1 point for each tap correctly made. Deduct 2 points for each error. Count each of these as errors:

a box you skipped
two dots in same box
dot striking a line

96 or more   Excellent
86 to 96   Good
80 to 84   Fair
Less   Poor

Test Your Sense of Spatial Relationships

(a) 27   (g) 10
(b) 15   (h) 22
(c) 15   (i) 13
(d) 18   (j) 20
(e) 19   (k) 50
(f) 40

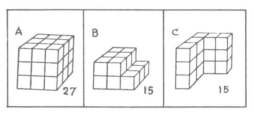

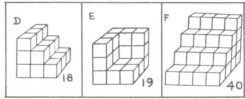

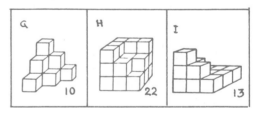

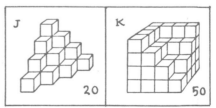

10 or 11 piles correctly figured   Excellent
8 or 9   Good
7   Fair
Less   Poor

Office Machine Aptitude Test—#1

1.	6	0	3	2	9.	4	0	1	5
2.	2	8	9	1	10.	0	3	6	1
3.	1	6	7	4	11.	1	7	1	6
4.	3	4	1	0	12.	1	2	3	1
5.	2	7	0	9	13.	5	2	3	5
6.	1	4	0	3	14.	6	9	3	5
7.	7	1	3	2	15.	4	1	4	9
8.	5	8	0	9					

If all 4 numbers on a line are correct, give yourself 1 credit. Deduct 1 credit from your total for any line containing 1 or more mistakes. Deduct $\frac{1}{2}$ credit for each line not completed.

14 or more	Excellent
11 to 13	Good
8 to 10	Fair
Less	Poor

Office Machine Aptitude Test—#2

1.	1	4	8	2	9.	3	6	9	1
2.	1	0	3	4	10.	7	4	5	6
3.	1	3	5	3	11.	4	2	6	7
4.	2	3	9	5	12.	6	3	0	4
5.	1	5	8	5	13.	8	2	3	7
6.	5	0	9	2	14.	5	9	3	0
7.	4	9	0	4	15.	7	2	4	3
8.	5	8	0	1					

Scoring is the same as the previous test.

Copyreading Aptitude Test—#1
The following lines contain errors:

1   2   4   6   7   9   10   11   13   14

Copyreading Aptitude Test—#2
The following lines contain errors:
1 2 3 4 6 7 9 10 11 12 15
Scoring for both tests: More than 3 errors in either test means that you are a careless copyreader. You can overcome this with practice.

Pattern Visualization Tests

Test—No. 1	1 and 3
Test—No. 2	2 (only)
Test—No. 3	1 (only)
Test—No. 4	1 and 2
Test—No. 5	3 (only)
Test—No. 6	1, 4 and 5
Test—No. 7	1 and 2
Test—No. 8	2 and 3

On the overall test of 8 pattern figures with 14 possible correct figures, credit yourself with 2 points for each correct figure picked but debit yourself with 1 point for each incorrect figure picked.

20 or better	Excellent
16 to 19	Good
12 to 15	Fair
Lower	Not everyone can visualize this way!

Literature—Quiz 1

Two-Point Questions
1. "Gone with the Wind."
2. Rudyard Kipling.
3. "The Legend of Sleepy Hollow."
4. "Black Beauty."

Three-Point Questions
1. Edgar Allan Poe.
2. "Gulliver's Travels" (which satirizes the faults of mankind through the Lilliputians and the Brobdingnagians).
3. Beau Brummel (real). Lady Godiva (real). George Babbitt (fictional—in Sinclair Lewis' novel). Cyrano de Bergerac (fictional—Edmond Rostand's play). Minnehaha (fictional—Henry W. Longfellow's poem). Copernicus (real).
4. Carl Sandburg.

Five-Point Questions
1. Robin Hood (who was allegedly born in Locksley, in Nottinghamshire, in the 12th century).
2. That the murderer had written the German word for revenge.
3. Dante's great love was Beatrice (Portinari).
4. The Fallen Angel was Satan; his children, Sin and Death.

Literature—Quiz 2

Two-Point Questions
1. "Kidnapped"
2. Jules Verne
3. "Don Quixote"
4. Sherlock Holmes

Three-Point Questions
1. "Utopia."
2. "Pilgrim's Progress," an allegory based on the adventures of Christian on his way from the City of Destruction to the Celestial City.

3. King Arthur.
4. Eugene O'Neill.

Five-Point Questions
1. Mrs. Malaprop.
2. "Robinson Crusoe" by Daniel Defoe.
3. (a) George Eliot (Mary Ann Evans),
   (b) Jane Austen,
   (c) Jan Struther.
4. "Ulysses" by James Joyce.

Literature—Quiz 3

Two-Point Questions
1. Oliver Twist.
2. Aesop.
3. Gilbert and Sullivan.
4. "Beware the Ides of March" (March 15).

Three-Point Questions
1. Abou Ben Adhem (in Leigh Hunt's poem).
2. Enoch Arden.
3. Edgar Allan Poe's "The Gold Bug."
4. The Elizabethan Age.

Five-Point Questions
1. "The House of the Seven Gables."
2. "Il Penseroso" and "L'Allegro."
3. Bassanio chose the lead casket.
4. "Strange Interlude."

Literature—Quiz 4

Two-Point Questions
1. O. Henry.
2. The Ancient Mariner of Coleridge's poem of that title: "Water, water everywhere, nor any drop to drink."
3. Dr. Fu Manchu.
4. The series that began with "Tarzan of the Apes."

Three-Point Questions
1. "The Sea Wolf" (Jack London).
2. "Ivanhoe" (Sir Walter Scott).
3. Gopher Prairie.
4. Grover's Corners.

Five-Point Questions
1. Jefferson.
2. (a) Mexico.
   (b) Poland.

3. (a) Peru.
   (b) France.
4. (a) Pantagruel.
   (b) Gargantua.

"Bad Guys"—Quiz 1

Two-Point Questions
1. Frankenstein's Monster.
2. John Dillinger.
3. Mr. Hyde.
4. Al Capone.

Three-Point Questions
1. William Bligh.
2. Macbeth.
3. Mephistopheles.
4. Rasputin.

Five-Point Questions
1. Billy the Kid.
2. Heydrich the Hangman (Reichsprotektor Reinhard Heydrich).
3. Blackbeard.
4. Israel Hands.

"Bad Guys"—Quiz 2

Two-Point Questions
1. Nero.
2. Sitting Bull.
3. Scrooge.
4. Attila.

Three-Point Questions
1. Iago.
2. Jean Lafitte.
3. Fagin.
4. The Devil.

Five-Point Questions
1. Javert.
2. General Zaroff.
3. Niccolo Machiavelli.
4. The Duke of Alva.

Mythology—Quiz 1

Two-Point Questions
1. Atlas.
2. Aurora Borealis.
3. Centaurs.
4. Love (also beauty and fruitfulness).

Three-Point Questions
1. He overcame her greater speed by tossing three golden apples in her path as she ran. She stopped to pick them up.
2. The Augean Stables.
3. Three-headed Cerberus.
4. Circe.

Five-Point Questions
1. The winged horse, Pegasus.
2. Caduceus, a winged staff entwined by two serpents.
3. Charon.
4. The father was Daedalus, the son Icarus. Icarus' wings melted when he flew too near the sun.

Mythology—Quiz 2

Two-Point Questions
1. Cupid.
2. The Golden Fleece.
3. Hercules.
4. Olympus, a mountain in Macedonia.

Three-Point Questions
1. Cyclopes (plural for Cyclops).
2. Alexander the Great.
3. Narcissus.
4. Janus, the god of doorways and entrances (January was named after him).

Five-Point Questions
1. Because Pluto, who had stolen and married her, had tricked her into eating a pomegranate there, thus making Hades her home.
2. Hector was the great Trojan hero. When he killed Achilles' friend Patroclus, Achilles slew Hector and dragged his body around the walls of Troy.
3. Proteus, from whose name we got the word "protean."
4. The Minotaur, a half-man, half-bull monster.

Mythology—Quiz 3

Two-Point Questions
1. Achilles.
2. Helen of Troy.
3. Bacchus.
4. River Styx.

Three-Point Questions
1. He was shot in the heel with a poisoned arrow by Paris.
2. The Argonauts.
3. Siegfried.
4. Thor (Thursday was named after him).

Five-Point Questions
1. Theseus.
2. (a) Menelaus.
   (b) Paris of Troy.
3. Perseus was able to behead Medusa by looking at her in the reflection of his bright shield.
4. Tantalus (hence, our word "tantalize").

The Bible—Quiz 1

Two-Point Questions
1. Goliath.
2. John the Baptist.
3. Jerusalem.
4. Jonah.

Three-Point Questions
1. Sea of Galilee.
2. Abraham (or Abram).
3. Saul of Tarsus.
4. At Jericho, the defending walls tumbled when the trumpets blew.

Five-Point Questions
1. Ham, Shem and Japheth.
2. Jacob first married the older daughter, Leah, and later married Rachel.
3. Procurator of Judea.
4. 969 years.

The Bible—Quiz 2

Two-Point Questions
1. Samson.
2. Solomon.
3. Thomas.
4. Sodom and Gomorrah.

Three-Point Questions
1. Stephen.
2. Miriam.
3. Joseph.
4. Elijah.

Five-Point Questions
1. Caiaphas, the High Priest; Pontius

Pilate, the Roman Procurator of Judea;
and Herod Antipas, Tetrarch of Galilee.
2. Saul, David and Solomon.
3. Instead of going to Nineveh, Jonah
sailed for Tarshish.
4. Joseph of Arimathea.

The Bible—Quiz 3

Two-Point Questions
1. Tower of Babel.
2. David.
3. Delilah.
4. Nazareth.

Three-Point Questions
1. Absalom.
2. Armageddon.
3. Bath-sheba (wife of Uriah).
4. Exodus.

Five-Point Questions
1. Ananias.
2. Belshazzar.
3. Cyrus (the Great).
4. Seven.

Legends, Tales and Fables—Quiz 1

Two-Point Questions
1. William Tell.
2. Simon Legree.
3. Midas.
4. Fountain of Youth.

Three-Point Questions
1. A beautiful lady behind one door, a
fierce tiger behind the other.
2. "Last of the Mohicans."
3. The Flying Dutchman.
4. The Mormons.

Five-Point Questions
1. John Henry.
2. Oliver Cromwell.
3. Sancho Panza.
4. Thomas à Becket.

Legends, Tales and Fables—Quiz 2

Two Point Questions
1. Friar Tuck.
2. Lady Godiva.

3. Sinbad the Sailor.
4. Huckleberry Finn.

Three-Point Questions
1. Athos, Porthos and Aramis.
2. The Jabberwock.
3. The phoenix.
4. Jim Hawkins.

Five-Point Questions
1. Jack and Jill.
2. Pygmalion.
3. Napoleon.
4. Modred.

Legends, Tales and Fables—Quiz 3

Two-Point Questions
1. Atlantis.
2. The Blarney Stone.
3. Ali Baba.
4. Lorelei.

Three-Point Questions
1. Androcles.
2. Excalibur.
3. Bruce (or Robert the Bruce).
4. Damon and Pythias.

Five-Point Questions
1. Anacreon (the original English song
was "To Anacreon in Heaven").
2. Bucephalus (meaning ox-headed).
3. Grendel.
4. John and Michael Darling.

Nursery Rhymes—Quiz 1

Two-Point Questions
1. Tea.
2. Nine days old.
3. A plum.
4. Under the haystack (fast asleep).

Three-Point Questions
1. His master, his dame and the little boy
who lived down the lane.
2. Some broth, without any bread.
3. Tuesday's child is full of grace.
4. A whale.

Five-Point Questions
1. "Over the Hills and Far Away."

2. Silver buckles.
3. "Are the children in bed? for it's now eight o'clock."
4. A very fine gander.

Nursery Rhymes—Quiz 2

Two-Point Questions
1. A spider.
2. The candlestick.
3. A pig.
4. He kissed them.

Three-Point Questions
1. Butcher, baker, and candlestick maker.
2. Pie ("Then you shall have no pie!")
3. A wooden shoe.
4. To see a fine lady, upon a white horse.

Five-Point Questions
1. They took some honey, and plenty of money, wrapped up in a five-pound note.
2. Dasher, Dancer, Prancer, Vixen, Comet, Cupid, Donner and Blitzen.
3. "Is bonny and bright and good and gay."
4. Ann (who had crept under the pudding pan).

Origin of Words

Two-Point Questions
1. Titanic.
2. Hieroglyphics.
3. Scintillate.
4. Bacteria.

Three-Point Questions
1. Lethargy.
2. Stentorian.
3. Laconic.
4. Chauvinism.

Five-Point Questions
1. Assassins.
2. Admiral.
3. Nepotism.
4. Ostracize.

Interesting Places—Quiz 1

Two-Point Questions
1. Africa.

2. Australia.
3. Europe.
4. The Alps.

Three-Point Questions
1. North.
2. The Himalayas.
3. An ocean area (no land).
4. Caribbean.

Five-Point Questions
1. The Bund.
2. U.S. 66.
3. The Appian Way.
4. Easter Island.

Interesting Places—Quiz 2

Two-Point Questions
1. Arctic Ocean.
2. Elba.
3. English Channel.
4. Dead Sea.

Three-Point Questions
1. Danube River.
2. Cairo, Egypt.
3. Austria and Italy.
4. Andes Mountains.

Five-Point Questions
1. Florence.
2. Peiping (Peking).
3. Fleet Street.
4. Sugar Loaf (Pao de Acucar).

Interesting Places—Quiz 3

Two-Point Questions
1. Fjord or fiord.
2. Ganges.
3. Iceland.
4. The Po (418 miles).

Three-Point Questions
1. Straits of Magellan.
2. Pampas.
3. Chile (over 2,600 miles long, often less than 200 miles wide).
4. Genoa.

Five-Point Questions
1. Pitcairn Island.

2. Stone Mountain Memorial.
3. Threadneedle Street (the Bank is often called "the Old Lady of Threadneedle Street").
4. Zambesi River.

Interesting Places—Quiz 4

Two-Point Questions
1. Alaska.
2. The Amazon.
3. St. Helena.
4. Sahara.

Three-Point Questions
1. Bangkok.
2. Pall Mall.
3. Shetland Islands.
4. Kansas.

Five-Point Questions
1. Bay of Fundy (over 50 feet).
2. Superior, Michigan, Huron, Erie and Ontario.
3. Sargasso Sea (named from the bladder-like thallus which keeps the seaweed afloat).
4. Hyde Park (Rotten Row is now used by riders).

Where Are These Rivers?—Quiz 1

Two-Point Questions
1. China.
2. Alaska.
3. Austria-Hungary (boundary); also Germany (where it rises).
4. United States-Mexico (boundary).

Three-Point Questions
1. India.
2. U.S.S.R.
3. Canada.
4. Germany.

Five-Point Questions
1. Vietnam, Cambodia and Laos.
2. U.S.S.R.
3. Australia.
4. Brazil.

Where Are These Rivers?—Quiz 2

Two Point Questions
1. Egypt.

2. Brazil.
3. Canada and United States (as boundary).
4. U.S.S.R.

Three-Point Questions
1. India.
2. Turkey and Iraq.
3. Canada.
4. U.S.S.R.

Five-Point Questions
1. U.S.S.R.
2. Colombia.
3. Turkey and Iraq.
4. U.S.S.R.

Famous Explorers

Two-Point Questions
1. Pacific Ocean.
2. Florida.
3. Mississippi River.
4. Straits of Magellan, or Philippine Islands, or first expedition around the world (accept any).

Three-Point Questions
1. Mexico.
2. Peru.
3. Mississippi River region.
4. Labrador or east coast of Canada.

Five-Point Questions
1. Grand Canyon and New Mexico.
2. St. Lawrence River.
3. Roanoke Island, Virginia.
4. Greenland.

Where Are These Famous Structures?

Two-Point Questions
1. Greece (Athens).
2. Egypt (Giza).
3. Italy (Rome).
4. England (London).

Three-Point Questions
1. India (Agra).
2. Italy (Rome); also France (Paris).
3. Spain (Granada).
4. Italy (Venice).

Five-Point Questions
1. Turkey (Istanbul).
2. Italy (Florence).
3. Spain (Madrid).
4. Israel (Jerusalem).

Where Are These Volcanoes?

Two-Point Questions
1. Italy.
2. Japan.
3. Hawaii.
4. Mexico.

Three-Point Questions
1. United States (California).
2. Mexico.
3. Sicily.
4. Africa.

Five-Point Questions
1. Japan.
2. Sumatra.
3. Alaska.
4. Mexico.

Famous People—Quiz 1

Two-Point Questions
1. Florence Nightingale.
2. Walt Whitman.
3. Sir Isaac Newton.
4. Mary Pickford.

Three-Point Questions
1. Socrates.
2. King John.
3. Benvenuto Cellini.
4. Vasco da Gama.

Five-Point Questions
1. Wilhelm Röentgen.
2. Titian.
3. Friedrich Engels.
4. Jean and Auguste Piccard.

Famous People—Quiz 2

Two-Point Questions
1. Alexander the Great.
2. Albert Einstein.
3. Henry VIII.
4. Pierre and Marie Curie.

Three-Point Questions
1. Sir Francis Drake.

2. Francis of Assisi.
3. William Randolph Hearst.
4. Karl "Baron" Munchausen.

Five-Point Questions
1. Sun Yat-sen.
2. Baron Friedrich von Steuben.
3. Voltaire.
4. Pythagoras.

Famous People—Quiz 3

Two-Point Questions
1. Davy Crockett.
2. Joseph Goebbels.
3. Antoinette.
4. Marco Polo.

Three-Point Questions
1. Sigmund Freud.
2. Euclid.
3. Haile Selassie.
4. King Farouk.

Five-Point Questions
1. George Goethals.
2. Aleksandr Kerenski.
3. Pliny the Elder.
4. Tomas de Torquemada.

Famous People—Quiz 4

Two-Point Questions
1. Nathan Hale.
2. Joan of Arc.
3. Alfred Nobel (founder of the Nobel prizes).
4. Captain Myles Standish.

Three-Point Questions
1. John Sutter.
2. Diogenes.
3. Martin Luther.
4. Sir Thomas Lipton.

Five-Point Questions
1. Charlotte Corday.
2. Stephen Decatur.
3. Zoroaster or Zarathustra, founder of Zoroastrianism.
4. Joseph Priestley.

Famous People—Quiz 5

Two-Point Questions
1. John Quincy Adams.

2. Amelia Earhart.
3. Thomas Edison.
4. Josephine (Marie de la Pagerie).

Three-Point Questions
1. Hannibal.
2. Clarence Darrow.
3. Nicolaus Copernicus.
4. Mary Baker Eddy.

Five-Point Questions
1. Kemal Ataturk (Mustava Kemal Pascha).
2. Demosthenes.
3. Blaise Pascal.
4. Pompey.

Science—Quiz 1

Two-Point Questions
1. Liquid and gas.
2. Gold.
3. Warm air. At 32 degrees Fahrenheit, sound travels at about 1,090 feet per second at sea level. Its velocity speeds up about 1 foot per second for each higher degree in air temperature.
4. Bauxite.

Three-Point Questions
1. Its specific gravity.
2. Osmosis.
3. Some energy must be expended in overcoming friction.
4. The Law of Conservation of Energy, or the First Law of Thermodynamics.

Five-Point Questions
1. That a body at rest remains at rest (possesses inertia), and a body in motion moves with uniform velocity in a straight line (has inertia of motion) unless it is compelled to change its position by an external force.
2. With every action (or force), there is an equal reaction in the opposite direction.
3. In most compounds, carbon has a valence of 4.
4. Hydrogen.

Science—Quiz 2

Two-Point Questions
1. The sun and the moon.

2. The barometer.
3. 186,000 miles per second.
4. Smallpox.

Three-Point Questions
1. The Greeks (of Iona).
2. Hippocrates.
3. Ptolemy.
4. Galileo.

Five-Point Questions
1. Aristotle.
2. Lavoisier.
3. Gregor Johann Mendel.
4. Dmitri Mendelejeff.

Pot Luck—Quiz 1

Two-Point Questions
1. Mercury is closest to the sun.
2. Solon was the Chief Magistrate of Athens who compiled the most equitable legal code the world had known. (He died in 559 B.C.)
3. Stonehenge.
4. A rook (from the Persian word "rukh," meaning castle) is one of the pieces used in chess.

Three-Point Questions
1. Jezebel.
2. Criticized for the appointment of friends to high political office, Andrew Jackson epitomized the "spoils "system with that saying.
3. The Sioux Indians for whom he led combined Indian forces at the Battle of Little Big Horn.
4. The abacus, probably first invented by the Chinese, but independently invented by the Egyptians in 500 B.C.

Five-Point Questions
1. .3.
2. Nimrod.
3. Miki Kuchi is Mickey Mouse.
4. The Parthenon, dedicated in 438 B.C. by its chief sculptor, Phidias.

Pot Luck—Quiz 2

Two-Point Questions
1. It was Old King Cole, who called for his pipe, his bowl and his fiddlers three.

2. Toga. It was the badge of Roman citizenship.
3. Governor Peter Minuit.
4. Pandora.

Three-Point Questions
1. The author of the Third Gospel and of the Acts of the Apostle was Luke, a physician.
2. It's from the Chinese words "ko" and "tou," which mean to knock the head on the ground, to prostrate one's self.
3. The song "Comin' Through the Rye" commemorates an old practice whereby a young man, who met a young girl on the stepping stones across the River Rye in Scotland, could exact a kiss.
4. The United States (southwestern states).

Five-Point Questions
1. The seal's popular maternity hospital site is the Pribilof Islands.
2. Queen Elizabeth I, daughter of Henry VIII and Anne Boleyn.
3. The pelican of the South Pacific is called a cormorant.
4. 62.4 pounds.

Pot Luck—Quiz 3

Two-Point Questions
1. Shakespeare's "Hamlet."
2. Pluto was the Greek God of the lower world.
3. The Aztec Indians (or Nehua).
4. Statue of Liberty.

Three-Point Questions
1. He referred to the press, people in the newspaper field.
2. The bat is a mammal; therefore it is more closely related biologically to the cow than to birds or insects.
3. On May 24, 1844, those words were sent over the first telegraph line (between Washington and Baltimore) by inventor Samuel Finley Morse.
4. A bushmaster is a poisonous snake, a member of the rattlesnake family.

Five-Point Questions
1. Scottish patriots stole the Stone of Scone, on which Scottish kings were once crowned. It has been returned.
2. A member of the Sultan's guard—an

organization which dates back to the 14th century.
3. Photosynthesis.
4. The hero of Salamis was Thermistocles (whom the Greeks exiled for life 9 years later).

Pot Luck—Quiz 4

Two-Point Questions
1. "Nessie," or the Loch Ness Monster.
2. Atlanta.
3. A German submarine torpedoed it.
4. Halley's Comet, which turns up every 76 years and was first recorded by man in 240 B.C.

Three-Point Questions
1. The female cuckoo.
2. The legendary founders of Rome were brothers Romulus and Remus.
3. The great city which straddles the Bosporus and is therefore situated in both Europe and Asia is Istanbul, formerly known as Constantinople.
4. Uruguay.

Five-Point Questions
1. Caries is tooth decay; myopia is near-sightedness; missing patellar reflex is missing knee jerk.
2. The horse-seeking king was Richard III.
3. Penicillin was discovered by Sir Alexander Fleming.
4. The Bubonic Plague ("Black Death") occurred in Europe in the 14th century, reaching its climax in 1348. The Hundred Years War between France and England ran, with truces, from 1337 to 1453. The plague was so severe that it interrupted the war.

Word Hunt

AMELIORATE

alarm	liar	mole	roil
alate	lime	molt	role
alit	lira	moral	rote
altar	liter	morale	tail
alter	loam	more	tailor
alto	loiter	mortal	tale
aorta	lore	mote	tame
area	mail	motel	tare
areate	male	omelet	taro
areole	malt	omit	teal
aria	mare	oral	team
aril	marital	orale	tear
aroma	marl	orate	teem
atelier	mart	rail	term
earl	martial	rate	tiara
elate	mate	ratel	tile
elite	matelote	ratio	time
emir	mater	real	timer
emit	material	realm	tire
emote	meal	ream	toil
eral	meat	reel	toile
irate	melt	relate	tole
item	mere	remit	tome
iter	merit	remote	tore
lair	metal	retail	trail
lama	meteor	rialto	trailer
lame	meter	riata	tram
lariat	mile	rile	tremor
late	mire	rime	trial
later	mite	riot	trim
leer	mitre	rite	trio
lerot	moat	roam	

CONSTRUCTION

coin	cousin	onion	scorn
conic	croon	onto	scour
consort	crouton	onus	scout
constrict	crust	oust	snort
construct	curio	roon	snout
contort	curt	roost	soon
contour	icon	root	soot
contusion	incur	rout	sour
coon	instruct	ruction	sort
coot	into	ruin	stint
corn	iron	runt	stir
cost	noon	rust	stoic
cotton	notion	rustic	stout
count	noun	scion	strict
court	occur	scoot	strut

stun	tonic	trot	union
stunt	toot	trout	unison
succor	torn	trust	unit
suction	torso	tunic	unto
suit	tort	turn	
tint	tour	unction	
tocsin	tout	unicorn	

DEVELOPING

deep	endive	lied	opine
deign	envelop	liege	oven
dele	envied	lien	ovine
delve	even	ling	pend
depone	evil	lion	pied
devein	geode	live	pile
develop	gild	liven	pine
devil	give	lode	plied
dine	glee	loge	plod
ding	glen	loin	pole
dinge	glide	long	pond
dive	glove	lope	pone
doge	golden	love	veil
doing	gone	need	vein
dole	idle	node	vend
dope	idol	novel	vile
dove	ingle	ogee	vine
dung	ledge	ogle	viol
edge	legend	olden	void
elide	lend	olive	voile
elope	levied	open	

ESTABLISH

abet	beat	hast	lest
able	belt	haste	list
aisle	best	hate	sable
alit	bias	heal	sahib
asset	bile	heat	sail
bail	bite	heist	sale
bait	blase	hilt	salt
bale	blast	hiss	sash
base	bleat	isle	sate
bash	bless	istle	seal
basil	blest	lash	seat
basis	bliss	lass	shale
bass	blithe	last	shalt
basset	east	late	shies
bast	habit	lath	silt
baste	hail	lathe	sisal
bath	hale	leash	slab
bathe	halt	least	slash
beast	hassle	less	slat

slate	stale	stile	tassel
slit	stash	table	teal
stab	steal	tail	this
stable	sties	tale	tile

IRREGULARLY

ague	glue	legal	regular
airy	grail	liar	relay
alley	gray	lira	rely
ally	grey	lure	rile
argue	grill	lyre	rill
argyle	gruel	rage	rule
aril	guile	rail	ruler
earl	gull	rally	ruly
early	gully	rare	rural
gale	gyre	rarely	ugly
gall	lager	real	urge
galley	lair	really	year
gayer	large	rear	yell
gear	largely	regal	yule
girl	layer		
glare	leary		

PRECIOUS

cope	ecru	puce	sirup
copse	epic	pure	sore
core	icer	purse	soup
corpse	osier	recoup	sour
coup	ours	rice	spice
coupe	peri	rise	spire
course	pier	rope	spore
crisp	pious	rose	spruce
crop	pore	ruse	spur
croupe	poser	scope	suer
cruise	pour	score	super
cure	precis	scour	sure
curse	price	scrip	user
cusp	prose	sire	

Hinky-Pinky
1. A killer gorilla.
2. Mighty nighty.
3. Gruesome twosome.
4. Dirty Gertie.
5. Sicker ticker.
6. Evil weevil (or sly fly—as a hink-pink).
7. Pocket rocket.
8. A chunky monkey.
9. A kickin' chicken.
10. Feed me a bear medium rare.

Famous Words That Were Never Said
1. Hamlet.
2. Jack the Giant Killer.
3. George Washington.
4. The Queen of Hearts.
5. King Arthur.
6. The Butcher, the Baker or the Candlestick Maker.
7. Rapunzel.
8. Jack Sprat.
9. Snow White.
10. Farrah Fawcett-Majors.

End of Party
The message: This party is over.

Party Psychoanalysis

WALKING IN THE WOODS
Question #1 is a test of your attitude towards other people.

If you answered (a), you are outgoing and friendly and sometimes, perhaps, not as cautious as you might be.

If you answered (b), you wait for other people to approach you, offering your friendship only to a few.

If you answered (c), your attitude towards others is based on common sense.

Question #2 is a test of your attitude towards your friends.

If you answered (a), your friendships are often casual and even when you are very friendly, you make few demands on relationships.

If you answered (b) you are easily offended and don't open up easily even to your closest friends.

If you answered (c) you are possessive of your friends, demanding and quite jealous.

Question #3 is a test of your attitude towards experiences.

If you answered (a), you test out new activities before you commit yourself to them.

If you answered (b), you rush into new things and often drop them.

If you answered (c), you are reluctant to participate in new activities and hold yourself aloof from things that might really interest you if you gave them a chance.

Question #4 is a test of your attitude towards life. If you answered (a), you run away from it.

If you answered (b), you wait to see what is going to happen before taking action.

If you answered (c), you go out to meet it, often without thinking!

IN A DREAM GARDEN

1. Your description of your ideal garden is a description of the way you want everyone to think of you.

2 & 3. Your description of the house and where it is in relation to the garden is a description of the way you see yourself in relation to the rest of the world.

4. Your description of the key is a description of your friendships—how simple or complicated they are.

5. What you do when you lose your key tells what you do when something goes wrong in a friendship.

6. Whatever you choose to describe represents the artistic side of your nature, your imagination.

7. The action you take reveals what you do when you are faced with an obstacle.

Are You an Extravert or an Introvert?

Give yourself 1 point for every "Yes" answer. Then deduct 2 points for any of the following questions which you answered "Yes": (1) (6) (7) (10) (13) (20) (26) (27) (28) (29) (31) (35) (37) (38) (39).
If you scored:

Between 16 and 25: You answered the questions as an extravert.

Between 6 and 15: Your answers fell in between the two.

Below 6: You answered the questions as an introvert.

Birthday Anagrams

1. Examine motive.   3. Don't be a donkey.
2. Not at this time.   4. Don't forget fun.

5. Give it best try.
6. Not impossible.
7. Plot and scheme.
8. Lend a hand soon.
9. Dreams are good.
10. Revamp quickly.
11. Keep the secret.
12. Build thy power.
13. Coming up roses.
14. You have spirit.
15. Spread the word.
16. Don't take dares.
17. Think it out now.
18. You know answer.
19. Don't lose heart.
20. You can do it now.
21. You are not sick.
22. Beware of ducks.
23. Be kind to kooks.
24. Mind your words.
25. You will change.
26. Surprise ahead.
27. Unusual future.
28. Stop being mean.
29. Watch your step.
30. You'll overcome.
31. It's not too late.

Biorhythm Puzzles

SCOTT'S EXAM

You're right, he did wonderfully. His cycles were as follows:
Physical Cycle: 5th day—High
Emotional Cycle: 3rd day—High
Intellectual Cycle: 15th day—High

ROD'S RACE

If you went along with Biorhythm, you'd tell Rod to stay home. His cycles look like this:
Physical Cycle: 10th day—High (but with a critical the next day)
Emotional Cycle: 15th day—Low (with a critical the day before)
Intellectual Cycle: 16th day—Critical
You can see that Rod is having three critical days in a row in this period and is not very likely to be at his best. As it happened, he didn't drive anyway. He got a terrible virus and was in bed for a week!

SARA'S TRY-OUT

Sara should wait. On March 26th, her cycles look like this:
Physical Cycle: 11th day—Critical
Emotional Cycle: 26th day—Low
Intellectual Cycle: 30th day—Low

But on May 5th, they look like this:
Physical Cycle: 5th day—High
Emotional Cycle: 10th day—High
Intellectual Cycle: 4th day—High
No, Sara didn't wait. But we don't want to say we told her so!

Guide to the Games

The games in this book are some of the best games in the world, the games that are the most fun. Children between the ages of 8 and 12 can play just about all of them. Younger children can play many of them, too, and so can adults.

If you're planning a party for 6- to 8-year-olds, look at the guide here and on the next page. A star in the first column shows the games in each chapter which are appropriate for 6- to 8-year-olds. Younger children—4 and 5 years old—can also play, depending on their development and their interests. These age range listings are merely guidelines. They are most useful when you refer to them to make sure you aren't overlooking a great game. Don't let them limit you.

If you're planning a party for adults or young adults (age 13 and up), look in the last column of the guide. A star in that column shows the games in each chapter which adults play just as enjoyably as children do—sometimes even more enjoyably! There are well over 100 of them in this book.

If you're planning a party for 8- to 12-year-olds, you can select almost any game here, but there are a few exceptions. If you're not sure, check the center column of the guide to see that the game is recommended for this age group.

Note: A divided box with the star at one side indicates that the game works better with one end of the age range than the other.

Example: ★| This indicates that the game is recommended for 6-year-olds (if in the first column), for 8–10-year-olds (if in the center column).

Games	6–8	8–12	13-Up & Adult	Games	6–8	8–12	13-Up & Adult
House of Cards **Solitaire Games** ALL—except		★	★	**Games for Travelling** ALL—except		★	★
Cave Man Game, 213	★	★	★	Buzz, 342	★	★	★
Wish, 215	★	★	★	Eagle Eye, 348	★	★	★
Card Games ALL—except	★	★		Ghost, 332	★	★	★
Calamity Jane, 251		★	★	House That Jack Built, 344	★	★	
Crazy Eights, 248	★	★	★	Super-Buzz, 343	★	★	★
Go Boom, 248	★	★	★				
Hearts, 250		★	★	**Quick Contests** ALL—except		★	
Whist, 249		★	★	Ampé, 354	★	★|	
Wild Jacks, 248	★	★	★	Anagrams, 376		★	★
Quiet Games **Pencil and Paper Games** ALL—except		★	★	Backward Alphabet, 357		★	★
Battleships, 306	★	★		Beautiful Baby Contest, 385	★	★	★
Dots, 302	★	★		Chicken Fight, 371	★	★	
Eternal Triangles, 302	★	★		Double Trouble, 364		★	★
Group Art, 300	★	★	★	Hand Wrestle, 361		★	★
Hangman Grows Up, 308	★	★		Mancala, 386		★	★
Longest Word, 321		|★	★	Penny Soccer, 358		★	★
Snakes, 303	★	★		Ransom Note, 384	★	★	
Transmigration of Words, 322		|★	★	Table Football, 355		★	★
				Table Wrestle, 360		★	★
				Toothpick in the Bottle, 365	★	★	
				Woollcott Game, 389		★	★

Games	6–8	8–12	13-Up & Adult
Party Games for ages 6–8			
ALL—except	★		
Buddies, 404	★	★	★
Catching the Stick, 408	★	★	
Full of Beans, 404	★	★	
Hot Potato, 410	★	★	
Ping Pong Hockey, 405	★	★	★
Sardines, 397	★	★	★
Shadows, 402	★	★	
Stop and Listen, 410	★	★	★
Swat Thy Neighbor, 413	★	★	
Musical Chairs Games			
ALL—except	★	★	
Cat and Mice, 419	★	★	
Deep in the Jungle, 422	★	★	★
Musical Chairs, 416	★	★	★
Noah's Ark, 422	★	★	★
Party Games Before the Party			
ALL—except		★	
Balloon Head, 430	★	★	
Elbow-Coin Trick, 426		★	★
Feelies, 425		★	★
Lottery, 427	★	★	★
Up Feather!, 430		★	★
Icebreakers			
ALL—except		★	
Bag on Head, 439		★	★
Blown-Up Fortunes, 433		★	★
Broom Dance, 443			★
Multiplication Dance, 443			★
Musical Grabs, 434		★	★
Talk Fest, 437		★	★
Who Am I?, 440		★	★
Pairing Off Partners			
ALL—except		★	★
Balloon Buddies, 444	★	★	★
Clay Mixer, 448	★	★	★
Lines, 444	★	★	★
Riddle Pairs, 446	★	★	★
Terrible Twosomes, 447	★	★	★

Games	6–8	8–12	13-Up & Adult
Party Games			
ALL—except		★	
Actions Speak Louder, 456		★	★
Camouflage, 453		★	★
Categories, 469		★	★
Dictionary, 476		★	★
End of Party, 478		★	★
Horse Race, 458	★	★	
Mad Ad Agency, 459	★	★	★
Murder, 450		★	★
Phonies, 476		★	★
Rumor, 456	★	★	
Scars, 474		★	★
See It! 463		★	★
Teakettle, 462		★	★
Time Bomb, 451		★	★
Truth or Consequences, 452	★	★	★
Ummm, 478		★	★
Up Jenkins!, 466		★	★
Who's Missing?, 453	★	★	★
Special Party Games Relay Races			
ALL—except		★	
Art Relay, 490	★	★	
Balloon Races, 487	★	★	
Dog Dash, 489	★	★	
Fancy Dude, 492	★	★	
Fast Lemon, 491	★	★	★
Pig Roll, 489	★	★	
Thought for the Day, 490	★	★	
Races for Small Spaces			
ALL—except		★	★
Hair Ribbon, 493	★	★	
Pinocchio Race, 494	★	★	★
Salty Whistle, 493	★	★	★
Acting Games			
ALL—except		★	★
In the Manner of the Word—with Words, 513			★
Carnival Games			
ALL—	★	★	★
Psychological Games		★	★